Also Available From
the American Academy of Pediatrics

Common Conditions

ADHD: A Complete and Authoritative Guide

Allergies and Asthma: What Every Parent Needs to Know

Waking Up Dry: A Guide to Help Children Overcome Bedwetting

Developmental, Behavioral, and Psychosocial Information

CyberSafe: Protecting and Empowering Kids in the Digital World of Texting, Gaming, and Social Media

Mental Health, Naturally: The Family Guide to Holistic Care for a Healthy Mind and Body

The Wonder Years: Helping Your Baby and Young Child Successfully Negotiate the Major Developmental Milestones

Immunization Information

Immunizations & Infectious Diseases: An Informed Parent's Guide

Newborns, Infants, and Toddlers

Baby & Child Health: The Essential Guide From Birth to 11 Years

Caring for Your Baby and Young Child: Birth to Age 5*

Guide to Toilet Training*

Heading Home With Your Newborn: From Birth to Reality

Mommy Calls: Dr. Tanya Answers Parents' Top 101 Questions About Babies and Toddlers

New Mother's Guide to Breastfeeding*

Newborn Intensive Care: What Every Parent Needs to Know

Raising Twins: From Pregnancy to Preschool

Your Baby's First Year*

Nutrition and Fitness

Food Fights: Winning the Nutritional Challenges of Parenthood Armed With Insight, Humor, and a Bottle of Ketchup

A Parent's Guide to Childhood Obesity: A Road Map to Health

Sports Success R_x! Your Child's Prescription for the Best Experience

School-aged Children and Adolescents

Building Resilience in Children and Teens: Giving Kids Roots and Wings

Caring for Your School-Age Child: Ages 5 to 12

Caring for Your Teenager

Less Stress, More Success: A New Approach to Guiding Your Teen Through College Admissions and Beyond

For more information, please visit the official AAP Web site for parents,
www.HealthyChildren.org/bookstore.

*This book is also available in Spanish.

Building
Resilience
in Children and Teens
Giving Kids
Roots and
Wings

2nd Edition

Kenneth R. Ginsburg, MD, MS Ed, FAAP
With Martha M. Jablow

American Academy of Pediatrics
DEDICATED TO THE HEALTH OF ALL CHILDREN™

American Academy of Pediatrics Department of Marketing and Publications

Director, Department of Marketing and Publications
Maureen DeRosa, MPA

Director, Division of Product Development
Mark Grimes

Manager, Consumer Publishing
Carolyn Kolbaba

Coordinator, Product Development
Holly Kaminski

Director, Division of Publishing and Production Services
Sandi King, MS

Editorial Specialist
Jason Crase

Print Production Specialist
Shannan Martin

Manager, Graphic Design and Production
Peg Mulcahy

Director, Division of Marketing and Sales
Kevin Tuley

Manager, Consumer Product Marketing
Kathleen Juhl

Published by the American Academy of Pediatrics
141 Northwest Point Blvd, Elk Grove Village, IL 60007-1019
847/434-4000
Fax: 847/434-8000
www.aap.org

Building Resilience in Children and Teens: Giving Kids Roots and Wings was created by Kenneth R. Ginsburg, MD, MS Ed, FAAP, and Martha M. Jablow.

Illustration on page 214 by Talia Ginsburg, age 10.

Second Edition—2011
First Edition—© 2006 as *A Parent's Guide to Building Resilience in Children and Teens: Giving Your Child Roots and Wings*

Library of Congress Control Number: 2010934613
ISBN: 978-1-58110-551-3

The recommendations in this publication do not indicate an exclusive course of treatment or serve as a standard of medical care. Variations, taking into account individual circumstances, may be appropriate.

Statements and opinions expressed are those of the authors and not necessarily those of the American Academy of Pediatrics.

Products and Web sites are mentioned for informational purposes only. Inclusion in this publication does not imply endorsement by the American Academy of Pediatrics. The American Academy of Pediatrics is not responsible for the content of the resources mentioned in this publication. Web site addresses are as current as possible but may change at any time.

Every effort is made to keep *Building Resilience in Children and Teens: Giving Kids Roots and Wings* consistent with the most recent advice and information possible.

CB0065
9-275/rep1213   6 7 8 9 10

What People Are Saying

Building Resilience in Children and Teens provides a rich and valuable resource for anyone who cares about overcoming the increasing pressures of student achievement. Dr Ginsburg has created a great way for adolescents to manage stress and offers effective strategies to prepare this often-overlooked age group to thrive. It was a super pick for our school and community books clubs—a must-read for any adult involved in middle schools!

    David Schrag
    Principal, Stanley Middle School, Lafayette, CA

This book is about recognizing your child's strengths and parenting from a place of what you *can* influence. By helping parents understand what is normal developmentally, [Dr Ken Ginsburg] helps us refocus our impression of teens as difficult, and in the process helps us enhance our child's feelings of competence, setting the groundwork for raising children who can cope on their own in today's complex world. As a parent of 9- and 19-year-olds, and as someone who has brought Dr Ginsburg to speak to parents and teens in our community, I can tell you his genuine concern for children comes through on the pages of this book. Not only is he a parent himself, but he is on the front lines with teens in his office every day. There's no magic answer, but this book gives parents well-thought-out advice on raising children so they have the tools they need for authentic success in life. This book is one you will keep on your shelf to refer back to and share with friends.

    Sharon B. Greenstein
    Parent Education Chairperson, Los Altos-Mountain View PTA Council

Dr Ginsburg has focused on one of the most critical traits necessary for students on their path to self-actualization. This book provides a commonsense approach and time-tested exercises for stress reduction for students. *Building Resilience* can be the "spark" to assist students in their social-emotional growth.

    Ray Piagentini
    Professional school counselor and Past President, Illinois School
    Counselor Association

Dr Ginsburg masterfully integrates cutting-edge theory and research with his rich, insightful, and compelling vision for enhancing the lives of youth. No book better serves parents, practitioners, policy makers, and educators in its respective effort to promote the health and positive development of children and adolescents.

> Richard M. Lerner, PhD
> Bergstrom Chair in Applied Developmental Science and Director, Institute for Applied Research in Youth Development, Tufts University, and author or editor of more than 70 books, including *The Good Teen: Rescuing Adolescence from the Myths of the Storm and Stress Years*

Dr Ken Ginsburg's work on resilience forms the basis of our entire adolescent medicine practice. Teaching young people to use their strengths to prevent and manage problems helps them to be in control of their own futures; teaching parents to recognize and build resilience in their children fosters productive family-based partnerships that last a lifetime and save lives. Whether 3 years old or 30, whether struggling with "normal" developmental issues or major medical or psychological stresses, Dr Ginsburg empowers parents to raise children who love, accept, and protect themselves. Isn't that what we all want for our kids?

> Susan Sugerman, MD, MPH
> President and Cofounder, Girls to Women Health and Wellness

[Dr Ken Ginsburg's] book…has become a vital part of our training and support resources for parents, professionals, and community volunteers. Over the years we have found…that Ken Ginsburg's research-based and evidence-informed training and practical scholarship is an incredible asset in helping us support parents and expand the convoy of other supporting adults that understand the challenges of mobility and transition faced by America's military-connected children and youth.

> Mary M. Keller, EdD
> President and CEO, Military Child Education Coalition

With love to my wife Celia,
who has taught me so much about good parenting,
and to Ilana and Talia,
who are growing up to be the generous, compassionate,
and creative people I dreamed they would.
I pray that
they will continue to find joy
in the simple pleasures
of life while remaining
strong enough to bounce back
from life's challenges.

Contents

Acknowledgments

It would not be possible to thank all the people who supported me in writing this book or inspired me to feel that it should be written. My colleagues at the Council on Communications and Media of the American Academy of Pediatrics (AAP), formerly chaired by Donald Shifrin, MD, FAAP, deserve special mention because they had the wisdom to know it is insufficient just to suggest what we *don't* want children to do. They knew that we must make clear all the wonderful expectations we have of youth. I thank the AAP for trusting me to take on this important project. In particular, I thank Carolyn Kolbaba and Mark Grimes for the vision to make this happen.

I thank Martha Jablow for her wisdom, patience, and clarity of thought. This book never could have become a reality without her skills and perseverance. And I never would have had such joy in writing it without her kindness and good humor. I am so appreciative of Mary Keller, EdD; Patty Shinseki; Donna Earle; and Avlyn Bolton of the Military Child Education Coalition for their critical appraisal and guidance that helped me to write Chapter 22. I am deeply grateful to Jed Michael, MOM (Master of Oriental Medicine), for contributing heavily to Chapter 27. We work together at Covenant House Pennsylvania to facilitate the healing of youth. He is one of the most gifted practitioners I have ever witnessed. I am also grateful to Princess Skyers for the wisdom and perspective she shared in the section about avoiding prejudice in Chapter 23.

I offer my heartfelt thanks and respect to the leaders of the positive youth development and resilience movements who have inspired me. In particular, Rick Little and his team at the International Youth Foundation first elucidated the importance of the primary ingredients needed for healthy youth development—confidence, competence, character, connection, and contribution. Although I have modified these a bit to include coping and control, they originated and solidified the core ideas. I have been honored to know Richard Lerner, PhD, of Tufts University, who was part of that team and is one of the great developmental psychologists of our time. Dr Lerner has spent decades demonstrating that positive youth development efforts indeed work and that caring is another core trait we must actively nurture through our own demonstrations of caring. In my own field of adolescent medicine, Robert Blum, MD, FAAP, and Michael Resnick, PhD, have led the way and motivated me to shift from a risk-based to a strength-based approach to youth; and Karen Hein, MD,

FAAP, has made us understand we need to support youth so they can reach their full potential. I am impressed by how Peter Benson of the Search Institute has helped communities and parents understand that we need to develop core assets in children and not just bemoan their deficits. The Communities That Care process developed by David Hawkins, PhD, and Richard Catalano, PhD, has advanced the field substantially by helping communities mobilize to promote the positive development of and prevent problem behaviors in youth. Karen Pittman of the Forum for Youth Investment has called for our nation to understand quite simply that "problem free is not fully prepared."

I thank my professional mentors, Donald Schwarz, MD, FAAP, and Gail B. Slap, MD, who have had the experience to guide me, the knowledge to enlighten me, and the passion and love of youth to transmit to me. Above all, they have repeatedly demonstrated they care not just about my academic career but about me. I also thank the best teacher I ever had, Judith Lowenthal, PhD, who inspired me (when I was an adolescent) to grasp the potential in every young person. I also need to thank my colleagues at the Craig-Dalsimer Division of Adolescent Medicine at The Children's Hospital of Philadelphia for teaching me so much and being uniformly supportive of these efforts.

My first mentors and first teachers, of course, were my parents, Arnold and Marilyn Ginsburg. I learned much of what I have come to see as good parenting in their home. I was also blessed to learn about the strength of family from my grandmother, Belle Moore, who demonstrated unconditional love better than anyone I have known, except for her daughter Marilyn. They were two of a kind. I hope that I have passed along in some small measure what I learned from them to my own daughters.

Above all, I thank the young people and their families who have let me into their lives. I am awed by the love I see every day by parents who bring their children to me at The Children's Hospital of Philadelphia, and I hope that I have served them well. I am moved by the resilience of many of my patients, but in particular the youth of Covenant House Pennsylvania who serve as a constant reminder of the tenacity and strength of the human spirit.

Preface

When we look at children today, we see them in the moment. We rarely picture a cute 5-year-old or a texting preteen as an adult. But we must prepare children to become healthy, productive, contributing 35-year-olds if their generation is to repair our world and lead us into the future. For them to thrive long term, we need to consider happiness and achievement today, as well as the skills they'll need to navigate an increasingly complex world tomorrow. We want them to be able to overcome adversity and view challenges as opportunities for growth and innovation. We need them to be *resilient.*

When I wrote *A Parent's Guide to Building Resilience in Children and Teens: Giving Your Child Roots and Wings* in 2006, my goal was to translate the best of what was known about positive youth development and resilience into strategies that parents could apply in their homes. Since then, I have been privileged to speak to thousands of parents and young people in scores of communities. From each, I have gained pearls of wisdom that I want to share. And from many, I received feedback about information they wanted. New research has come to light in the last few years that offers concrete advances in our knowledge of how to guide children more effectively.

The first edition of this book was written as a parent's guide, but I found that many communities, schools, and professionals also used it. We know that children thrive best when they have many layers of support, so I was gratified to learn how many people who care for children, in addition to parents, used the book to develop young peoples' strengths. I soon realized that it was important to produce a book that would remain useful to parents but would better serve other caring adults who are so critical to building a child's resilience.

Building Resilience in Children and Teens: Giving Kids Roots and Wings updates information in the first edition and expands it significantly in response to reader feedback. For example, parents told me that they wanted to know more about how to monitor their kids effectively, and more details on stress-reduction strategies. New chapters include one on redefining success by supporting children to thrive while withstanding so many pressures that drive perfectionism, stifle their success, and undermine their creativity and happiness. Another new chapter, 4, prepares parents and communities to stand together against those toxic messages that lead children and adolescents to believe they're the source of trouble rather than the solution.

Chapter 22 is a timely new chapter that pays tribute to families of our military service members by addressing ways to maintain vital connections despite multiple moves and deployments. The ideas in that chapter came from military families themselves. Others may want to read it because these military families serve as models of resilience and because all of us have to deal with challenges to our important connections at some level.

Anyone who works with children may want to begin by reading Chapter 38, Community-based Resilience-building Strategies.

Finally, resilience is a wonderfully positive concept, but it should never be confused with invulnerability. Just as children can reach their limits of resilience, so too can the adults who love and care for them. For that reason, I've added Chapter 37, which discusses what adults can do when their own resilience reaches its limits. I hope it serves you well when you need to reboot.

We can all work together as parents, schools, communities, and policy makers to nurture our children today so they can become the compassionate, creative 35-year-olds we need tomorrow.

PART 1

Resilience and Stress

CHAPTER 1

Why Resilience?

Every parent's dream is to raise children who lead charmed, happy lives free of physical pain, worries, and emotional hurt. They'd never break a bone, lose a ball game, or receive a grade lower than an A. Never smoke a cigarette, use a drug, or wreck a car. Never have sex until they're married...

We would love to live in a world so idyllic that children wouldn't have to be concerned about peer pressure, bullying, parents fighting or divorcing, lurking strangers, disease or death, poverty, crime, terrorism, and war. We fantasize that we could safeguard them from every possible loss, heartache, and danger. We'd like to wrap our children in a downy quilt and insulate them from every misfortune. But even if we could, would it really benefit them?

If we could immunize children from all disappointments and stress, would they ever have the chance to experience the satisfaction of facing a challenge, recovering, and discovering that they are able to cope with tough situations? Would they be able to revel in success or experience joy and pleasure if they never faced some struggle, failure, or rejection? Would they recognize and appreciate good fortune if they never knew its opposite? If we could wave a magic wand to isolate children from the pain around them, wouldn't we produce cold individuals incapable of empathy and unable to feel and express love, compassion, or a desire to help others? Would they be prepared to make the world a better place?

No parent wishes any adversity to befall a child, of course, but realistically we have to expect problems. We cannot raise totally invulnerable kids. Our goal, then, must be to raise children who can handle the bumps and bruises that the world has in store. We need to prepare them to cope with difficult challenges and bounce back. We must help them find happiness even when things aren't going their way. We want them to develop deep, strong roots now so that their wings will carry them successfully and independently into the future.

If we want our children to experience the world as fully as possible—unfortunately with all its pain, and thankfully with all its joy—our goal will have to be *resilience*. Resilience is the capacity to rise above difficult circumstances, the trait that allows us to exist in this less-than-perfect world while moving forward with optimism and confidence even in the midst of adversity.

Resilience is commonly defined as an ability to recover from setbacks, the quality of bouncing back. Resilience is similar to buoyancy. When pushed under water, our bodies instinctively rise back up to the surface. That's a useful image to keep in mind as we consider resilience throughout this book. It's what we want our children to be able to do: when pushed under, rise to the top again.

Resilience is a mindset. Resilient people see challenges as opportunities. They do not seek problems, but they understand that they will ultimately be strengthened from them. Rather than engaging in self-doubt, catastrophic thinking, or a mindset of victimization *(Why me?)*, they seek solutions.

Resilience is uneven. A person might be highly resilient in one aspect of life and need much higher levels of support in another. Resilience is not invulnerability, not perfection, not isolation from all risk. Resilience is the trait that parents hope to develop in children so they will be equipped to navigate a stressful, complicated world while relishing its abundant pleasures. Resilience is not a trait of "perfect" people. Perfectionists fear making any mistakes. They perform well but don't take chances to perform at their very best. Resilient people are more successful because they push their limits and learn from their mistakes. Resilience may be a core factor in determining not only who will adapt, but who will thrive.

Stress and Resilience

All children are born with a natural resilience. If you watch a group swimming lesson, it's apparent that kids have different degrees of natural buoyancy. Some float more easily than others, but all children can learn to float. In terms of resilience, some children seem naturally graced with an ability to recover from obstacles, while others need extra support. But all children can become *more* resilient. Contemporary society continues to place increasing pressure on their young shoulders, so it's impossible to *over*-prepare children with resilience-building supports.

We all recognize how real stress can be. Families are endlessly rushed. Kids are heavily scheduled with academic and extracurricular activities. Friends dare them to take bigger risks. Parents and teachers push them to get higher grades. Coaches demand better performance. The media bombard youth with messages that they aren't thin enough, cool enough, sexy enough, or attractive enough.

In this pressure-cooker atmosphere, children need to tap into their strengths, acquire specific skills to cope, recover from adversity, and be prepared for future challenges. That's a huge order for young people. They cannot do it completely on their own. Parents take the lead in building resilience, but children's ability to thrive is also deeply affected by the community of adults that surround them.

On These Pages

I hope to reinforce the best approaches you already use and help you support children in developing skills that will make them stronger, happier, and more resilient. I will discuss building resilience in children as young as 2 years and as old as 18 years. I will suggest ways to help them learn to reduce stress and cope with challenges as well as deal with peers and self-doubt. As you read through this book, I hope you will become increasingly confident about substituting ongoing *resilience development* for that figurative protective quilt.

While resilience is the theme of this book, I want readers to understand from the outset that much of this is commonsense parenting. Don't expect each page to address dangers or risks. This is not a doom-and-gloom book. It's about building on children's existing strengths. Many of the situations that I address may not seem obviously related to resilience development. For example, discipline strategies will be discussed, as they are in every parenting book. The difference is that I intend to show you how to approach some of these issues in ways that tie into an overall strategy to enhance resilience.

Chapter 39 is a special chapter to share with children and teenagers. This stress-management plan can be individualized for every child.

The Resilience Movement

The resilience movement began as an effort to determine why children from the same challenging environment might achieve different levels of success and happiness. It looked at what protective forces in children's lives buffered them from all that was wrong. This approach remains a stark contrast to the more commonly used approach—learning what went wrong. The leaders of the resilience movement come from a wide variety of disciplines and perspectives. Sociologists look at the social fabric and how it supports or harms communities. Psychologists examine individuals' thoughts and experiences and how they influence their ability to bounce back from difficulties. Anthropologists study human survival and how culture and communities influence resilience. Most books about resilience favor the discipline or interest of the author. In this book, I want to offer you the best from all disciplines because kids are whole human beings whose behavior never can be fully explained by any textbook or single theory. So while we have to understand how kids think, we also have to consider the social and community forces that affect them.

There is no way, in one book, for me to do justice to every good idea out there about building resilience. If there is an approach that you feel is important to explore further for your child's individual needs, I want you to know where to turn. The Resources section at the end of this book can guide you to explore further areas of interest or special concern.

My goal is to present many different ideas about building resilience. I will introduce the *7 Cs* model of resilience in Chapter 3. Those Cs are *competence, confidence, connection, character, contribution, coping,* and *control.* I want you to realize that every C is a different layer or individual piece of a total approach to blanket your child with protection, while reinforcing his own strengths.

Several essential themes weave through the book. Here is a preview.

* To be strong, children need unconditional love, absolute security, and a deep connection to at least one adult.
* Sometimes the best thing parents can do to help children learn is get out of their way.
* Children live up or down to adults' expectations of them.
* Listening to children attentively is more important than any words parents can say. This applies to routine situations as well as times of crisis.
* Nothing parents say is as important as what children see them doing on a daily basis.
* Children can only take positive steps when they have the confidence to do so. They gain that confidence when they have solid reasons to believe they are competent.
* If children are to develop the strength to overcome challenges, they need to know that they can control what happens to them.
* Children with a wide range of positive coping strategies will be prepared to overcome stressors and far less likely to try many of the risk behaviors that parents fear.

There's no absolute guarantee for doing everything right. If there were, I would tell you. This is not an instruction manual. I won't give you a list of steps and say, "Proceed from step 1 to 2 to 3." I wish raising resilient children were that easy. It's more like putting together a recipe, making sure first that you know all of the right ingredients are in place. I want to give you a wealth of material that stimulates thought and debate. I hope you will discuss these ideas with your partner or other significant adults in your child's life. I believe you will recognize that you already know most of this information on an instinctual level. I want to reinforce the best of what you know. Never trust an "expert" more than your own instincts about what is right for your family. From working with families for nearly 25 years, I know that I could learn a great deal about parenting from each of you. In fact, much of what I will share has been taught to me by my patients and their families.

Using This Book

I hope you will think about the ideas on these pages, play with them, try them on for size, and see how they fit your individual children, depending on each one's character, temperament, likes and dislikes, and strengths and weaknesses. Because I hope you will return to this book as your children grow, examples apply to different stages of development.

You will find that most of these techniques require practice and reinforcement. You'll probably need to go back from time to time to reteach skills and adapt guidelines as your child backslides or moves to a new developmental milestone. You may think you've taught your child a particular lesson or helped him acquire a certain coping skill, but he may not retain and use it. Kids need ongoing support—not nagging, lecturing, or criticism, but gentle reinforcement and practice. Like developing a good jump shot or mastering a musical instrument, skill-building takes time, practice, and patience.

You'll also discover (although you probably already know it) that children mature in fits and starts. Whenever an important, new situation is about to occur, such as entering a new grade or school, moving to a different community, or starting summer camp, your child will probably regress a bit. You may notice this pattern with some children in even less momentous circumstances, such as going to a sleepover for the first time.

Most children take a few developmental steps forward and, just as parents are taking pride in their progress, something new and challenging appears on the horizon that's beyond their capabilities. Then they regress a step or two, behave as they did last year, or lash out at their parents. This is normal!

Think about how you'd leap across a chasm. You wouldn't stand still on the edge and just jump across. You'd take several steps backward to get a running start before you leap, and then cover your eyes as you soar across. Visualize every major developmental stage or challenge as a chasm that children worry about crossing. Don't be surprised when they take 2 or 3 steps backward before their next attempt to move forward. And don't be shocked if they sometimes leap with blinders on.

Please don't feel defeated if you do your best to help your children across that chasm and your efforts seem to fall short. Children are listening, even when they roll their eyes or ask, "Are you done yet?" Keep plugging. Keep caring. You can make a big difference even when it feels like you've slipped backward once in a while.

The standard line I was taught over the years in every lecture I attended and every chapter I read about child development was, "Consistency is the most important ingredient in parenting." If that means consistency of love, I agree. But I can't be completely consistent with my own children. Each of my daughters has her own temperament. On any given day, they may live the same experience, but each requires a different response from me.

I don't mean we have to just go with the flow. We certainly need to have clear, unwavering values, and our love for our kids has to be the most consistent, stable, and obviously expressed force in our homes. Children benefit from knowing that there are reliable routines in their lives. But life is always changing, so we need to give our children and ourselves a break by being flexible. To be resilient, we must be able to adapt as circumstances require, for our own sake as well as to model this valuable quality for our children.

The truth is, though, that we do want to make crossing that chasm a bit easier when we can. We know our children need to get across on their own, but we'd like to help them build a bridge. This book is about giving kids the tools they need to construct that bridge while maintaining the kind of relationships that will make them more likely to welcome our presence alongside them. I have written another book, *Letting Go With Love and Confidence: Raising Responsible, Resilient, Self-sufficient Teens,* that will help you develop the concrete strategies to prepare your child to take each of life's challenges step-by-step.

Why Me?

My life's work is about guiding youth toward an emotionally and physically healthy life. I am a pediatrician who has degrees in child and human development and who has specialized in adolescent medicine for more than 21 years at The Children's Hospital of Philadelphia and the University of Pennsylvania School of Medicine. Early on, most of my guidance tended toward telling kids what not to do. I learned pretty quickly that this problem-focused approach sometimes instilled shame, and it rarely worked. On the other hand, when youth are noticed for their strengths and expected to rise to their potential, they become self-motivated to overcome their challenges. It also took a short while to grasp that, while my service could spark their motivation, it was really their parents' support that made the long-lasting difference. In short, there is nothing I can do that carries even a fraction of meaning compared to what parents do at home and what communities do to support children and youth. That is why I write books.

Outside of medicine, my purest joys have included teaching in nursery school, where I learned more than I ever taught. Much of what I believe about resilience was absorbed on a Lakota Native American reservation in South Dakota. There I learned about the power of community to help individuals overcome great hardship.

I am a qualitative researcher—that is, I learn about children and teens from kids themselves. I have developed a method with one of my mentors, Gail B. Slap, MD, that helps adults essentially get out of the way so that we can learn from the wisdom of youth. This research allows young people to teach us how they determine whether adults are trustworthy and what they think makes a difference in whether they will thrive.

The majority of my knowledge has been acquired from working directly with young patients and their parents. I have a medical practice that is widely varied—I treat suburban and urban youth, children of college professors and children in poverty, some who have thrived despite social inequities and some who have not.

From homeless families, children, and youth, I have learned great lessons about individual strength and the extremes from which people can recover. As the health services director of Covenant House Pennsylvania, I work with homeless youth who have survived lives that would have destroyed me. I am showered with their wisdom about what it takes to move beyond pain and what ingredients could have been in place that would have enabled them to thrive. From them, I know that children and teens have the capability to overcome almost anything. Because many have absorbed a great deal of condemnation and low expectation, some begin to see themselves as problems. I sometimes help them identify and build on their strengths. While I may serve as a guide, they do the heavy lifting. I have learned that they possess a different kind of credential, one that is earned through survival. I am consistently amazed by how many of them want to devote their lives to guiding children to overcome difficulty. I know that with the right kind of investment in them, we would find many of the healers of tomorrow. From my colleagues who work at Covenant House, I have learned that a loving, strength-building environment that offers structure permits young people to flourish and move beyond a troubled past.

I have recently been honored to work on building resilience among the children, adolescents, and families of those who serve our nation in the military. As our country has been fighting wars for several years, there are almost 2 million young people whose connection to their parents has been challenged through frequent deployments overseas. I am privileged to work with the Army's Child, Adolescent, and Family Behavioral Health Proponency, as well as the Military Child Education Coalition, which serves all military branches, in an effort to support our service members' families by designing resilience-based strategies to support emotional health and well-being. I am truly inspired by the strengths I see in these families and their communities.

❖❖❖❖❖

Just as parents fantasize a safe, idealized world for their children, I wish all the kids I care for would be protected and headed toward a positive future. In truth, most of the kids I see, from all backgrounds, are using their built-in resilience and are ready to tackle whatever lies ahead. But nearly every day I see some young people in trouble—drug-abusing, depressed, and suicidal kids; pregnant 14-year-olds; homeless youth who ricochet from the streets to shelters and back; kids with sexually transmitted infections; victims of gunshots on street corners; and those who wield the weapons. It would be incorrect to assume that only the homeless youth I serve or those who live in urban areas of concentrated poverty have problems. I care for young patients from upper-income suburbs who binge drink; are anxious, depressed, and suicidal; use drugs; get pregnant; have sexually transmitted infections; and have eating disorders. Most of them attend "good" schools and some get top grades, but they are so overstressed that they deal with pressure in destructive ways.

These similar yet diverse groups suffer the consequences of poverty and the different but very real pressures of affluence. In between these extremes, many other young people struggle to make their way through childhood and adolescence. But take a deep breath because I want to remind you that although all will take some bumps and bruises, most will use them to become stronger, more adaptable people. You can make a difference in making sure children will become healthy, emotionally intelligent adults; that's why you are taking the time to read this book. You are already proving your commitment, and that bodes well for your children.

While children have many natural abilities and strengths, they can always develop greater resilience, but it's difficult to do this on their own. All children need caring adults to guide and support them. It will take a coordinated effort on many levels if we are to raise future generations of resilient young people. The best starting point is at home, with parents, as early as possible in a child's life. Parents are the pivotal force in children's lives. The actions they take years before adolescence, starting even in infancy, can make a difference in the health of teenagers and their success and well-being as adults. Regardless of a child's age, keep in mind that it is never too late to begin new approaches to building resilience. The fruit of your efforts will grow throughout childhood, culminate in adolescence, and serve your child well through his adult life. Parents' efforts, in turn, must be supported by professionals, communities, and society.

This brings me to my utmost joy, my greatest challenge, and my most important job—I am the parent of wonderful teenaged daughters, Ilana and Talia. I certainly learned more about children, and infinitely more about parenting, after I was privileged to become their daddy. I know, just like you, what it means to have your heart on the outside of your body, love like you never imagined possible, and have worries and fears that didn't exist until you knew that you had something so very precious to protect. You can be sure that I come very humbled to these pages. I know there is no magic plan for raising children, only love and the very best of intentions.

Stress and Its Effects

In 21st-century America, stress seems to permeate everyone's lives 24/7. Individual families are strained by financial and work tensions. Separation and divorce are common. Children are stressed at home and at school ("Hurry up, finish this, do your homework, try out for the team, audition for the school play, do your best, stay out of trouble, make more friends, don't drink or do drugs..."). Their peers continually pressure them ("Be cool, try this, show us you aren't a loser, don't hang out with those dorks..."). Many children put even more stress on themselves ("I need to lose weight, wear the right clothes and shoes, get a tattoo, show my parents I'm not a baby and can do what my friends do...").

Contemporary society and the media add to family stress every time we turn on the television, click on a news Web page, or open a newspaper—terrorism, school violence, hurricanes, tsunamis, nuclear threats, economic instability, globalization that threatens to take your job overseas.... Unless you've been living in Antarctica without a cell phone, you certainly recognize this picture.

Adults deal with ongoing stress in various ways—exercise, meditation, long walks, turning down overtime or weekend work, painkillers, smoking, or another glass of wine. How do children deal with stress? Depending on their ages and temperaments, some kids choose healthy, positive strategies like play, exercise, or talking, but others withdraw, sulk, or zone out. Still others act aggressively, talk back, and toss tantrums. Older children may turn to the coping mechanisms that they see peers using—smoking, drugs, fighting, sexual activity, eating disorders, self-mutilation, and delinquency. Adults usually see these activities as "behavior problems" and underestimate the amount of stress that young people are under. In actuality, these negative behaviors are often attempts to counter stress, push it under, chill out, and make it all go away.

When kids are stressed, their first impulse is to relieve the discomfort. They don't sit down and rationally think about the best way to do it. They find relief by acting impulsively or by following the paths most readily available to them, the ones they see other kids taking. Many young people simply don't know more healthy and effective alternatives. Unless we guide them toward positive ways to relieve and reduce stress, they choose the negative behaviors of peers or the culture they absorb from the media. They become caught up in a cycle of negative coping methods and risky behaviors. We need to help them avoid that cycle.

Before a child or adult can change a behavior, it's critical to understand its function as a coping mechanism—how it works, why we do it, and what need it fills. Simple examples: when pressures build at work, an adult may relieve the tension for a while by stepping outside for a cigarette or venting about the idiot boss to a coworker at the coffee machine. When a child is hassled on the school bus, she may withdraw and act unaffected or slug the child who's bothering her. When friends are drinking at a party, a teenager feels pressure to be accepted by the crowd so she guzzles beer to keep up with them. She does this partly as a response to peer pressure, but other factors also come into play. The dilemma of whether to drink increases her stress. She has seen how alcohol relaxes her parents after a difficult day at work or in stressful social situations, so she decides to drink to relieve her own social stress.

Most of these behaviors are actually effective—in the short term—at relieving stress. The child who's hassled on the school bus lets off steam by punching the kid who's bothering her. A teen who feels that she has little control over her life may seize control of whatever she can. Although she may have no control over how her parents treat her, where she lives, or what school she must attend, she decides that she can control her body size and shape. By denying herself food, she takes some control, which temporarily decreases her stress, but the long-range result can become disordered eating. A young person who feels little love or connection with family may turn to a gang for a sense of belonging, loyalty, and protection. Although the gang may fill a void in this young person's life, the choice to join it is deeply destructive. A child who is anxious about living up to expectations of parents or teachers may turn to drugs for relief. Her feelings of inadequacy or fear of failure are diminished in that haze of marijuana. The feelings resurface after the high wears off, so she is likely to use drugs more frequently to keep her stress at bay.

Negative strategies are easy, quick fixes that do relieve stress, but they have consequences that are harmful to individual children, families, and society. Our job is to convince young people that although stress is part of life, healthy ways of coping with it can ultimately be protective, productive, and satisfying.

Can Stress Be a Good Thing?

The word *stress* is often used in the midst of a complaint. "My boss is stressing me out." "Raising kids has to be the best thing I've ever done, but I don't know if I can survive the stress." While stress can be a problem, it is too simplistic to see it only in a negative light. In fact, stress is designed to be a lifesaver. In times of danger, stress gets our adrenaline going so we can move quickly to dodge a harmful threat.

An appropriate level of stress may be a driving influence that leads us to positive achievements. A little stress, for example, pumps us up to perform well for a presentation at work or make a tough sale. A little stress energizes a child to play a musical instrument at a recital or train for a race. Without some occasional, well-timed stress, we might become too passive, decreasing our ability to reach new heights. Problems arise, however, when stress becomes chronic or we don't manage our stress level well enough to perform the many tasks and responsibilities before us. Then stress can become a destructive force that harms our bodies, paralyzes our efforts, or drives us toward dangerous behaviors. It's been said so often that it has become a cliché, but it's still true— it's all about balance.

Stress as a Lifesaver

The human body is absolutely amazing. It can transform quickly to meet multiple needs. Intricate connections between nerves, hormones, and cells allow for rapid changes to occur based on the emotions, thoughts, pleasures, and fears that our brain experiences. Our bodies are finely tuned machines whose functions differ depending on our surroundings and states of relaxation, vigilance, arousal, or fear.

But our bodies were designed long ago. They were not designed to survive 21st-century lifestyles. If they were, our bodies would grow stronger when fed fast food. Our skin would welcome that extra ultraviolet light that the hole in the ozone layer offers us. We would become temporarily deaf when our boss threatens to fire us.

Our bodies were designed to survive in the jungle when, at any moment, a tiger might leap out of the brush. Imagine that moment. Our great, great ancestor, feasting on some berries and basking in the warmth of the sun, is as relaxed as he can be. Suddenly he sees a tiger. His brain registers terror before he can even bring the grave danger to consciousness. His nervous system immediately begins firing, which causes hormones to surge throughout his body. Some of those hormones, such as adrenaline, give him the needed initial burst of energy to get up and run, while others spark a cascade to mobilize his body's immediate needs (increased blood pressure and a release of sugar for energy) and prepare for some of its longer-term needs (replenishing water and sugar).

The first feeling of our ancestor—let's call him Sam—is one that we're familiar with: butterflies in the stomach. Sam has that sensation partially because blood that was circulating in his gut to digest food now swiftly shifts to his legs so he can run as fast as possible. In times of rest, muscles use only about 20% of the blood that the heart pumps every minute, while the kidneys and gut each use another 20%. Within an instant of a stressful event, the strenuously working muscles use up to 90% of the blood that the energized heart is able to pump. Because the heart pumps much more vigorously than it did at rest, the muscles are actually bathed in 18 times more blood than during calm times. In the meantime, the kidneys and gut are only receiving about 1% of the blood during these stressful times. No wonder we don't want to eat during times of extreme stress.

When Sam leaps to his feet, he notices his heart is beating rapidly to pump blood as quickly as imaginable. As he runs from the tiger, he breathes quickly to oxygenate that blood. The sweat dripping down Sam's body and brow cools him as he runs. His pupils dilate fully so he can see any obstacles in his path; even in the dark, he won't trip over a log or rock. He won't think about anything but running because he is not supposed to stop, turn around, and suggest to the tiger that they figure out a way to settle their differences amicably.

Stress as a Helpful Factor

Without the stress reaction, our ancestors would not have survived. But stress has helped us do more than run from tigers. It keeps us alert and prepared. You can be sure that the next time Sam sat down to munch berries, he was attuned to the sounds of brush rustling nearby. That heightened vigilance, caused by low stress levels, can help us today. It's what helps us finish reports and helps our children study when anticipation of a test generates just the right amount of stress.

Few of us need to race from tigers today, but 21st-century crises, such as violence in our homes and communities, war, natural disasters, and major illnesses, require intense efforts for survival. But most of the events that cause stress for us are not immediately life-threatening—a fight with a spouse, pressure at work, economic worries, or the ongoing challenge of balancing our many roles. Yet our bodies are not designed to meet those needs repeatedly, day after day. Imagine if they were. Your boss warns you that she might fire you. Immediately that part of your brain that stored her favorite joke becomes energized and you retell the joke to lighten her mood, or your emotional centers help you come up with the perfect flattering comment. You need no sleep because you know that your survival at work requires you to clock those 92-hour workweeks. Eating no longer feels necessary because your body has learned to stretch last Tuesday's dinner for a full week. You needn't waste any time on frivolous meals! Bathroom breaks? No reason. Your kidneys have conveniently shut down.

Let's return to reality. When your boss first warns you that she may let you go, your first sensation is that you may vomit because you just ate a huge lunch. Suddenly there is not a drop of blood in your gut. All your blood has rushed to your legs and, for the life of you, you just want to escape her ferocious words. But you don't. You stand still because somehow you remember that it would be inappropriate office behavior to race out the door.

Your heart, however, beats as fast as it would if you were running. Your breathing intensifies. You sweat and have hot flashes because the adrenaline coursing through your veins is confused about why you aren't listening to it. Why are you standing still when the tiger—your boss—is ready to devour you?

Wouldn't it be great if we had multiple sets of hormones to help us deal most efficiently with each crisis? Hormones that made us regress to lovable 4-year-olds when we have fights with our mothers? Hormones that turn us into study machines with no biological needs—no sleep, no food, no bathroom needs, and certainly no sex—when we have to prepare for examinations? We only have the hormones that prepare us to escape from the tiger and other, more subtle jungle-based problems.

If Stress Is a Survival Tool, Why Is It Eating Us Alive?

When the tiger chased him, Sam had few options. Either the tiger ate him or he escaped. As cynical as it sounds, if he had been eaten, he wouldn't have had much to worry about anymore. If he survived, you can be sure that his burst of energy allowed him to outrun the tiger, or at least outrun Zok (his slower friend who never had the chance to become our ancestor because the tiger ate him instead of Sam). In his sprint for survival, Sam used up every hormone, reveled in his success, and in time, his body was able to return to normal. In the modern world, those same stress hormones remain in our bodies because, unlike Sam, we don't react as fully to our hormonal bursts. We don't sprint away. Instead, our stress hormones continue to circulate, unused and confused—why did my body remain seated when that tiger attacked?

In truth, we have more subtle varieties of hormones than those generated during a carnivorous attack. The body's intricate wiring allows us to meet a broad variety of needs. Blood pressure, for example, ranges widely during the day. During sleep, it can be quite low. At times of crisis or maximum exertion, it can become quite high. When we're functioning in the midst of a hectic day, blood pressure is somewhere in the middle range. Factors that control blood pressure—heart rate, how constricted the blood vessels are, salt and water load—are in a constant dance to meet the body's needs. That dance is carried out through the movements and fluctuations of nerves and hormones, all magically choreographed by the brain. The brain is not an objective choreographer, however. It is heavily influenced by emotion and passion. Sometimes blood pressure goes up because of a real need, such as the need to run or even to stand up after lying down. At other times, blood pressure goes up because of an intense emotion or stays up in a state of vigilance for a coming crisis. And the world is always ready to offer us another crisis.

Why do poor people suffer more diseases? The answer is profoundly complex. Certainly part of the answer is the pervasive presence of stress in their lives. They remain under constant siege so their blood pressure remains raised, and high blood pressure leads to disease. Two other factors explain why stressed people generally suffer ill health. People who are stressed are more likely to do whatever it takes to escape that stress. Many types of escape are profoundly harmful, such as smoking and abusing alcohol and drugs. People with persistent stress also tend to eat more, and obesity leads to ill health.

Let's return to Sam for a moment. Stress helped Sam survive other conditions beyond escaping a famished animal who thought he might be delicious. When Sam was hungry, he couldn't simply open a refrigerator or go to a supermarket. Plentiful seasons would be followed by leaner times and sometimes by famine. Sam's body was designed to adjust to a feast/famine cycle. In fact, he could predict when leaner times were likely to come. His body generated just enough stress signals that his metabolism adjusted to store more food as fat to get him through coming shortages. His body produced hormones to increase his appetite so he could eat as much as possible while food was still abundant. Are we surprised that people under low-level but persistent stress tend to overeat? Isn't this level of stress equivalent to a kind of foreboding that our ancestors experienced as they prepared for lean times?

Tying It Together

As you proceed through this book, please keep in mind the following key points from this brief overview of stress:

- ☀ Stress is nothing new. We'll always have some degree of stress in our lives.
- ☀ Stress is an important tool that can aid our survival.
- ☀ The body's reaction to stress is mediated through a complex interplay of sensory input—sights and sounds—as well as the brain and nervous system, hormones, and the body's cells and organs.

❋ Emotions play an important role in how we experience stress because the brain is the conductor of this system. The way we think about stress and what we choose to do about it affects the impact of a stressful event.

With these points as a backdrop, let's turn the discussion to parenting. Despite our parental desire to shelter our kids, we cannot completely eliminate stress from their lives. But we can play a vital role in helping them learn to respond to stress in the most beneficial ways. One of those important ways is understanding how emotions help us distinguish a real crisis from a bump in the road. A tiger running at us is an authentic crisis. A hurricane forecast mobilizes us to act quickly and evacuate. An oncoming car suddenly veering into our lane instantly energizes us to steer out of its path.

Milder stressors, such as a pressing deadline, a test to prepare for, or some nagging symptoms that require a doctor's checkup, deserve some extra vigilance. If a young person blows a mild stressor (such as cramming for a test) way out of proportion, she will be unable to prepare well because she will lose her ability to focus. She'll run from that tiger and be incapable of concentrating on anything but escape. In situations like these, parents' subtle (or not so subtle) messages can determine how children define *crisis* and how their stress hormones mobilize. Do you want your child to perceive a B- or a messy room as a major crisis?

I don't want to mislead you. I do not think that parents control their children's worlds and determine entirely how they define crises. Parents can't control poverty, racism, and all the other isms that plague humanity. Parents can't control the weather, disease, random violence, or war. But we can prepare children to navigate a range of crises by helping them realistically assess the immediacy of a threat, develop strategies to deal with and address problems, and develop counterbalancing relaxation tools that help them modify the effects of stress throughout their lives. Perhaps most importantly, we can *model* for them how to handle stress in a healthy way (more information about modeling is included in chapters 3, 27, and 28).

Ingredients of Resilience: 7 Crucial Cs

Remember when your child was an infant? So helpless and dependent. Most parents hold babies closely, pick them up whenever they cry, and make sure they're always warm and fed and dry. We buckle them snugly in their car seats and strollers. We protect them from every possible discomfort and danger. We rarely let them out of our sight. And when we must leave them, we make sure they are safely in the hands of dependable caregivers. We love them so much we want to hold them, tickle them, and make them smile and laugh all the time. We know how vulnerable infants are, and we handle them like fragile porcelain.

Then they grow up. They learn the word "no," start walking away, talk back to us, go to friends' homes for sleepovers, and want to hang out at the mall instead of home. We still yearn to protect them from any possible risk. We know they have to grow up, become independent, and experience the external world of school, peers, and community, but we wish we could wrap them up in that downy comforter, hug them close, and insulate them from every danger.

That natural instinct is bred into our parental bone marrow, probably going back scores of generations in our genetic makeup. But realistically, it is impossible and probably not all that wise when carried to the extreme. Why? Because kids *aren't* as fragile as we tend to think. They are born with strengths and abilities to cope with adversity, learn from their mistakes, and mature into responsible, competent adults. Yet they cannot develop and energize their inner resources unless we allow them opportunities to do so.

We don't want children to get hurt, of course, but we also need to acknowledge that they must be exposed to some risk to develop and practice coping skills if they are to grow up. If we rob them of opportunities to develop resilience or undercut their abilities by doing too much for them, solving all their dilemmas for them or overprotecting them, we actually send a damaging message—"I don't believe you're capable. You're not good enough." This hardly breeds competence or confidence in children. Our challenge instead is to give them some room to err, fall off their bikes and scrape their knees, and at the same time teach them *how* to ride steadily and confidently over the rocky paths that lie ahead.

Throughout this book, 3 essential themes are at the core of how adults affect children's resilience: 1) unconditional love is the bedrock of resilience because it creates security; 2) children meet adult expectations, for better or worse; and 3) children watch what we do more than they listen to what we say. Let's look at these themes more closely.

- Unconditional love gives children the deep-seated security that allows them to take chances when they need to adapt to new circumstances and the knowledge that in the long run all will be okay. Parents' unconditional love and acceptance will be discussed further in Chapter 15. For now, I simply urge you to keep in mind those feelings of protection that you had toward your child when he was a baby. As he grows up and away from you, pushing your buttons and trying your patience, show him your unconditional love. Don't assume that he knows it or takes it for granted. We must never let a child think we don't love and believe in him, even when we dislike or disapprove of his behaviors. Unconditional love doesn't mean unconditional approval. The child is not the behavior. Parents can reject certain behaviors and simultaneously love the child completely. The key is that love is never withdrawn or threatened to be withheld based on a behavior. It is about your child knowing that you are not going anywhere, no matter what. Hopefully parents will be the source of this essential ingredient of resilience, but a grandparent, an uncle, an aunt, a teacher, a health professional, or a counselor can also fill that role. The more supportive adults in a child's life, the more firmly rooted and unshakable his security will be.

- Youngsters live up or down to their parents' expectations. If parents expect the best of their children, kids tend to live up to those standards. High standards really matter, but let me be crystal clear—by high standards, I am not referring to achievements. I don't mean straight-A report cards, consistent 10s in gymnastics, or pitching perfect Little League games. I mean being a good human being—considerate, respectful, honest, fair, generous, responsible...you know, the qualities you hope your children have. On the other hand, if parents expect children to be lazy, argumentative, thoughtless, selfish, or dependent, kids sense those negatives. "Why," they figure, "should I try to be any different? I guess I'm dumb, slow, a loser, or whatever," and "I have nothing to lose. My parents already think I'm sneaky [or fill in an adjective of your own], so why shouldn't I just lie to them?"

Young people also absorb messages from outside the family and change their behavior to meet those expectations. Sometimes these messages support the positive image that parents want their children to have of themselves. Other times parents must shield their children from harmful portrayals of youth and low expectations.

As children's most powerful models, parents are in the best position to teach them about stress and resilience. Whether they're toddlers or teens, children observe parents closely. If we show them negative ways of coping with our own stress, they will follow our example. If we rant at the driver who cut into our traffic lane, our kids will assume that road rage is acceptable. If we drink heavily after work each evening, we're sending the message that alcohol is an acceptable stress reliever. If we binge on junk food whenever we're anxious, they are likely to do the same.

Here is a common example of how a parent unintentionally models negative coping. "Michael, why don't you ever help your mother? Take your dishes to the sink! Pick up your junk—look at that mess! Crap is spilling out of your book bag all over the floor. Why are your shoes and jacket on the sofa? Jeez, I want to stretch out and just watch TV tonight. I've had a horrible day at work. C'mon, get your stuff out of here.

"Oh, Gladys, as long as you're up, bring me another beer."

Dad has clearly had a bad day, but what lesson does he model for his son? Yell, criticize, vent your anger at others, slump on the sofa, and wash it down with another beer.

On the other hand, if parents talk about their anger or discuss how the day's work was tense and exhausting, they send the message that talking about frustration and stress is a healthy way to vent. They also can demonstrate constructive coping methods by going for a walk or jog after a bad day at work, taking time for themselves to relax before rushing to make dinner, or practicing deep breathing or yoga.

As we show children beneficial ways to deal with stress, we are not only offering them good role models but also treating ourselves well. That's a generous gift to ourselves and our children. We may not think that children always pay attention to what we are doing, but they do. We probably won't be perfect models every time we're stressed, of course, but each time we attempt to offer children a constructive model, we reduce the potential that they will turn to negative ways of coping with stress.

Roots of Resilience

As we've seen, resilience is usually defined as an ability to bounce back or recover from adversity. Resilience has another, similar definition—the power or ability to return to the original form or position. Think of a bent twig. It can be held or tied down, but it will eventually straighten up to its original position. Or compare resilience to those rubbery stretch bands used for exercising. They can be pulled to several times their original lengths, but when you let go, they spring back to their original size and shape. Here's the point of these analogies—resilience is a quality that's part of the original. It's already packaged in our kids' makeup. It's not something we need to go out and acquire for them; rather, it is already within them. We just need to nurture it.

It's vital to remember that all children come equipped with assets and abilities, strengths that have been described as "islands of competence," that can become sources of pride and springboards to ongoing accomplishments. Our job is to help children gain appropriate confidence by helping them recognize that they possess various abilities and inner resources. This confidence is an essential ingredient of resilience and can be nurtured at any time in life. Just as we develop and strengthen our muscles by exercising them, we can develop resilience by paying attention to those strengths and building on them.

Seven Crucial Cs of Resilience

To build resilience, it is helpful to begin by organizing many action steps into a few categories. A common language about resilience also allows us to collaborate better with spouses, neighbors, and communities as we work together to build supportive strategies for children. I organize the steps and language into 7 integral, interrelated components that I call the 7 Crucial Cs—*competence, confidence, connection, character, contribution, coping,* and *control*. Many of these Cs are borrowed from great thinkers on positive youth development and resilience whose paths have informed mine. The original 4 Cs—*competence, confidence, connection,* and *character*—were coined by Rick Little, who founded the International Youth Foundation.

Each C will be explained individually in succeeding chapters, but to begin this discussion, I will summarize each component and pose a series of questions about each C. Let these questions rattle around in your mind for a while. Instant answers aren't necessary. The questions are designed only to help you reflect.

Competence

Competence is the ability or know-how to handle situations effectively. It's not a vague feeling or hunch that "I can do this." Competence is acquired through actual experience. Children can't become competent without first developing a set of skills that allows them to trust their judgments, make responsible choices, and face difficult situations. In thinking about your child's competence and how to fortify it, ask yourself

- Do I help my child focus on her strengths and build on them?
- Do I notice what she does well or do I focus on her mistakes?
- When I need to point out a mistake, am I clear and focused or do I communicate that I believe she always messes up?
- Do I help her recognize what she has going for herself?
- Am I helping her build the educational, social, and stress-reduction skills necessary to make her competent in the real world?
- Do I communicate in a way that empowers my child to make her own decisions or do I undermine her sense of competence by giving her information in ways she can't grasp? In other words, do I lecture her or do I facilitate her thinking?
- Do I let her make safe mistakes so she has the opportunity to right herself or do I try to protect her from every trip and fall?
- As I try to protect her, does my interference mistakenly send the message, "I don't think you can handle this"?
- If I have more than one child, do I recognize the competencies of each without comparison to siblings?

Confidence

True confidence, the solid belief in one's own abilities, is rooted in competence. Children gain confidence by demonstrating their competence in real situations. Confidence is not warm-and-fuzzy self-esteem that supposedly results from telling kids they're special or precious. Children who experience their own competence and know they are safe and protected develop a deep-seated security that promotes the confidence to face and cope with challenges. When parents support children in finding their own islands of competence and building on them, they prepare kids to gain enough confidence to try new ventures and trust their abilities to make sound choices.

In thinking about your child's degree of confidence, consider the following questions:

- Do I see the best in my child so that he can see the best in himself?
- Do I clearly express that I expect the best qualities (not achievements, but personal qualities such as fairness, integrity, persistence, and kindness) in him?
- Do I help him recognize what he has done right or well?
- Do I treat him as an incapable child or as a youngster who is learning to navigate his world?
- Do I praise him often enough? Do I praise him honestly about specific achievements or do I give such diffuse praise that it doesn't seem authentic? (More information about praising effectively is in Chapter 7.)
- Do I catch him being good when he is generous, helpful, and kind or when he does something without being asked or cajoled?
- Do I encourage him to strive just a little bit farther because I believe he can succeed? Do I hold realistically high expectations?
- Do I unintentionally push him to take on more than he can realistically handle, causing him to stumble and lose confidence?
- When I need to criticize or correct him, do I focus only on what he's doing wrong or do I remind him that he is capable of doing well?
- Do I avoid instilling shame in my child?

Connection

Children with close ties to family, friends, school, and community are more likely to have a solid sense of security that produces strong values and prevents them from seeking destructive alternatives. Family is the central force in any child's life, but connections to civic, educational, religious, and athletic groups can also increase a young person's sense of belonging to a wider world and being safe within it.

Some questions to ponder when considering how connected your child is to family and the broader world include

- Do we build a sense of physical safety and emotional security within our home?
- Does my child know that I am absolutely crazy in love with her?
- Do I understand that the challenges my child will put me through on her path toward independence are normal developmental phases or will I take them so personally that our relationship will be harmed?
- Do I allow my child to have and express all types of emotions or do I suppress unpleasant feelings? Is she learning that going to other people for emotional support during difficult times is productive or shameful?

* Do we do everything to address conflict within our family and work to resolve problems rather than let them fester?
* Do we have a television and entertainment center in almost every room or do we create a common space where our family shares time together?
* Do I encourage my child to take pride in the various ethnic, religious, or cultural groups to which we belong?
* Do I jealously guard my child from developing close relationships with others or do I foster healthy relationships that I know will reinforce my positive messages?
* Do I protect my friends' and neighbors' children, just as I hope they will protect mine?

Character

Children need a fundamental sense of right and wrong to ensure they are prepared to make wise choices, contribute to the world, and become stable adults. Children with character enjoy a strong sense of self-worth and confidence. They are more comfortable sticking to their own values and demonstrating a caring attitude toward others. Some basic questions to ask yourself include

* Do I help my child understand how his behaviors affect other people in good and bad ways?
* Am I helping my child recognize himself as a caring person?
* Do I allow him to clarify his own values?
* Do I allow him to consider right versus wrong and look beyond immediate satisfaction or selfish needs?
* Do I value him so clearly that I model the importance of caring for others?
* Do I demonstrate the importance of community?
* Do I help him develop a sense of spirituality?
* Am I careful to avoid racist, ethnic, or hateful statements or stereotypes? Am I clear how I regard these thoughts and statements whenever and wherever my child is exposed to them?
* Do I express how I think of others' needs when I make decisions or take actions?

Contribution

It is a powerful lesson when children realize that the world is a better place *because they are in it.* Children who understand the importance of personal contribution gain a sense of purpose that can motivate them. They will not only take actions and make choices that improve the world, but they will also enhance their own competence, character, and sense of connection. Teens who contribute to their communities will be surrounded by reinforcing thank-yous instead of the low expectations and condemnation so many teens endure.

Before we can foster this sense of contribution, here are some things to consider.

- Do I communicate to my child (at appropriate age levels, of course) that many people in the world do not have as much human contact, money, freedom, and security as they need?
- Do I teach the important value of serving others? Do I model generosity with my time and money?
- Do I make clear to my child that I believe she can improve the world?
- Do I create opportunities for each child to contribute in some specific way?
- Do I search my child's circle for other adults who might serve as role models who contribute to their communities and the world? Do I use these adults as examples to encourage my child to be the best she can be?

Coping

Children who learn to cope effectively with stress are better prepared to overcome life's challenges. The best protection against unsafe, worrisome behaviors may be a wide repertoire of positive, adaptive coping strategies. Before we begin teaching children this repertoire of coping and stress-reduction skills, some basic questions to ask ourselves include

- Do I help him understand the difference between a real crisis and something that just feels like an emergency?
- Do I model positive coping strategies on a consistent basis?
- Do I allow my child enough time to use imaginative play? Do I recognize that fantasy and play are childhood's tools to solve problems?
- Do I guide my child to develop positive, effective coping strategies?
- Do I believe that telling him to "just stop" the negative behaviors will do any good?
- Do I recognize that for many young people, risk behaviors are attempts to alleviate their stress and pain?
- If my child participates in negative behaviors, do I condemn him for it? Do I recognize that I may only increase his sense of shame and therefore drive him toward more negativity?
- Do I model problem-solving step-by-step or do I just react emotionally when I'm overwhelmed?
- Do I model the response that sometimes the best thing to do is conserve energy and let go of the belief that I can tackle all problems?
- Do I model the importance of caring for our bodies through exercise, good nutrition, and adequate sleep? Do I model relaxation techniques?

* Do I encourage creative expression?
* As I struggle to compose myself so I can make fair, wise decisions under pressure, do I model how I take control rather than respond impulsively or rashly to stressful situations?
* Do I create a family environment in which talking, listening, and sharing are safe, comfortable, and productive?

Control

When children realize that *they* can control the outcomes of their decisions and actions, they're more likely to know that they have the ability to do what it takes to bounce back. On the other hand, if parents make all the decisions, children are denied opportunities to learn control. A child who feels "everything always happens to me" tends to become passive, pessimistic, or even depressed. She sees control as external—whatever she does really doesn't matter because she has no control of the outcome. But a resilient child knows that she has internal control. By her choices and actions, she determines the results. She knows that she can make a difference, which further promotes her competence and confidence. Some questions about control include

* Do I help my child understand that life's events are not purely random and most things happen as a direct result of someone's actions and choices?
* On the other hand, do I help my child understand that she isn't responsible for many of the bad circumstances in her life (such as parents' separation or divorce)?
* Do I help her think about the future, but take it one step at a time?
* Do I help her recognize even her small successes so she can experience the knowledge that she can succeed?
* Do I help her understand that no one can control all circumstances, but everyone can shift the odds by choosing positive or protective behaviors?
* Do I understand that discipline is about teaching, not punishing or controlling? Do I use discipline as a means to help my child understand that her actions produce certain consequences?
* Do I reward demonstrated responsibility with increased privileges?

A Web of 7 Cs

Before we consider each of the 7 Cs individually and in depth, I want to emphasize how interrelated they are. I hope you will envision them as a carefully constructed web as they relate to resilience. Here is a brief, whirlwind description of how intricately interwoven these 7 ingredients of resilience are.

Children need to experience *competence* to gain *confidence.* They need *connections* with an adult to reinforce those points of *competence.* They need *character* to know what they should *contribute* to their families and the world, and *character* is forged through deep *connection* to others. *Contribution* builds *character* and further strengthens *connections*. Children who *contribute* to their communities gain *confidence* as they feel more and more *competent*. All of this leads them to recognize that they can make a difference and change their environments, and this gives them a heightened sense of *control*. Children with a sense of *control* believe in their ability to solve problems so they will more tenaciously attack a problem until they find a solution. This newfound area of *competence* then enhances their *confidence,* which will be used the next time they need to reinforce their beliefs in their ability to *control* their environment. When children know they can *control* their environment, they will more likely use healthy *coping* strategies because the need to deaden the senses or escape reality will be lessened. A key *coping* strategy is turning to people with whom you have strong *connections.* And so on.

As you think about the building blocks of resilience, do not be surprised when you notice that your child is already strong in one or two of these categories and that you need to focus your energies on other areas. Similarly, your community may be expert at supporting some components of resilience and be in serious need of other strategies that will support its young people to adapt and thrive.

Not Letting Others Undermine Your Child's Resilience (or Psych You Out!)

Ask any mother, teacher, or coach—we know in our gut that youth live up or down to our expectations. That's why we went out of our way to catch our children being good when they were 2 years old. They delighted in our pride and kept doing what it took to earn our praise. Teenagers would be no different, but as they grow up they quickly learn that people begin to expect the worst of them. Many parents are too busy to notice the continued miracles of normal development and have just enough time to focus on the problems that arise. Messages from society portray teens as the source of problems; they are viewed as challenging, even dangerous.

As my twin daughters were turning 13, I experienced an onslaught of warnings from near-strangers and friends alike. "Get ready...just remember they can't help it." "It'll get better." "Oh well, you'll look sophisticated when you're gray." I think I got an extra dose because of my well-known respect for teens. "Dr Ken, the world is watching you," was my favorite comment. I heard, "We'll see what you think of teens once you have them," more times than I can count. I usually smiled because it was so much easier than launching into a tirade. "How dare you hold my girls to low expectations," I wanted to say. Of course, to prove I was not naive, I would have liked to continue, "Yes, they will test me and my boundaries. I hope they do. How else will they test their limits? I know it won't always be fun, but I sure am not going to make it worse by fearing them. I will continue to expect the very best from them!"

Media Misrepresentation of Teens

Books that portray how crazy teens are and popular media that reinforce their self-indulgence reinforce the sense of dread, urgency, and foreboding that parents feel about the arrival of adolescence. Even exciting new medical knowledge about the teen brain is sometimes presented in ways that suggest teens are all impulse and no control and that a part of their brains are missing.

New imaging techniques prove what we have always known—the teen brain is a work in progress. The emotional center of the brain, the amygdala, develops more rapidly than the thinking center that regulates emotions, the cerebral cortex. The brain is not fully developed until about age 25. This does not mean teens are broken. It means we need to nurture them and pay special attention to helping them avoid situations in which they would find it harder to regulate their emotions and equip them with tools that make it easier for them to do the right thing, even when their emotions are spinning out of control. Don't worry, a lot of this book is about just that!

If parents weren't already frightened by stereotypes of adolescence, they receive media and even some public health messages that hype teen sexuality, drug use, and violence—"Crisis in America!!!" This hyperbole may make for good ratings and fear always catches people's attention, but this "Teens at risk!" mentality that promotes the storm and stress of adolescence does great harm to our youth. Beyond increasing parental anxiety, it leads to the negative behaviors we worry about and the counterculture that interferes with youth taking the positive steps they need to thrive.

The offensive portrayal of youth creates a self-fulfilling prophecy for 2 key reasons. First, remember that one of the fundamental questions of adolescence is, "Am I normal?" Teens tend to do what they think "normal" is. If a teen sees a stereotype often enough, she will believe it and might behave negatively just to fit in. The second point follows directly: Because teens live up or down to expectations, they will behave in ways they believe others expect. The more we allow these negative images to circulate, the more youth will do what it takes to match them, the more uncomfortable they will feel with themselves when they don't, and the greater difficulty they will experience navigating peer relationships when they choose to do the right thing.

I have counseled students going to college whose biggest anxiety had nothing to do with academics. Instead, they worried they wouldn't be able to keep up with the drinking. I know countless teens who feel badly about their virginity because they are 16 and know with certainty they are abnormal. I know many who are having sex, not because they are ready but because they think they are supposed to. I watch painfully as youth in underperforming schools don't believe they're supposed to study because they've incorporated a toxic message about their potential to become highly educated into their self-image and have grown to accept that academics are not for them. These underserved teens have investments directed toward them in the form of prevention programs but have few enrichment activities. Despite the best of intentions, they may receive a message that the very issues the prevention programs target must be what normal teenagers like them do. If prevention programs were better balanced with strength-building enrichment programs, teens would have positive alternatives clearly defined and a better understanding that they were expected to develop into creative, future-oriented people.

With the best of intentions, public health messages want to illuminate the problems of youth. "Did you know that X% of teens have sex before the end of high school?" "An alarming X% of adolescents use drugs." "In the city of X more than X% of teens drop out before graduating high school." "Binge drinking is a growing problem on campuses; at X University, X% of freshman say they have blacked out after a night of drinking."

News outlets hype stories of teen crises to draw parents in. Because "dog bites boy" isn't news, they rarely tell the stories of the kids thriving and contributing to society. Instead, lead-ins ensure that parents will tune into the news. "Is your child having sex in your house at 3:00 in the afternoon? Parents, you'll want to hear the startling finding of a new study on teen sexuality, right after these messages." Then the story airs. "Crisis in our community—38% of teens..."

When herds of youth converge on a designated location in response to a viral text message (aka, a "flash mob" organized through social media), it's news. If anyone gets hurt, it's a 48-point headline and leads the evening news. When every expert asks, "Where are the parents?" and talks about "kids nowadays," youth learn that adolescents are supposed to frighten us. The news needs to be reported, of course, but as a rare phenomenon. Stories should include facts without hype. And wouldn't it be nice if some stories focused on helping teens resist peer pressure by giving them face-saving techniques they can use to leave a risky situation while following their own internal compass? (See chapters 11, 12, and 13.)

Countering the Negative News

There are better ways, and my ideas are not revelations. Social marketing experts understand the power of the media in shaping self-perceptions and behaviors. Jeff Linkenbach, EdD, of Montana State University has created a vigorous response to popular messages about adolescents. With www.mostofus.org, he strives to teach communities and policy makers that drive the self-perception of youth to transform how youth are portrayed.

What if the binge-drinking story said, "Although X% of college freshmen say they are drinking to dangerous levels on the weekends, the good news is that most teens are choosing better ways of spending their time." What if the story on school dropouts sounded more like, "Clearly schools in X city are not performing well because some kids are not able to be successful and X% are leaving. The good news is that most teens are working hard to keep their stake in the future." Imagine how much better youth who wanted to delay sexual activity would feel if stories on teen sexuality ran like this: "Despite the fact that popular shows focus on teens having sex, in a recent study by X Foundation, fewer than half of teens were choosing to have sex by age X."

So what can a parent do? First, never stop catching your teen being good. Second, set clear positive expectations. Third, ignore the hype that creates anxiety in you and subtly transmits lowered expectations to your child. Fourth, as best as you can, insulate your children from the negative messages swirling around them by reframing the hype. If the news will not point out that 22% is not a crisis, then you do it. Listen to the story and note, "Too bad for those kids, but the good news is that most kids, more than 3 out of 4 actually, are not doing it."

What can a parent do within the community or as a community leader?

* Spread the good news messages.
* Advocate for the positive portrayal of youth in the community. Ask for a shift away from media coverage where only the highest achievers and delinquents get noticed. Make sure acts of generosity and compassion shown by everyday students are noticed as well.
* Advocate for enrichment programs in communities and schools, especially in those areas most at risk that currently only have prevention programs. This doesn't mean you should suggest that risk-based programs (like those for drugs, violence, teen pregnancy, bullying, or sexually transmitted infections) be cut—they have tremendous value. But we must guard against a situation in which only youth who engage in worrisome behaviors get our added attention and those who don't view themselves as outside "expected" behaviors in their community. Sports, art programs, and academic enrichment activities running in parallel send the message that we expect youth to be creative, have strong bodies and minds, and be prepared to lead us into the future.
* Give youth opportunities to contribute to their communities. When they are serving others, their value will be noticed and they will receive vital reinforcing displays of gratitude.

☀ Work with parents of your teen's friends and with your community so that many more young people have the rules and boundaries you have for your own child. Adolescents who see these boundaries as normal have no reason to rebel against them.

The next time a friend tells you, "Uh-oh, she's 12, put on your safety belt," smile and say, "I'm ready for the ride. There will be some bumps, but I expect her to come through just fine. She has already shown me what a fine person she is."

PART 2

Competence and Confidence

Competence is ability rooted in experience. Children acquire competence by mastering tasks and facing challenges. Competence is cumulative; the more they master life experiences, the more children realize they can tackle new challenges, and thereby they develop genuine confidence in themselves. Along with a strong sense of competence comes tenacity, the ability to stick with tough tasks and solve difficult problems. Safety also follows competence because children who trust their abilities have an easier time standing firm in their values and making their own decisions when faced with unsafe situations.

Competence is not a vague feeling that "I can handle this." If it were, it would not only be empty and unfounded, but it could also be dangerous. For example, a 4-year-old who has just learned to ride a "big kid's" bike may *feel* capable of cruising around the neighborhood and crossing major intersections, but obviously she is not yet able to do so. A 14-year-old might argue, "I can take care of myself, Dad. If there's beer at the party and other kids start drinking, I can handle it. I just won't drink." But under pressure to be accepted by friends, young people can become overwhelmed. They often *assume* that they will be able to handle challenges, but they haven't yet been in a real crunch. They haven't been tested by experience. They haven't developed and demonstrated enough competence—yet.

Competence derives from a wide range of achievements, from almost invisible steps to major leaps. A toddler experiences accomplishment when he whizzes in the toilet instead of on the floor. A child becomes competent when she learns to build a sand castle and demonstrates tenacity when she rebuilds it over and over after waves wash it away. A child demonstrates bravery and confidence when she crosses the threshold on the first day of kindergarten, turns around, and gives her parents a nod that says, "I'll be okay." She knows she is competent when she makes it through the day despite her fears, and she is ready to go back the next day.

The first time a child can cook eggs by himself may be a small deal to adults, but it's a milestone for him. A child experiences a new level of competence when a teacher helps him understand that his history report is much better written than his last attempt. A youngster owns his own sense of competence when, after getting hit in the nose with a hardball, he goes back out and practices fielding until he's no longer afraid to take his position at third base. A teenager experiences a rich, satisfying competence when he is able to stand on his convictions and not shoplift or try drugs when his friends are doing so.

Competence is the first of the 7 Crucial Cs to consider because it provides the bedrock for resilience. Without genuine competence, it is unlikely the other 6 Cs could be developed. Competence is the largest area to cover in this discussion because fostering competence requires an understanding of several key principles.

- **Getting out of the way!** Normal child development occurs because children are wired to build new knowledge and skills from each experience. Sometimes adults do their best when they get out of kids' way.

- **Play is one of the major jobs of childhood.** It is filled with opportunities for children to discover their competencies. We must allow plenty of time for free child-driven play, the most effective type of play for children to discover their competence in the world.

- **Noticing, praising, and criticizing.** Competence is enhanced or hindered by the ways that we communicate and interact with children. New skills and abilities are reinforced when adults notice and praise them. Criticism, when given harshly or insensitively, can undermine a child's ability to become more competent. When criticism is offered as constructive, targeted feedback, it can enhance growing competence.

- **Striving for authentic success.** If we are to prepare children to thrive in the future, we must think beyond the grades and extracurricular schedules that seem to measure success today. We must ask whether children possess tenacity, love of learning, and creativity. We should consider whether they are under so much pressure that those critical ingredients will be stifled.

- **Thinking clearly.** Sometimes the way we think prevents us from recognizing our competence and paralyzes confidence. This is true for children too. To be able to get past difficulties, we first have to be able to stop thinking in a self-destructive manner.

- **No more lectures.** Though our advice is offered with good intentions, it often undermines children's growing competence. In short, lecturing backfires. We need to know how children think so that we can put them in the driver's seat as they develop solutions for themselves.

- **Guiding children to find the right choices.** Parents can use specific skills to steer kids toward making their own wise, safe decisions in the face of peer pressure.

- **Media literacy.** Young people need to be able to sift through all the media-driven messages so that they can be in control of their own opinions and self-image.

Getting Out of the Way

As children develop, they increase their competence over time. Think about your own child's development and how nearly every day brings new skills and abilities. How parents react to these miracles is key to a child's motivation to continue striving. If a child takes a significant step and no one notices or cares, she learns that her accomplishments don't matter. These achievements are often ignored because busy, stressed parents take normal events for granted—after all, every child learns to roll over, to walk, to talk, to go to school for the first time.

Think about the biggest challenge of your adult life or your most difficult task at work. I bet it pales in comparison to the huge leap that occurred when you learned to stand up and take your first step as a toddler. Children accomplish these tasks all the time, but some parents don't build on the spirit of growing competence innate to childhood because they ignore their child's everyday milestones.

Other parents do anything but ignore their children. They hover, praise incessantly, and protect, protect, protect. While involved parents are more likely to produce motivated kids, we have to find some balance. Overly involved parents can unintentionally get in the way of children's acquisition of confidence and drive to achieve new competencies. If we push too hard to master the next step, we may push children into feeling incompetent. We also may inadvertently interfere with natural processes that allow them to become increasingly competent.

To foster their competence, we need to recognize when and how our parental involvement helps or hurts. As situations arise throughout childhood and adolescence, we need to understand when to do the following 3 things:
* Get out of the way.
* Join in and help a child build new avenues of competence.
* Guide a child to think through situations wisely and safely.

Getting out of the way is a tough challenge. We want to help, fix, and guide kids. But we have to remind ourselves that when we just let them figure things out for themselves, we communicate the powerful message, "I think you are competent and wise." When we allow them to finish their arts-and-crafts projects without our interference, we're saying, "I think you are creative." When we let them build blocks to their unique specifications, we are communicating, "I think you are capable." And when the blocks tumble down and they rebuild them without our intervention, we convey the message, "I like it when you try again."

Every time we try to solve children's problems for them, we undercut their growing sense of competence. If we solve all their problems, they will remain dependent on us. While it may be an attractive prospect to have our children always need us, we have to remind ourselves that our job is to create capable individuals. When we support their problem-solving skills by getting out of their way or by offering gentle guidance only when necessary or when they ask for it, we foster their growing sense of self-reliance and independence. When we recognize their capabilities, we diminish the number of power struggles with them. As a result, our children will be more comfortable returning to us for the nurturance and support that has no age boundaries.

The Parent Alarm

Why do many parents have so much difficulty trusting in their children's competence to learn how to face and overcome challenges? It's our *parent alarm*—that menacing feeling that arises whenever we sense that our children might be in trouble. As soon as the parent alarm goes off, we immediately proclaim restrictions that prevent them from even getting close to a sticky situation. The alarm is also a major barrier to effective communication.

"Mom, I met this girl..." The parent alarm response: "You're too young to date!" That's a lost opportunity to discuss feelings, sexuality, and respect for others when building relationships.

"Dad, I think the guys on the next block are smoking some weed..." Dad's parent alarm blasts, "Never go over there! Don't you dare hang out with them!" That's a lost opportunity for a discussion about drugs, peer pressure, and especially how grateful Dad is that his son comes and talks to him about drugs.

The parent alarm is an instinctual rapid response we use to steer children away from danger when our sensors shout, "TROUBLE!" The parent alarm is beneficial, of course, when a situation involves danger. Don't worry about building competence at that moment; let the alarm ring and rescue your child. Don't worry about the psychological ramifications of preventing a young child from running into the street—just grab her! If you have to scream and take quick action to prevent a 4-year-old from toppling a pot of boiling water off the stove, yell loudly! If your teenager is drunk and getting in a car, grab the keys and prevent tragedy at all costs. These are lessons that we cannot afford to let children learn on their own.

Short of scenarios that challenge safety, we should try to let children figure things out on their own. Sometimes doing nothing is precisely what they need. Wendy Mogel speaks of this in her aptly titled book, *The Blessing of a Skinned Knee*. Paying attention but doing nothing to interfere sends children the wonderful message, "I trust you to handle this."

Some problems clearly require guidance. In *Parent Effectiveness Training*, Thomas Gordon offers considerable wisdom that can help parents decide when and how to intervene. He suggests that parents first decide who owns the problem at hand. If the child owns it (when the problem is one that a child experiences in her own life independent of her parents, such as a conflict with a friend or teacher), parents can be most helpful if they don't try to solve the problem. They can get out of her way or help her to problem-solve by using techniques like role-playing or choreographed conversations (explained in Chapter 11). On the other hand, if parents own the problem or if a child's behavior interferes with the parents' lives (such as coming home late and waking parents), the parent has the right to be more directive.

Many parents believe that they know exactly how to get children to figure out what's wrong—they tell them; they lecture about every possible dire consequence of their behaviors. Parents' protective instincts want to steer children far away from dangerous outcomes and toward safer, immediate solutions. What are some reasons that we jump in as soon as our parent alarm rings and try to fix their problems or correct their mistakes?

- We worry that they will not be successful.
- We think that they are not trying their hardest.
- We worry that they will embarrass us or reflect poorly on us.
- We see our children as reflections of ourselves; they become the product we have produced, and we want our work to seem perfect.
- We are uncomfortable when we make mistakes and assume our children share that insecurity. We wish to spare them the same discomfort.
- We have strong standards of right and wrong, and we don't want our children to stray too close to the boundaries of what we believe is wrong.
- We think that criticism is the best kind of guidance, and we offer our judgments as keys to self-improvement.

Interference Versus Getting Out of the Way

Let's consider some examples of how parents interfere or get out of the way as a child develops from toddlerhood through adolescence. For each scenario, first imagine what your parental impulse would be if this were your child. Then consider whether you could let go enough to allow her to boost her own competence. Look for the subtle messages you might convey with your desire to protect your child.

Eleven-month-old Sophia pulls herself up on wobbly legs and takes her first step. What a wonderful metaphor for life! She takes an almost unimaginable leap—she has just changed her entire perspective on the world. What's next? She inevitably falls. Will anyone notice her great achievement? Or will the tall people around her simply see this as a normal event and ignore this magnificent moment? Will they applaud, cheer, and encourage her to use her legs, strength, and ingenuity to stand right back up? Or will they worry that she might get a bruise, run to pick her up, and prevent her from experiencing the thrill of getting back up by herself?

A few months later, Sophia is an avid walker exploring her environment. She wants to climb over the sofa and up and down stairs, and explore the kitchen (with all its knives, electric appliances, and other dangers) and the living room (with all its fragile knickknacks). Will her parents get down on their knees to see the world from her perspective and childproof the house so she can move around freely and safely? Will they grab her every time she gets near a breakable object, shout "No!" and make her wonder why her parents seem to think all glass objects are intrinsically evil? Will they let her hold and turn them in her little hands, cupped gently by their own palms, while she observes and touches? (Afterward, they put fragile items out of her reach and replace them with plastic toys.) Will they yell at her every time she climbs because they worry that she may fall, or will they stack a pile of pillows on the floor and let her climb and tumble to her heart's content? Will they let her explore her home freely but safety, or will they restrict her to a playpen?

At age 4, Sophia is proudly building a house with blocks. Do her parents watch and praise her as she adds piece by piece and encourage her to go further? Or do they say, "That's going to fall down if you don't put the bigger blocks on the bottom?" They're trying to be helpful by teaching her basic physics, but they're sending her the message, "I don't think you're a very good builder." Perhaps they will tell her, "Your brother built a really tall tower this morning," which may make her feel less capable and make her believe that life is a competition.

Do they sit down next to her, join in the project, and ask her where to place each block? If they let Sophia be the construction foreman while they play the carpenter's role, they have the joy of playing alongside her and entering her fantasy world, while allowing her to experience the wonderful, powerful feeling of control. But if her parents sit beside her and build a bigger, sturdier house than she could ever build, they leave her feeling somewhat incapable and inferior. If they simply remind her, "Don't forget to clean up that mess," when she finishes building and fail to notice her accomplishment, what message are they sending her?

At age 6, Sophia paints a picture of a garden under a bright blue sky. She uses vivid colors to paint flowers that are all larger than the brown dog in the corner. Do her parents tell her, "That is the most perfect picture in the whole world," which makes her question their assessment skills? Or do they say, "What beautiful colors," which offers praise that she knows she has earned? Do they tell her, "The flowers are out of proportion to the dog," which shows her they are displeased? Do they say, "We have to get you art lessons now," which may make them feel like wonderful parents, but forces her to specialize when she only wanted to play with paints? Do they encourage her to proceed at her own pace by saying, "I really like your picture. Here's another piece of paper. Please draw me another wonderful surprise"? Do they support her creativity with open-ended remarks such as, "Tell me about your picture"? This type of neutral comment opens an opportunity to learn from her imagination and avoids the embarrassment she would feel if they made a faulty guess about the images in her picture.

When Sophia is in fourth grade, she has her first group assignment for science. She and 2 classmates are studying endangered rain forest animals, but her partners aren't pulling their weight. Sophia gets frustrated but does her own work well. Do her parents encourage the work she is doing and stay nearby so that they can answer her questions as they arise? Or do they tell her, "We are going to make the most wonderful project in the whole school," and spend the whole evening completing "our" science project?

When they see her class's completed projects, do they say, "Yours is the best science project I've ever seen! You're my little environmentalist!" and sign her up for an after-school club for future scientists? Or do they say, "You really did a nice job. I especially liked the piece on the gorilla," which is authentic, reality-based praise, and then ask her if she wants to take a trip to the zoo?

Or do they tell her they like her work, but if she had put in more time it could have been even better "like Soyun's," which clearly tells her that her parents are dissatisfied? If they really think she could have done a better job, they might say something specific, such as, "I really liked your section on the red-eyed tree frog. You put a lot of heart into that. I noticed there were other animals you didn't include. Were there any other animals you wish you had more time to study?"

At age 12, Sophia is about to enter that phase of middle childhood that parents dread—the "mean girl" stage. Her best friend abruptly rejects her for "not even liking boys yet and still playing with dolls." Sophia comes home devastated, runs to her mother, and cries, "Courtney's telling everyone I'm a baby."

Oh, no! Her mother's parent alarm blares, "I'd better fix this. I've got to make her feel better." Does she tell Sophia, "This isn't such a big deal," which devalues Sophia's hurt and lets her know that her mother thinks she's emotionally immature? Does she reply, "I never liked Courtney anyway," in an attempt to bond with her daughter? That response implies that her daughter has bad taste in friends. And at some future point, if Mom needs to offer advice or guidance about avoiding negative influence from Courtney, this comment sets Mom up for the retort, "You never liked her anyway," after the girls repair their friendship (which preteen girls do even as we parents continue to hold grudges for the hurt our daughter has endured).

If Sophia's mother says, "You know, Courtney's mother is my friend, so you'd better work this out," she sends the message that her priorities do not include her daughter. If she says, "I once had a friend who dumped me. Let me tell you how I handled it," that statement translates into, "I have to give you the solution because you are not competent to fix it yourself." Or does she listen closely to her daughter's feelings, acknowledge how upsetting the situation is, and then ask, "How do you think you can handle this?"

Now Sophia is 15 years old and has just broken up with her first boyfriend. She brushes past her parents and says, "You just wouldn't understand." An hour later, she sulks into the living room, cuddles between her mother and father on the sofa, and talks about a fight she and Tyler had. Do her parents say, "What a creep he is! You're better off without him," which prevents her from saying she's still madly in love? Do they say, "You know, if you just lost a little weight, boys would find you so attractive?" Do they say, "You were too young to start dating anyway. We knew you'd get hurt"? Or do they just listen quietly and help her think it through and communicate with their supportive presence that it's okay to be sad?

Finally, Sophia is a senior preparing for college. Do her parents help her exaggerate her application résumé, which clearly tells her that who she is, the authentic package, is just not good enough? Do they rewrite her essay, sending the unspoken message that they see her as incapable of doing it well enough herself? Do they tell her that she must go to the college that family members attended, or that they have worked so hard only so that she can go to the very best college? Who will she think they're really concerned about? Whose needs and reputation are her parents really looking after? Will she feel like a failure if she doesn't get into her first-choice school? Will she feel as though she has failed this initiation into adulthood because she did not meet her parents' goals?

Or do her parents sit down with her, listen closely to her interests, and help her clarify what she is looking for in a college environment? Will they guide her to find the best possible match to meet her interests, needs, and desires?

Like Sophia, all children have almost daily opportunities to demonstrate and shore up their natural capabilities from their first toddling steps to their senior year of high school. As parents, we can support their efforts by getting out of the way.

Sibling Rivalry

It sometimes seems impossible to get out of the way when siblings are squabbling. One whines, "She started it. Punish her!" The other argues, "No I didn't. He did. It's all his fault. Punish *him!*"

Sibling rivalry has a bad reputation. Mention it and most parents groan. But there's a positive side to sibling rivalry. As brothers and sisters argue over everyday issues, they have an opportunity to become competent at negotiating and peacemaking, if we allow them to settle their differences on their own. This means refraining from interrogating ("Who started it?"). It means staying out of sibling fights unless someone is getting physically hurt. Each child usually wants parents to jump in and take his or her side. Instead, we can remain neutral and calm. "I'm sure you can both come up with an answer. You might not like it as much as if you got your own way, but I know you can work something out together." Then walk away.

When we don't allow kids to draw us into their battles, they are often quite capable of problem-solving on their own. When both work out a compromise, each will be more likely to stick to it because they are invested in it. They have contributed to the solution rather than having it imposed on them. When parental judgments about who is right or wrong, good or bad, or more or less favored are removed from the scene, siblings have less to fight about.

It isn't easy to avoid jumping into your children's battles, especially when one plays the "see, you *do* favor her" card. All children want as much time, resources, and attention from parents as they can get, and sometimes it's hard to share. A friend who is a single father of 3 explained how he helped his youngest understand that his love would never run out, even if it had to be shared. "Love is not a pizza," he said. "It's not something with only so many slices and people have to compete for the biggest or last piece." Even as he needed to focus his attention on another child, his love for his son would never be challenged or diminished. It would last forever and only grow as his son grew.

The Value of Play

For too many young people, childhood is a time of crammed schedules and heightened pressures. Their afternoons, evenings, and weekends are slotted into tight segments for soccer, drama, homework, music lessons, tutoring, ballet, homework, hockey, gymnastics, and more homework. Some children are so busy that they give up critical sleep time to complete their school-work. Even during the summer, their hours are filled with scheduled activities through camp and child care programs to keep them occupied and safe while parents work.

While most kids thrive, some react with anxiety and other signs of increased stress. Highly scheduled children have less time for child-driven creative play that is central to healthy development. When adults over-schedule children's free time, it isn't really free at all. Two important elements are for-gotten amid these hectic schedules. Unstructured free play (or downtime in the case of adolescents) not only offers benefits that protect against the harmful effects of stress, but play also gives children unlimited opportunities to discover their own interests and competencies. Play allows them to use their creativity while developing imagination, dexterity, and physical and emotional strength. When adults aren't directing or organizing them into activities, kids create and explore worlds they can master. They can conquer their fears while practicing adult roles ("I'll be the astronaut. You can be the engineer."). Play helps them develop new competencies that lead to enhanced confidence and resilience needed to face future challenges. Undirected play allows them to learn how to work in groups—to share, negotiate, and learn to advocate for themselves.

When play is allowed to be child-driven, kids move at their own pace, discover their own talents and interests, and ultimately engage fully in the passions they wish to pursue. In contrast to passive entertainment like watch-ing television, play builds active, healthy bodies. Above all, play is a simple joy that is a cherished part of childhood.

Play also offers parents a wonderful opportunity to engage fully with children. Here's an opportunity *not* to get out of the way entirely! The key is to let them choose and direct the playtime activity. We can be on the sidelines and ask how they would like us to be involved, but we have to remember it is *their* play, not ours.

When we observe children at play or join with them, we have a unique opportunity to see from their vantage point as they navigate a world perfectly created to fit their needs. The interactions that occur through play tell children that we are fully paying attention to them. Parents who take the opportunity to glimpse their children's world through play also learn to communicate more effectively with their children and gain another setting to offer gentle, nurturing guidance.

If we want children to enjoy the many benefits derived from play, we need to make a determined effort to limit the over-scheduled, overstretched atmosphere in many families. We have to make more time for free, exploratory play. Unfortunately, we may feel like we're swimming upstream because we receive carefully marketed messages that "good" parents expose children to every opportunity to excel, buy a plethora of enrichment tools, and ensure that children participate in a wide variety of activities. As a result, much of parent-child time is spent arranging special activities or transporting children between those activities.

It is not clear whether this rushed, jam-packed routine is offering a developmental benefit or producing children who are better prepared for the future, but it is clear that this lifestyle has repercussions. Many parents experience frustration and feel that they're running on a treadmill to keep up, yet they dare not slow their pace for fear that their children will fall behind.

We need to take a deep breath and find an appropriate balance between preparing for the future and living fully in the present through play and rich parent-child interaction. That balance will be different for every child, based on individual academic needs, temperament, environment, and family situation. With so much pressure to prepare kids for the future, it is important to have a professional to turn to who can reinforce the importance of some of the basic, tried-and-true aspects of child-rearing. Talk with your child's pediatrician and teachers about turning down the pressure, trimming some activities from your child's schedule, and allowing your child more time to play in an unstructured, relaxed way.

Children aren't the only victims of over-scheduling and lack of free play. The whole family may suffer. Parents who are burdened by work responsibilities and maintaining a household find themselves sacrificing their own downtime because they need to arrange activities and drive children between appointments. The pressures they feel to meet every single need they perceive (or are told) their children require to excel make them feel inadequate and ultimately have less personal satisfaction as parents.

Most importantly, parents miss opportunities for high-quality time with children. Some of the best interactions occur during downtime—just talking, preparing meals together, working on a hobby or an art project, playing sports together, or being immersed in child-centered play. To the extent that over-scheduling interferes with essential parent-child time, it is a problem that may lead to less competent, less resilient children.

Play offers an ideal opportunity for parents to engage fully with their children. Some play should be entirely child-driven, with parents not present or observing passively from the sidelines, because play builds many assets that children need to develop and remain resilient. Spontaneous, creative, unstructured play is a terrific opportunity for children to become more competent on their own and thus more confident. Studies have shown that when adults drive or direct play, children acquiesce to adult rules and lose much of the benefit of play (creativity, learning, negotiation, and a sense of control). If we regulate children's time and activities to the exclusion of free, leisurely play, we deny them the opportunity to figure out what they're good at and what they enjoy doing.

When children play alone or with friends by engaging their imaginations and talents in a wide-open arena without hovering adults, they explore a variety of interests and discover what they like to do. The more they enjoy it, the more they do it and the better they become at it. But all too frequently, an adult steps in and says, "I see you and your friends like putting on puppet shows. Maybe you'd like to take a drama class. I'll find one and sign you up."

Before you know it, child's play is no longer play because parents have turned it into "practice" or "lessons." Some children may genuinely enjoy pursuing these interests in a structured way. Others will be turned off quickly. If they'd been allowed to pursue their interests in an unstructured way, they might have enjoyed mastering new skills. Perhaps most important in terms of enhancing resilience, they learn what kinds of activities or hobbies can take them away on an instant vacation as a means to relax (see Chapter 28).

Going With the Flow

The phenomenon of losing oneself in a pleasurable, rewarding experience is often called *flow*. It's becoming absorbed in a deep, genuine interest or passion that has bubbled up from inside. A cellist loses herself in the music she's playing; an athlete practices over and over while time stands still. Mihaly Csikszentmihalyi's books, *Flow: The Psychology of Optimal Experience* and *Finding Flow,* explain this complete absorption in activity. Flow can produce experiences that are simultaneously demanding, enjoyable, and valuable.

Parents sometimes tell me that their children are self-driven in avidly pursuing a sport or other activity, but this may not always be flow. When the drive truly comes from within a child, it is wonderful and should be supported. On the other hand, if a child's drive is motivated more by a desire to please parents than self-satisfaction or joy, this drive can become one more stressor in the child's life. It is far better to let children explore their interests freely, discover their own flow, and follow it without imposing too much structure on their activities. We can put a little wind behind children's sails to support them, but the direction should come from them.

At the moment I am writing this, a gaggle of little boys is playing in an alley behind 20 Philadelphia row houses. No parents are in sight. The boys are 6-, 7-, and 8-year-olds of different heights and sizes. The smallest run to keep up with the bigger boys. From their enthusiastic shouts, it's easy to tell that they have devised a new twist on hide-and-seek. They break into teams and split up. Some dash up steps and through a neighbor's yard before hiding behind a garage. The other team grabs their bikes and races down the alley.

This could be a Dick and Jane scene from the 1950s or Wally and the Beaver in the 1960s when children played outdoors by themselves all day long. Unfortunately, concerns for kids' physical safety and the need for working parents to enroll children in after-school programs have nearly placed free play on the endangered species list.

The importance of play in strengthening family ties will be addressed in Chapter 19; my point here, as play relates to competence, is simple—give your child as many opportunities as possible to play freely if you want him to discover his likes and skills. Your child will reap an internal satisfaction from being good at something, whether it's building towers of blocks when he's 4 or staging plays when he's 14. Don't you wish you had more time to play now? Wouldn't your work life be more productive if you had that right balance of work and pleasure? Your child learns this balance by choosing how to spend his unscheduled time while still getting his chores and work done. He will be a happier, healthier, and more successful adult if he learns to mix achievement and pleasure now.

Please don't misread my advocacy for play as anti-enrichment activities. It would be wonderful if enrichment activities were available to all children. I wish every child had an opportunity to build athletic and artistic prowess and reach academic heights. I also want every child to have the balance that includes enrichment and play, schoolwork and sleep. My concern is that unscheduled, free playtime is considered expendable when different forces compete for a child's time. It is not; it is the work of childhood.

Noticing, Praising, and Criticizing

When children demonstrate their competence, we can reinforce it by noticing and praising them, or we can undercut it through inappropriate criticism.

As busy as we are, we can't let ourselves become too distracted to notice or take their achievements for granted. If we have the casual attitude, "Isn't that what 7-year-olds are supposed to do, after all?" we will miss opportunities to reinforce their competence. Perhaps our 7-year-old struggled to read the whole chapter, do that gymnastic flip, or walk to the corner store alone for the first time. We can help her recognize her own competence in reaching those relatively minor achievements if we use a little praise. "That was a long chapter. You really stuck with it, didn't you?" "I know you've been practicing that flip. Now you really do it well." "How did it feel to go to the store all by yourself? Pretty grown up?"

A few words about praise—don't lather it on too thickly. If we hype an accomplishment like blocking a soccer goal and imply that it's equivalent to winning an Olympic medal, our child will see right through it and she won't believe us. She also won't be able to recognize or appreciate an achievement whenever she does something particularly meritorious because all the praise she receives seems the same.

The opposite—no praise or attention—takes the luster out of every achievement and stifles motivation. Genuine praise, however, goes a long way in reinforcing positive behaviors. To do so, praise should be specific. For example, "Wow, you used a lot of great colors in that painting. Look at those bright red and blue birds!" is more specific and authentic than simply saying, "You're a great artist." The first comment shows the child that we're really looking at her creation and appreciating it. The second comment sounds vague and canned. She knows she's not Picasso. It sets a high expectation that a child may feel she cannot meet in the future.

I was reminded of the importance of clear, specific praise by my daughter Ilana when she was 10 years old. In 1 hour, she taught herself to do a flip off the diving board at a community pool. She transformed from a child scared to consider it into a giggling, proud girl who could do a well-polished flip and a half. She first let her legs go slightly over her head just before entering the water; she landed flat on her back in pain, but she grinned. Within minutes she taught herself to curl and tuck. I (who can't do a simple dive without belly flopping) stared in amazement. I oohed and aahed sincerely for the whole hour. When she got out of the pool, I burst out, "Ilana, I am so, so proud of you!" She asked, "What are you proud of? That I was able to do a flip? That I tried to teach other kids how? Or that even though I was really excited, I always waited my turn?" (Come to think about it, perhaps Ilana should be writing this section about praise...)

Praise Effort, Not Intelligence or the End Result

If you want your child to reach her potential, one of the most important traits to nurture is *tenacity*—the "I'll stick with it" approach to challenges. Carol Dweck, PhD, professor of education at Stanford and author of *Mindset: The New Psychology of Success*, wrote a classic research study that demonstrated how well-intentioned but misguided praise could go awry. She conducted a relatively simple experiment that demonstrated the dramatic differences in children's performance based on the type of praise they received. Fifth graders were given a series of puzzles designed so that all children would do fairly well. After the first part of the test, the children were then told their scores and given a single line of praise. One group was told, "You must be smart at this"; the others were praised for their effort: "You must have worked really hard."

The students were then given a choice of which tests to take for the second round. Students could choose a test that would be harder but from which they'd learn a lot, or an easy test similar to the first. Ninety percent of children praised for their *effort* chose the harder set of puzzles, whereas the majority of those praised for their intelligence chose the easy test. Next, all the students were given a difficult test that was 2 years above their grade level. As expected, it was difficult for all of them, and most were not able to complete the tasks. The students who had been praised for their effort on the first test assumed they simply hadn't worked hard enough. Those praised for their intelligence took their failure as proof they were no longer smart or maybe never were. Their discomfort was visible. Then a final round of tests, as easy as the initial test, was given after the "failure round." The children who were praised for their intelligence initially did worse than their very first attempt, and those praised for their effort showed improvement.

This study suggests that we should recognize the process, not the product, and praise effort rather than grades and test scores.

The Downside of Criticism

All children have their own personal strengths, but too often we overlook them because we're focused on what they do wrong or what their shortcomings are, especially as they grow from sweet babies to independent children and sometimes rebellious adolescents. Instead of noticing, appreciating, and praising their assets, we pay more attention to their weaknesses or faults because we want to improve them. This is where criticism creeps in.

Adults usually criticize with good intentions. After all, we have the mature wisdom children lack. But pointing out only their mistakes or what's wrong usually puts them on the defensive. Instead of thinking objectively about what we've said, kids want to defend themselves. Criticism also shames them, which can breed anger and resentment. Criticism can make children feel inept—exactly the opposite of competent.

We must not be afraid to point out how they could do better, however. If criticism is offered without denigrating a child in a personal way, it can be helpful. Two basic points—the most important guideline is that criticism, like praise, must be specific; and when we want to help children get past a shortcoming, it's more effective if our constructive criticism also recognizes their strengths.

Specific criticism points out errors that a child should avoid in the future. But no matter how upset you are by what your child has done, be careful to target the specific behavior and avoid making personal statements about your child. Two examples follow:

Jordan runs into the house, topples over the umbrella stand, tracks mud on the carpet, and leaves his rain-soaked jacket puddling on the kitchen floor. It's fine for his parents to say, "You've left a mess all over the place. We expect you to clean it up." It's not helpful to say, "You are such a careless slob. What's wrong with you?"

When Takesha ignores her mother's request to help with the dishes, it's appropriate to say, "I really need your help now. You're acting selfishly, as if your going out with friends matters more than my being able to relax after working a 10-hour day." It's not appropriate to say, "You are a thoughtless, selfish girl."

When we need to point out children's errors or shortcomings, it's far more effective to build from their strengths. This is particularly true when they are stuck and don't know how to accomplish or finish a task. Point out what they've done well in the past, ask what they've learned from that experience, and invite their suggestions about how they might use past experiences to handle current problems.

If we want to help children build competence, we have to help them develop their own strengths. We need to capitalize on real experiences in which they have learned appropriate skills and allow them to practice those skills and apply them to new settings. When they fall into difficulties, we can help them draw on those experiences as opportunities to learn to avoid or prevent similar difficulties in the future. When we're about to open our mouths and utter a critical comment, we should stop and ask ourselves, "How can I use this experience to help my child learn from this mistake without destroying her confidence or instilling shame?"

Unintended Criticism

Our criticism needn't be blatant or intentional to be harmful. Children sometimes simply don't understand where our criticism is directed. The following example illustrates how these misunderstandings occur:

Thomas, a curious 3-year-old, is playing for an hour by himself. He industriously rearranges some furniture. He moves little chairs around his table and cleans up all the clutter on the table as he prepares to draw pictures. When he finishes, Thomas wanders over to his blocks and builds the tallest tower he has ever created. He then demolishes it because he has magically transformed into a pterodactyl whose wings crash into the tower. He stops his pterodactyl noises and rebuilds the tower.

Watching him play contentedly, his mother is pleased by the way he entertains himself while she prepares dinner. As it gets dark, Thomas notices that a lamp is unplugged. He picks up the plug and reaches toward an outlet, which fortunately has a childproof plug. His mother suddenly shouts, "No! No! Don't do that!"

How does Thomas interpret her message? "I've been bad." He assumes her harsh tone covers all his recent behaviors (rearranging furniture; cleaning up clutter; drawing pictures; building, smashing, and rebuilding towers; creating an imaginary dinosaur; attempting to illuminate the room). He doesn't understand that she thought he was terrific until that one dangerous moment with the electric plug.

Criticism (or directly changing behavior) is necessary whenever there's imminent danger, but we have to be careful in how we express it. We need to be clear about giving kids an appropriate amount of information that they can process. If criticism is not focused and specific, it leaves a great a deal of room for misinterpretation. Thomas's mother might have said, "Don't touch that plug!" After he dropped it, she could have reminded him that he'd been told to stay away from electric outlets, then immediately tell him what a good job he had done with his tower and drawings and redirected him to those activities.

Because she is human, it is all right that she shouted "No!" loudly. She should be concerned that he might get an electric shock. But after she shouts, it's important that she make it crystal clear that it was only the plug that's forbidden, and that she really liked how Thomas was playing before that moment.

Unspoken Criticism

Not all criticism is verbalized. Sometimes a parent's actions can be unintentionally critical without saying a word. For example, a 10-year-old loved spending time with his father. One of his favorite activities was helping his dad with weekend projects. When a table needed painting, Dad opened a can of paint and handed his son a brush. Sounds easy enough, but as the boy proceeded, he couldn't smooth out the brush marks. The more he painted, the more brush strokes appeared. He grew frustrated and asked his father for help. His father took the brush from the boy's hand and repainted the table himself.

Years later the boy recalled how insignificant and criticized he felt. His father probably thought he was helping his son, but he really hadn't. By stepping in and taking over, the father criticized his son's work and failed to help him become more competent—without uttering a word.

A Word on Teens

As our children grow and our family lives become busier, it often seems that teens would rather be with their friends than us. Our time with them becomes a premium and we want to make the most of every moment. Sometimes we use these few precious moments to get in all our criticisms and "instructions." When they were little, we knew that the most effective way to elicit good behavior was to catch them being good, notice their progress, and show appreciation for it. Teens are bigger, but they are no different. Never forget that core point of building resilience—our children live up or down to our expectations. Couple this with the fact that teens want our attention as much as young children do—though they would deny that emphatically—and you can better understand why focusing on negatives will backfire. Teens will continue to do whatever gets your attention, good or bad.

Authentic Success

Our goal has always been to prepare children to thrive and succeed far into the future. Generations of Americans have dreamed that children will have better, more successful lives than their parents and grandparents. For many, that dream became a reality. But today we fear this dream may no longer be achievable. Especially in difficult economic times, we realize our children may have to outperform us just to keep up. We feel the pressure. So do they.

To maximize their chances, we try to instill in them the cornerstones of enduring success—commitment to hard work, tenacity, and love of learning. When possible, we expose them to a variety of opportunities so they will be prepared to flourish. With the best intentions, we begin building their résumés at earlier ages than ever before.

For these and other reasons, many young people internalize society's stresses and absorb the pressure to succeed. They believe that they need to become all things to all people to make it. Some children use this pressure as fuel, perhaps even reaching levels of success they may not have attained otherwise. Others become so stressed that they lose the love of learning, and their innate curiosity is crushed. Some create an image or posture that allows them to pretend they just don't care—they walk off the playing field before others have an opportunity to judge them.

Resilience isn't only about overcoming external challenges. Sometimes it is about overcoming voices from within that tell us we are unacceptable unless we consistently perform at the standards that please everybody.

Defining Success

I frequently ask parents and teens, "What is success?" Parents often remain silent with mouths agape while their teens respond, "Having money"; "Getting into the right college"; "Driving a nice car"; and "Power." (In fairness, there are always some teens who talk about their desire to make the world a better place.) Parents then speak of the importance of happiness, service, and relationships. Where did this disconnect happen? Are we raising a selfish generation, or are teens absorbing messages we don't think we are sending?

Let's attempt to define *authentic success*. No one has a corner on its meaning. Every family needs to define it for themselves. I speak as a parent when I say that I will consider my daughters successful adults if they remain happy, generous, and compassionate. Ideally, they will improve our world and maintain their creative and innovative potential. I speak as a concerned citizen when I say that creativity and innovation are needed to lead us into the future.

We can be successful and contribute to the world in many different ways. We certainly need an educated population, but college is not for everyone. Some people's gifts come through their hands, others through their compassion, and still others through artistic expression. Our challenge is to recognize the gift in every child and create circumstances in which all children have support and resources to reach their potential. While we recognize that many avenues lead to success, this chapter focuses on teens who are likely college-bound and the consequences of the pressure that many feel about that prospect.

A Choice Between Happiness and Success?

Teens aren't completely off base when they say success is about money, education, and a good job—they're just being honest. But many parents might worry, "If we define success more broadly to include happiness and compassion, might we destroy the motivation and drive that lead to a competitive educational spot and ultimately a good job? If we protect children from pressure, will they languish in mediocrity?"

Today's teenagers have more impressive college applications than a decade ago—far more impressive than their parents. On paper they look almost too good to be true—socially committed, brilliant, athletic, musical, artistic, and widely experienced in summer jobs, internships, and community service projects.

But as we prepare these paper-perfect students for higher education, we may be undermining their ability to succeed in life. As we mold them to be "well-balanced," we actually may be making them feel unsure of their own footing. They may be so committed to being perfect that they fear being anything less. In fact, the most worrisome thing about this generation of driven students may be the fear of imperfection that's being instilled in their psyches. This fear can stifle their creativity, impede their innovative potential, and diminish their ability to experience joy.

We must never forget that our ultimate goal is to raise healthy, successful 35-year-olds, not high school seniors whose success is narrowly defined by the college that admits them.

So the choice is not between happiness and success. Happiness leads to success. Pressure sometimes fuels fear of failure, *impostor syndrome* (more about that later), and fear of the B+. All of these can crush healthy risk-taking that leads to new ideas. Young people who believe a B+ is the end of the world will never think outside of the box. Instead, they will make safe, guaranteed choices. They may have the grades, but they are not destined for authentic success.

Isn't It Good to Be a Perfectionist?

No. We want children to be healthy high achievers who reach their potential, but that's not accomplished by being a perfectionist. Perfectionists are not resilient; they live life always feeling unsettled. Why? The answer lies in the process, not the product.

The product—an A, a piece of art, a 10 in gymnastics—does not distinguish the healthy high achiever from the perfectionist. It's the process. For example, a maestro who composes the finest symphony may be driven by a healthy desire to achieve or by an inability to accept anything less than a masterpiece. The difference is in how much he enjoys the process, how much he celebrates rather than disparages his creation, and how quickly he may burn out. The end product might be the same, but the process is tortured or exhilarating.

The world is run by high achievers. Many of them describe themselves as perfectionists because they aren't satisfied until they've done their best. But they prove resilient when they fall short of perfection. Healthy high achievers get genuine pleasure from putting every effort into producing the finest-quality product—an effective business plan, an award-winning presentation, a well-designed computer program. They enjoy the process and excitement that bubbles up from within as they work their hardest. They react to deadlines by generating just enough anxiety to stay energized.

Healthy high achievers see a mistake as an opportunity for growth and as an impetus to learn to do better the next time. They see failure as a temporary setback from which they will rebound. They appreciate constructive criticism because it informs them about how to improve.

High achievers have passion, creativity, and flexibility. They excel at something but maintain other interests as well. Every new venture is flavored by past experience because every disappointment was used as a learning experience. They remain open to looking outside of the box for the solutions or strategies not yet tried. They propel colleagues forward through enthusiasm, love of the process, and willingness to take healthy risks.

In sharp contrast to healthy high achievers, perfectionists reject anything less than a flawless product or performance. They don't enjoy the process of creating because they worry endlessly about not performing as well as they think they should. Their fear of failure is greater than the joy of experiencing success.

When perfectionists do well, they may not even notice because they are so worried about mistakes they might make or focused on how they could do better. The perfectionist soccer star scores 3 goals but when carried off the field on his teammates' shoulders, speaks only of his penalty kick that went wide. The perfectionist gets a 96 on an examination but is frustrated that she didn't score 100.

Perfectionists see every mistake as evidence they're unworthy or not good enough. They don't trust others' praise because they see themselves as "impostors" whose faults are just waiting to be discovered. When criticized, they become defensive, embarrassed, or ashamed. They experience constructive criticism as reinforcement of their ineptitude. Perfectionism is a state of unease driven by an intense sense of being unacceptable.

Perfectionists fear adversity. They lack the flexibility to rebound from difficulty because challenges paralyze them. The thought of not doing something well prevents them from taking chances that successful people take to reach their greatest potential.

Authentic success is rarely achieved because perfectionists become paralyzed before getting there, lest they disappoint the harshest critics (usually themselves). They may be graced with creativity but are hesitant to tap into it for fear that coloring outside the lines will disappoint others. Innovations are too risky.

Young People Who Don't "Live Up to Their Potential" Aren't Necessarily Lazy

Not all perfectionists are high producers. Their fear of failure may prevent them from initiating or completing tasks. They may avoid a task entirely for fear they can't do it well enough. They may procrastinate because starting a project that they fear will have flaws is too overwhelming. Sometimes they invest heavily in an image that will make the pressure stop. They may pretend they just don't care, or they may feign laziness because it is too hard to confess the depths of their anxiety about failing.

If your child isn't doing as well in school as she used to or isn't "living up to her potential," consider that she may act like she doesn't care because in truth she cares too much. I have known many young people who work very hard to create an image of nonchalance. Lazy is cool. Being riddled with anxiety is not. I've even met perfectionists who use drugs to medicate their stress and support the image of the burnout who couldn't possibly care.

Some of my most inspirational experiences in the practice of medicine have been watching the healing that occurs when a teen who has become a source of disappointment is able to turn to his parents and confess, "I never stopped caring. I care too much."

If you think this pattern may resonate with your child, think about the sources of the pressure she might be receiving. It may be from you, but it could just as likely come from school or peers. Your less-than-enthusiastic child may be reacting to an older sibling's achievement and may fear being unable to live up to that reputation. No matter the source, your child needs to learn that she needn't fear being unacceptable, and she is loved unconditionally by you.

What Goes Wrong? Whose Fault Is It?

Certain character traits may make people susceptible to messages that they aren't good enough unless they are flawless. But to become a driving force in a person's life, those inherent traits have to be reinforced from somewhere.

There are no villains here, certainly not among parents. All parents want the best for their children. So how do parents know if a child is self-driven or if it is a parent's fault? That was a trick question. Give yourself a break and delete the word *fault* from your vocabulary. If a child is experiencing too much pressure and some of it came from you, certainly you applied that pressure with the best of intentions. What may feel like helpful encouragement to one child may be experienced as overwhelming pressure to another. In fact, what feels like encouragement to one person may feel like pressure to the same person at a different time in a different mood. This is why we need to take the scrutiny off ourselves and look at our children. Are they thriving or struggling? Do they relish their achievements or fear their inadequacy? Whether or not parents are part of the problem, we certainly can be part of the solution.

I am willing, however, to be clear about some common parental behaviors that are counterproductive. If your child has studied her hardest and comes home with a C, you should be proud. Children need to be encouraged to put in a good effort, not to strive for unattainable goals. If you show dissatisfaction with a grade or project when your child has tried her best, you are setting her up to never to be satisfied with her *efforts*. If your child sees a B as adversity or failure, how will she ever learn how to face real challenges?

Do not lead the battle for higher grades for your child. If your child comes home with a B and you think she deserves or, worse, *needs* an A and you go into battle with her teacher, you will be harming her in 3 ways. First, you have made clear that nothing short of perfection is acceptable. Second, you have communicated that the prize matters more than how the game is played. Third, you have impaired her ability to be successful later in life. When she is 32 years old, will you call her employer and demand that her job evaluation be upgraded? In the real world, grades don't get changed. People work harder to attain greater successes. And they find the resilience to do this by using their creativity, ingenuity, and tenacity—all driven by passion for what they do.

It might seem that we should simply urge children to "just try your best." But teens tell me that this statement drives them crazy. This generation is largely motivated by the D word—fear of *disappointing* parents. No one ever really does their best, so they always feel they are underperforming. Instead of the general statement, "Do your best," keep your feedback and encourage- ment more targeted and understand that someone can try really hard yet per- form very differently in 2 different subjects. Talents and strengths are uneven (more on this later). For example, instead of saying, "Don't worry, I just expect you to do your best," a parent might say, "All I can expect is that you put in a good effort. It is not your grades I care about; it is that you are learning. I'm good at some things, and with a decent effort I will always score high—for you, that's math. In other subjects you might work hard and still not get the grade you wish. But all I want from you is to stretch yourself; it's not the grades that matter. I know writing is hard for you; just keep working on it."

Finally, allow yourself a moment of self-reflection. In this age of over- stretched adults, many of us see our children as a product that, to some degree, reflects our success as human beings. This may be particularly true for parents who are highly prepared for the work world and have given up that world temporarily for child-rearing, or who are still working but apply the same standards of efficiency, productivity, and performance to home and family as was learned for the workforce. When we do this, our children may become products of their successes, and their successes or setbacks become markers of our own. This is not good for children or our relationships with them. Of particular note here is that when they learn somehow that they are our prod- ucts, it sets them up to want to be perfect to please us.

Overstretched Children

Some young people may have jam-packed lives and flourish. They are driven to succeed and relish their accomplishments. They remain joyous and self- confident. Others exhibit signs of weariness or stress, but their parents may see it as the price to be paid for success. As long as grades remain high and they continue to be involved in many extracurricular activities, their parents believe they must be doing well, regardless of outward or inward signs of stress. They believe that happiness sometimes needs to be sacrificed in the name of accomplishment. (From time to time, it may be useful to reread Chapter 6 to remind ourselves of the value of play and free time in the lives of all children.)

More parents need to understand that while some children say they are fine, their stress often manifests with physical concerns such as headaches, fatigue, insomnia, dizziness, and belly pain. To evaluate whether children are moving toward authentic success, we need to look less at their accomplishments and more at the kids themselves.

A College Admissions Process Gone Awry

The college admissions process is a big offender here. It has generated the myth that only perfect, well-balanced, brilliant candidates are worthy of admission, as proven by thick applications with high SAT scores, grade point averages, class rankings, and lengthy résumés of extracurricular activities—even better if candidates have built a water purification system in a South American village or organized a fund-raising event for earthquake victims.

People who mistakenly believe that success is tightly linked to only select colleges will do anything—or pressure their children to do anything—to grasp that precious acceptance letter. But the truth is that success is linked to the individual. Higher-profile colleges may help a graduate get his first job, but most people stay at that job only a couple of years. Their performance in that job leads to the next one. In other words, if pressure produces individuals with perfect résumés—perfect enough to get into the best colleges—but crushes their creativity and innovative spirit and interferes with healthy development of their interpersonal skills and capacity to rebound from setbacks, their long-term chances for success are seriously harmed.

Let's look at some of those myths that drive the frenzy of the college admissions process.

Myth no. 1: The SATs or ACTs will determine your life. If you score well on this single test, life will be handed to you on a silver platter. It is worth forgoing pleasure in the present to prepare for this test that hands you the future.

The truth is that no single test determines anyone's life. It is equally as true that nothing is ever handed to you on a silver platter. All of life requires hard work and tenacity. That's why each day should be a balance of work and pleasure. Never avoid living in the present to prepare for the future.

Myth no. 2: Successful adults are good at everything. That is why you must prove you are brilliant in all subjects, a gifted athlete, a talented artist, and a great humanitarian.

How many adults can honestly say, "I'm good at everything"? When was the last time you could say that? Probably in second grade when you got gold stars on spelling papers or when you were praised as a great artist for making a Thanksgiving turkey out of brown construction paper.

The truth is that successful people excel at something. What makes them interesting is that they also do other things that challenge or intrigue them. Colleges know this; that's why there are various majors. But we as parents, physicians, and educators must apply pressure back on colleges to stop making teens believe they need to wear a cape, mask, and tights to be worthy of their school. Unrealistic expectations foster the drive toward perfectionism that is bound to crash-land.

The college admissions process has had a trickle-down effect. Parents pressure schools to perform, and in turn schools pressure teens to get into top-rated colleges to demonstrate the school's excellent preparation. They do this even while knowing that each teen needs to find the right match for herself, not the highest-rated school.

Peer groups also generate anxiety in a climate when success is defined by college stickers on parents' car windows. Teens pressure each other about which colleges they're applying to and which accept them. Guide children to keep their grades, awards, and college acceptances close to the chest. Not only will it tone down the competition, it will teach them humility.

A Toxic Society

We live in a culture that reveres success and barely notices regular people doing their best. When we know the names of sports stars and great actors but forget to acknowledge the generous acts of our neighbors, are we teaching children that to be noticed you have to be a star? Who can remember a bronze medalist from the last Olympics? What does it mean when third best doesn't count? To be noticed, you need the biggest prize. And what happens when someone does become a star? How quickly do we jump on their first transgression, and for how long are we captured by the media frenzy? What does it do to children when they are raised in a culture where, to be noticed, you have to be the very best? And to be destroyed, you need only be caught making a mistake. In case the big stories are missed, commercial media subtly and not-so-subtly communicates endlessly, "To be successful, you need to look this way, talk this way, own this, dress this way."

The Fear of Creating Pain for Parents

Sometimes perfectionism has nothing to do with internal or external pressure. Instead, it stems from an intense need to spare a parent. For example, if your children sense that you have been through so much, perhaps because of an illness, divorce, or stress at work, they will do anything to spare you more pain. They will try to be perfect children. Of course, this is exacerbated if parents make statements like, "Do you think I need to worry about you with everything that's already on my mind?" But chances are you don't have to say a word. If your child knows you are suffering, she will do anything not to add to your burden. She'll strive to get straight As to make you proud and keep her anxieties and struggles a tightly held secret, always showing you her very best face.

If this discussion hits home for you, help your child understand that there is nothing more important to you than being a good parent. Tell him that he does you no favors by protecting you. Here is an example of a helpful statement. "You know I'm going through a lot, but you're always the most important thing to me. Please don't spare me by holding back the details of your life. I'm your [mother/father]. Even when I wonder what I can still do well, I know that I can do that well. Please give me the chance to do what I care about most—being your parent."

The Solution Starts With Parents

"I never asked you to be perfect." Most parents firmly believe that they never said anything directly to their child to imply that they expect perfection. Many are adamant that their words always reinforce the importance of happiness. Certainly most parents do send the right verbal message of unconditional acceptance. For many children, perfectionism derives from other forces in their lives.

But we need to consider the possibility that some children pick up parental signals that reinforce the need to be perfect, despite the words parents speak aloud. Ask yourself the following questions, but be gentle on yourself if some of the answers make you realize that you might be part of the perfectionism problem:

- Are you a perfectionist yourself? Are you highly self-critical? Has your child seen you accept your own flaws?
- Do you judge people easily? Your other children? Neighbors? Other kids? Teachers? Might you have communicated that you can be highly critical? Is it possible your child will do anything to avoid your judgment?
- If you and your spouse or ex-spouse fight frequently, might your children act "perfectly" to prevent you from fighting?

- Are you so busy that you forget to notice your children's achievements unless they get a trophy, a ribbon, or an A?
- Are people in your home uncomfortable with expressing emotions? Or do they recover easily, even have healthier relationships after expressions of emotion? Is the only way to achieve harmony in your home to suppress problems and pretend that everything is just wonderful?

Expanding the Definition of Success

Make it clear to your children that your definition of success includes happiness. Show them that you appreciate it when they challenge expectations and are willing to color outside the lines and think outside of the box. Let them know a creative spirit is one of the greatest predictors of success. Help them to understand that the best ideas are usually rejected at first and that everyone fails sometime, but truly successful people can recover and learn how to do better next time.

You define success, but please include some of the following worthy contenders:

- Happiness
- Resilience
- Generosity
- Compassion
- Desire to contribute
- The capacity to build and maintain meaningful relationships
- Creativity
- Innovation

Recognizing Real Heroes

Do you only notice champions, or do you acknowledge others who have played a good, fair game? Do you admire the runner-up or bronze medal winner who overcame huge challenges? Who are the heroes spoken about in your house? Sports stars? Oscar winners? Please notice the teachers, doctors, nurses, police, firefighters, military service people, and social workers in your community. Applaud the woman who has sacrificed so she could care for her mother with Alzheimer disease, or the man who spends his weekends mentoring disadvantaged boys in his community.

Opportunities for Self-discovery

Many parents assume that more is better—more activities will "perfect" their children. Enrichment activities are good, but we need to consider the kinds of activities, how many are really good for our children, and who is choosing them. As discussed in Chapter 6, child-driven play is vital. Downtime is critical for young people to discover who they are. If they participate only in adult-directed, back-to-back activities, when will they learn what they might choose to do?

Young people's self-acceptance is fostered when they trust that they are competent. If they believe in their ability to manage their own problems, trust their own decision-making capabilities, and develop their own solutions, they needn't catastrophize their mistakes. We nurture their competence by getting out of the way and by encouraging them to take control of their own lives. We want them to discover that they each have a compass and can follow its direction.

Dialing Down the Competition

The first step toward authentic success is redefining success. Once you have done that, you've clarified that your child is living for herself, not to become a product you can display. When parents reject anything less than the perfect product, they promote perfectionism. When they suggest that their children "just beef up" their activities a bit, they are making a statement that their children are not good enough as they are. If a parent treats a rejection as an unmitigated disaster, how will a child feel about being accepted "only" by her second-choice college? Won't she feel that she has failed? She will feel rejected and unaccepted twice, most importantly by the people whose acceptance really matters most—her parents.

Professional Help

A child's anxiety or drive for perfection may make him so uncomfortable that he needs professional help to unlearn his catastrophic thinking patterns and replace them with healthier ones. Professional therapists can be very helpful in this regard; an investment now in your child's emotional health will pay dividends of happiness, contentment, and success throughout his life (see chapters 9 and 36). Ask a school counselor or pediatrician for a possible referral.

Unconditional Acceptance

The bottom line is that perfectionism drives people toward exhaustion for fear that anything less than the best makes them unacceptable. We must look at our children and notice how they are experiencing the process rather than push for a result. If they are driven to achieve to please others, we need to consistently reinforce that they are acceptable to us just because they are ours.

Changing a perfectionist's style is not easy. A perfectionist has a lot invested in being flawless. Giving up that style brings the risk of failure or a conflict that the perfectionist is trying so desperately to avoid. A parent's job is to let children know they are adored regardless of their accomplishments. If you directly criticize perfectionists for being hard on themselves rather than absorbing the lesson you hope to convey, they may just use this as more fuel to reinforce their sense of inadequacy. It is better to notice that they seem uncomfortable or are struggling more than they should. "Darling, I see you're really worried about your grade in English in a way that seems really uncomfortable." "I notice you seem disturbed that Ms Singh gave you a B- on your history project. It makes me sad to see you this upset. Can we talk?"

Remember, the most essential ingredient in raising resilient children is an adult who loves or accepts them unconditionally and holds them to high but reasonable expectations. High expectations are not about grades or performance. They're about integrity, generosity, empathy, and the traits our children need if they are to contribute to the world.

Parents need to accept children for themselves, not compare them to siblings, neighbors, or other students who win full scholarships. Such comparisons are damaging to children feeling comfortable about themselves.

When you think you should comment about how your children could do better, base your statements on the fact that they *already have* done better. Use an example of past successes to remind them that they're already equipped with the talent, experience, and resources to address new challenges. Remind them of some obstacle they overcame or a problem they worked creatively to resolve for themselves.

Parents must be cheerleaders. We get excited when our children win, but we have to learn to encourage and praise more effectively. We usually tend to praise an outcome or accomplishment—"I am so proud of your winning goal, your blue ribbon, that A on your science test." The unintended message is, "I wouldn't be as proud if you had come home without the prize." Instead, we have to encourage the *process* and display our pride over how they are playing the game of life with integrity, genuine effort, and, yes, joy.

Accepting Yourself

Self-acceptance is a very basic ingredient we all need if we value ourselves. We accept that we are still basically good, even when we don't hit the ball out of the park. We remain worthy of others' love even when we are in a foul mood. We feel good about our efforts even when the guy across the hall scored higher, produced more, or received more recognition. We are okay because we see ourselves as more than a package of achievements. We don't have to be the best all the time, and we're comfortable that no one can be a star on every stage.

As you struggle at work, let your children know how you are trying a new strategy. And when you don't succeed the first, second, or seventh time, model how you learned from each new effort. You are not destroyed or worthless. You are not an impostor. You do not become paralyzed. You become energized! You take disappointment with grace and good humor. Your B- at work is not a catastrophe.

One of the greatest gifts you can give your children is to accept yourself. Perhaps the largest contribution to their achieving authentic success is seeing it in you.

CHAPTER 9

Thinking Clearly

We have seen how a child's competence can be helped or hindered by the amount and style of parental involvement. We recognize the importance of giving children time and opportunity to play so they can discover and strengthen their areas of competence. We've considered how the chances of achieving real success are hampered by perfectionism, which is driven by thoughts of being unacceptable. Now let's look at how competence is affected by thinking patterns.

The way children think about challenges can undermine the confidence they need to tackle adversities. On the other hand, young people who use their thought processes to address issues realistically and resolve them wisely can enhance their growing sense of competence, and they will become increasingly resilient.

Understanding how thinking patterns affect kids' capability of dealing with difficulties is essential to your ability to support their natural resilience. Some of the best studies that demonstrate the importance of thinking patterns began with the Penn Resiliency Project, headed by Martin E.P. Seligman, PhD, of the University of Pennsylvania. After many years of studying abnormal psychology, Dr Seligman came to understand the importance of looking at what makes people resilient in the face of difficulties. He mentored several leading experts in resilience, including Karen Reivich, PhD. Dr Seligman, Dr Reivich, and their colleagues worked with hundreds of schoolchildren and their families and demonstrated, in a nutshell, that children and adults can become more resilient, more optimistic, and better able to cope with life by changing the way they think about problems. People don't have to remain stuck with their first impulsive, negative thoughts when they become frustrated, disappointed, anxious, or sad. They can use their cognitive abilities to rethink the situation, reframe it, "decatastrophize" it, and find workable solutions. Rather than feeling defeated or depressed, they can find a path that leads to optimism and greater resilience.

They can reduce their stress levels and become more effective problem-solvers. Ultimately, they become more confident about facing the next obstacle.

All children can benefit from becoming resilient thinkers, but if you believe that your child's way of thinking or processing events is rather negative or creates unnecessary anxiety or sadness, I suggest you read *The Optimistic Child* (Seligman, Reivich, Jaycox, Gillham) or *The Resilience Factor* (Reivich, Shatté). These works can be helpful in preventing young people from becoming self-defeating thinkers. *The Resilience Factor* is not just directed toward children; it is also designed to help adults become more resilient. Because children learn more from observing parents' behavior than words, adults who want to become more resilient would find this book a wonderful start for modeling a more constructive path to resilience for children.

Some key points of Seligman or Reivich's work include

- ❋ Children come up with their own explanations of why they succeed or fail. This is called their *explanatory style.* The essential question that they need to answer in response to failure is, "Why?" In arriving at an explanation for why, children are likely to weave a story. How that story unfolds makes a big difference in the way they respond to failure. Will their story generalize the disappointment and paralyze them from taking further action, or will it be used as a springboard from which they will try again?

- ❋ The first part of the answer to why lies in who is to blame. Is it the child's fault or was it someone else's? If children always blame themselves for problems, they will tend to see themselves in a negative light.

- ❋ The second part of the answer lies in "How long will it last?" The answer to this permanent or temporary situation may make a big difference in their chosen responses. If they truly believe the causes of their problems are going to last forever and are outside their control, they are more likely to give up.

- ❋ Children use the third part of their story to explain how much their failure has affected them—is it a small bump or a catastrophe? Children who catastrophize are much more likely to become anxious and feel incapable of coping with the situation.

- ❋ It is important for parents, teachers, and coaches to help children correctly assess their successes and failures. A first step is having an accurate, rather than a catastrophic, story line. Resilient people can realistically distinguish when they have control over a situation and when they do not. They gather their resources for situations in which they do have control and conserve their resources when they do not. They can assess when something will pass easily and quickly; they're able to talk themselves down when they start to magnify events in their story lines to catastrophic proportions.

As we interact with the world, automatic thoughts fly through our minds and heavily influence how we respond. Four steps to taking control of these thoughts include

1. Learn to recognize your negative thoughts at the times when you feel your worst. Dr Seligman, Dr Reivich, and their colleagues call this *thought catching.*
2. Evaluate these thoughts for accuracy.
3. Develop more accurate explanations or story lines when bad things happen.
4. Decatastrophize to let go of particularly harmful thoughts that can make you worry that a small mistake or failure is leading to inevitable disaster.

Drs Seligman and Reivich use a cognitive technique originated by Albert Ellis, PhD, a renowned expert on cognitive behavioral theory, called the *ABC technique.* The A refers to the *adversity* itself. The C refers to the *consequences* that flow from the adversity. B is the connector, and it is critical because it stands for the *beliefs* and interpretation about the adversity. These beliefs determine how a person reacts to adversity and therefore produces the consequences.

Much of cognitive behavioral therapy works by identifying beliefs that are not accurate. Dr Reivich points out that in conversation, especially those that adults have with children, we tend to focus on the A ("What happened?") and C ("How do you feel now?" or "What are you going to do?"), while ignoring the B connectors. We need to help children hear that silent voice in their heads (sometimes called *self-talk)* that explains their beliefs, forms their interpretations of events, and guides what will happen next. We can begin helping children get in touch with their beliefs by first verbalizing our own beliefs. Talking out loud can help them see the connections.

A good time to help children listen to their self-talk is when you notice a sudden shift in their mood. This may be a clue that they have experienced something stressful and that their beliefs about it are in process. At this time, you could simply ask, "What are you thinking about?"

Whether we're trying to help children hear their self-talk or listening to our own, here are some primary points to consider.

- Identify the adversities that consistently push your buttons; notice which negative emotions and behaviors they trigger.
- Watch your patterns of reacting. Do you usually blame things on yourself or others? Do you tend to see problems or their causes as permanent or temporary? When you observe your reaction patterns, you'll probably notice a theme. Perhaps you fall into certain traps or ways of instinctively reacting in negative ways ("Why do I always do that? I'm so dumb." "It always happens to me.").

❋ Once you recognize your habitual reactions, you can begin to pull them apart and think of alternatives. If you always magnify the possible outcomes of a situation and expect a disaster, you can begin to train yourself to look for other ways to balance that negative tendency. Rather than blame yourself as usual, you might ask yourself, "What did I do well in that situation? What good things came out of it? How much of the difficulty was caused by me or someone or something else?" You may not have all the answers or solutions, but you can begin to break your pattern and stop reacting reflexively.

Dr Seligman suggests that we can ask children leading questions to help them understand the complexity of problems rather than jump to a quick, emotional response. Children think in concrete terms, as I will discuss in greater detail in Chapter 10. They tend to see problems as entirely their fault or never their fault. By posing leading questions, we can guide them step-by-step through a series of possibilities so that they arrive at the realization that yes, perhaps they contributed to the problem, but it may not be completely their fault. Or there may be another, entirely different way to look at and interpret the situation.

Take the following problem as an example: Derrick frequently comes home with bruises, scrapes, and torn clothes, and he complains about the schoolyard bully. "Frank is always picking on me. He always starts these fights. It's his fault I get sent to the principal's office."

By asking leading questions, his father helps Derrick see a pattern—Derrick rises to the bully's bait by arguing with him, but Frank is at fault for hassling Derrick first. Once Derrick recognizes the pattern, he is able to think of ways to respond differently, like walking away from Frank, defusing the situation with a joke, or hanging out with another group of kids.

Children also tend to make excuses when they feel defensive ("My teacher hates me." "You just don't understand." "It's not mine, I'm just keeping it for a friend."). This defensive thinking pattern can be redirected if we help kids pull a problem apart and think it through one step at a time. Instead of lecturing children or denying their feelings or statements ("Your teacher doesn't hate you—don't be silly." "You're lying."), we can listen calmly and nonjudgmentally before we even open our mouths to speak.

To listen effectively, we need to be quiet and *not* formulate our responses while children are speaking. If we're focusing on what to advise them, we will miss their message. But if we listen silently with an open mind, children will know that we care about what they're saying. Only then can we move ahead to ask them questions that give them an opportunity to think about the situation in a new way. ("Why do you think your teacher hates you?" "Maybe I don't understand. I'll try if you'll tell me more about it.")

Building resilience in children involves more than helping them change their thinking patterns. Specific social and problem-solving skills are also required (as explained in chapters 11–13), as well as coping strategies (chapters 25–28). But the first step is to help kids think differently and break the pattern of negative emotional reaction. If your gut says that your child suffers from negative thought patterns in a way that interferes with his happiness or success, I suggest you start by reading one of the books referred to in this chapter and speaking to your pediatrician about a referral to a cognitive behavioral therapist.

No More Lectures

Why is it so easy to slip into a lecture when we notice children's shortcomings, faults, or weaknesses? We want to offer sound advice because we have the life experience that they don't yet possess. We want to fix their problems and solve their dilemmas. We want to prevent future problems. Our intentions are good, but lectures just don't work—they backfire.

When we launch into a lecture, children tune out before our second sentence is complete. We can list 20 reasons why they should finish their homework and get to bed by 10:00 pm ("You were up late last night talking on the phone." "You'll be too tired to pay attention in class." "You need to bring up your grades." "Why don't you listen to me? I know what's best for you."), but all they hear is, "Waaa...waaa...waaa."

We need to shorten our speeches, be direct, and get kids involved by asking them to make a choice. "Do you want to finish your homework before dinner so you can watch your favorite show, or do it after dinner and skip the program?" Short, sweet, and simple. The child hears your parameters and has a choice, which gives him some control of the situation. If he doesn't finish his homework before dinner, he can't watch television or have computer time. He determines the outcome.

Lecturing doesn't work for several other reasons. As soon as many parents sense a problem, the old parent alarm goes off. They think they must provide instant answers and wisdom to solve their child's problem, so they jump in and start lecturing. But the child rarely has a chance to express his concern, so he feels cut off, unheard, disrespected, or even shamed.

When an adult lectures, children often feel stupid. No wonder they tune out. Who wants to listen to someone who disrespects you or treats you as though you're brainless? Kids not only tune out, but some will also become hostile or defensive. Lecturing certainly does nothing to enhance their sense of competence.

I know many parents who think that long, reasoned explanations that connect all the dots and link all potential consequences with each choice will teach a child to do the right thing. But too often, parents talk to children in ways they don't understand. This undermines competence. ("I don't get it. I must be stupid. I can't do it.")

To appreciate why children don't get our reasonable cause-and-effect lectures, we need to understand how they think. Children think concretely. Think about *concrete*. When a concrete block is split in half, it's 2 chunks of concrete. It's exactly as it appears, nothing more, nothing less. Concrete thinkers don't think about future consequences of behavior, only how a behavior affects them *right now*. Ask a 5-year-old whether he'd prefer using a dollar to buy a chocolate bar or invest the dollar for his college education. (It may be worth $3.37 in 15 years!) He'll take the chocolate bar.

Children also think egocentrically. "What will she do for *me?*" They see the world as it revolves around them. They observe and interpret human interactions in terms of what people will do for *me,* to meet *my* needs. They see people as good or bad, depending on whether those individuals give them what they want. Of course this makes children vulnerable to exploitation because some very bad people can easily convince kids, with ice cream or a few choice words, that they are good people.

As children grow, they become more open to abstract concepts. Abstractions are possibilities, ideas they do not have to see. Abstract thinkers can imagine the future and recognize that choices they make will lead to different outcomes. Most late adolescents are abstract thinkers, but it is important to know that some people will never get there. It is also critical to understand that *all* people think concretely during times of extreme stress.

How does this transition from concrete to abstract thinker occur in children? During adolescence, the brain transforms as new brain pathways become more activated and allow young adults to process information in new ways. Do you recall from your own adolescence when you suddenly just couldn't stop thinking? Things began to make sense in ways they never had before, but you also realized that some things made no sense at all. "Okay, if the universe goes on and on, it is infinite. But how can something be infinite? It must stop. But if it stops, then what's there?" Your head spun with confusion and excitement.

Another change occurs in adolescence to transition from concrete to abstract thinking—life experiences teach consequences. With each consequence, the young person begins to get it. ("Oh, so that person is manipulating me." "Oh, because I did X, then Y happened the next day." "I never even imagined that could happen; it just felt so good at the moment." Or: "He said we were best friends, but he was just using me so I would get caught instead of him.") The bottom line is we learn through our mistakes, especially those that bring hurt or pain. Kids learn about their own ability to screw things up and the bitter consequences. Perhaps more importantly, they ultimately learn that people are far more complex than *good* or *bad.* They can be manipulative; smooth, flattering words can mask an ulterior motive. This new cynicism leads to an understanding of how consequences follow behaviors, and this is highly protective for young people.

As parents and abstract-thinking adults, we desperately wish to protect our children from needing to learn the hard way. We know how mistakes lead to pain. We know how manipulative people can be, and we want our kids to learn as quickly and painlessly as possible.

Childhood is potentially dangerous because kids can't think about the far-reaching consequences of their actions and can easily be fooled by ill-intentioned people. So we watch children as closely as possible. We try to explain to them—often emphatically or dramatically—all the future consequences of their behaviors. And we easily slip into the lecture mode.

Let's break down a typical parent lecture. "What you are doing now, let's call it behavior A, will very likely lead to consequence B. What were you thinking? And then consequence B will go on to consequence C, which almost always ends up with D happening! Look at me when I'm talking to you!!! At this point, you'll almost lose control—here comes consequence E. Then, depending on several factors completely out of your control, consequence F, G, or H will happen. No matter what, we're talking disaster! You might even die!"

With the best of intentions, we lecture children to spare them the fate of learning through painful life lessons. I have no problem with this, provided we pay attention to 2 points. First, sometimes kids have to learn from mistakes, and this kind of learning is very effective. We hope they learn from their minor, less dangerous mistakes while we steer them away from the major ones. Second, we have to lecture wisely. That means taking a completely different approach. No more A leads to B, which leads to C, and so on. The typical lecture has a somewhat algebraic pattern—variables affect outcomes in all sorts of mysterious ways. But there's a reason why algebra isn't taught to preadolescents—their brains aren't ready for abstract thinking. If we lecture them in an algebraic cadence, it only frustrates them because they're not yet capable of following it. When we lecture that way, kids hear our anger, condescension, and threats, but not the content of our message. Just like in the *Peanuts* comic strip, adults sound like, "Waaa waaa, waaa, waaa."

Before puberty, children think in a more concrete, mathematic cadence. They grasp simple math, like 2 plus 2 equals 4. If we switch to a simple mathematic cadence, they'll get the content of our reasoning. Even a 4-year-old can grasp simple math—one thing added to another can make something different happen.

Our challenge is to put kids in the driver's seat so they can figure things out themselves. If they dissect a problem, the lesson will be long-lasting. If we learn to use a simple mathematic cadence, children can follow and understand what we are saying. Our words need to promote their growing competence by guiding them to figure out for themselves how to be wiser and safer. We have to move away from the traditional lecture format that undermines developing competence, shames kids, and creates anger within families. Yes, anger. When children, especially adolescents, feel parents' passion, understand their fear, but cannot grasp the content of their words, they feel stupid and incapable, which makes them act out. Parents who passionately communicate from their hearts to protect their kids become frustrated and hurt when they are ignored, often causing them to react with fury.

Another significant reason to stop lecturing in the traditional way is that it may make children do exactly what we dread. This is particularly true of teenagers, who try desperately to prove to parents (and more to themselves) that they control their destinies. Younger children do it as well. When they think parents believe their decisions are wrong or dangerous or that they are naive or stupid, kids have a lot invested in proving parents wrong. If a lecture make them feel incompetent, they want to prove they are competent. And the result may be the opposite of parents' intended message. Unless we guide them to come to different conclusions by giving them some choice and control, they will go to great lengths to follow through on their original plans just to show parents that their dire predictions were off base.

A Better Way

What's a more effective way to get our points across without lecturing in the tired, old way? How can we break the cycle? Let's look first at 2 traditional lectures and see how ineffective they are.

Carl got a D on a history test and is in danger of failing unless he buckles down to study. He finds it easier to say, "History is boring," and refuse to study than to face his fear of failing the class.

His father launches into a typical lecture. "You refuse to study? What are you, crazy?! You think I work this hard so you can be lazy and become some dropout? You'll only be able to get a lousy job, living paycheck to paycheck! You think you'll have enough money for food? Then what happens? Your job gets moved overseas. You'll be on the street. No son of mine will be a failure!"

Does Carl get the message? Hardly. He's not studying because it's an easy way out in the present moment. He doesn't even follow what his father is thinking. How does not studying for tomorrow's test make him a bum later in life? Carl says to himself, "I know lots of dropouts who have jobs and own their own cars. My father is lame. I'll prove it and he'll tell me he's sorry in 10 years."

Then there's the lecture that ends with the favorite hysterical saying, "But I know this—you are going to *die!*" In the following typical lecture, a father catches his 11-year-old son smoking:

"What? You put that trash in your lungs with my money? If you start smoking, you'll get addicted. Then half your money will be spent on your habit. You'll stink. Your teeth will be yellow. And yes, then you'll get lung cancer or heart disease. Cancer will spread throughout your lungs to other parts of your body, or your arteries will get messed up and you'll have a heart attack. But I know that if you smoke, you'll *die!*"

What does his son hear? "Waa, waa, waa, waa, *die!*" He understands that his dad considers him naive at best, foolish and incapable at worst, but he misses the point because Dad's reasoning was too abstract. The son feels stupid and frustrated. He knows his father usually trusts his judgment but has lost faith in him. He thinks his father is making a huge deal of nothing. His father just doesn't get it. He wants to prove Dad wrong. He is more motivated to do what he initially wanted. Besides, smoking is a sign of growing up, and his father is still treating him like he's a little kid. His father's intervention has backfired.

If these parents shifted from an algebraic to a simple mathematic cadence, their children could follow their reasoning. Instead of a string of abstract possibilities (A to B to C to D), parents' reasoning needs to be broken down into separate steps. "Did you see how A could go to B? Do you have any experience with something like that? Tell me about that experience. Do you see how B might lead to C? Have you ever seen that happen?"

We need to speak in ways young people understand—short, concrete phrases. Then listen to their responses before moving to the next step. This approach makes kids feel competent because we're asking them to go through possible consequences step-by-step with their own ideas rather than those we dictate. They learn the lessons well because *they* have figured them out. They learn by breaking problems down in multiple steps, and they no longer have to learn only through experience. They have no need to rebel, only to listen to their inner wisdom.

"I Get It!"

Once we stop lecturing and learn to talk and guide children in ways they can clearly grasp, we need to teach them specific skills to make wise, safe decisions. This chapter offers several approaches designed to put children in the driver's seat and headed in the direction of reaching their own well-thought-out conclusions.

The Cognitive "Aha!"

When a child sees a solution or finds an answer by thinking through a situation, it's like a cartoon lightbulb turning on above her head. I call this the *cognitive aha!* experience. Suddenly, a child realizes, "I *get* it."

The cognitive aha! is our goal in guiding children through the process of absorbing the information we want to teach. We want them to comprehend and internalize that information and make it their own. When we steer them through real and hypothetical experiences, we help them break down abstract concepts into concrete, understandable steps. We guide them down the path, but they themselves take each sequential step until they reach the end of the process and suddenly they get it—aha!

Using the previously explained simple mathematic cadence (in Chapter 10), we can present one step at a time in a logical sequence so that children can follow us. They figure things out on their own so they don't have the conflict that comes with our telling them just what to think or do.

Choreographed Conversations

An effective way to teach problem-solving and build competence is to stage a *choreographed conversation.* This is simply a casual conversation between parent and child, but the parent has a hidden agenda—to steer the child through a problem so she can come up with her own sensible solution. Choreographed conversations are best held during a relaxed time, not in the heat of an argument or confrontation.

Here's an example: Dad has heard rumors that older kids are dealing prescription medications to younger kids. He's sure his fifth-grade daughter isn't involved, but Dad wants to prepare her for the possibility of being approached. As they're driving to a movie, Dad raises the subject in an offhand way.

"So, Michelle, I heard at work that somebody's teenager was stealing his little brother's ADHD medicine and selling it to kids in middle school."

"Oh, yeah?"

"Do you think it's true?"

"Maybe. I don't know, but I've heard some stories."

"I heard that the older kids start offering free pills to younger kids. Why do you suppose they do that if they aren't getting any money?"

"Maybe to be nice, or make friends?"

"I wonder. You know how the corner store sometimes gives out free samples of candy or chips?"

"Yeah, Dad, I get 'em sometimes."

"Why do you think the store owner gives them away for nothing?"

"'Cause he's nice. He likes his customers and wants to keep them happy."

"I think you're right. He does want to keep them happy, but when he stops putting out free samples, what then?"

"I guess the customers will buy the same kinds of candy or chips because they've already tasted them and liked them."

"You got it! He's a pretty smart businessman, right?"

"Yeah. He'll start selling 'em and make more money."

"Do you think that's something like the older kids who hand out free samples of pills to younger kids?"

"Sure. They're not going to keep giving away freebees to be nice. They'll start charging money. I wouldn't fall for that."

This father has carefully guided his daughter through a series of ideas and questions that lead to her recognizing the reality of a problem—"aha!" If Dad had simply proclaimed, "I forbid you to take drugs from anyone, ever!" or lectured about the dangers of drugs, Michelle may have heard the words but not absorbed the message.

Michelle is too young and inexperienced to think logically and in an abstract manner about the ulterior motives of older kids. By choreographing or stage-managing their conversation, Dad asked leading questions that guided Michelle to reach her own sensible conclusion. Because she walked through the scenario, the lesson at the end was authentic and meaningful to her.

One or two choreographed conversations like this certainly will not guarantee that Michelle will never try drugs in the years to come. But if her father continues to use choreographed conversations to raise issues of potential harm, he will reinforce lessons that Michelle can understand and internalize. At the same time, he will enhance Michelle's competence to anticipate and deal with challenges.

Role-playing

In addition to choreographed conversations, we can role-play to get children to the aha! moment. This strategy allows children to explore hypothetical situations and grasp how certain decisions or actions will determine outcomes. Think of it as a rehearsal for real life.

I use the term *role-play* loosely. It doesn't mean that you have a script or you and your child will step into actor's roles. It's simply a way for parent and child to spin out a what-if situation and see where it leads. If it doesn't lead to a successful conclusion, that's okay. In fact, it may even be more effective than a happy ending because it can show your child the various possible results of unwise decisions and actions. When you role-play, keep the following suggestions in mind:

Try to set up a role-play casually. Don't make it obvious or announce, "Let's role-play. I'll be your friend. What are you going to say if he asks you to help him cheat on a test?" If you do that, children will groan and roll their eyes. Instead, be subtle and relaxed. Work "what if..." and "what'll happen when..." scenarios into conversations. When you start a role-play, use neutral situations that don't involve your child or her friends directly because that approach makes children feel defensive. They will think you are being nosy or trying to find out about their friends. This will take their attention off your central message. Instead, spin the role-play around television characters or fabricated strangers, such as the nieces and nephews of a coworker whom your child doesn't know personally.

Keep the tone light and avoid confrontational dialogue. Regardless of where the role-playing leads, stay calm so your child can think instead of react. Don't jump in with answers. Let her fill in the blanks and come up with her own suggestions or solutions. Use short phrases and let your child do most of the talking. You can nudge the conversation along if it's stalling by inserting, "Uh, huh...I see...okay...I hear you...then what?" Don't try to sound like a cool kid yourself. If you sprinkle phrases like "My bad," or "Awesome, dude," into the conversation, your child will see that you're trying too hard. Truly cool parents don't talk in kid speak or wear nose rings. Truly cool parents are nonjudgmental adults who respect children and don't try to act like kids themselves or be their best friend.

You can begin a role-playing situation almost anywhere. A car ride, waiting in line, a movie, or a television show can provide an opening. "What would you do if you were in that situation?" As your child steps into the role, you can take another part, such as the best friend. As you would in a choreographed conversation, walk your child through various scenarios with a series of what-ifs.

If you use a television program as a chance to role-play, you could start with something like this: "If Brad does X, how do you think Jenna will react?" You are in effect playing the Brad role by tossing out possible actions and suggestions that he might make. "What other choices does Jenna have? What else could she say or do? How could she get out of that situation?" Have some fun with these role-playing activities. Don't make them drip with heavy meaning. Listen carefully to your child's responses and take it from there. Perhaps your child will suggest an action that you know will lead to embarrassment or failure. That's okay! You're just role-playing. When that disaster occurs in a role-play scenario, no one gets hurt, but your child will recognize that specific actions and choices can lead to the misguided end. In other words, by acting it out, your child can learn a lesson far more effectively and safely than if you had lectured to make the same point.

Here is another twist on the role-playing technique. In this example, mother and daughter technically don't take on roles, but the mother takes a real-time situation and helps her daughter foresee possible outcomes.

Mom and daughter are shopping for back-to-school clothes. The dressing room is one of those wide-open spaces where curtains divide the changing cubicles. As her daughter is trying on another pair of jeans, Mom notices a group of girls whispering nearby. For a half-second, she wonders why 2 of them are wearing baggy jackets in August. Then she sees one girl layer a sweater over a sweater over a blouse and finally zip her jacket over everything. Mom nudges her daughter and whispers, "Look over there."

The daughter responds, "What?"

"See what those girls are doing?"

"Oh my god..."

"What do you think will happen?"

"I bet they'll try to sneak past the cashier."

"Then what?"

"The guard at the door will probably catch them when the security tag sets off an alarm."

"What will the guard do?"

"I don't know. Call their parents?"

"Maybe he'll call somebody else."

"Oh, yeah, the police. Will they have to go to jail?"

Their conversation continued on the ride home. The daughter revealed that some of her friends shoplifted makeup from the local drugstore, but she hadn't. Mom replied, "I bet those girls really wanted you to steal some makeup, too. It must have been hard to resist their pressure, but you made a good decision. You can be proud of yourself."

"Yeah, I know. But I really liked that mauve eye shadow!" her daughter laughed.

What happened here, and what didn't? The mother could have ignored the shoplifters or used them as an example to lecture her daughter. ("Don't you ever try anything like that! I never want to be embarrassed by you or have to come and bail you out for shoplifting!") Instead, she took advantage of a situation at hand and used it to walk her daughter through the possible consequences of shoplifting. By discussing strangers instead of her daughter or her daughter's friends, this mother prevented her daughter from needing to become defensive.

By calmly steering the conversation along instead of getting hysterical, she got her daughter not only to think about those situations, but also to open up and talk about her friends. When Mom learned that her daughter's friends had shoplifted, she remained nonjudgmental and praised her daughter for making a good choice. She sent her the clear message, "I trust you. You're a good person who can make good decisions."

Learning to Recognize a Line

Parents can use almost any daily situation to create a teachable moment without their child's direct involvement. These ordinary events are often more effective as teaching opportunities because the focus *isn't* on your own child. For example, Dad walks into the living room and notices an about-to-get-steamy scene on the television screen. He sits down beside his daughter Kim and watches silently for a while. At the commercial break, he asks her, "Why do you think that girl fell for that guy's line?"

"What line?"

"When he said, 'If you really love me, you'll show me...'"

"Oh, I don't know. I guess he was trying to get her into bed."

"Yeah, and she fell for it. What could she have said instead?"

Television programs are great opportunities to springboard into conversations. The story lines are usually predictable, so it's easy for parents to plan their questions and comments. When talking about fictional characters, parents can use a confrontational or critical tone ("How could he be so stupid?")

that would send kids into a defensive frenzy if it were directed at them or their friends.

Television offers ample opportunity to teach kids to distinguish a line. Adults are used to hearing lines. The telemarketer tells us we'll get all sorts of terrific free gifts if we sign up right now by charging it on a credit card. We know there's a catch. But children, and even most teens we think are sophisticated, often don't see a line for what it is—manipulative. This father used the television opportunity to open a discussion with his daughter about recognizing a line. When the program ended, he asked her several hypothetical questions that could occur in real life. "What would you think if your friend said X, Y, or Z?"

By using a television program that presented a dilemma, at a calm time when there was no pressing conflict with his daughter, this father wisely set up an opportunity for Kim to problem-solve in a safe, objective way. If he continues to teach and reinforce problem-solving skills, he will help her rehearse and prepare for challenges that undoubtedly will arise in the future.

Picking Times and Places

The car is a great place to launch a choreographed conversation or role-play. You have a captive audience in your 2-ton moving vehicle. You pass various scenes that can spark a discussion, which allows you to bring up tough topics without having to talk about your child or her friends. You'll drive by kids smoking, kids being disrespectful to adults and each other, inappropriately dressed kids, children out alone when they shouldn't be, children being bullied, and kids making out. Maybe most importantly, you will be able to talk about those significant topics while avoiding eye contact. This can be especially important for boys. It is usually quite difficult to sit down with your son, hold his chin firmly in your palm, look straight into his eyes, and say, "Tell me how you FEEEEEL." It's easier to bring things up sideways and keep the conversation laid back. Let him stare out the window. All the while he will look like he doesn't care, but you will be talking about incredibly important matters.

But a cautionary word if your teen is driving and you're in the passenger seat: It is vital that he keep all his attention and focus on the road. Teens don't have enough experience to engage in thoughtful conversation while driving. If he wants you to be his driving teacher, agree ahead of time that you need to create another space for your best conversations.

As you look for teachable-moment situations with your child, here's a summary of 3 general guidelines to remember.

- Keep your tone relaxed. Children are more likely to listen and even be curious about what you're about to say if you open with offhand questions like, "What would you do if...?" If your child doesn't respond with interest, drop it. Other opportunities will always pop up.

- Avoid end-of-the-world scare tactics. Whether you're talking with your child about actual events or hypotheticals, don't overdramatize. She'll never take you seriously if you say, "Smoking will kill you by the time you're 30." First of all, kids don't think about being 30, 40, or 50 years old—it's far too distant and abstract. Secondly, they know you're trying to scare them because they know smokers who have lived into their 80s. ("But Craig's grandpa still smokes.") Even if you use scare tactics that children might believe, they will react emotionally or defensively rather than think about possible consequences. Scare tactics only increase children's stress; they don't help them problem-solve.

- Avoid hurtful criticism. When a child has done something foolish or harmful, parents tend to blurt out phrases like, "How could you be so stupid? Why didn't you think first? Was your brain out to lunch?" Labels, sarcasm, and shame are ineffective responses because they put children in the position of having to defend themselves or retreat into anger and resentment. Even worse, these negative criticisms make children feel inept. ("I guess I am a loser. I can never do anything right.")

Before moving ahead, I want to circle back briefly to the cognitive aha! technique. Choreographed conversations, role-playing, and learning to recognize lines can all lead your children to reach a cognitive aha! As long as these techniques are done casually, they can and should be used whenever a teachable moment arises or you can create one. You will want to fine-tune these techniques as your child grows so they will be age-appropriate. If you use these strategies often and in a relaxed way, you may prevent many behavior problems. But trying times will inevitably arise, no matter how diligent you are. When your child has a behavior problem, you'll want to be prepared to deal with it. The starting point is an understanding that behavioral change must occur in sequential steps.

CHAPTER 12

Changing Behavior Step-by-step

If we want children to change a certain behavior and become more competent, we need to understand that this is a sequential process that takes time and practice. We guide them through this process so they will become more responsible for their choices and therefore more competent to handle other challenges.

Whether we want to prevent a problem, redirect negative behavior in a more constructive direction, or promote an entirely new, positive behavior, we need to steer children through 5 related steps in the following order:

1. Become aware that a problem exists.
2. Recognize that the problem affects them so that they become motivated to change.
3. Acquire the skills to find a solution.
4. Weigh the costs and benefits of changing the behavior.
5. Make a decision to change and commit to it.

Behavioral change is a step-by-step process, so you need to give targeted guidance tailored to where your child is at the moment. If you offer guidance that's too many steps ahead of where he is and what he's ready for, he will become frustrated and you'll stifle his competence. If your guidance is a few steps behind where he is on the behavioral change spectrum, he won't benefit because he has passed beyond your suggestions. The goal is to recognize the stage where your child is right now. Then he will be comfortable, and you can offer an opportunity to move to the next step.

For children who don't even see the problem (not even at step 1), offering information makes a lot of sense. At some point, though, you'll find that your child does know there's a problem (step 1). He knows the problem affects him and wants to change the situation (step 2). He doesn't yet have the skills to change the situation, however, so he's stuck. This is where you can step in and teach him skills to find a solution (step 3). You may use choreographed conversations or role-playing. Once he has some skills to address the problem, he needs to weigh the benefits and disadvantages to changing the behavior (step 4). Then he has to decide which direction to take—to change the behavior or continue it. Your child's ability to maintain his behavioral choices will be reinforced or undermined by important influences in his life like parents, peers, teachers, and the media.

If the problem is drinking at parties, for example, 15-year-old Camela is at step 2. She knows there's a problem behavior because she has gotten drunk, thrown up, embarrassed herself in front of friends, and her parents have caught her staggering in after her curfew. Camela may want to refuse to drink, but she doesn't have the skills to change her behavior. At step 3, her parents need to teach her those skills. Even after she acquires them, she may not be sure that changing her behavior is worth losing the acceptance of her partying peers. She will have to weigh the benefits against the cost of alienating friends (step 4). If she does decide to stop drinking at parties, she will have to commit to her decision and stick with it (step 5), which will require the ongoing support of her parents and nondrinking friends.

Because Camela is at step 3, her parents can use role-playing or choreographed conversations to help her figure out ways to refuse alcohol at these parties or find other alternatives, such as hanging out with a nondrinking group of friends. Here's another skill-building technique they might use.

Decision Trees

A *decision tree* can break down vague lessons ("Don't drink—you're too young, it's illegal at your age, and you can get in big trouble...maybe die.") into concrete segments that a child will see on paper and quickly grasp. Remember, Camela is 15 years old. She may not yet be thinking as abstractly as an adult. While her parents talk with her about the drinking situation, they sketch out various possibilities that Camela suggests in response to their leading questions. Some branches of the tree may lead to dead ends or unwanted results. Others may produce viable solutions.

Camela's parents begin in the present.

"Okay, your friends tell you there's a party next Friday at the Williams' house." They draw a little square at the bottom of the paper. "What's going to happen?"

"Everybody will go," Camela immediately replies.

"Will Mr or Mrs Williams be home?"

"Probably not," Camela answers sheepishly.

Her parents sketch a line from the box and write in "parents not home." They ask her what would happen next. As Camela suggests various possibilities, such as, "James brings a keg," "More kids show up," and "We don't know some of them because they're older and from another school," her parents write down these events in a sequence. Her parents easily foresee alarming scenarios—a raucous party, neighbors calling police, arrests for underage drinking, date rape, alcohol poisoning, rushing to the hospital—but Camela doesn't acknowledge these possibilities until she sees them sketched out on paper. She begins to see how A (no parents home) can lead to B (lots of underage drinking) to C (arrest or worse).

Her parents don't just leave it there with a scary outcome. They then lead Camela along other tree branches and suggest other possibilities.

"What if someone called the Williamses to see if they'd be home? What if the Williamses are home, but older kids who drive have alcohol in their cars and kids sneak outside to drink? What if you're uncomfortable and want to get out of there? What if someone offers you a ride home and you know they've been drinking?"

As they sketch their way through these possibilities, Camela begins to see that there are alternatives to going along with the crowd, which was the only path she imagined before this decision tree exercise. Her parents ask, "What else could happen? What other choices do you have?" This leads to other tree branches. "Maybe I could skip the party and go to another friend's house overnight." (This friend isn't in the drinking crowd.) "Or maybe I could tell my friends that I have to babysit that night because I need the money for our class trip. Or maybe I could stop by the party for only a little while and then say I have to get home because you've lowered my curfew."

As Camela comes up with these alternatives, her parents sketch them on the decision tree and connect them to the ultimate goal—Camela doesn't get drunk, comes home safely, and doesn't lose face with her peers. She now has a concrete lesson, in black and white, on paper. She can see how the dots connect. She now knows she has choices. She sees how each choice can lead to a certain outcome. She is now competent to make wiser choices than drinking with the crowd.

But will she? The next step (4) in the behavioral change model is to weigh her options. Is she willing to risk friends' disapproval or rejection if she chooses not to drink? Does the chance of getting home safely outweigh the chances of getting into a car wreck or swept up in a police raid? If she makes the less wise choice, her parents will have to continue to work with her on problem-solving skills. But if she makes the smarter, safer choice, her parents will still need to be involved in a supportive role because new challenges will inevitably arise to test her resolve.

As you use decision trees, if your child gets stuck or suggests an unwise or impractical action, you can redirect the discussion back on point with comments like, "Uh huh. Let's see. I think that might be a mistake to try that. Let's think about this and see what could happen if…" Guide your child along with specific questions, but don't supply the answers. Remember, this is an exercise on paper. Your child can always retrace his steps or turn in another direction if he makes a poor choice. One cautionary note about decision trees—they are most effective if not used too often. Save them for major issues.

Decision trees can work with younger children too, as long as you keep the discussion at a level your child understands. In the next example, the behavior problem is fighting.

The teacher called 8-year-old Eric's parents to report that he is often getting into playground and school bus skirmishes. First his parents want to be sure Eric is aware of this problem, so they say in a nonjudgmental tone, "Your teacher called last night to say that you've been having some problems on the playground and bus." Notice that they don't grill him or make an accusation on the assumption of guilt. Their even tone allows Eric to open up and say that, yes, he'd gotten into a couple of push-and-shove matches because he felt bullied by classmates.

His parents take it to step 2 to see whether he's motivated to change. "So, do you like fighting?"

"No, it stinks," he answers. "I don't like getting shoved around in front of my friends, but I don't know what to do about it. Two of the guys are bigger than me." Eric has recognized the problem, knows it certainly affects him, and wants to change the situation. He has the motivation to change, but he isn't at step 3 because he doesn't have the skills.

At this juncture, his parents step in with pencil and paper to sketch out some decisions he might make. They walk Eric through a series of events one at a time. One branch of the decision tree leads Eric to more fights, a black eye, the principal's office, and eventually suspension from school. Another branch leads to avoiding the bullies by sticking close to a group of friends. Another branch points to sitting near the driver at the front of the bus instead of the rear where the bullies sit. Still another branch leads Eric to defusing these confrontations with self-deprecating humor whenever the bullies approach him. Yet another leads to taking karate lessons so he becomes more confident (but not aggressive) about facing them.

More Skills for Your Repertoire

When we think about the skills needed to promote safe behaviors or move toward a successful future, there's almost no end of desired skills. The skill to put on a bike helmet or seat belt properly and consistently count here. Academic skills certainly count because even highly motivated students will not succeed without academic skills. For our discussion, I want to focus on the skills that children need to navigate the suggestions, pressures, and influences of their peers. These potentially life-changing skills can be broken into 3 categories.

- Learning to say no
- Recognizing manipulation and responding to it
- Shifting the blame to save face

The Unique Power of "No"

It is unrealistic to expect young people to stand up to their friends and say, "No, I won't do that. It's just not right or ethical." It is equally difficult to expect them to say no effectively to a peer or refuse to go along with the crowd because the very word no has become so overused and weakened. Many parents say, "No, you can't have that toy," when a child begs at the checkout counter. The child whines and pleas and the parent replies, "No, I said NO! Okay?" Okay? Is it really necessary for a parent to ask a child's permission?

Many children grow up hearing wishy-washy noes. They learn early in life that if they stick to their guns, continue to beg and argue, and wear us down, they can turn our initial no into a "Well, maybe," and finally a "Yes." To compound the problem, many parents overuse no. The word spills from our lips instinctively and often.

If we use the word no less frequently, children learn that we mean it. Learning that "no means no" in their early years can make it easier for preteens and teens to understand that message clearly when they have to say no themselves. I urge parents to feel comfortable saying "Maybe," or "I'll have to think about it," instead of a spontaneous no, when they don't really mean no.

I have learned from many of my teenaged patients that equivocal noes lead to conflicting double messages, particularly in sexual circumstances. Although gender roles are certainly changing and girls are more forceful in pursuing boys than in past generations, the following is still a common situation:

A boy comes on to a girl, flatters her, pressures her to have sex. She finds him attractive and says no with a smile or giggle. He doesn't hear no in a manner that prompts him to walk away; he hears, "Maybe. Keep flirting with me, keep asking." Such mixed signals could lead to date rape. Girls and boys need to say no like they mean it. Too often, I have heard girls explain that they don't like to say no because "it sounds mean."

We need to teach children to say no in a clear, firm tone and make it non-negotiable. An ideal way to teach this lesson is through a role-play. For younger children, you could set up a role-play around almost any issue for which you want them to be able to refuse a behavior. Take stealing, for example.

Aneesh and his father notice a skateboard that someone has left near the sidewalk. Dad sets up the role-play by saying, "I bet somebody will be tempted to steal that. What if some kid asked you to take it?" (Here, Dad steps into the role.) "'Let's take it. Nobody will know.'"

"I'd tell him, 'Somebody might see us,' because I really don't want to steal it."

"'Nobody's around. C'mon, let's take it. Don't be a wuss, Aneesh.'"

"Well, I don't know. No, I don't think we should."

"That doesn't sound like no to me. Can you say it like you mean it?"

"I guess I could say..." (Aneesh's voice gets stronger.) "'No, I don't want to take it because I already got a skateboard,' or 'No, I saw someone looking out a window and they'll tell on us.'"

"Right, that's good and clear. You said it strongly enough that you made me believe you."

Dealing With Manipulation

Adults have a distorted view of peer pressure. We tend to imagine that it comes from a sinister-looking child or teen who threatens our dear, sweet, innocent child. "Do this or die." "Do this or I'll flush your head in the toilet and give you a swirly." In fact, peer pressure is much more subtle. Words are not even exchanged most of the time. Peer pressure usually is internally driven. "If I wear a bike helmet when none of my friends do, I'll look like a mama's boy." "If I just take a drag of this cigarette, the sixth graders will think I'm cool enough to hang out with them." "I better not hang out any more with Susanna because then Emily will think I'm not good enough to be her best friend."

There's no magic way to prepare children to manage this internally driven peer pressure. The best we can do—and it does make a big difference—is to help them develop strong character and always be available to listen to them when they need a sounding board to work out their dilemmas.

Although most peer pressure is internally driven, young people still do receive pressure-filled, manipulative messages from peers. Some of these messages come from "the group"; others come from individuals. Much of childhood, and particularly adolescence, is spent figuring out who we are, so kids tend to know which groups they fit into and which they don't. Quite a bit of child culture is defined by telling kids why they are out and what they must do to get in. "We all have our ears pierced. If your mom doesn't even let you do that, then you couldn't have any fun going to the mall with us. We don't go to little kid shops," or "I really like hanging out with you, but it's just that after soccer, the 5 of us go out to the field and slam back a few beers, that's all."

The best a parent can hope is that their child is so bathed with security and so solidly clear about his values that he won't stray too far. It's also helpful for a child to have more than one circle of friends (as I will address in Chapter 20). If he has only one circle and that group moves into behaviors beyond his comfort zone, he'll become isolated if he doesn't go along with them. But if he has other sets of friends, he can turn to them for other options.

Parents can prepare children to handle another kind of peer pressure, the type that comes in the form of manipulative messages from someone who tries to get a child to do something he wouldn't choose to do on his own. It's rarely delivered in a rude or confrontational tone; rather, it's couched in friendship, even love. It says essentially, "C'mon, haven't I done enough for you already?" and includes lines like, "I really love you and I want to be able to show you," or "I want to hang out with you, man. I just really, really want to get high too." With younger kids, it sounds like this: "C'mon, I'm your best friend, aren't I? I just really want you to..."

The most commonly taught way to prepare children to deal with these manipulative lines is to teach them first to recognize a line and then to respond by pushing the pressure back on the other person. For instance, "I really love you and I want to show you," would be countered by, "No, you don't. If you really loved me, you would wait!" Or, "C'mon, we're buds, let's get high. Everyone does," would merit a response like, "Well, I'm not everyone, and I don't need to be your friend."

I believe this push-back approach is seriously flawed because it ignores the fact that kids, especially preteens and teens, want desperately to be loved and accepted. So while they understand this push-back technique, I don't believe they actually will use it in the real world. I realize that many parents want their children to stand up to and abandon friends with riskier behaviors, but I'm afraid it just won't happen.

A more effective way to handle this kind of pressure fits into youth culture and allows kids to keep their friends while controlling their own actions. This technique has 3 stages.

❖ First, kids need to be able to recognize a line. You can help even younger children to recognize manipulation by pointing it out on television, in the neighborhood, or wherever you see it. "My goodness, he sounds like he wants to help me, but I know that he really wants me to..."

❖ Second, children need to be taught how to state their positions clearly, with no ambivalence, in a direct way that isn't argumentative, accusatory, or self-righteous. "I don't want to steal that." "I won't cut school with you." "I'm not ready for sex." "I'm not doing drugs." "I'm not cheating."

☀ Third, they quickly offer an alternative that allows them to maintain the relationship on their terms but doesn't end the friendship. "If you want to come over to my house instead, I've got a new game we can play." "But I love you too, and I still want to be with you and have fun in other ways." "I won't get high, but if you aren't too wasted, I'll shoot hoops with you later." "I won't cheat, but I'm not bad at math, so if you want, I'll help you study."

The best way to prepare kids to learn these strategies is by role-playing, as discussed earlier. But be subtle—if you practice role-playing about how to say no to sexual advances before your daughter's first date, she will be mortified. Remember to look for external situations to teach these skills.

Shifting the Blame to Save Face

We can further strengthen children's competence in dealing with peer pressure and other negative influences if we teach them skills to reject certain behaviors or get out of jams without losing face. This is particularly important for teenagers. We often believe that they will do the right thing based on their own moral compass or our best parental advice. But if their decision doesn't play well in teen culture, they often choose not to follow a well-thought-out strategy. The following techniques are designed to offer a way out while still fitting in. But don't wait for adolescence. Even if your children aren't yet teenagers, you can prepare them at a younger age. They will be able to use some of these techniques before they hit double digits.

Code Words

You and your child choose a code word or phrase that will only be used in an emergency and not shared with friends. Make sure you and your child agree on what an emergency is. Your child may assume it means, "I'm in a burning building. Come rescue me." You may assume it means anytime your child needs to be pulled out of a risky social situation. Discuss what you mean and reach a clear understanding. Then rehearse how you and your child could use the code word technique in future situations.

When I discuss the use of code words with my patients and their parents, I describe an emergency or dangerous occasion as any situation in which a child feels uncomfortable or at risk and can't get out of it safely on his own. For example, 12-year-old Andre is at a friend's home when other kids show up with bongs. Andre has never tried marijuana and he feels on the spot. If he turns it down, his friends will think he's a wuss. He's clearly uncomfortable and doesn't know what to do.

If he and his parents have already agreed on a code word and rehearsed how he can use it, the scenario can lead to Andre's getting out of the situation.

He tells his friends that he has to call home or "my Dad will be really angry." He phones home in front of them so they can clearly hear his end of the conversation.

"Yeah, Dad. I'm over at Sandy's. We're doing homework. I know, I know. I'll be home as soon as I can. But I didn't have time to walk Shaggy. Can you walk him for me?"

Shaggy is their code word. When Dad hears it, he knows his son is in a tight spot, so Dad raises his voice loud enough for the friends to hear him yell through the phone, "You're already late! I told you to be home by 8:00! Get home this minute or else!"

If Andre thinks he can leave immediately and still save face with his friends, he will say, "Okay, all right, Dad. I'm leaving right now," slam down the phone, and complain to his friends, "I gotta go or my old man will kill me." If it's too far to walk or he can't get a ride home, he can ratchet up the phone conversation as a way to let his father know he needs to be rescued.

"What do you mean, I have to come home this minute? I'm staying. I don't have to listen to you!" That's the warning sign to his father that Andre needs to be picked up. So his father yells—again, loudly enough for the friends to hear— "What's Sandy's address? I'm coming to get you right now. You'd better be waiting at the door when I get there."

Andre can then turn to his friends and complain about what a pain in the butt his father is. Andre has gotten himself out of a potentially risky situation without losing face or wimping out. In fact, his friends sympathize with him. When they get home, Andre's father doesn't blame him for getting into a tight spot or hanging out with bad friends. Instead, he praises Andre for using their code word effectively. Andre now feels more competent and confident because he has mastered this skill and is prepared to use it again the next time he's in a difficult spot.

A code word can also be used to help children face uncomfortable social situations because they know that can always call on a parent to get them out of the predicament without embarrassment. A shy child, for example, may find that going to your office party with you would be overwhelming. She wants to go to please you, but is afraid you'll be too busy networking to notice how bored and uncomfortable she is. She won't tell you any of this, but you will sense it. To make her more comfortable, you could say, "You know, all you have to do is tell me that you have homework to do [or you forgot to feed the fish— the phrase doesn't matter] and I'll make sure we leave." That will make her feel brave enough to know she can handle the party.

Using a code word is an ideal addition to the Contract for Life promoted by Students Against Destructive Decisions (SADD). In that contract, the teen promises to call for a safe ride if there are any substances that might decrease the driver's focus. Ideally teens will call readily because they value safety so highly and trust their parents. But that is a gamble not worth taking. If a code word is added to the contract, it makes it easier to call home.

Another common situation that creates a great deal of anxiety for children is the roller-coaster friendship ride—the shifting status of *best friends,* especially among girls. It's difficult for children to repair friendships after an argument. Parents can help by first listening to their child's hurt or angry feelings and then using a choreographed conversation to help her think about how to face the friend the next time they meet, such as at a sleepover next weekend. The final step, which lets her know in advance that she can handle anything no matter what comes, is having a code word to use if she becomes uncomfortable and wants to come home early.

Just Blame Me

A similar technique teaches children to blame parents or use us as the bad guys to get themselves out of a tight spot. Tell your children that it's perfectly fine with you if they want to paint you as the meanest parent in the world. You're happy to be the bad guy if it will help them stay away from risky behaviors or situations.

Many young people want to avoid or stop negative behaviors of their peer group, but they are afraid that rejecting these behaviors will cost them friendships and acceptance. So shifting the blame to their nagging, ridiculous parents is an acceptable way to avoid those behaviors. Other examples of how kids can paint parents as the enemy to get them out of a jam or protect them from risky behaviors include, "My parents are so mean, they'll ground me for a month if I don't get home on time," or "I can't drink with you or smoke weed because my mother sniffs me when I get home. Yeah, you don't believe it? She actually smells my clothes and hair and breath and stares into my pupils. She thinks she's a cop."

Create a Rumor

A similar strategy is to suggest that your child create a rumor or spin out a tale of what will happen if she does something you won't approve of, such as, "My parents said they'll take my DVD player to the pawn shop if I do that again," "They'll send me to another school if I get caught cutting classes again because my grades are already slipping," "They won't let me get my license if I don't study," or "If I get one speeding ticket, they said they'll take my license away."

Your child can also blame someone else, such as the school principal or guidance counselor who "will expel me if I cut class again" or a doctor who tells her not to smoke. If a child doesn't want to smoke, she can tell friends, "I have asthma and my doctor says I could end up in the hospital if I smoke. I don't want to be in any hospital."

You may never have threatened to give away the DVD, send her to another school, or deny her license, but these white lies are an effective out for children or teens who are in situations in which they want to avoid trouble or change a behavior but still retain standing with their peers.

I have been teaching these techniques for 15 years, and I know that they make some parents uncomfortable because on some level I am advocating lying. I truly wish all children could have the ability to handle everything— they would never be frightened of a new situation or in danger of succumbing to bad influences. I wish they could say, "I disagree. I won't participate." But I know that they cannot, even if they have a full rational understanding of the consequences. Peer culture can be so tough to navigate that if they don't have a face-saving maneuver that allows them to make a sound decision and do the right thing, they often will take risks rather than confront or lose their friends. So while lying is not consistent with the values we want to teach children, living up to their own standards definitely is a major value we hope they hold. These techniques make this possible. Above all, it reinforces the parent as the person they can always rely on to get them out of trouble.

CHAPTER 14

Media Literacy

To be competent in today's world, children have to deal with many powerful forces that try to influence them. They need to understand the motivations of people who try to affect their behavior or the way they think. I have addressed some ways to prepare children to evaluate peers' motivations, control their own choices, and form their own values in the face of peer pressure. But there is another strong and sometimes dangerous influence on our children—the media.

In the 21st century, the media have an ever-present effect on how children view the world and perhaps even themselves. We need to prepare our children to be media literate so they can properly understand, interpret, and reject media messages when necessary.

Kids spend more time in front of a screen than ever before—television and movies screens, computers, video games, and all sorts of handheld devices, including cell phones with pictures, e-mail, and easy Internet access.

The Henry J. Kaiser Family Foundation conducted 3 studies between 1999 and 2009 that revealed a dramatic increase in the amount of time children and teens spend with entertainment or electronic media. With technology allowing almost around-the-clock media access, young people aged 8 to 18 years spend an average of 7 hours and 38 minutes a day—more than 53 hours a week— using computers, televisions, cell phones, video games, and other electronic devices. And much of that time they are multitasking—texting and listening to music while watching television or surfing on the computer, for example— so they're actually cramming 10 hours and 45 minutes into those 7 hours and 38 minutes each day.*

I don't want you to assume that all of this is bad. Some media exposure is preparing children to navigate an increasingly wired and computerized world. I have 2 major concerns. First, once children begin communicating primarily through texting and social networking, they do less face-to-face interacting;

*Information from *Generation M²: Media in the Lives of 8- to 18-Year-Olds*,
The Henry J. Kaiser Family Foundation, 2010.

therefore, be sure your child knows how to have a polite interaction and deal with people before entering the cyberspace world. Second, all of this multi-tasking may not be producing people who are actually better able to multitask. People who spend their lives doing 2 or 3 things at once tend to genuinely believe they're adept at this juggling and can stay focused on each task at hand. Research proves that this is not true. People are not as good at multitasking as they think. In fact, teens who consistently multitask are found to lose focus with straightforward tasks because they get bored.

Almost 70% of US children have televisions in their bedrooms, and solid research shows that televisions in bedrooms affect school performance. An increasing number of kids also have DVD and video game players in their bedrooms. By the time you read this, I'll bet even newer technologies which children "absolutely need" will be the rage.

In addition to hours and hours of screen time, children are exposed to scores of advertisements each day, from the logos on T-shirts to ads on bill-boards and buses. They are also inundated by messages in the music they listen to and magazines they read.

These powerful influences often don't project the values we want children to hold. I'm not just talking about violence or sexual activity. In an attempt to promote certain products or simply keep the child consumer tuned in, many media messages target a child's insecurity. These messages imply that the child isn't slim, good looking, cool, or rich enough because he doesn't eat certain snacks or have the "right" sneakers, clothes, phone, backpack, or even car.

Have you noticed how many commercials include children who, of course, cannot even use the advertised product? Advertisers aren't just interested in making children consumers themselves; they're attempting to turn them into little lobbyists who will influence parents' buying habits.

If children accept these media messages at face value, how will they ever become competent to stand up and say, "No, I don't need to buy that," "I don't want to do that," "I don't have to own that," and much more importantly, "I am okay the way I am," and "I am happy with what I have."

Isn't contentment a piece of happiness and resilience? Is it possible to feel content in a world that says you never have enough? No one can have every-thing, but what does it do psychologically to children and families who can't afford what most middle-class families can buy? And how does this never-enough advertising blitz affect middle-class children who are led to believe that they won't be good enough unless they are affluent?

We need to raise media-literate children if they are to rise above these dangerous messages and feel satisfied with their own capabilities and identities. I strongly urge my patients and their families to put the family television in one room of the house where they can watch together and ban televisions from children's bedrooms. Televisions have become so ubiquitous that they are even used as babysitters or entertainment on family car trips—kids watching televisions in the back seat while Dad or Mom are up front, talking on a cell phone or listening to the radio or a CD. This hardly promotes family connection.

I am not suggesting we ban television altogether; there are ways to control its influence and enlighten children. We can begin immediately by watching television with kids and discussing commercials. I started this with my own daughters when they were about 3 years old. At that age, children can't yet tell the difference between commercials and programs, but it was important to me that they begin to understand when the program stopped "because right now someone is trying to sell you something," I explained to them.

As you watch television with your children, you can ask questions like, "Why do those people do that? Do you really think other kids will think you're a superstar if you wear those sneakers? What is behind those ads? What does the manufacturer want you to think or do?" By asking leading questions and listening to your child's responses, you can guide your child toward the conclusion, "They're out to sell me something. I have choices. I don't have to be manipulated."

When a toy is promoted through a television commercial or used as a tie-in between a fast-food purchase and a movie, you can ask your child, "Why do you think they're advertising [or selling] that toy right now? Is it to get you to go see the movie? If kids have already seen the movie, do you think they'll want to buy the toy?" Even 7-year-olds are savvy enough to understand this marketing manipulation when you guide them along. That doesn't mean, of course, that they'll say, "Don't buy it for me. I won't cave in to such a manipulative, commercial scheme!" They'll probably still want the toy, but they'll start to become more media literate. If you continue to reinforce these messages by raising similar discussions over time, they will further integrate the message, "I have choices here."

With children approaching adolescence, it's important to begin contrasting the truths of heavy alcohol and cigarette use with their media exposure. The next time you see a beer commercial or billboard featuring a handsome guy with perfect abdominal musculature (his own six-pack!), lifting a beer with beautiful, unnaturally thin women at his side, ask your son if your heavily drinking neighbor resembles the guy in the ad. I'm guessing your neighbor probably doesn't have six-pack abs or beautiful women hanging on him. He's more likely to have a wonderful, normal-looking wife who begs him to drink less and pay more attention to her. Your son will get the picture.

As children mature and become better able to distinguish between pro-gramming and commercials, encourage them to be more discriminating about what they watch. Again, by asking leading questions, you can steer them toward judging whether a program is clever, engaging, and thought-stimulating, or mindless drivel. Ask them questions like, "What did you like about that program? Could you figure out what was going to happen? If you hadn't watched it, do you think you would have missed something important?" You can help your kids become competent television critics while keeping your own opinions to yourself.

Teaching opportunities don't always have to spring from a television com-mercial. They could arise from a video game. Video game makers want children to buy more video games, so they make the games fast-paced and often incorpo-rate violence to capture children's anger, rage, aggression, or desire for control.

Talk to your children about how they feel when they play these games. Help them recognize the underlying motives of the game makers. Explain that sit-ting in front of a game and pretending to kill people desensitizes some people to real tragedies. In my experience, kids always tell parents that this won't hap-pen to them. You can reassure them that you don't believe they will become desensitized, but as a matter of household policy, you can limit the amount of time they are exposed to violent material. While you should limit screen time altogether so children will find more creative, physical, or intellectual pursuits, you can be more lenient with nonviolent video games. Your kids may not swear off playing video games forever, but hopefully they will find alternatives to the offensive games.

Not all media are manipulative. Some are educational, informative, and purely entertaining. (I have discussed how media offers a prime opportunity to engage kids in role-playing or spark a choreographed conversation.) But even educational or nonentertainment media, notably the news, can have a profound if unintended effect on children.

As much as we worry about children becoming numb to violence through movies and video games, we also need to monitor their exposure to the news. Some families leave the television on continuously, almost as background noise. Sadly, we can become numbed by the tragedies of the world—famines, wars, acts of terror, and disappearances of children. I strongly urge parents to limit the around-the-clock reporting of huge stories like terrorist attacks, hurricanes, plane crashes, kidnappings, and abductions. That repetitive exposure can sear images into the consciousness. Many younger children are appropriately terrified by nightly news stories but will usually not tell their parents because they see the parents watching the news so passively—it all seems so normal.

Don't assume that older children and teenagers can handle the news without being deeply affected. They have a greater understanding of what is happening and may have lingering, unstated worries. It is important for older kids to know what is happening in the world. As with all media, the amount of exposure should be monitored and parents should help them process it.

Media Dos and Don'ts

There is much more to learn about how to make children capable of dealing with media messages. The Resources section at the end of this book has several suggested books and Web sites for you to explore. The following table of media dos and don'ts includes some ideas that will build competence, others that will foster important family connections, and still others that are just good parenting:

Do	Don't
☀ Read to and play with your child every day.	☀ Let your infant or toddler be exposed to television and computer games.
☀ Expose your children to a wide variety of ways to entertain themselves.	☀ Let your children think there is nothing to do except watch television or play video games.
☀ Watch television with your children and use it as a tool to explore values and human interactions.	☀ Watch your show in another room because the kids are watching "some nonsense."
☀ Have media-free family dinners together.	☀ Read, talk on the phone, or watch television during meals.
☀ Enjoy family time together (sometimes) with media, but limit your home to 1 or 2 televisions.	☀ Have a television in every room.
☀ Encourage good study and sleep habits.	☀ Allow television in bedrooms. (It interferes with sleep.)

Do	Don't
☀ Help children with computer-based homework (and monitor the sites they visit).	☀ Allow computers in kids' bedrooms. (It interferes with sleep and is harder to monitor for inappropriate use.)
☀ Discuss the motivations of advertisers.	☀ Leave the news programs on, assuming it's "just news."
☀ Help children to understand that no one can be as perfect as the people on commercials (even if they do use that breath-freshening, tooth-whitening, cavity-fighting, great-tasting toothpaste!).	☀ Let children or teens keep cell phones in their rooms after bedtime. (They will receive texts all night. Instead have a mandatory recharging dock in the living room.)

CHAPTER 15

Not Being Broken

In any discussion about competence, some parents worry, "My child has a learning difference. What if she is never competent? Will she never be resilient?"

In the 21st century, we seek perfection and quick fixes that will make every child fit snugly into an idealized mold. When a child doesn't fit into that mold, we look for a label and solution. I am thrilled by the progress we have made in diagnosis and early intervention. I strongly support asking a child's pediatrician and teachers when parents are worried about a child's delayed developmental milestones or sense that she's not performing as well as she should or is having social and school adjustment difficulties. My biggest worry, however, as we identify more children with learning differences (differences, *not* disabilities), is that we will see them as somehow broken or in need of fixing.

We forget that there are different kinds of thinkers and learners. Some of us learn best visually, others through listening, and still others by tackling a problem with our hands. Most of us are flexible and can learn fairly well by using a combination of our senses. Some of us find it particularly challenging to integrate one of those senses well enough to learn when information is delivered primarily through that sense. For example, people who have difficulty with visual processing won't be able to learn best by looking at pictures. Some of us focus well, despite lots of distractions, and others lose focus on the task at hand and concentrate instead on the distractions. Different ways of thinking, different ways of being.

Each of these different styles may be balanced by enormous strengths. Children with learning differences in one area are sometimes gifted in other areas. We all know people who didn't do well in school but are masterful with their hands, and others who were brilliant in the classroom but can't use a screwdriver. We know individuals who are too fidgety to read a book but whose creativity and passion for the expressive arts are inspirational.

For every child's well-being, it is important to be able to function in school because school is where society teaches children. The problem is that schools are generally designed for people who fit into a particular mold—those who can sit still and focus for hours and learn by hearing and seeing—which brings me circuitously back to our caveman ancestor, Sam. (I'll use some poetic license here rather than the science I learned in a classroom.)

Hunters and Lookouts

When Sam needed food, did he go to the local supermarket, stroll down air-conditioned aisles, and peer through plastic wrap for the best cuts of meat? No, he hunted while other tribe members foraged through shrubs and fields for berries, herbs, and roots. Sam and 20 caveman buddies prepared for the great hunt, sharpened their spears, and planned how they'd track game. Intent on finding a herd of deer, they entered the forest with the knowledge that they could not survive the coming winter unless they brought home some deer. Twenty-one men focused on the deer...what happened? Did they kill the deer? You bet they did. That was a powerful lot of human concentration focused on one goal. The tribe ate through the winter. But what else happened?

Twenty-one men were in a forest, a dangerous haven for lions, tigers, bears, and snakes. If all 21 hunters were focused only on the deer, they would not have survived the perils of the forest. Some of them needed to be lookouts to prevent the other deer hunters from becoming prey themselves.

Generations later, the scenario still applies. We need lookouts, people who are easily distracted by the rustling brush, a distant sound, or an unusual smell. We can label people who have trouble focusing and are easily distracted, and we should help them to learn more effectively in school. But we dare not see them as broken because it may be precisely their differences that ensure our survival. The lookouts may have trouble focusing on the blackboard or text-book, but their distractibility and great attention to their environment can be important strengths.

There is a full life ahead for children who are now labeled as *distractible* or have other learning differences. If this speaks to your child, I suggest that you get extra tutoring (especially the kind focused on organizational skills), consider medicines, explore early interventions, and allow your child to burn off that "lookout energy" with exercise. Ask your pediatrician to join you in maximizing your child's chances of learning as much as she can in her own way. But trust in your child's wisdom that she will find a career path that uses her strengths.

Children with learning differences are not broken; they are different. If parents view them as broken and in need of fixing, their learning differences will hold them back. If parents find appropriate interventions while reveling in and supporting their children's strengths, they will thrive. For parents who are worried about competence and resilience in children with learning differences, I suggest thinking again about what resilience is—bouncing back, overcoming difficulty. If you refuse to see your child as broken, if you recognize and build her strengths, you will help her overcome hurdles and she will indeed become a master of resilience.

Chronic Conditions

Parents of children with chronic diseases also worry about competence and resilience. These conditions do bring limitations that can affect some capabilities, but that doesn't prevent children from becoming resilient. Children with chronic diseases are often blessed with particularly strong characters and competencies that healthier children could only dream about. If they are viewed as broken or treated as fragile, their conditions can affect their resilience because they will never know how to take a chance or believe in themselves. When parents can overcome the challenges and fears that come with raising a child who has a chronic condition and see the whole child, they can help their child become highly resilient.

I've had the privilege of taking care of hundreds of children with chronic diseases over the years. I can assure you that they're not only usually resilient, they are often remarkably mature, insightful, and committed to contributing to the world. When parents recognize their kids' strengths (and contain their own anxieties about the disease), children learn to view the ailment as a challenge to overcome. They are deeply resilient. They have character traits that often surpass their chronologic age. Most adults go about their lives, caught up in the daily grind, until they lose a parent or have a serious challenge to their own health. Then they get serious about living life to the fullest. What do normal kids worry about? Finishing their vegetables so they can watch their favorite television show or go outside and play. What do normal teenagers worry about? The zits on their faces. Children with chronic conditions often have a well-honed sense of what really matters. They understand the importance of family and health. This strengthens their character. They've often developed tremendous competencies to compensate for their challenges. This builds confidence to meet or overcome other, unrelated struggles they may face. They are certainly not broken.

I would add that parents of children with learning differences or chronic conditions can use the same competence-building strategies discussed earlier. You may need to adapt role-playing or choreographed conversations, for example, to your individual child's age and ability level, but like all children they too need parental guidance in these areas.

A Competence Recap

As you work on competence-building skills with your child—and it will be work, although it will have its humorous and joyful moments, I promise you—notice your progress and hers. You will become a better communicator; you will lecture less; you will notice and praise your child's assets; you will become more adept at guiding your child to become a problem-solver; and you will show her how to break apart complex, often confusing challenges and take them one step at a time.

Your child will become more competent along the way because you are guiding her with a supportive hand and specific skills. As she practices these skills, she realizes that she has a variety of alternatives. Your child can make choices; she is capable; and she is competent. By helping her increase her competence, you are boosting your child's resilience. As she recognizes and uses her competence, she will be more confident, which leads straight to the next chapter.

Building Confidence

Confidence is rooted in competence. Children can't gain genuine confidence without experiencing their own competence. They have to manage challenges to know they are able to succeed. Only then will they be truly confident.

Why is confidence so important? It feels good, of course, to know that you can do something well. But confidence is especially critical to children because it is necessary to navigating childhood and adolescence successfully and safely. That journey involves taking risks at every step of the way—risks in walking into a new school for the first time, trying to make friends, or looking foolish by speaking up in class or not making the team. Without solid confidence, children won't take necessary risks. If they have an unrealistic, hollow sense of confidence, they may take chances recklessly. But authentic confidence, which they have earned by demonstrating competence, assures children that they have some power over their environments. They are more likely to persevere and have an optimistic outlook instead of feeling passive or powerless. Confidence earned during childhood and adolescence will be a springboard toward success in adult life.

Before discussing confidence in more detail, I'd like to clear up some misconceptions. When I use the word *confidence,* I do not mean the same thing as the overused, feel-good term *self-esteem.* For about 30 years, a self-esteem movement has urged parents and teachers to build a child's self-esteem as if this quality can be bestowed by piling brick on brick. That external approach presumes that adults can construct a child's self-esteem by telling him 3 times a day that he is terrific, beautiful, or brilliant. If every child in the class wears a sticker proclaiming, "I am special," all of them are supposed to soar up the self-esteem scale. If all 25 children are special, of course, how can each one be special? Kids aren't dumb. They quickly figure out that empty words and labels are meaningless. Don't get me wrong—I want children to have a high degree of self-esteem. I just want it to be deep-seated, authentic, and permanent.

All children are indeed special, but I want them to learn that with genuine, targeted information that helps each child know why he is unique and valued.

I have another problem with the way self-esteem is often reinforced. When we are so concerned that children "feel good," we emphasize their moods over their experiences. Watch how this typically happens.

Marcus is learning to ride a 2-wheeled bike. He's been practicing with training wheels until he feels ready to pedal without them. His mother unscrews the training wheels and Marcus bravely takes off. He immediately begins to wobble. Neighborhood kids start laughing and calling orders to "steer straight." Marcus naturally becomes flustered. He zigzags a few feet, veers over the curb, and falls off. His mother rushes over, brushes him off, checks for scrapes (there are none), and pours out a litany of, "You did great! Look how far you went the first time without training wheels! You're a terrific rider. Don't look so sad!"

Marcus's mother is doing what many well-meaning parents do. She's so focused on his feelings that she isn't thinking about how to promote resilience—in this case, Marcus's ability to get back on the bike and practice until he masters the 2-wheeler. Instead, she wants to make him feel good. Most parents worry terribly when children fail at something or feel sad and discouraged, so we respond by saying and doing *anything* to brighten their moods. We deny it was a failure. We tell them that it was a wonderful success. We blame someone else or reassure the child, "It just wasn't your fault." We try to deflect their feelings by cheering them up—"Let's forget about it. Are you in the mood for a hot fudge sundae?"

Responses like these are dishonest and misguided because they send the message that feeling bad is a disaster. This can be a setup for problems later on, as every sad, uncomfortable, or anxious feeling takes on a disastrous meaning because "I'm supposed to feel special, so what's wrong with me because I don't feel happy now?"

Rather than trying to cheer up a child every time he experiences failure or disappointment, we should focus on resilience. We all have failures. Resilient people learn a bit from every failure. They learn how to do better the next time. They are persistent. They use those bad feelings to motivate themselves a little more.

Emotions like sadness and dismay are beneficial when based on an authentic event. They exist for a reason. If we paint over those emotions with a "feel better" approach, we do not support resilience. We want children to feel good as a result of what they have done, not believe naively that they will do good things because they feel good about themselves.

How could Marcus's mother have better responded to his bike spill? She might have strolled over less dramatically, asked him if he was hurt, and said something along these lines: "Well, that was your first spinout on a 2-wheeler. Do you know how many minutes you stayed up before the fall? How do you feel? Yes, it's a bummer. Ready to try again? I'll time you if you want. I like the way you keep trying even when things are hard." These responses don't deny the failure or his feelings. She simply reflects on what happens, acknowledges that he's disappointed ("Yes, it's a bummer."), and shows him that she is proud of his efforts. She doesn't dwell on his feelings or smother him with cheerful words.

Real confidence, as opposed to self-esteem or "confidence-lite," fosters resilience because it results from demonstrated, proven competence. A child knows in his bones that he has mastered a task, so he believes in his ability and is truly confident. Adults can certainly nurture his confidence by teaching problem-solving skills and providing safe opportunities to use and practice those skills. We can recognize children's assets and help them use those strengths to overcome difficulty and bounce back. It is not enough simply to tell them they are terrific or unique or dress them in "I am special" T-shirts.

As we teach children a repertoire of skills and they become more competent at making good decisions and solving problems, we cannot assume that they will automatically overflow with confidence. Even when they are in the process of becoming more competent, they may feel insecure or unsure that they really are capable. Confidence needs support and reinforcement. We can do this in 3 basic ways—catch them being good, offer genuine praise, and set reasonable expectations.

Catch Them Being Good

We do this all the time with very young children. We make a big deal of every developmental milestone and minor accomplishment. "Ooh, you ate all your cereal! You put away your books! You're such a big girl to brush your teeth all by yourself!" Fast-forward to age 12 or 14—"Why can't you ever pick up your things? Why do I have to remind you every morning to take your lunch and not to forget your homework? Are you *ever* going to finish your chores?"

What has happened in the intervening few years? We stopped being thrilled by their good behaviors and achievements. Why do we become so concerned and focused on what's wrong with them? We should still try to catch them being good by reinforcing their good behaviors, kind gestures, and unprompted acts of kindness by offering a few words of appreciation and praise. It's just as important to older children as it is to toddlers. Remember, they still crave our attention and approval.

Offer Genuine Praise

Effective praise was discussed in Chapter 7, but I want to relate it here to confidence. The best way to praise children is not with empty or vague words ("You're wonderful!") but with words that show children we really notice and appreciate what they have done. "It was so thoughtful of you to help Grandma with her shopping and carry her heavy grocery bags." "You really make me happy when you help get dinner without my having to ask you first."

If we want to support and reinforce a child's sense of confidence, our praise must be genuine. Excessive praise won't ring true any more than false praise will, but try for a balance. Look for one or two things *every day* that your child has done that are worthy of a verbal pat on the back. Remember that praise is a powerful way to encourage positive behaviors. If you want your child to continue a good behavior, pay attention and praise it.

Sometimes we get so caught up in our love for our kids that we heap enormous amounts of praise on them and tell them how perfect we think they are. On some level we may do this in hopes of creating a self-fulfilling prophecy. "If I keep telling him how wonderful he is, he will become that wonderful person." On another level, we do this to build a child's self-image and, we hope, self-confidence. "You are the kindest, most wonderful child in the world. You don't have a mean bone in your body. You're the perfect child I'd always dreamed of."

Well, no one is perfect, even your child. And if anyone knows your child isn't perfect, your child himself does. It is difficult living on a pedestal. A child (or an adult) can become too hard on himself. If a child is told he doesn't have a mean bone in his body, for example, how will he feel when he's justifiably angry at someone and wants to strike back? It's a setup for denying emotions or anxiety when upsetting emotions surface. Taking it a step further, a young person can consciously or unconsciously decide to jump off that pedestal to show the world he isn't perfect. It can be much harder to bounce back after a failure because perfect people aren't supposed to fail. It's okay to tell your child something like, "You are the perfect child for me," as long as it's combined with clear messages that no one is truly perfect and that you love him unconditionally.

Set Reasonable Expectations

Children live up or down to our expectations. I repeat this frequently because it's so easy to forget. As children's competence and confidence grow, we need to continue to hold up high expectations to keep them moving in the right direction. I don't mean unrealistic expectations. The NBA or WNBA will not draft every young basketball player. Not every child can get into an elite college.

We cannot expect children to be perfect, but we can expect them to be honest, caring, and responsible. We can hitch our expectations not to their achievements, but to their human qualities.

You may be thinking, "Okay, I get it. Hold them to high expectations for their human qualities, but what about the day-to-day accomplishments—don't I have to keep holding the bar just above their reach?" I have no simple answer to that question because the answer has to be individualized for your child's temperament. Children gain confidence through their successes, and that gives them the push to test whether they can master other, more challenging tasks. If the next task is far more difficult than they can handle, they will undoubtedly fail and perhaps lose confidence. They may tie that failure to your high expectations. They are struggling to please you, so their failure is magnified. If this is the case, they may experience shame, which can prevent them from reaching for achievements they certainly are able to master.

Our challenge as parents is to monitor children's responses to achievement and failure and have a handle on their capabilities. Some questions to consider include

* Does a particular achievement seem like a stepping stone to the next one?
* Is your child energized by a failure to try again, or does he become paralyzed by that failure?
* After a success, does he like to stay on that level for a long time until he feels comfortable enough to move forward, or is he eager to proceed quickly to the next level?

When your child is ready to try the next challenge, see where he would like the bar to be set. Support him to determine what he can handle. If you set the bar too high, he will fail you (emphasis on *you*). This has to be about him, not you. If you set the bar too low, he will think you haven't been watching him closely enough to know his capabilities.

Most importantly, react supportively when your child does come up short. It's crucially important for children to know that we all fail, we can recover, and those people who are successful are the ones who try again. Thousands of opportunities arise in childhood to support your child to try again—the first time he walks and falls, when he misspells words on a test, when his art project ends up in spills and splatters. Numerous opportunities also arise during your child's growing years for you to model how you try again without shame and with good humor when you haven't always succeeded. I believe we have just defined resilience again.

De-emphasize Incompetence

I've discussed various ways to foster competence, but in this discussion of confidence I want to mention *in*competence. One of the greatest ways to destroy confidence is by emphasizing incompetence and shaming children. First we return to the lecture. As soon as we fall back into an old pattern of lecturing, we undercut children's sense of competence and their growing confidence. As discussed previously, lecturing robs them of opportunities to make decisions and learn from them. It is often triggered by something they have done wrong. Lectures disempower children and do damage by making them feel small, inept, stupid, unheard, and shamed. (Just a reminder.) Lecturing is not the only tool we use as we try to change children's undesirable behaviors. Sometimes they make us so angry or worried that we focus only on what they are doing wrong. We want to shout repeatedly, "Stop that, you fool!" in the vain hope that they will come to their senses. That doesn't work.

Some adults blindly assume that kids will change when they become aware of all their dangerous behaviors or human frailties. I work with a lot of young people who engage in worrisome behaviors like drugs or early, unprotected sex. I watch as adults, parents and professionals with the best intentions, point out everything these youth are doing wrong as if to rattle some sense into them. As the adults get frustrated with the young people's inability to change, they begin pointing out every character fault. I call this *mudslinging*. It usually sounds something like, "Maybe you're not ready to quit drugs because you have no motivation. You're too lazy. How can I trust you, even if you say you're going to quit? You're such a liar. You're really shaming your mother and me. You've always been trouble from the time you were a small child." Mudslinging creates a series of blots on young people's self-image and robs them of the confidence they could have used to rise above a challenge.

Children will never have the confidence to change when they feel denigrated or are made to focus repeatedly on their faults. They know they can change or improve when they are reminded that they have, in fact, already done better. They have more than enough strengths and capabilities to overcome the bad stuff they've done.

The best way to promote positive behavior is by accentuating children's strengths. If we want them to get past negative behaviors, especially those they do by habit, their chances of success will be much greater if they have developed confidence. It takes confidence for anyone to change direction or alter habits, stop a dangerous but comfortable behavior and move toward something safer but less familiar. Confidence comes from knowing that success is possible. This strength-based approach allows us to build on something. Simply being highly aware of our problems and faults can lead to paralysis, but a ripple of positive energy can flow from each strength, each island of competence. When we allow that to happen, problems begin to disappear amid a sea of success.

Know your children so well that you see all of their wondrous accomplishments and good traits, and allow yourself to be constantly reminded of why you are so crazy about them. This knowledge will serve you well when you need to redirect their behaviors back to something that will make you proud.

Playing to Strengths in the Midst of Problems

Recognizing strengths and building on them is particularly important when a child is having difficulty. Look for past experiences when your child overcame a challenge or dealt with a problem effectively. Help him go back and draw on that successful experience and use it for the difficulty now facing him.

A child who procrastinates about homework will not respond to "You are so lazy!" or "You can't go out with your friends until you finish your homework." He may be paralyzed by anxiety or feel that the task is insurmountable. Being called lazy only shames him and certainly doesn't convince him that he can handle the homework. Prohibiting him from going out won't help if his roadblock is anxiety. If his problem lies with his organizational skills, keeping a child inside may prod him to take the right direction. It's more likely to be effective if he is reminded how overwhelmed he was last week when he couldn't organize his social studies report. But once he got started, he felt much better because he divided the large assignment into small sections and tackled them one at a time without fretting about the others.

When children are engaged in worrisome behavior, look for the good that also exists. Children who act out in class may be bored because they are so far ahead in a lesson. Adolescents doing drugs often have a deep sensitivity that they are trying to deal with, albeit in a troublesome way. A 4-year-old who hits her 2-year-old brother may be frustrated that he's not following the rules that she has learned so well. She needs to learn not to slug her brother, of course, but punishment alone will not teach her how to channel her energies. After she is told clearly that hitting is inappropriate, she could be reminded of how proud her parents are that she cares about the rules and how well she follows them, and she could be encouraged to teach her brother all the good behaviors she knows. The goal is to create a ripple of confidence that flows from a child. When she knows she's competent, she can build on those positive attributes and move away from the negative activities.

I used a strength-based approach with Rita, a 14-year-old patient, when she started smoking marijuana and her grades began to slip. Rita used to talk about wanting to go to nursing school to become a pediatric nurse. When her mother took a second job to save for her education, Rita had to watch her younger brother and sister in the afternoons and evenings. She had less time to study and became anxious. "To chill," she said, she began smoking weed "only after they went to bed. I never smoked in front of my brother and sister."

I could have reprimanded her or given her 40 reasons not to smoke marijuana, which would have shamed her and probably changed nothing. I could have begun mudslinging and challenged her character, lack of resolve, or failure to appreciate her mother's sacrifice. All of this would have increased her stress, leading directly to increased marijuana use. Instead, I listened silently to her story. I didn't interrupt or criticize. By listening to her intently, I discovered all the things she was doing right. When she finished talking, I simply said, "We need you to be a pediatric nurse. Look how good you are with little kids. You get your brother and sister's dinner. You make sure they're safe. You bathe them and put them to bed. You're really responsible. You've already proven how good you are at caring for people." In other words, I spoke to her strengths. Then I said, "I'm worried, though, about how much marijuana you are smoking and how that may interfere with your future plans. Can we talk about this?" We talked about healthier ways to chill (relaxation techniques are discussed in chapters 26, 27, and 28) so that she would be less anxious and better able to cope with her schoolwork.

I often use the following pattern or choreographed conversation:

Step 1: I notice what you are doing right. (I demonstrate that I have noticed by reflecting it back.)

Step 2: I am feeling worried about you.

Step 3: Can we address this problem?

It is so much easier for young people to deal with why we are worried if we first note their successes. And when we get their permission to address the problem, we get buy-in and offer them the kind of control they need to be willing to consider taking steps to change.

❖❖❖❖

Confidence is the key ingredient that allows a young person to take those chances needed to excel and be brave enough to take the first steps toward positive behavioral change. Confidence derives from trusting in one's capability, knowing that one has strengths. Many adults undermine young people's confidence by focusing on their risk-taking, faults, or mistaken behaviors. Although they may do this with the best intentions, they undercut the potential for progress and feed into the cycle of shame, hopelessness, and powerlessness that prevents children from recovering from mistakes. Just to drive this critical point home, look again at the 5 steps of behavioral change described in Chapter 12. Those steps are a simplification of many existing behavioral change theories, but I think they are missing a key point. People do not even allow themselves to get to the first step—to become aware—unless they have the confidence to believe they can change. Focusing on problems alone instills shame, undermines confidence, and therefore impedes progress.

Children will make mistakes, perhaps even serious errors. Our job is to set them straight, not make them feel good regardless of their behaviors. But if we focus only on what they do wrong, it's as if we're attaching weights to their legs that make it harder for them to bounce back. If we recognize their strengths and remind them of their abilities to succeed, we energize them to transform failure into a learning experience from which they can rebound.

Children get constant messages about their capabilities and deficits from teachers, coaches, and peers. We cannot protect them from all of the messages that lower their confidence, but we can ensure that their connection to us remains a protective force that emphasizes their competencies and builds their well-deserved confidence, which is critical to resilience.

PART 3

Connection, Character, and Contribution

CHAPTER 17

Connection

Human connection provides reassurance that we'll be okay despite tough times, and it gives us deep-seated security that convinces us we can take chances. Connection to other people tells us, "We can get through this together." We support others during their troubles, which helps us realize we have a place to turn when we need their support. Human connection allows us the luxury of being weak at times and letting others care for us while we reenergize. During times of crisis, we turn to people with whom we share our deepest connections to regroup and remind ourselves that we're part of a family or community and that our purpose in life remains intact.

Connection isn't just about getting through hard times, however. It also lets us experience a higher level of security that gives us joy and a comfortable base that permits us to take chances that allow us to come closer to our potential. When we forge a secure connection with our children, they have absolutely no doubt that we're crazy in love with them. With this solid base at home, they will connect with others more comfortably. Children without this secure base may turn inward and focus more on their own needs or do whatever it takes to connect with others, even if it is not in their own best interest.

How well connected to other people are most children today? Yes, they live in families, some with 1 parent, others with 2. Children of blended families may have 3 or 4 adults in a parental role. They may have other familial connections with siblings, grandparents, uncles, aunts, or cousins. They have friends and classmates, teachers and coaches. For a great many children, though, connections to others are weak or limited. Weak because families are so busy and have so little time together; quality time is hurried and often scribbled on a calendar to squeeze in next weekend. Limited because families move frequently, which requires children to leave friends behind. Extended families are spread around the country. Many children see grandparents only a few times a year, if at all. Other adults pass in and out of their lives on an irregular basis.

Instead of having strong ties to a network of relatives, friends, and adults in the community, many children are increasingly isolated and disconnected. Even in their own homes, family members may pass each other like ships in the night. Each has a separate thing to do or place to be. As pointed out in Chapter 14, children average more than 7.5 hours a day (more than 53 hours a week) watching television, using computers, downloading music, and instant messaging. For most of that time, each child is alone, unconnected to other people. PlayStation, Nintendo, Xbox, video games, cell phones, Internet chat, and 100-plus cable stations are not substitutes for human relationships. I strongly urge parents to keep televisions out of bedrooms; instead, have a central room where the family is entertained together. And for a variety of reasons, including your ability to monitor its use, try to keep computers in a central common location. As soon as we no longer need each other's company to avert boredom, the connection to family begins to wear away.

In this increasingly tech-driven world, youth are in some ways more connected than ever before through social networking sites, instant messaging, chat lines, and cell phones. These technologies offer a connection that has no geographic boundaries. This can be wonderful for a youth who may have concerns not shared by many in his community and for others, such as children in military families, who move frequently. Will these connections offer better support or further dissolve the need for authentic human connection? Time will tell.

Meanwhile, we need to be aware that electronic connection shouldn't be relied on as a substitute for the real thing. One anecdote illustrates this concern. Dad was torn between attending his kids' different activities on the same day. He decided to go to one child's concert rather than the other's ball game. He was then thrilled to discover that another parent had a Twitter feed to the game so Dad could follow the score from the concert hall. He thought this was a terrific solution. Of course, Dad couldn't be in two places at once, but following a child's game with Twitter isn't the same as cheering from the bleachers where your child actually can see and hear you.

Independence or Interdependence?

Before we consider various kinds of connections that benefit children, the following point should be made about resilience and connection: Resilience isn't simply self-reliance or independence in a narrow sense. Yes, children who have strong resilience are self-sufficient and independent, but they also are *interdependent* with other people. It's unrealistic and probably undesirable to expect children to be highly independent until they reach adulthood. We want them to exhibit gradually increasing independence, especially as they move through adolescence. But we don't want to send children the message that independence means isolation or disconnection. As independent as we want them to become, we also want them to recognize that the healthiest adults remain interdependent on family, friends, and community. After the throes of adolescence, when independence is demanded but interdependence is secretly craved, young adults become much more comfortable restoring a warm, secure connection.

The Security Connection

Close bonds to people who provide stability and attention are essential to healthy child development and fostering resilience. One adult can make this critical difference in a child's life. Resilience research and literature consistently demonstrate that guidance and support from a caring adult are pivotal in determining whether a young person can overcome challenges. Hopefully children will have several supportive people in their lives—parents, relatives, peers, teachers, and clergy.

Connection to others gives children an essential sense of belonging, from infancy when parents are the center of their world to an ever-widening circle as they grow and step into a larger community. Most parents recognize the significance of infant-parent bonding, but we may forget that forging new ties to other people is important throughout childhood and adolescence. These connections are necessary for children to develop trust.

When children know that other people care for them and will support them through thick and thin, they gain a strong sense of security that is essential if they are to be resilient. Without that social foundation, kids are reluctant to test themselves and try new ventures. If they won't take such risks, they may remain isolated and timid. They won't move forward to develop new competencies and confidence.

Children need multiple circles of connection to feel secure and protected at home, at school, and in the community. We don't want them to form these connections naively because some people aren't trustworthy. However, we must be very cautious about not instilling stranger anxiety in our children. When we teach children they mustn't talk to strangers because they can be dangerous, we limit our children's ability to reach out for that instant connection they may need one day. The truth is that it's likely they'll need to turn to a stranger for help if they are ever lost, being followed, being chased, or even hurt. We do our children harm if we instill a fear that prevents them from seeking needed help. It is better to give them clear instructions on when and how to reach out to adults at the same time you teach them how to avoid danger. Most parents tell children to find a police officer if they're in trouble. That is good advice, but an officer is usually not in view. So teach children to turn to a woman with children if they don't see a police officer. Gavin De Becker offers other safety strategies in his book *Protecting the Gift: Keeping Children and Teenagers Safe (and Parents Sane)*.

The Starting Point

Empathy is an important ingredient in making human connection. Empathy isn't sympathy or feeling sorry for someone else. Empathy is about trying to imagine what a situation feels like from another person's perspective. It is about not judging before thinking about what it would be like to stand in someone else's shoes. It is not "understanding"; sometimes we'll never understand. But at least we can try to grasp that an issue has a special personal meaning to another. Sometimes saying, "I can't imagine," with warmth and honesty is more effective than pretending to understand. It can be especially effective and sincere to say, "I'm trying; please help me to better understand."

When we try as best we can to have empathy toward our children, we let them know that their experiences and perspective are important. Too often, parents see children as extensions of themselves, problems to be managed, or little creatures to be trained. Sometimes parents see childhood as carefree and can't imagine that their children have significant problems. "How can a silly fight with a friend be compared to my struggle to earn a living? How can a scraped knee produce such a flood of tears when my friend is dealing with cancer?"

We are tempted to say, "Get over it," but children's problems and emotions are real. If we belittle or dismiss them, we produce shame and prevent them from coming back to their most valuable resource—us.

Children need to be heard and understood on their terms. Adults need to grasp that childhood, with all of its play and carefree joy, has its own share of turmoil. Children deserve empathy to feel listened to and respected; they also need to see parents project and model empathy to grow up and become caring young people and adults. Without developing an ability to see and feel things from another's point of view, it will be harder to forge positive relationships in the future.

Empathy is protective and preventive. When we are empathetic toward children, we create an emotional safety net. They feel secure in coming to us with problems. When they're in trouble, they know we will listen without sarcasm, criticism, or blame. When they make a mistake, they know we'll help them correct it without condemnation. When they come to us with problems because they know we'll be empathetic, they are more likely to let us guide them toward solutions, and they will feel safer in working out their own strategies to prevent the problem from becoming worse.

A Special Mention About Boys

I must make a special plug for allowing boys to have and express emotions. You might think that our gender-enlightened society would have put this issue to rest by now, but studies show adults continue to react quite differently to little boys and little girls from an early age. Girls are held more. Boys are wrestled with to make them tough. Boys who cry are told, "Don't act like a baby," or "Don't act like a girl." This attitude flies in the face of empathy. Adults who say this not only fail to see the problem from the boy's viewpoint, but they also shame him for having unhappy feelings. If we cause boys to become disconnected from their real, justified emotions, we deprive them of an important tool they need to connect with other people and recover from difficulties later in life.

Our Responses to Children's Emotions

Children pay a great deal of attention to how we respond to their emotions. How often have you seen a child take a mild tumble? Usually he has 1 of 2 reactions. If the adults around him get hysterical, he cries. If they calmly reassure him he's okay, he gets up, laughs, and goes on playing. When emotions are real and deep—let's say his best friend has made fun of him and he's completely disheartened—and adults lack empathy, ignore him, or denigrate his feelings by saying, "It's nothing," or "It'll be okay," he may not let himself feel those emotions again. He may not trust his own feelings. He may not go to his parents or other adults the next time he's sad or worried. He has lost a profoundly important coping strategy for dealing with challenges when he no longer feels emotions or goes to others to process them.

If we cause children to be disconnected from their emotions and therefore not share them, we deprive them of an important tool that they will need later to recover from adversities. We know that people who have experienced tragic events recover best when they hold deep connections to other people.

Children who grow up in a caring environment learn to be caring. They measure the "caringness" of the environment by whether they are listened to and whether adults in their lives pay attention to or deny their emotions. A simple, "Tell me how you feel," or "I really want to understand how you're feeling now. Please tell me so I can try to understand," can go a long way toward preparing children to use other people as a support system throughout their lives.

Useful Unpleasant Emotions

There's yet another reason not to let children become ashamed of their negative emotions. Even unpleasant emotions are useful because they inform us when we should be cautious. Anxiety tells us that we have stepped outside our comfort zone and may be approaching danger. Sadness reminds us how much we care when we experience a loss and teaches us that we need to appreciate what we have. Fear teaches us to be vigilant. Anger tells us that someone has stepped over our boundary zone, and we may need to defend ourselves.

When we empathize, children learn to listen to their own emotions. When we help them name their feelings, they learn to lessen their frustration when they're unable to express themselves, to better inform us when we should worry, and to show us how we can offer support. When we allow them to process real versus perceived slights or dangers, we support them in becoming more emotionally mature and healthy. But if we don't listen with empathy or if we belittle their emotions, children learn to suppress feelings and perhaps lose some of the protection those emotions provide.

The Art and Importance of Listening

My young patients often say, "My parents never listen to me." More than anything else—more than an iPod, time on Facebook, or a trip to Walt Disney World—kids want parents to listen to and respect them. They crave our attention, even when they seem to be pushing us away. The best way to show them we're paying attention is to listen closely and with empathy.

Parents tell me they often don't know what to say to their kids when their children are troubled. They worry that they'll mess up by giving the wrong advice. My response is consistent. "Don't worry, just listen. If you can be a sounding board, you will help him figure things out."

Part 2 discussed listening as a component of building competence. Again, I want to stress how critical good listening is to forging connections. Listening is the starting point of every good human interaction. We may think we're listening to children when we are only hearing their chatter. Hearing the noise and listening to the meaning in their words are entirely different.

This may be the most important section of this book because nothing else will work if you don't become a good listener. Give yourself the gift of losing the fantasy that you're supposed to have all the answers. Free yourself from the myth that says good parents always have ready solutions. If you believe that myth, you'll never feel adequate as a parent because no one, not even people who write books, have all the answers. Instead, know that if you listen well, your children will always have someone on their side to help them unload their worries and develop their own solutions. Sometimes there are no solutions and only time will fix the problem; even then, listening offers the gift of unconditional respect.

Earplugs

We need to recognize and overcome barriers to listening because we miss so many wonderful opportunities for the frank, deep discussions essential to strengthening family connections. One of those common barriers—the earplugs that keep us from listening to our children—is jumping in with our parental wisdom too soon. This only stifles the conversation. Here are 3 earplugs we need to remove.

- *The old parent alarm.* "My child is in trouble!" We jump in with a solution before the child finishes a sentence. "Mom, Brian was caught cheating in—" "I told you he was a bad influence. You will never play with him again. I'm calling your teacher. I want your desk moved away from his." This is a lost opportunity to talk about honesty, the value of hard work, and the satisfaction of accomplishing something yourself. Perhaps it's even a lost opportunity for your son to say that he considered cheating and feels bad about it. You'll never know.

- *Our discomfort with silence.* Most of us have been taught that silence is supposed to spark further conversation, but we still find silence awkward. When children are groping for the right words, struggling to tell us something that's bothering them, or simply thinking about what to say next, we tend to fill those silent gaps with our own words of wisdom. It's better to allow some silence and give children time to put their thoughts into words. If they seem to be struggling, you can use some brief coaching words like, "Hmm, you're really thinking."

- *Discomfort with kids' mistakes.* Most of us are uncomfortable when children make mistakes. Instead of letting them think things through, we wish to correct their ideas before they get out of hand. So we start talking, telling them how to prevent or correct mistakes, instead of listening as they try to figure out their own solutions. It is important to remember, and sometimes hard to accept, that a person (even a medium-sized person) is usually the best expert on himself.

How Do We Know When Children Want to Talk?

If only children held office hours. If only we could have time delegated for deep discussions. (Wednesday from 8:00 to 9:00 pm would work perfectly in my schedule.) If only kids would start conversations with, "I'd like to talk now. Do you have some time?"

Children are rarely direct when they want to talk. They don't come to us with a well-organized agenda of concerns. Instead, they approach us in as many different ways as there are children and temperaments, often depending on their mood at the moment. Sometimes they come to us in silence, perhaps with a furrowed brow that says they're upset. At other times they feign indifference, casually signaling something with that "What, me care?" look to see if it sparks our interest. Or they may open with the classic, "I have a friend who..." stories so they can seek advice without making a confession.

There's the one-step-at-a-time approach—they reveal just a small piece of the story, not just to whet our appetite, but also to test us and see how we'll react. If we leap in, judge, criticize, condemn, or give lame advice, we fail the test. Then, of course, there's the bombshell—"Take this, Mom and Dad—what are you going to do now?" If we jump in with punishment, we have lost an opportunity to understand what the bombshell means.

Rage is the most difficult approach of all and is common in adolescence— red hot anger that blames parents for the problem. Why us? Because we are the only safe people to blame, the only ones who will receive their rage and still love them. Let them let it out. Tell them if they have been inappropriate, but stay calm, don't punish. Say something like, "You seem to need to get that off your chest. I'm here to listen." Other times you may need to give yourself a time-out before being able to remain calm and nonjudgmental. That makes you human. You could say, "I hear your anger, but if I just get angry we won't get anywhere. I'm going to take a walk; when I come back, I'll be ready to really listen." Not only have you prevented an escalation, you've modeled a healthy coping strategy.

Next Step: Availability

If you are alert to the wide range of clues your children offer, you will have taken the first step toward becoming an effective listener. The next step is availability. The timing of children's needs usually doesn't meet our schedules, so flexibility is key. No matter what you planned, listening becomes the most important thing you can do. Of course, children have to respect your schedule. You don't need to allow them to interrupt your phone calls, for example. You might say, "Hold that thought. I'll be off the phone in 3 minutes." It's not always realistic to be flexible at every moment. When your sensors are raised but the world gets in the way, explain to your child that you know he needs your time and attention. Then tell him precisely when you can give it to him. If you know he has something on his mind that you've put off discussing, call him during the day (after school or at the sitter's) to let him know you're thinking of him.

Spontaneous Opportunities to Listen

Family meetings provide a time for adults to listen to children and offer a great way to work on issues that can improve connection. Realistically, a child's need to talk usually doesn't coincide with scheduled meeting times. Some of the most fruitful conversations may occur spontaneously when you're building a model together, baking birthday cupcakes, or riding in the car. For boys in particular, who are somewhat more comfortable talking about their feelings when they can look around and act like they don't care, car rides are opportunities for conversations, as are spur-of-the-moment talks that arise while throwing a ball or playing a game. Remember, many boys don't do as well with those eye-to-eye, "Tell me your feelings" conversations.

Quantity Versus Quality Time

In our harried, over-scheduled lives, we often talk of making *quality time* for our children. I agree—a few moments, when parents are truly present and undistracted, can be most meaningful. At the expense of saying something unpopular, though, *quantity* matters too. All parents are stretched to make ends meet and fulfill their multiple obligations, but we need to make available as much time as possible for our children. To some extent, the quality of our time with them is influenced by the quantity of that time. I'm not suggesting that you quit your day job. I am saying that there will be more opportunities to listen if we spend more time with our children. We won't always be there for the crises, triumphs, or heart-to-heart moments, but the more time we spend with them, the more likely we will be available to listen during a significant moment. Enrichment activities are important, but never forget that time with us is the best way to enrich their lives.

Curb the Interruptions

When we interrupt children, 2 things happen. The first is that most of us find silence uncomfortable. The second is that it's difficult to withhold our parental wisdom. So rather than listen in silence, we blurt out our opinions. We may not think that we're voicing our views directly because we may make comments just to keep the conversation going. But children are hyperalert to our views and attitudes, especially our critical opinions, and their antennae pick up even the smallest clues about how we feel.

We can learn to limit blatant criticism for the big issues, but we are frequently unaware of how loud our subtler messages can be, even when we are trying to be supportive listeners. In routine daily conversations, we drop clues when we're judging, fixing, moralizing, minimizing, negating, catastrophizing, belittling, and shaming. The following is an example of how a parent's various responses may be heard and interpreted by a child:

Thirteen-year-old Nate comes home and mumbles rather shyly, "Mom, I met this girl, Emily, and I don't like her or anything, but Phil and Bryheem say that she has a crush on me."

If his mother replies, "Oh, how cute!" Nate will hear it as minimizing, belittling, or even negating his experience.

If she says, "Well, why wouldn't she? Now what you want to do is play hard to get," he will see her as trying to fix a problem that doesn't exist.

If she intones, "You are way too young to date," he will feel she's judging, moralizing, and perhaps even shaming him.

If she says, "Well, don't listen to them. What do Phil and Bryheem know, anyway? You know I don't like them," she is being judgmental, criticizing his friends, and again trying to fix something that isn't broken.

If she cries, "Oh, no, is my little boy growing up?" she is making a catastrophe out of a normal event.

If she says, "You don't have to get caught up in this nonsense," her words are belittling, shaming, judging, catastrophizing, moralizing—you name it.

Here is another example. Seven-year-old Madeline comes home from ballet class with a furrowed brow and eyes brimming with tears. Gradually, she reveals pieces of the story. Her teacher has said she's improving but may never learn to plié well enough for the recital. A parent's comment like, "What does she know?" will undermine Madeline's confidence in her teacher, belittle the problem, and hardly support her in trying to improve her pliés.

If her mother says, "Sweetheart, you will be the star of that recital," Madeline will question her mother's grasp of reality, feel more pressure to perform well, and conclude that her real fears are not taken seriously.

If her mother suggests, "Fine, quit ballet if that's what you want," she is turning the situation into a catastrophe that doesn't exist.

If she says, "Oh, don't cry, darling. It's not that bad," she minimizes a problem that is really upsetting her daughter.

If she says, "Your teacher has no right to say that to you!" she creates a moral judgment and prevents further discussion, especially when Madeline thinks her teacher is wonderful.

Keep the Ball Rolling: Encourage Them to Talk

The key to getting a child to open up is to say very little. Simply use short phrases that reassure and prompt more conversation. This is particularly important at the beginning of a conversation because we want children to reach a point where they're comfortable enough to express whatever is on their minds. To reach this point, they must know that we are present, paying attention, and have only their agenda in mind.

I am about to describe a way to talk to children that may seem stilted on first reading. It requires some practice to be able to sound authentic, rather than like someone who's trying to impersonate a therapist. (Therapists are trained to withhold comments because this is a tried-and-true way of making people feel listened to and accepted despite whatever they have to say. This keeps them comfortable enough to continue disclosing their thoughts.) Trust me that this is important. I suggest that you practice this technique with another adult until you can do it in a natural way, one that makes conversation flow, without your child thinking you're a robot.

First point: Remember the power of silence. Saying nothing, while being in the present moment, sends a loud message that you are accepting of the person who is talking. This doesn't mean that you approve of everything he says; it means only that you are glad he's saying it.

Second point: As your child warms up and gets comfortable talking about an uncomfortable subject, listen attentively and silently. When you feel you will burst if you don't utter something, feel free to nod and say, "Hmm," and "I see."

Then, when you are about to spew forth your wisdom, refrain! Just continue to give brief statements that let your child know you're impressed that he is talking and you are eager to hear more. Some examples of these phrases include

- Tell me more.
- Wow, you have quite a story to share.
- Please keep talking. I'm really interested.
- It sounds like you have a lot on your mind, so I'm glad you're talking.
- I love that you're so open and honest with your feelings.
- It means a lot to me that you feel comfortable talking to me.
- You're doing a great job of describing what happened.
- Could you repeat that? I want to be sure I understand what you're going through.

You'll know when your child has unloaded. He finishes what he wants to say and feels an emotional release. The pace of his conversation may slow. His body language may soften. He may even blow you out of the water with, "What do you think?"

When that happens, be certain you are completely clear that you have gotten the story straight. If you aren't quite sure, you might say, "This is what

I heard. Did I understand you correctly?" or check his emotions by saying, "It seems that you are feeling…. Is that right?" or "When something like that happened to me, I felt like…. Do you feel a little like that?"

We know that when 12 people hear the same story or witness the same event, the result is 13 different interpretations. It is important that we understand our child's interpretation because that is what matters here. He will greatly appreciate that you want to understand it correctly and that you've listened so carefully to his story that you can recount it.

How to Respond

Sometimes, there may be absolutely nothing else we should do but be fully present as a sounding board. At other times, though, a child needs direct guidance. The best way to figure this out is to ask a simple question: "How can I be most helpful to you?"

When you sense your child needs guidance, you may not think your ideas can actually help him get out of a jam, or your own experience may not match his. But you can take the first step by starting with, "Hmm…how are you thinking of handling this?"

Occasionally, children come to us for advice. When that happens, go ahead and give it, following this approach. Always try to avoid lecturing and critical judgment. Break your wisdom into separate digestible servings by speaking in a tone and cadence that your child understands. If you offer 10 brilliant pieces of advice in one broad swoop, you may overwhelm or confuse your child and he'll miss much of what you are saying.

Mind Your Body Language

Parents can master all the effective listening skills previously discussed and still blow it if their body language projects a different attitude. A frown, rigid posture, clenched teeth, or furrowed brow doesn't indicate an open, accepting willingness to listen without judging.

If a child is trying to talk about a worrisome situation, it is difficult to listen without tensing up. We tend to concentrate on a child's words, not on our body language. Try to remember the following points because off-putting body language can stop a conversation as easily as insensitive spoken words. When a child, especially a small child, feels that a parent is angry or fearful of the subject, he will clam up.

- If you tell your child you have time to listen, show it. Sit down. Get down to your child's eye level instead of hovering over him. Eliminate distractions. Turn off the television and cell phone. Just be there.

- Take deep, soothing breaths to turn off those surges of adrenaline that make you turn red or perspire or make your legs tremble with anxiety. Fool your body into thinking you are relaxed. This helps you think more clearly and prevents outbursts that could stop the conversation. Sometimes deep breathing won't work, especially if your child's concerns generate fear or anxiety in you. In that case, step away and run in place. Remember, stress makes you feel like you're being attacked. Sometimes, you just can't think until you've run from danger.

- Watch the defensive postures that say you're uncomfortable with the subject under discussion. Avoid tightly crossed legs, folded arms, finger tapping on the table, or leg shaking that convey anxiety, boredom, or annoyance.

- Make sure you give lots of hugs because they make everyone (you too) feel better. Children receive hugs as the ultimate sign they are safe and protected.

❖❖❖❖

In my experience, nothing is more important to being an effective parent than making children know they are truly heard. This doesn't mean we have to agree with everything a child says or condone every behavior. But before we can impart any useful guidance, we have to send the clear message that we're really listening to a child's words and trying to grasp the emotions beneath them. In communicating with children of any age, we need to create a zone of safety that makes them know we are trustworthy. Otherwise, they are likely to shut down, tell us nothing, or lie to defend themselves and get us off their backs. Whether children come to us with serious troubles or everyday matters, we can create a safe zone by listening patiently and nonjudgmentally, without interrogating them or interrupting with a solution or advice. This projects a clear message that we love them unconditionally. We're not going anywhere. There are no requirements to receive our love; we don't trade it for good behavior or achievements.

Strengthening Family Ties

Listening is the best way to connect with children. How else can we increase and strengthen our children's connections? Even when our time is limited, we can create special times and establish simple, regular family rituals. We don't have to spend 2 hours a night or all day Saturday or Sunday on togetherness projects, but we can lavish attention on children by getting into the habit of doing routine events together on a consistent basis, such as preparing meals, walking the dog, or doing chores like laundry. (Why should Mom and Dad have all the fun? Kids can put clothes in the dryer or fold laundry while they start another wash load.) We can use these occasions as opportunities to listen to our children, encourage them to talk to us, tell us jokes, sing songs, dance around the kitchen—whatever you both can enjoy at the moment.

These don't have to be heavy, tell-me-your-deepest-thoughts conversations, although they can be sometimes. For the most part, they are simply pleasant moments together. When you encourage children to help around your home and work alongside you, you are also sending them the message that they are team players who contribute something and are important members of the family. The family is connected and only functions well when everyone does their part.

Part of the Family Team

Volumes have been written about sibling rivalry. I won't attempt to repeat that advice. In the context of strengthening connection as a building block of resilience, this point is basic—sibling rivalry is not only inevitable, but it also serves a purpose by giving kids a chance to work out differences and practice negotiating skills in the safety of their families. Sparring with a brother or sister is a normal way to test strengths and weaknesses and define separate identities. In other words, a child can practice individuality and independence while still being part of the family team.

Of course parents get headaches from sibling fights, but if we avoid taking sides or assigning blame and strive instead for fairness, we can encourage siblings to work out their differences. This builds their competence at problem-solving and encourages family cohesiveness.

Susan Beris, MD, coauthor of *Beyond the Visit: From Pacifiers to Piercing, Toilet Training to Tattoos*, shares some advice that she frequently gives parents: Each child in the family should be encouraged to excel in, or at least love, something different. A son may love photography; a daughter is at her peak on the soccer field; a younger son adores baseball. They may all share the same passion or interest, such as swimming. But if they also have separate interests, they are less likely to get entangled in the negative aspects of sibling rivalry. A younger one won't have to go through years of insufferable comments like, "When your big brother was on my team..." (which the younger one interprets as, "You'll never live up to him."). Encouraging different interests also gives each child an experience of being a star in her own arena. It gives other siblings a chance to cheerlead for the one currently in the spotlight.

Creating Family Rituals

You can enhance family connection by establishing rituals such as eating at least one meal a week together, though more is better. On weekends, choose an evening in the coming week when your family will all be present. No matter how busy everyone is, set a firm date. Be respectful of your teenager's social schedule by being flexible about the day and time, but plan in advance and stick to it.

Attendance is required (dress, optional). Take no excuses, no last-minute "But I have to go to my friend's house," or "I forgot." If you're especially busy, prepare something in advance or bring in takeout if you have no other choice, but make the weekly sit-down dinner a routine. You may want to turn off phones during dinner or light candles on the table, but make it an event.

Some adults today fondly remember visiting a grandparent's home every weekend and sharing dinner with cousins, aunts, and uncles. While those occasions are rare today, many families still find that a certain evening or the Sabbath offers a perfect opportunity to ensure the family will be together. Even in smaller-sized families today, no matter how difficult the rest of the week has been, no matter how many different directions each family member has been flying in, there is always the guaranteed connection and calm of that certain evening or the Sabbath.

Other valuable family traditions include reading bedtime stories, sharing hobbies, and spending regular special time with children, as a group and one-on-one. You can designate 10 or 15 minutes each evening or alternate evenings to spend separately with each child. This may sound counter to family connection or togetherness, but the point is to devote individual attention to all your children one at a time. Karyn will understand that you're spending special time with Derek on Tuesday, and you will spend the same amount of time with her on Wednesday. This approach avoids sibling jealousy, while giving parent and child time to spend together doing something they enjoy.

This special time with each child is especially valuable in my family because we have identical twin daughters. We split up and have an Ilana-Mommy and a Talia-Daddy day (or the reverse) about every 2 weeks. This allows us to focus on the uniqueness of each child. While this may be particularly important in a household with twins, many parents tell me that when life gets chaotic, their children blend together—bad for children, bad for parents, and a setup for sibling rivalry. There is less of a reason to make sure you are at the top of the pecking order by putting down your sibling when there is not a competition for attention.

Specific Techniques for Connecting

When your children were babies, you probably had certain rituals like the evening bath and bedtime story. As life got busier and they grew, they took their own baths or showers and read themselves to sleep.

I have a suggestion—reestablish that ritual with a twist. Children may feel too old to be read to, and they certainly don't need your help with a bath when they're 10 or 11 years old. Do something together each evening, even if it takes only a few moments—a guessing game, telling jokes, or singing a song—and make it a routine, nightly event. And always, please *always*, say good night to each child or have her come to you and say good night before she goes to bed. This is particularly important when she becomes a teenager, so I strongly suggest you establish this pattern as early as possible.

The *nightly check-in* is a technique that I have been promoting for years with preteens, teenagers, and parents. It is not meant to be punitive, but it does work as an effective disciplinary tool with adolescents because it ensures a safe return home when they have been out. Here's how it works.

Make sure your child understands this clearly. You expect her to come in and tell you when she gets home. Even if you are asleep, she is to wake you up and tell you she's home safely. Ask her to talk with you for a few moments. Don't ask for details about the evening—she will see this as interrogation—but remain open if she wants to share details. Tell her you're happy to listen to her no matter how tired you are.

Be firm and don't permit any exceptions or excuses like, "I didn't want to wake you because I knew your were tired and it was late," or "I forgot because I was so sleepy." If you establish this rule early and hold your child to it, she will understand that there will be a predetermined consequence or loss of privilege if she breaks the check-in rule.

The rule has several benefits. It is an effective way for parents to monitor adolescents. It reduces your worry that your child is drinking or using drugs because you will be able to determine her coherence as soon as she gets home. It also gives her a great refusal skill to use with her friends. "I can't smoke weed with you because I have to check in with my parents as soon as I get home. They smell my hair and clothes!" Their friends will sympathize and reduce the peer pressure because of your "stupid check-in rule." Essentially, it is a great tool to allow her to self-monitor and create her own boundaries with peers.

If you use the nightly check-in in a loving spirit, as in, "I'm glad you're home safe. I need to know you're okay. I love you," your child will view this ritual not as controlling but as caring. She will see your concern as positive attention, not interrogation or distrust. This in turn helps her feel even more connected to you.

Fun and Games

Play and humor are often overlooked or underappreciated contributors to family connection. The value of unstructured play was addressed in Chapter 6, but I mention it again here because play provides one of the most pleasurable ways for parents and children to connect.

Parents pressed for time may think they have little opportunity to play with their children. But kids never outgrow having fun with their parents, even when they become adolescents. If you have time for only a short, simple game, try to squeeze in some fun with your child. You don't have to take her to a professional ball game and spend 4 hours and $200. Free, unstructured, spontaneous play is cheaper and usually more fun.

There's a lot more benefit to playing with your child than getting to know her better and watching as she builds her competencies and resilience. There's the pure joy of play. When children play, they remind us of a very basic lesson—make the most of every moment and appreciate what we have.

I was reminded of this when we were on a family vacation. I grew impatient and wanted to get moving. It was time to pack up and drive to the next spot, but my daughters were enthralled with a sandy hillside that they had transformed into a sliding board. They wanted to keep sliding. I kept rushing them. Then I suddenly caught myself—why was I so worried about where we should be in the next hour, when they were having such a good time now? My needs were instantly put into perspective and were so insignificant in comparison to the joy my daughters were experiencing.

Give children a few sticks of wood and they can make endless games from them. Of course they'll beg for fancy toys too, but left to their own devices they can discover purposes for objects that no adult could fathom. We adults are always so future-oriented. Think of a road trip with the family. Sure, kids are always asking, "Are we there yet?" But wherever they are, it is good to learn *they are there!* Every stop seems like the best. They can't imagine going to the next site and leaving that most perfect sliding hillside behind. Parents, with our adult minds, miss out on the present because we are focused on the future ("How long will it take to get there? Where will we stay? When will we be able to clean all this trash out of the car?"). We have lost the ability to relish every moment, enjoy little things thoroughly. We hear all the folk wisdom ("Take time to smell the roses!") that tells us to slow down and cherish the beauty and pleasure we usually overlook, but children really get it! They seem to know innately how to appreciate and live in the joyous moments, if only we allow them to do so.

Children and adults who can draw pleasure from the little things have a fundamental trait that helps them spring back from difficult challenges and misfortune. We're all surrounded by inspiration, if we only choose to see it and allow it to rejuvenate us when things get us down. When we play with children, we're reminded of this essential truth. When we meet them where they are—on their playground, governed by their rules—and we don't force them to change, we encourage them to stay just the way they are. And our own adult resilience is enhanced as we learn to find little vacations everywhere.

CHAPTER 20

Widening the Circle

Outside the nuclear family, children need connections to multiple groups of friends, relatives, community, and the world. Think of it as a chain of interlocking circles—the more strong circles that build the chain, the more children feel a sense of belonging and support.

Friendships

Circles of friends shift like the tides during childhood and adolescence. School friends move away or get dropped for a cooler group of peers. Your child's neighborhood friends since they were toddlers go on to different schools and cliques. Preadolescent girls in particular seem to change friends almost daily. On Tuesday, Tasha is your daughter's inseparable best friend forever. By Friday, Tasha won't talk to her and moves on to a different group that excludes your daughter. Probably by next Wednesday, Tasha will be back at your house.

I know it sounds sexist to ascribe this pattern to girls, but it happens. Boys seem to work out their differences with name-calling or a shove and get over it quickly. Ten minutes later, they're skateboarding or tossing a ball around together. Girls tend to hurt each other with psychologic weapons, such as gossip and nasty remarks, and weep over it for days.

Children can be deeply hurt and isolated—left unconnected—when suddenly dumped by a close friend or group. In the worst-case scenario, children may do whatever it takes to fit in again rather than risk isolation. To avoid the perils of social isolation, it is important to ensure that they have more than one circle of friends—some at school, some in the community, and others through scouts, sports, or religious organizations.

Relatives and Neighbors

Relatives form another strong link in the chain of friendships. Cousins in particular can offer a child good role models and guidance. If your child is having a problem with friends or at school, he may be more willing to open up and discuss it with a favorite cousin who is a few years older and has been through similar dilemmas. What if there are no cousins nearby? Older neighbors can be good models for your younger children—perhaps the 19-year-old college student down the street who holds a part-time job and plays in a band, or the babysitter who volunteers at a homeless shelter. If you ask these young people simply to keep an eye out for your child, to inquire how he's doing from time to time, you will be offering both a valuable opportunity. For the older ones, it's an opportunity to be influential and have someone look up to them. You're letting them know you have respect and confidence in them. For your younger children, you're expanding their circle of connections and exposing them to examples of healthy contributing teens.

Multigenerational relationships also strengthen a sense of connection. A doting grandparent, a favorite aunt, or a cool uncle gives children valuable support and makes them feel part of something bigger than themselves. For centuries, children grew up amid many generations. They worked on a family farm or in a family-owned business alongside grandparents, parents, and other relatives. As they grew, they developed increasing abilities and took on more responsibilities that prepared them for adulthood. As adults, many took over those family enterprises.

Today it is rare for a child to grow up in such a tight-knit family environment. We cannot recreate the family farm or open a general store with Grandpa Henry behind the counter and Aunt Emma at the cash register, but we can try to strengthen family ties for our children's sake, whether our extended families are large or small. Today we can encourage them to e-mail Grandpa Henry on the other coast and phone Aunt Emma during unlimited time on the phone. We can encourage young children to make drawings and small homemade gifts to send to relatives and write thank-you notes when they receive gifts from them.

The more family connections children have, the more they have to fall back on. More security will envelop them. The more support they have, the more content they'll be, and the better equipped they'll be to spring back during rough times.

Adolescents and Connection

Relationships with people outside the family can come in particularly handy during adolescence. Preteens and teenagers go through periods of hating their parents, or so it seems. This is an upsetting but normal part of their growing independence. It is helpful to remember that much of their reaction stems from how much they actually *love* their parents. To figure out who they are and who they want to become, adolescents need to reject almost every idea their parents have and try out a few new ideas of their own. But rest assured, they don't hate everybody, not even every adult.

If parents have wisely supported adolescents in forging a variety of positive connections, teens will turn to other trusted people for guidance during that 2- to 3-year period of mid-adolescence when everything parents say is ridiculous.

Here's a hint—be subtle about fostering these other connections. If they seem too forced or directed by you the parent, teenagers may think these other people are your stooges and their views will also be seen as tainted. So don't be obvious and suggest, "Why don't you hang out with that mature college kid down the street?" Instead, set up situations in which someone like this model neighbor can interact spontaneously with your teenager (maybe drive him to the mall), and let the relationship develop from there. If your child has a favorite older cousin, aunt, or uncle, make it possible for your teen to spend more time with him or her.

Community Connections

When children are old enough, they need to gain a sense of broader connections beyond their individual families. By belonging to sports, civic, and religious organizations, children learn that they have a place in the larger community. And that community—a team, scout troop, church, synagogue, mosque, or temple—values them as members. These connections show children that they're part of a safe and supportive community. If parents locate or help their children find and join organizations that promote the same values they cherish, parents' efforts to instill these values can be reinforced by those groups. Children who participate in these organizations learn that parents aren't the only ones who expect them to play fair, be honest and loyal, and show responsibility, for example. Others also expect these standards. As discussed in the next section, connections like these contribute to a child's character.

Many children do not feel connected to people outside their immediate family. A lot of kids don't even know their neighbors. After school, many children return to empty homes and stay indoors. Whether they live on city blocks, rural farms, or suburban cul-de-sacs, they are physically isolated—disconnected—from people nearby. One way to foster some connection is as simple as setting up a safe house with neighbors so children know where to go if their parents aren't home or they feel any danger. If they know that the retired fireman who lives across the street is usually home every afternoon and they can always phone him or ring his doorbell, they'll feel more securely connected to their neighborhood. Setting up safe houses in your community is similar to planning and practicing a home fire drill. If your children don't know the neighbors who live in the safe house, introduce them and make them comfortable, be clear about where to go or when to call, and make sure your children know where those phone numbers are posted in your home.

You will undoubtedly think of other ways to create and support relationships between your child and other people in your community. In our disjointed, harried, and often chaotic world, it is more important than ever for young people to have as many adult connections as possible.

Who's Watching the Kids?

That answer may seem all too obvious—it's the parent's job, of course. But all adults have responsibility to watch out for the children being raised in our communities. I was privileged to see how well community involvement in child-rearing can work when I lived on the Cheyenne River Sioux Reservation in South Dakota. Outsiders used to pass through Native American communities quickly and draw the erroneous conclusion that no one was watching the children. Kids wandered throughout the community, well beyond the boundaries of their homes. So who was watching the children? Everyone was.

Despite some social problems linked to poverty, these children were cherished and protected. They were everyone's responsibility. Each adult in a parent's generation was regarded as an aunt or uncle, and numerous grandparents of the elder generation were all treated with veneration. Any of these adults could watch children, correct them, and keep them from harm.

We have moved so far from this ideal that we now fear correcting other people's children. Where are the community standards? We need to have serious conversations within our communities about the importance of adults' watchful surveillance for children's safety and well-being.

Connection With School

For most children, school provides the closest community outside their families. Children spend nearly half their waking time in school, where they not only learn but also are socialized. Children who are well connected to their schools are more likely to thrive educationally, emotionally, and socially. If they view school as a safe, protected place and understand that the adults at school care about their well-being, children are more likely to soak up knowledge and absorb the invaluable life lesson that learning is pleasurable and rewarding.

Parents also need to get involved and stay connected because children sometimes need advocates to negotiate their world at school. Parents who are connected with their children's teachers will know what's going on in school and be better prepared to help their children navigate school successfully. Teachers are valuable allies because they may pick up on difficulties that parents might miss, especially social difficulties or learning differences. As child professionals, they also can help parents evaluate certain concerns, like moodiness, to sort out the difference between normal development and a more serious problem.

Connection With Nature

An often overlooked factor that can enhance a child's resilience is a connection to nature. It's easy to overlook because many children today are increasingly *disconnected* from the natural world. They spend most of their time indoors. Even when they take a school trip to a nature center, for example, the experience is limited and usually structured by adults. Few kids have leisure opportunities to explore nature on their own.

When was the last time your child walked in the woods, looked under a mossy rock, and watched a tiny critter wiggle, or poked a stick into a pond and discovered a tadpole? Yes, children may attend summer camps, but fewer and fewer revolve around nature hikes and singing around the campfire. Many of today's camps focus on specialties like computer instruction or weight loss.

What does nature have to do with resilience? Children need to understand that they are part of the natural world as well as the human community. Nature can nurture their sense of belonging. Children can learn that they are the future stewards of the planet. In observing nature, young people are exposed to countless examples of resilience—pinecone seeds, for instance, that survive forest fires to sprout new seedlings, or recurring seasons that bring birth, maturity, death, and rebirth. Mother Nature is a great teacher of resilience.

Some Cautions About Connection

Is it possible to love our children too much? No, but it is possible to be too centered on our children. While they should be central to our lives, children cannot be our sole focus. Many parents today are so committed to parenting that the lines become blurred between their lives and their child's. This is the "We go to school at Shadyside" or "We are worried about the test on Thursday" phenomenon. Children need their own lives that are interdependent with, but clearly independent from, parents' lives.

When children perceive that they're the sun, moon, and stars in a parent's universe, it is too much pressure. They often feel the need to be perfect, as discussed in Chapter 8. Every shortcoming is magnified because they have to worry about their own disappointment and letting parents down. Children who worry excessively about parents' emotions may not be willing to try new ventures. If they believe that their actions are the sole determinant of parents' well-being or sense of self, they may try too hard to be trophy children and will become frustrated and ashamed when they don't excel. Their fear of failing their parents will prevent them from success—they'll lack confidence in their own resilience to take the very chances necessary to succeed.

We certainly want kids to experience security and connection, but at the same time we need to maintain our adult lives—to preserve our own time, personal relationships, and connections to our communities. If we maintain connections to spouses, friends, and coworkers, we will do a great deal for keeping our families happy and together, and at the same time we'll model for our children a good example of meaningful relationships.

As a child advocate who desperately wants parents to cherish their children, I strongly urge you to take care of yourself, savor your accomplishments, and nurture your adult relationships for the good of your children and yourself. If nothing else, you will find it easier to bounce back as your children inevitably grow up and lead the independent lives for which you've prepared them.

When Connection Verges on Control

When children are small, we naturally must protect them. As they get older and more competent, we loosen the reins gradually. They're allowed to cross streets by themselves when they've demonstrated that they watch traffic, check the stoplight, and look both ways before stepping off the curb. Later we let them go out with friends when they've shown us they can be responsible by calling us to check in and coming home on time.

Throughout this process, we try to balance their increasing independence and separation with our need to know they're safe. This is one of the greatest challenges of parenting—giving just enough freedom or rope. If we let the rope out too much, they may figuratively strangle themselves; if we give too little rope or hold it too tightly, the rope may snap.

We are mindful that children need to separate from us gradually. We know that the job of an adolescent is to find her own identity and ultimately separate from parents to become an adult. But we're often tempted to hold the rope too tightly or step in and fix something for the child. Then what happens to adaptability?

Cell phones make that rope readily available and easy to clutch tightly. They provide a great way to stay in touch, but this electronic connection can be overused. If parents expect teens or college kids to call in throughout the day to report minor matters ("I just ate lunch."), perhaps the parent-child connection is too taut. We need to be aware that this sort of "connection" is really verging on *control*.

Even as we recognize that connection is intertwined with the other 6 Cs of resilience, we have to be careful that connection does not feel like control. If parents forge an overly tight connection with children, it can subtly transform to unhealthy control. These parents don't intend to be overly controlling; they certainly aren't harsh disciplinarians or dictators. But taut emotional ties can be smothering and restrictive.

I grow concerned when parents tell me that they don't worry about what may be going on in their child's life "because she tells me everything—we're like best friends." Remember that an adolescent's job is to become an individual, separate and distinct from parents.

Until adolescence, most of children's values and perspectives are directly formed by observing their parents. Teenagers cannot become independent adults until they confront their parents' values, decide to reject some of them (that's when they tell you how uncool and ridiculous you are), and form their own values. When teens go through this normal process, they need parents to be a stable rock that they can keep referring to by saying, "That's not me.

I'm not at all like Mom or Dad." Parents are like a yardstick—teens measure themselves against us.

If parents try to be their teenager's best friend by dressing alike, using teen lingo, or smoking and drinking with their child and her friends, how will this young adult figure out how far she has to go to come up with her own stands? I worry that well-intentioned parents may drive children over the behavioral cliff as they force them to move closer to outrageous choices just to differentiate themselves from their parents. Children need loving, connected, even fun and friendly parents, but they don't need parents to be their best friends. If your teen tells you that you're no fun, remind her that she has lots of friends but only one mother/father.

What Gets in the Way of Connection?

Let's look at connection from another perspective. What gets in the way of parents staying connected with children from infancy through adolescence? In our early discussion of resilience, I described how we snuggle with our precious, vulnerable babies. They smell so good. We play with their tiny fingers. But what happens over the years that makes us feel so burdened as parents? What takes away so much of the joy and replaces it with seriousness and even anger? I don't have all the answers—no one does. But it is an essential question to examine if we are to figure out how to maintain an ideal connection with our children. We may not achieve that ideal, but it is our goal.

I become teary as I consider the prospect of my 14-year-old twins going off to college. My house will transform in an instant. Suddenly my wife and I will be alone. How will my babies handle it? (Hint: Dr Ken, they will not be babies. They'll be 18 years old.) How will I handle it? Sage parents of high school seniors or college freshmen always assure me, "Don't worry. You'll be ready." I think they sometimes mean, "You'll be glad to have them gone." I cannot imagine that now. Remember you will not be sending your small child or young adolescent away. They will be different—taller, at least; wiser, I hope. And they will prove that they will be ready to go!

Perhaps it is biological. All animals grow up and leave the nest. They go through their playful phase, practice adulthood, and then are on their own. Our human children just play longer and we parents just worry more.

If our children didn't prove to us that they were ready to go, would we let them? It's not just about going to college or moving out to start working. Throughout childhood, children become increasingly independent. First their legs begin working and we don't have to carry them everywhere. We lose a lot of snuggle time because they are always scampering off on another exploration.

This process goes on through adolescence, when it becomes painfully obvious that they do not believe we are needed, or so they tell us.

During this march toward independence, part of what happens is that they really don't need as many protective bonds with us. They also need to break these bonds to create the appearance of independence, if only to deal with the turmoil and anxiety within themselves as they take those next steps.

Yes, children may be excited when they reach new developmental milestones, but they are also human. They may not be able to tell us clearly, but they worry about whether they will succeed. They worry about whether they will lose us, their parents. Remember the metaphor of leaping over a chasm? Think of every milestone (like learning to walk and talk, staying overnight at a friend's house for the first time, a first date, or going to college) as a huge, gaping chasm that needs to be crossed.

A child can't gingerly slide her feet across the ground or she will fall in. She must jump across if she has any chance of getting to the other side. Swinging her arms won't propel her across. She must go back several steps and take a running start. She has to stop thinking, suppress her fears, and leap!

Is it any wonder that children seem to regress just before their milestones? Remember how irritable your baby was before mastering those first steps? Is it any wonder that a 10-year-old about to start a new middle school or a ninth grader about to enter high school sometimes seems cranky and irrational before these necessary leaps?

What about us, the loving parents? Why don't our children simply come to us for support and ask us to help them build that bridge across the chasm? There are 2 answers. First, they do. They constantly do, but they don't ask directly. They sometimes seek our attention in ways that anger or frustrate us, but they do get our attention. Don't be fooled into believing that they need us less during major transitions. They actually need us more. Second, if they told us how much they needed us or how confused or scared they are, they'd be unable to take those next important steps. They need those figurative blinders for a moment. It is very difficult for even the most emotionally intelligent adults to be so in touch with their feelings that they can articulate them clearly, especially in times of change or crisis when we suppress our emotions. Rather, we come up with rationalizations that help us move forward sometimes against our better judgment that yearns for comfort and familiarity.

Remember when your child was ready to take those first steps? Rocking on her legs, wiggling her bottom in the air just before she pulled herself up to stand on those little legs? Did she cry or push your arm away when you approached her to offer help? She wanted to say, "Gosh, thanks, Dad. I sure do appreciate your effort, but I'm struggling here to assert this new step toward my independence."

When your child was learning to talk, she knew what she wanted to say, but couldn't. She couldn't express, "Guess what? I'm on the cusp of a whole new world—suddenly able to use language! I will be less dependent on your doing everything for me because I will command attention." Instead, she cried in frustration, grunted, and pointed toward the objects whose names she could not yet pronounce.

And what about the first date? What a wonderful opportunity to have a conversation about sexuality, puberty, and morality—the talk that you looked forward to (with dread) since the first day of kindergarten. Here goes: "Darling, I think that you are a maturing young lady, and there are some things I think you are ready to learn." A noble try. Why did she respond, "You're such a dork, Dad. I don't need you to tell me anything!"? That was much easier for her to say than the truth—"I'm really scared, Dad. This emerging sexuality is really overwhelming. Only 3 years ago, I wanted to marry you. I still think you're the most wonderful man ever. That's weird."

When children are ready to go to college, parents want that last year at home to be so special. It's the last opportunity for family togetherness. It should be a perfect time. (Incidentally, it is absolutely *not* the final opportunity. Parent-child relationships last a lifetime.)

You want the last family vacation before your child leaves home to be an ideal opportunity. Why then does your daughter say, "Mom, I hate you. I'd rather be with my friends. It's a good thing I'm leaving in August because I couldn't stand one more minute in this prison"? Why does she say this? Because it's so much easier than saying, "I love you so much that I can't even find the right words. You've done everything for me. I'm terrified. Do you think I'm ready to go off on my own? Do you think you'll miss me as much as I'm going to miss you?"

Kids challenge us because they need to loosen one kind of connection with us—the connection that involves our assuming full responsibility for them. As they challenge us, we get hurt or even angry until we are ready for them to go. This is completely understandable, even predictable, and perhaps even partially necessary. But if we understand what is happening and learn to celebrate our children's growing independence, we will all be healthier. Otherwise, every time they push us we will tighten control. This will only breed resentment and harbor ill feelings. When you receive push back, you must set appropriate rules and boundaries that ensure safety. Your child needs to understand that these boundaries will get looser as he demonstrates responsibility. Then remind yourself that your baby is becoming more independent, and that means you are doing your job well. If we can all do that, we can celebrate and grow more comfortable with our evolving connections.

It wouldn't be honest of me to say that every time children behave badly or speak meanly to us, it reflects their growing independence or inability to say something much kinder because of their conflicted emotions. Sometimes kids might just be acting meanly. They know our vulnerabilities. Whether they are justifiably or unfairly angry, they can be masters at saying hurtful things. Often it's a way of shouting, "Listen to me!"

Perhaps they're testing the waters to grab your attention before they can bring up something that's troubling them. If you respond with anger and shut them down, they may feel justified for not sharing their concerns—"Remember, I was going to tell you, but then..." Yes, even our angels can be manipulative. While this book is primarily about children and much of it is about their emotions, it's also about parents. It's really okay to tell kids when they hurt your feelings—not in a way that makes them feel guilty, but just a clear statement of fact that their behaviors are inappropriate and hurt you. That is an important part of your job in building their character. You deserve empathy too.

Even during times when children challenge our connection to them, we must remain consistent about one thing—our love is unwavering and we will always be there for them. With this clear message, we say to them, "Go ahead—grow. I've got your back."

Supporting Resilience in Military Families

The next time you say, "Thank you for your service," to one of our men and women in uniform, please think about the family members who also serve our nation. Only a small portion of our populace chooses to serve, and their families deserve our gratitude for sharing the burden. This chapter is a tribute to the spouses and nearly 2 million children of service members. It is rooted in patriotism but is not political. Our service members do not create the policy of our country; they live it, as do their families. This chapter focuses on strategies parents and caregivers can use to maintain healthy connections and reinforce positive experiences even while facing the challenges that come with being connected to the military.

I invite you to read this chapter even if you have no direct military affiliation so that you are aware of the needs of military children, adolescents, and families. Odds are, though, that you know a military-connected child whose parent, brother, or sister is serving our all-volunteer forces or is a post-9/11 veteran. Ongoing conflicts have created a generation of 21st-century military children whose parents have been repeatedly deployed (sent into action, usually overseas). These parents haven't been able to share important parts of their sons and daughters' childhood, missing developmental milestones and opportunities to offer guidance. Non-deployed spouses have needed to act largely as single parents. This is a resilient population that has by and large endured this with grace, but resilience does not mean invulnerability. The stresses on family life have been prolonged, and the families are tiring. We know they do better when communities and neighbors recognize their contribution, and your awareness will be an important step toward creating the supportive environment that contributes to their well-being. If you want to know how you can best help, the answer may be in supporting the families of those who serve.

You may benefit from gaining a better understanding of how these families are trying to remain connected whether or not you know a child directly affected. Many other children also deal with separations, including children of divorce and others who deal with frequent moves. We can use the experience of the military-connected family to learn about values, strength, sacrifice, courage, resilience, sense of service, purpose, pride, and even the frailties of the American family. These children and families are not alone in needing to worry about the well-being of one or both parents who sacrifice to serve. In your own communities and within your own lives, consider first responders and other professionals who are regularly called to serve, such as police officers and firefighters. We tend to take them for granted instead of honoring their commitment and thinking about their families' special needs. We need to acknowledge the real heroes in our midst, rather than those who get attention because of money or athletic talent. When we recognize that heroes are those who offer service to society and their communities in one way or another, we build children with stronger character and a desire to contribute.

If you are a service member or spouse, remember that how you model resilience is more important than what you say about it. Don't be surprised if you repeatedly hear about the importance of your well-being. Your kids will learn how to problem-solve and manage stress by watching how you cope. They will learn from you that strong, capable people sometimes reach out to others for support. In uncertain times, they need to know that you can protect them, and you will be more capable of offering security when you are emotionally, physically, and spiritually healthy.

Why Many Military Families Are Models of Resilience

Military families deal with challenges that many civilians can only begin to imagine. I don't want you to think, however, that you merit a special chapter in this book because the choices you have made have hurt your children's healthy development or resilience. Let's start by recognizing what you are giving your children. Being military-connected may build your children's ability to adapt to challenges far into the future. Let's look at the benefits your children are likely to gain before we even consider how to prepare your family to minimize the challenges.

First, whether a parent is on active duty, in the reserves, or part of the National Guard, your child is raised within a culture of service. You or your spouse have determined that contribution matters; the benefit to your child of being raised by parents who are mission-focused and maintain a commitment to service is immeasurable.

Second, your children are being exposed to a very diverse institution in which the importance of cohesion and performance takes precedence over division. There are untold benefits to your children of having friends and sharing experiences with peers from varied backgrounds and experiences who come from all over the country and perhaps the world. In a nation that is increasingly diverse and whose future is dependent on cooperation and communication, your children will be prepared.

Third, one of the greatest challenges of military life, frequent moves and school changes, can contribute to a sense of pride in one's adaptability. Children may learn to make friends quickly and introduce themselves and interact with many adults, including teachers. As a result, many of your children become confident in their social skills. To maximize the likelihood your children will gain the benefits, it's important that educational transitions occur as smoothly as possible and that relationships with important friends and caring adults are maintained.

Finally, many military families have a cultural connection that comes from a shared experience and common mission. Families who live on base often benefit from neighbors who care about each other, check in frequently, and have common concerns. This layer of neighborly support is missing for many American children; it is a gift to raise a child in an authentic community. Our National Guard and reserve members, however, live throughout the nation, and even most active-duty families don't live on base. For these families in particular, it's important that the rest of us recognize and value their contribution, and create a supportive community.

Connection: Core to the Well-being of Children and Adolescents

All children need to feel safe, valued, and confident to develop to their potential. The vital connection to other people in their homes, schools, and communities supports their resilience. One way to visualize this is to imagine a child in the center of a series of protective circles, each layer surrounded by another; rings within rings, each offering security and appropriate challenges. The most important connection is to parents, but siblings and extended family form the next layer immediately beyond parents. Healthy friendships form the next ring and can offer a lifetime of support.

We know that children who feel connected to school are more likely to succeed there. During the school year, teachers often spend more time in a day with children than parents do; they can be a profoundly important layer of support. Coaches can help build character and instill important traits like perseverance. Community forms the outermost layer and can blanket the entire family with support and protection. A wide array of community-based forces can make life richer and create the kind of opportunities that help children thrive. Spiritual centers can offer a sense of purpose and security. Recreational centers create spaces where kids can safely play, learn to be physically healthy, and express themselves through art or music programs. The advantage of having multiple layers of supportive connections is that if one layer is weakened, the others can compensate to ensure children's healthy development.

The military mission and its requirements can significantly affect each layer of connection. The core connection to at least one parent is challenged by repeated deployments. The connection to the remaining parent is changed, largely because that parent has to function as a single parent during deployments. The relationship may become stronger, but the stress of single parenting can also create tension. Sibling connections can be altered because older siblings may take on some of the role of the deployed parent. Sibling relations often become stronger because as families move, brothers and sisters serve as built-in peers who understand what each is going through. Connections to grandparents and other extended family members may be tighter if they become more actively involved to compensate for the distant parent. On the other hand, it may be that the military family residing on or near a base is far from extended family. Even without deployments, the military lifestyle includes frequent moves, sometimes over great distances. Schools and friendships change more often than among civilians. This certainly creates challenges to maintaining a strong, secure connection to schools. The good news is that when children are engaged in a range of school and community activities, those connections can remain strong, and some community and cultural connections may be particularly strong and supportive when people share a common experience.

Deployment as THE Challenge to Connections

Preparing psychologically and physically to deploy can take months, and relationships within families can be altered long before the actual time to say goodbye. Similarly, returning is a complex process; it is not just about walking through the door. Especially for parents who have been in combat, it may require significant resettling. It may involve processing trauma and readjusting to family life after being in a war zone. For these reasons, the effects and adjustments of deployment and separation on family life may last as long or longer than the deployment itself.

Military services are very sensitive to the stress that deployment takes on its families, and a great deal of attention is paid to ease the transitions associated with deployment, separation, and reintegration (returning home).

Although I will offer some tips on these pages, your best resources are military resources such as family readiness and support groups and the professionals who devote considerable effort toward providing military family services. Remember, strong people seek help, and they use those circles of support *and* the extensive tools and resources available to them.

As you think about your family thriving through these times, your goal has to be to maintain a continual connection despite the disruptions to that connection. This may sound unrealistic, even illogical, given the likelihood that the service member may be living thousands of miles away in a parallel universe. There is no feasible way to have this ongoing continual connection feel natural or seamless. Although the goal may feel elusive, I believe there are steps you can take to maintain the best connections possible given the circumstances. If you have assumed your spouse would be totally absent during the time away, consider adopting a mindset that prepares for the reality of separation but plans for connection.

Let's first consider how to maintain positive connection with siblings, extended family, schools, and friends even in the setting of school moves, separations from a parent, and the significant family adjustments associated with deployment. Then we'll focus on strengthening the most important connection—the one between parents and children. We will discuss how to remain close despite geographic distance and how to avoid pitfalls that may strain parent-child relationships.

Sibling Connections

There are few greater pleasures than watching your family pull together, especially when your children care for and support each other. As your spouse deploys, the entire family needs to contribute to make sure the house functions as smoothly as possible and the burden does not fall entirely on the remaining spouse. Children can reasonably be expected to take on more age-appropriate chores, as long as they have time for schoolwork and play. Older siblings can take on more responsibility at home or perhaps in caring for younger ones, including babysitting and getting younger siblings to different activities. This will benefit older children because anything that makes adolescents feel their contributions matter serves as a powerful reinforcement toward continuing positive behaviors.

Despite the clear advantages (and even necessity) of having siblings care for one another, I caution you against having siblings take on a parenting role during deployment. It is common in stressed families and single-parent households (which yours is temporarily during deployment) for the oldest siblings to become "parentified." Adolescents need to focus on school. They deserve to be teenagers, to have friends so they can develop social skills, and to have downtime so they can reflect on their place in the world.

When teens assume too much responsibility, they may consciously or subconsciously resent their missed childhood. This resentment may build up to anger that could turn on you. More likely though, teens may fear disappointing you so much that they could lose the ability to express themselves freely to you. If authentic communication is damaged, that has major implications for your relationship. I also worry that parentified children may have role confusion when the deployed parent returns home. The last thing families need is for adolescents to feel demoted when parents return or to have resentment toward the returning parent because they're losing a valued level of responsibility. In the worst-case scenario, parentified children may reject parental authority even more than usual for a developing adolescent. They may perceive that they were functioning as an equal adult or even parent, and now resent monitoring and guidance. The bottom line is that all siblings should play their role, and contributing to family function should be an important part of that role. But at the same time, make sure that kids get to stay kids. Their "job" is to grow, learn, and develop into healthy, productive adults.

Before we leave the discussion about siblings within your family, let's take a moment to remember that many service members have siblings of their own who are still children and adolescents. They too need a supportive community and to stay connected with their deployed brother or sister.

Extended Family Connections

For your family, it may be that frequent moves have made it harder for children to know grandparents and other relatives. On the other hand, these family members may play a vital supportive role to your children during deployments and will have the opportunity to forge close lifelong relationships. If extended family will play a greater role in caring for your child during deployment than they did previously, there are 2 key things to keep in mind to allow smoother transitions.

First, *plan.* Try to make transitions between caregivers go as smoothly as possible. For example, grandmother may arrive in advance of the deployment so she will represent continuity and be associated with the loving nature of your home. Beyond that, children will benefit by seeing that the temporary caregiver has genuine respect for the deployed parent. If she arrives the day of departure, she may be associated with confusion or be viewed as a replacement. No child will appreciate anyone replacing a parent, and that can breed unnecessary resentment. Fostering closeness between your children and a temporary caregiver far in advance will make your children feel more secure.

Try to have the caregiver connect prior to deployment through visits, phone calls, or social media. If you will be relocating to a family member's home while your spouse is away, try to visit there prior to the move or, if that is not possible, use digital photos to familiarize your children with the environment.

Next, *communicate.* Children and adolescents need to know "who will take care of me" and that the adults around them are sensitive to their needs. You and your spouse should have a discussion with your children and caregiver. The discussion should be targeted to the age of your children and should include the following key points:

- You have given a great deal of thought about who can best help to care for your children.
- Explain why this person was chosen. Ideally, you should be able to say that you have chosen someone who also loves your children.
- Reinforce that this is temporary and that the caregiver does not replace the deploying parent.
- The caregiver represents you and should be respected.
- Explain that the distant parent will always be thinking of the children and will stay in contact whenever possible, but because of distance will be unable to give the daily attention the children deserve. Because you care so much for your children, you have carefully chosen someone who will do a good job of caring for those everyday needs.

You and your spouse should also find the opportunity to discuss your parenting approach with the caregiver. It's important that your children experience consistency of care rather than having to adjust to new approaches. You should discuss parenting style, and the blend of control and rules with warmth and support (see chapters 29 and 30). Ideally we strive for a balance between rules and warmth, remembering that discipline means guidance, not control, but adults disagree about these things. Even married couples don't always see eye-to-eye on parenting style, but well-functioning households do the best they can to disagree behind the scenes to present a united front to the children. When they don't, children learn to play parents off of each other. It's important that you discuss this openly in advance so children don't receive confusing messages. If the temporary caregiver clearly understands your approach, hopefully she will remain as consistent as possible in maintaining that approach. Don't be surprised if your extended family member from a different generation holds a different parenting philosophy than you do. She may be more lenient, or she may think you are too passive and she would be stricter. This is all the more reason to work this through openly in advance. This will make the household run more smoothly during deployment and hopefully prevent the returning service member from having to respond to a 7-year-old shouting, "Grandma never told us what to do."

Friendships

Everybody dreams of that best lifelong friend with whom you share a history of memories. This may not be a reality for military children. Many move frequently and have to make new friends, often having to try to break into long-standing friendship groups. For young children this may be as easy as an afternoon on the playground, but it may be difficult during adolescence when cliques run rampant and kids decide they are "normal" by arbitrarily deciding who is not. The good news is that most children navigate this successfully, and the skills military children develop in doing so may serve them well over a lifetime.

If your child goes to a school with a high proportion of other military children or other highly mobile children, he may adapt more quickly because the school's peer culture may be welcoming to newcomers and expect to maintain distant friendships after a move. In general, long-distance relationships are easier to maintain now because we have a more mobile population and children are used to others entering their lives at different points and may enjoy having friends all over the country.

The new era of social networking may hold a great benefit for these kids. Real friendships in teen culture are largely built in the virtual world. Teens who live next door to each other sometimes prefer to talk by video chatting, texting, or social networking sites. Let me be clear—this is a mixed blessing at best, and I have serious concerns about the implications to communication and human relationships. Despite my misgivings, it is a reality now and its benefit here is that the military child is closer to the mainstream when his friendships are largely virtual. These online communities may offer a way for teens to connect and create virtual support groups with others who can relate to their experiences. As with any online community, monitoring is recommended as outlandish ideas can spread quickly and, rarely, dangerous relationships can be formed. (See Resources for Internet safety on page 380.)

As your child moves into a new community, it's important that he has several entry points into the peer world. He will be more likely to find a suitable peer group if he has the opportunity to meet peers in a variety of different settings beyond school, including clubs, athletic activities, youth development programs, and spiritual centers. Another reason children need multiple peer groups is so they never feel completely isolated when friendships shift. This is particularly important during middle school when bullying, in-groups, and out-groups are unfortunately a way of life. If your child has 2 or 3 circles of friends as well as healthy in- and out-of-school activities, he will feel more secure. As one group of friends rejects him, he can hang out with another until he is likely re-welcomed into the first after a few days.

Even with efforts to build new friendships, you can expect that when your child is new to a community, he may initially be quite lonely. Plan events he can look forward to because filled calendars and activities help time to pass more quickly. Weekends and holidays may be especially challenging, so plan special outings for these times.

Your child needs to have some particularly important social skills as he attempts to enter existing peer groups. Because he will be so eager to make new friends, he may be particularly at risk of falling into a crowd that may negatively influence him. As an outsider to the community, some of the most welcoming kids may be other outsiders. These are often the most interesting kids with the best values. Sometimes, however, they are youth who have rejected adult values altogether. You can't choose your child's friends, but you can prepare him for this possibility. Encourage him to be friendly but not to dive into friendships until he has had time to observe. Prepare him to be observant rather than believe what he hears from the gossip mill. If he too quickly buys into the labels teens give other kids to "orient" new peers to the social landscape, he may close himself off to the best friendships. Finally, because he will find himself among new peers whose values he does not yet fully know, it's particularly important that he can shift the blame to you when he needs to get out of an uncomfortable or dangerous social situation (see Chapter 13).

School Connections

One of the greatest challenges for some military families is to ensure children receive a fine education despite frequent moves. Your involvement here is key. In general, children whose parents are involved in their education stay in school longer, do better academically, have fewer social issues, and are more likely to continue on to college. Imagine the message you send to your children about the value of education when it remains a priority to you as you move and especially when a deployed parent shows continued interest and involvement in your children's school activities even from a war zone.

It is beyond this book's scope to offer an in-depth discussion on smooth school transitions and I suggest you use available resources that are expert in this area. However, some general guidance on school moves follows on the next page:

❖ Preparing for the move may set the stage for success. Several months before the move, parents can begin to familiarize the family with schools in the community. The Internet is a great resource for this. Parents and children can visit the district and school Web sites looking for academic credentials and programs, athletics, and clubs available. Many Web sites have posted additional information and news updates about the campus. Such information can help allay your child's fears. A less formal source of information comes through friends who have lived in the new community and whose students have attended schools there. It's important to remember, though, that in addition to whatever facts they provide, they will include opinions, and some people exaggerate challenges because they make for better stories.

❖ A school's Web site may provide information about schedules and calendars, including start dates, holidays, and end dates. These are not standardized from state to state, nor even within a state. Incorrectly assuming your children's new school schedule is similar to their current school's can result in their enrollment being days and even weeks later than the official start date of the district. Classes in which they wish to enroll may be full, friendships are already solidifying, and athletic teams may have a cutoff date for students wishing to make the team.

❖ Hand carrying school records is vital in a school move. These records may include a photocopy of a cumulative folder, withdrawal paperwork, report cards, information on textbooks used, and a copy of the student's health record. Calling the person in charge of registration, likely a counselor or registrar, several weeks prior to the move will give time to copy these documents. It will also give the counselor or registrar the opportunity to let you know what you need to do to withdraw your child from the school.

❖ You need to hand carry documentation related to any special programs your child is enrolled in, whether enrichment, gifted, accelerated, special education, or 504 services. The receiving school may send a formal request for records to the sending school, and the documents you provide at the time of registration may be the only information the new school has to make informed placement decisions. This is extremely important for students receiving special education and 504 services. The information you provide may be instrumental in your child receiving services seamlessly; without that information your child may experience a lapse in services.

❖ When you arrive at your new community, a trip to your child's campus can give him an idea of what to expect. The school may give him a tour and a map so he can familiarize himself with the facility. Knowing where the cafeteria, auditorium, restrooms, and counselor's office are can go a long way to helping a student settle in to a new routine. This presents an opportunity to explore what clubs and athletics are available for your child and how to go about joining them. Remember that although your biggest concerns may be about academics, your child's biggest concern may be about finding his locker or a group to sit with at lunch.

❀ Parents can read and discuss the school's expectations for conduct and dress with their child.

❀ Meeting your child's principal or assistant principal, counselor, and teachers will go far to establish a personal connection. They may go further out of their way to ensure your child adjusts well.

❀ Volunteering on your child's campus or joining a parent organization such as the PTA can help you make contacts at the school while making you and your child more comfortable in new surroundings.

❀ Fitting in is vitally important to children and adolescents. A visit to the school's Web site can show pictures of students in the new community. Once you have arrived, look around the community to see what clothing, shoes, hairstyles, and accessories local kids are wearing. It may be that a few purchases would be all it takes to ease your child into his new life in his new community.

Many organizations work to help students transition to new schools. One organization particularly worthy of notice here is the Military Child Education Coalition (MCEC). It is devoted to helping schools and military installations deliver accurate, timely information to meet transitioning parent and student needs. It focuses on ensuring quality educational opportunities for all military-connected children affected by mobility, family separation, and transition. The MCEC offers online support and materials at www.militarychild.org, including a checklist for transferring students, a compilation of resources that provides information about each state's school requirements and resources, and SchoolQuest.org, a secure online resource to help families make decisions on schools as they relocate.

Here are a few additional thoughts related specifically to parental deployment.

1. Have a conference with teachers in advance of the deployment and let them know both parents want to stay involved. Give teachers self-addressed, stamped envelopes to send copies of tests and report cards.

2. The service member can visit the school Web site to see what is going on in the classrooms and, in some schools, can even access current class grades on a weekly basis.

3. Parents with regular computer access can even help children review papers and projects and give advice before turning them in. Some deployed mothers and fathers correspond with the class and send cultural artifacts and information about the country where they are stationed.

4. Deployed parents can even help their children learn to love reading. For younger children, they can read books on videotape before deployment and the caregiver can have the child sit on her lap and turn pages as the recording plays. For older children, you can choose books that the deployed parent and child will both read and decide the order you'll read them in. You can have "book club" discussions about the books even during deployment.

The Connection Between Parent and Child

The most important source of security to a child is the connection with parents. It's naive to believe that deployment will have no effect at all. The goal is to minimize that effect by maintaining strong connections through ongoing communication, effective listening, and family rituals that will serve as reminders of the presence of the distant parent. When parents are involved in any way in children's daily or weekly activities, it sends a strong message that they love and value their children and despite working in a war zone, are going to keep that connection strong. It's also important to avoid some of the pitfalls of separation, including having children who fear disappointing their parents so intensely that they lean toward perfectionism, or others who rebel, if only to pretend they don't care.

Concrete Reminders for the Youngest Children

It's nice to have reminders around the house of the deployed parent. Photographs and favorite clothes certainly fill this need. One suggestion that is a little more creative is Flat Daddy or Mommy. Make a cutout of the service member with Dad's or Mom's picture on the face. Make it at least 12 inches tall, but feel free to make it full-sized (if you have a big enough car!). Take pictures with Flat Daddy or Mommy at family or school events and then send them via e-mail or photo album, telling about the events. This sends a clear picture to deployed parents that they are wanted and needed and serves as reminders to children about how much they want to be there. Parents can do something similar with Flat Child, taking pictures in the tent or mess hall to show that the son or daughter is always with them in their hearts.

Young children frequently ask very basic questions about where their parent is sleeping or eating while deployed. Have your spouse send pictures of himself in his quarters, shaving, eating in the mess hall, and near his vehicle, and make a little album that the child can carry around.

Maintaining Family Rituals

With frequent moves and deployments, family life doesn't feel routine. During a deployment, chores have to be divided among fewer people, leaving less time to spend together as a family. If you have special family rituals like dinner, going to a game, or working on a hobby together, try to do as many of them as possible even if one parent is overseas.

Listening

Many parents worry endlessly about what to tell children about difficult topics. When's the right time and right place to say the perfect words? This search sometimes leads them to put off any conversation at all. My concern is that when we don't discuss really important topics, children learn that they should put away their emotions, or they even feel shame for having them. When subjects are avoided entirely, children are left to imagine the worst or make up their own endings. At the least, they worry alone and miss out on discovering that one way to get through difficult times is to connect with loved ones.

Whenever you wish you knew exactly what to say, let your children guide you on what they want to hear. Free yourself from struggling for the right words by reassuring yourself that it's more important to listen than to speak. When you listen, your child has an opportunity to express emotions. When you ask leading questions like, "What would you like to talk about?" you learn the right time to talk. If the child is not ready to talk, it is wise to respect that choice. When you ask, "What is on your mind?" you learn how a child is interpreting events. When you ask, "What have you heard?" you learn what messages a child might be receiving from others. This last point is particularly important for news events.

Listening is about more than asking leading questions; it's also about noticing behaviors that offer a strong hint of what is going on. A silent child who acts out with rage is actually speaking quite loudly. Rather than react with anger yourself, sometimes it's best to help your child find the words to match his expressed feelings so it is easier for him to use words next time. (See Resources for building emotional intelligence on page 379.)

Finally, try to be available when your child is ready to talk. Because you can't be everywhere, increase the odds you will be there at the right moment by learning the special places where your child is usually in her comfort zone. You may find the best conversations start while working on a project together, watching television, during bedtime, at bath time, or while driving in the car.

Talking

Communicating in ways that kids can hear what you are saying has already been discussed in this book, but a few key points deserve underscoring here. To remain calm and reassuring, you may need to think through or sit with your emotions for a while before you talk with your child. Talking about feelings is important, but do so when you can focus on your child's feelings. This will allow him to share rather than have to worry about you. Remember that his feelings focus on needing to be protected and secure. Assure him of your plans to make sure he is safe. He is also worried about the service member; therefore, it may reassure him to hear that his deployed parent is well trained to do his job.

For advice on talking about difficult subjects once a child has guided you to the right time, see "Talking With Children About Upsetting News Events" on pages 187 to 190 at the end of this chapter. You also may wish to turn to another trusted resource, the Center for the Study of Traumatic Stress (CSTS) of the Uniformed Services University of the Health Sciences (www.centerforthestudyoftraumaticstress.org). The CSTS offers guidance to parents on communicating with children about very difficult subjects as well as coping during deployment.

Maintaining Communication With the Deployed Parent (as Best as Possible)

Technology allows communication at levels that would have been unimaginable not too long ago. Separated parents can often be involved in making family decisions and in keeping up, to some degree, with family events. Because these communications are so highly anticipated and their timing is unpredictable, the pressure associated with them can sometimes diminish their pleasure and benefit. Let's frankly discuss some of the potential problems so you can think through how to get the most out of these cherished moments.

First, take care not to make the conversations something children would rather avoid. While it's important to have the deployed parent involved in family function, it's equally important that these touch points not be used only as opportunities to discuss tough issues. As we will discuss further in a few pages, don't make these "wait until I tell your father" moments. They certainly should be moments to receive guidance, the best kind of discipline. But make sure children have the opportunity to focus mostly on the things in their life that make them proud and to get advice on their concerns.

I am told that it's common for deployed parents to have difficulty finding the right words or setting the right tone because switching mentalities from war zone to parent is sometimes hard in these all-too-brief communications.

As a result, they may become frustrated with their inability to shut out their environment. Even though they would rather be present with their spouse and children more than anything in the world, they may have trouble even getting the conversation started. Their frustration may be masked by inattention or even anger. But the truth is that the weight of parental guilt they feel in their inability to have a normal conversation with those they most cherish may damage their self-image as an effective parent and could have later implications for reintegration into the family.

Plan ahead to try to minimize the likelihood this situation will occur, although I expect it may happen sometimes to even the best-prepared families. You and your spouse might first create an advance code word that suggests that a check-in is desired but it's not a good time for a deep conversation. If the code word is activated, the conversation can remain light and reassuring to the children, while avoiding straying into harder topics they are not currently prepared to address. With or without a code word, try to accept the spoken or unspoken cues that this isn't a good time to talk. And as best as possible, remind yourself that this is no reflection on your relationship. Next, the parent at home can "drop seeds" to the deployed parent addressing what to talk about. Some military families have told me they have used e-mail to prep the deployed parent on topics of interest to the child and even the child's struggles or accomplishments. This assistance with conversation starters may help the deployed spouse avoid the shame or guilt he feels when he's unable to connect with his children.

Spouses have shared with me that they struggle knowing how much to share long distance. They want to include their husbands or wives but don't want to upset them. A recently deployed mom shared with a group of military spouses that she didn't need to know everything going on, but she did need to know that she was wanted, needed, and loved. She told the group that all deployed parents desperately shared this need. Others in the session suggested that the caregivers agree prior to departure what the deployed parent needs to know. That way, individuals can specify the level of detail important to them. This takes some of the weight off the caregiver or parent at home who is concerned about worrying the deployed parent. Even if this understanding is made prior to deployment, situations can change on a daily basis, and the home parent should remain open to the cues that a given conversation needs to remain lighter.

The pressure of making the most of the few minutes may sometimes be too much for children as well. Parents have related that children sometimes feel shy or awkward trying to summarize their week or express their emotions on the spot. They proposed creating a communications center to alleviate this awkwardness. The communications center consists of a bulletin board and a supply of pens, markers, Post-it notes, and a calendar. The caregiver encourages children to make notes on the communications center board so they can share them during the call to the deployed parent. Children can post notes about sports, grades, or just important stories or feelings. When the parent calls (and you never know when that is going to happen!) the children, no matter their age, run to the board to remind themselves of all they wanted to talk about. This can be great for caregivers and spouses too because it's sometimes hard to remember all they needed to talk about as well.

A final point. Families have shared with me that children are sometimes scared of the sounds and images that come across via video-chatting technology. To the extent possible, the deployed parent should call from a place that's relatively quiet and should try to keep frightening objects or weapons out of view as they may serve as a reminder to sensitive children that their parent is in danger.

Staying Connected to the Mission (the Whole Mission)

Families tell me that one of the greatest frustrations they have is their inability to serve at the level the deployed parent is serving. Children understand that the parent is on a difficult, dangerous mission. It is hard to feel as brave as a parent serving in a war, and the potential exists for children to feel inadequate. They have trouble understanding how they can contribute.

They can take actions to feel connected to the parent's mission. They can "support the troops" and do their part by joining together with other families and doing things on the home front to make it easier for their own parent; they can also "adopt" a serviceperson by working with Family Readiness Groups to make care packages for soldiers without families. While they have trouble relating to the part of the mission that involves war, they can become young activists on the home front by working to collect resources to improve the lives of children and families in the war zone. This will give them a sense of shared mission that will allow them to feel more connected with the parent.

A first step is helping children to understand and appreciate the complex and important contributions being made by our service members. I consistently hear frustration from military families about how poorly the news media covers the rebuilding efforts. They feel that nearly all of the media attention goes to bad news stories and misses out on human interest stories that many troops share. For children in particular, it is important that some of the good news is heard because they can relate to and contribute actively toward that part of the mission.

Building Memories

Time is irreplaceable. I cannot imagine how difficult it is for the deployed service member and his family to miss out on developmental milestones; major events like graduations, birthdays, and sporting events; and even daily routines like bedtime. Perhaps before deployment the service member can record DVDs or write letters to be brought out periodically or during special events. Maybe most importantly could be "I love you" recordings, messages, and notes. These remind children of the unbroken bond of unconditional love and reassure them that their parent has gone to serve the nation, not because they want to be away.

Equally as important is for the "home team" to prepare memories to share with the returning parent. Sure, watching a video of a child's winning goal or first steps will never match being there, but it is the next best thing. Even recording favorite television shows or major professional games can allow the family to experience those missed opportunities together. Annotated photo albums can serve as tools for children to tell richer stories about past experiences. This may spare the returning parent from being limited to typical conversations like, "How was that dance performance?" "Fun."

Scrapbooks of special projects, creative expressions, and homework will allow a parent to see how the child progressed over the time they were apart.

These memory tools will be invaluable for returning parents because they will reinforce how closely parents were held even while they were away. They also may be helpful for the home team by giving them a project to focus on together. Important conversations can be held about the deployed parent while working on the projects. Opportunities for listening and talking may abound when the focus is on the missing parent. Memory tools do not have to be prepared only for the return home. Many families prepare care packages for the deployed member to receive treats from home. These might include special clothes or foods, but the real treats are the drawings, report cards, and family DVDs that can be included to spark conversations and maintain connections.

Avoiding Perfectionism

Your children deserve to be children, with all the stumbles that present opportunities for learning. One of my greatest fears for military families is that your children will try too hard to be good to spare you from added stress. Good little boys learn not to go to their parents when things aren't going well; they fear being the source of disappointment or an added stress. Good little girls become afraid of thinking outside of the box or scribbling outside of the lines for fear that what they produce won't be good enough. In Chapter 8 we talked about all of the reasons "perfect" children aren't and, more importantly, why perfectionism interferes with long-term success.

Some military children may be at risk for perfectionism for several reasons. The primary reason is that one of the leading causes of perfectionism is children's desire to spare stressed-out parents. Children worry about us and sense when we are at our limits. They may sense the extra stress you are under while your spouse is away, or that your spouse may need emotional recovery time during reintegration, and push themselves hard to behave perfectly. Next, by necessity, the military has a low tolerance for mistakes, and that may trickle down to families. And a service member is sacrificing so much and being put at such potential risk that families may feel that they too must be strong. This holds the potential of backfiring if strong is misinterpreted as being problem-free. No one is problem-free, but when people feel as if they must portray themselves that way, they become afraid of revealing any imperfection.

Some perfectionists act like anything but good little boys and girls. The pressure of being perfect, of always being strong, makes them go out of their way to prove that they just don't care. Acting-out behavior builds a strong case for indifference, and some preteens and teens are happy to misbehave if it hides their true feelings of vulnerability. These children sometimes need professional guidance to learn how to say, "I act like I don't care because I care too much."

Parents can be the antidotes to perfectionism. Let your kids know that you don't expect them to be strong all of the time, and listen to them so they can express their real feelings. Tell them that although you might be burdened, your greatest pleasure and most important job is to parent them. Help them understand that they do not spare you when they withhold feelings from you; instead, they make it harder for you to do what you care most about, which is parenting them. Above all, model for them that strong people understand their own limitations. You don't have to feel guilty about your frustrations and your angry feelings either. You don't need to be perfect yourself.

Maintaining a Consistent Parenting Style and Appropriate Discipline

Prior to having the privilege of hearing concerns about parenting from so many military families, I had made some pretty naive assumptions about the way they would likely parent. Sorry about that. I had thought they would be more likely to take an authoritarian, "You'll do as I say. Why? Because I said so," approach to parenting because military culture is rule-oriented. In fact, I have learned that many parents feel that their kids have to go through so much that they deserve a break. Some families, therefore, may take a more lenient or permissive, "I love you so much that I trust you to do the right thing," approach with their children. I've been told some families move in this direction during deployment as a "reward" to the children for having to endure deployment. In other words, guilt affects their discipline style and frequently leads to permissiveness. Adolescents especially are experts at working our guilt feelings and may push us toward permissiveness.

The balanced, authoritative style of parenting—"I love you so much. I trust you. I'm going to let you make some of your own mistakes, but for the things that really matter, you'll do as I say"—produces the best results for children and adolescents. You really are not doing your children a favor by rewarding them with leniency. Don't get me wrong—I am not promoting a strict approach either. Rather, I recommend that parents unconditionally and consistently demonstrate love and allow opportunities for self-growth all while blanketing their children with the protection that comes from watching them closely and giving clear boundaries.

If you become more permissive as a "reward" for children enduring separation from a parent, they may associate deployment with the time they get away with more. This isn't good for the smooth return of the deployed parent because children may resent his presence and associate it with lost freedoms. Similarly, if you become more authoritarian because you feel your children need more rules to keep them from trouble, perhaps because only one parent is around, they will resent deployment even more and could harbor anger toward the deployed and remaining parent or caregiver.

It is important that the deployed parent remain as involved as possible in big decisions of parenting, including discipline. This means that whenever possible, the deployed parent should help make disciplinary decisions. If this is possible online, the involvement could be in real time. I would caution strongly, however, against waiting for the next video chat to mete out a consequence because you will lose the benefit of immediacy. Discipline loses its effectiveness if children cannot clearly and directly associate the consequence they receive with the action they took. Especially for younger children, a significant delay can dampen the effect of any lesson. This is true even if that delay is to gain your partner's participation and agreement. On the other hand, never feel the consequence has to be so immediate that you have to give it while still in a rage. If you do that, you are more likely to give a punishment in which the child feels like a victim, rather than offer a lesson from which the child can learn. Additionally, the moments of communication your child has with the deployed parent are precious. If the parent at home threatens, "Wait until your [mother/father] hears what's going on!" those conversations will be dreaded. But to exclude deployed parents entirely from participating in discipline removes them from the opportunity to share wisdom, guidance, and life lessons.

The best solution is found in the meaning of the word *discipline* itself—to teach or to guide. Discipline is not about punishment or control. As discussed in detail in chapters 29 and 30, the key to discipline is that children and adolescents learn that the freedom and privileges they have are earned through demonstrated responsibility and actions. This means that discipline can be discussed in advance of any problem; in fact, the best discipline prevents problems. When parents lay out clear expectations that are associated with privileges, children learn exactly what it takes to earn those privileges and what it takes to be able to keep them. Consequences can be immediate—when children shirk responsibilities or break the prearranged rules, they lose the associated privileges. These agreements can even be done in formal contracts— "For me to feel comfortable with XXX, I need to know that you will do YYY."

If these kind of agreements are made as a family in advance of deployments and perhaps revisited every 3 months while deployed, the separated parent will in fact be "present" with every major disciplinary opportunity. Rather than needing to summon the authority of the distant parent with potentially damaging statements like, "You're lucky your mother isn't here," "Wait until your father gets back," or "Well, now we have something to tell your father on Wednesday night's call," you will be able to say, "Both us agreed that we expect you to XXX, and that the consequence would be YYY if you were not able to show responsibility." That is real discipline, authentic teaching, that includes both of you.

Although prearranged contracts of understanding allow the deployed parent's views to be represented in big decisions, the reality is that with distance and especially with repeated deployments, the home-based parent or caregiver will have to take more of the day-to-day discipline. Over time, the deployed parent will likely lose authority. This is why it's so important that these parents are kept in the loop. One parent described how she put it on her teenage son to keep his father in the loop. She would say, "Well, this is a decision your father needs to be involved in, so you should e-mail him and CC me." She found that making her teen demonstrate responsibly by including his father in any big decision before he got an answer helped her son stay connected to his father.

Some military families have shared with me that the real inconsistencies in parenting and disciplinary style occur during R & R leaves and with reintegration. The home spouse who has become the primary disciplinarian sometimes says, "Okay, it's your turn!" and gives up authority. There are several problems with this. The returning spouse may not be ready to assume authority, or it may generate a great deal of confusion in the children. More families have shared that the returning service member wants to be indulgent and limit his interactions with the children to good times. In those cases, the home spouse remains the authority figure, and the returning parent becomes overly permissive. Although kids may shower the returning spouse with affection for their new-found indulgence, this isn't the best way to rebuild a fully functional family unit in which both parents ideally share the pleasures and tough decision-making of child-rearing.

With regard to discipline, reintegration in the family is difficult whether the returning parent chooses to take a permissive or authoritarian stance. The balanced style—warmth, love, and appropriate rules—remains the best approach. But any rule giving may be met with resistance when the parent has been away. One woman who counsels military families shared that her own father was in the military and although he was very secure in his place in the family, he did not come crashing in with a heavy hand when he returned from deployments. Instead he would walk softly, listen and observe, and take a little time to reenter the system. That way he did not inadvertently undermine the authority and routines his wife had established, and this made his children less likely to rebel against his reemergence into their lives.

There is no way to make any approach to discipline always work in all circumstances when you are dealing with something as complex as a long-distance parent who is fully preoccupied with survival and another parent who is temporarily pulling the weight at home. Nevertheless, any steps you take to keep the deployed parent in the loop and his concerns about rules and expectation understood will make it easier to manage this complex dynamic.

Advanced planning prior to deployment on how to keep the distant parent involved is a critical step that likely will pay meaningful dividends before, during, and after separation. One idea previously discussed is the contract whereby big decisions and expectations are well understood in advance of the parent's departure. Another idea I particularly like is to have constant reminders of the parent's presence. One father told me that he and his wife sat down months before deployment and thought about the behaviors they wanted to promote in their children. They even thought through some of the tough spots their children might go through and some of the words of encouragement that might help them through those bumpy times. The father wrote notes to his children about how pleased he was with certain behaviors and how they made him proud. Similarly, he wrote about challenges and strategies that he had learned to overcome those challenges. The mother then distributed those notes at the appropriate times. The father wasn't present but his wisdom and encouragement were. Most importantly, their children absorbed the message that although Dad was away doing his job, his primary commitment was to his family. This effort took a lot of work and a tremendous amount of thought and planning. The yield was tremendous and allowed for much easier integration because the father's presence was always felt.

A Word on Teens

Some research suggests that teens may have the greatest difficulty when the deployed parent returns. This should not be surprising. The developmental task of adolescence is to learn to stand on one's own 2 feet and ultimately to become independent. This is why adolescence can often be challenging; teens simply must go through a phase of rejecting your values to be clear about their own. A year in the life of teens brings significant changes and great strides toward independence. These changes might be accelerated if they need to take on more adult responsibilities because of an absent parent. Teens experience these advances toward independence with a great sense of pride and confusion. They want to be able to fly on their own but at times wish that they could curl into a ball, cuddle in your lap, and be fully protected.

Add the strong mixed feelings teens have about their parents to the existing confusion over increasing independence. The reason teens sometimes act like they hate us is because of how much they can't stand how deeply they love us. There is a good chance that although your teen may never say it or even be consciously aware of it, the distance and separation of deployment has increased your teen's awareness of how much he cares about, or worse yet, *needs* his parents. No wonder adolescents' emotions swirl during deployment; they love their parents more than ever and hate them for making them become aware of those emotions.

When the deployed parent returns home, the teen's independence may suddenly feel challenged and some deep emotions may surface. It's no wonder the service member's return may not go smoothly. For these reasons, it becomes even clearer that the return should not be an event as simplistic as getting off of a plane and walking in the front door. An ongoing connection while away will likely make reintegration into the family easier. Maintaining a role in discipline while away will prevent the abrupt "I'm back in charge now!" return that is likely to trigger teen rebellion. An ongoing connection to discipline also might prevent the returning parent from applying the rules and orders associated with a smoothly functioning military command; they are not well suited to a household in which a teenager is appropriately testing her wings and pushing her limits.

The returning parent should honor the teen's growing independence and celebrate milestones achieved. It is likely the teen perceives that she has become the adult in the house and will highly resent being treated as a child. As previously mentioned, this is why the "parentification" of a teenager will likely backfire. But most teenagers will struggle in some way with being treated "just like a kid" when they see themselves as having grown so dramatically. There is no easy solution here. The best way to deal with this is to maintain parental connections, communication, and heartfelt presence during deployment and return with a celebration and acknowledgment of your teen's growth.

Above all, returning service members (as well as the parent at home) have a responsibility to model self-care, appropriate coping strategies, and reaching out to others for support. No one can or should be expected to return home without a lot to work through. Children, and especially teens, will be watching closely to make sure the parent is okay and to see what actions he takes to return to a state of equilibrium.

A Note for Single Parents

If you are a single parent, your concerns about deployment may be even stronger. You have likely worked out arrangements with extended family, close friends, or community members to care for your children in your absence. The key here is that your children know you are thoughtful about their safety and have carefully chosen people you trust and that you know will protect them. Let them be aware of the plan and if appropriate, contribute to it. Have a long, detailed discussion with caregivers before you go about your parenting style (see Chapter 29) and your discipline style (see Chapter 30) so they can do the best they can to maintain a home life that will feel consistent with your own and maintain your values and expectations of your children. This will likely make your deployment easier on you and your children and your transition home smoother.

A Note for Blended and Divorced Families

As you read any parenting advice, you are likely thinking, "If only it were that simple!" The preceding advice made an assumption that one spouse was at home and committed to maintaining a positive relationship between deployed parent and children. This may not be your reality. If you're part of a blended family, it will take greater efforts to maintain a relatively consistent parenting and discipline style. If you are part of a divorced couple, there may be some animosity remaining between you and your former spouse. As difficult as this may be, all adults can agree that we want what is best for our children. The children of deployed service members are already under a great deal of stress, and hearing conflicting messages about adult expectations of them and even hostile messages about their distant parent can be harmful to them. For this reason, all the adults need to agree to disagree behind closed doors and present a more unified message to the child. This will take hard, behind-the-scenes work and may require professional support, but the effort will pay off in the well-being of the child.

Pulling It Together

This book is about the 7 crucial Cs of resilience—competence, confidence, connection, character, contribution, coping, and control; all will add to your children's resilience, but 3 apply to you in a very special way. First, thank you for your *contribution;* it really will prepare your child to be someone who expects to give back. Next, the key to your family's thriving despite these enormous stressors is to stay *connected.* Your maintaining a strong connection, despite the challenges put on your family in service to our nation, is key to your being able to *cope* and to your child thriving. Most critically, if you want your child to *cope* with these special challenges and even to thrive, take care of yourself and your primary relationship with your spouse. Certainly the health of the relationship between you and your spouse may have more to do with your children growing up secure than anything else. Finally, demonstrate that strong people reach out to others and care for themselves with the same willingness that they care for others. If you struggle with that one, believe me when I tell you that you must care for yourself, for the sake of your children.

❀❀❀❀❀

To conclude this chapter, I include the following useful educational material written by my colleague Paula K. Rauch, MD, a consultation child psychiatrist at Massachusetts General Hospital, who directs programs for military-connected families (Home Base Program) and for families in which a parent has a serious illness (Marjorie E. Korff Parenting at a Challenging Time Program).

A Dozen Lessons Learned From the Parenting at a Challenging Time Program

These lessons are from Paula K. Rauch, MD, and colleagues at the Marjorie E. Korff Parenting at a Challenging Time (PACT) Program (www.mghpact.org) and the Home Base Program (www.homebaseprogram. org) at Massachusetts General Hospital.

1. **Begin by telling your child about the upcoming deployment.** Decide together with your spouse how you want to describe the separation, what you can share about what you will be doing during this time, and what ways you plan to stay connected during deployment. You may want to share with your child the reasons you chose to serve. Let your child know that he is loved and that you are serving to help protect your family, not because you want to be away from them.

2. **The worst way for a child to hear difficult news is to overhear it.** News learned by accident is often confusing and inaccurate. Keep the lines of communication open by letting your child know what is happening and what to expect, straight from you. Direct communication lets your child know she is important.

3. **Welcome all of your child's questions warmly.** Let your child know you are interested in questions about any topic. Be mindful of the settings in which your child is more likely to talk with you, such as in the car, at the kitchen table while you cook, or at bedtime. Try to be available at those times to make it easier for your child to share what is on his mind.

4. **Try to tease out the "real" questions your child wants to ask.** Ask your child to tell you what she was wondering about, or if there is something else she wants to know. You may find that there's a specific concern or worry that is the "real" question. Many times this specific worry can be more easily addressed than the initial question asked.

5. **Not all questions require immediate or detailed answers.** It's all right to say, "That's a good question. I'll need to think about it/discuss it with my [spouse, friend, minister, other family member] and get back to you."

6. **Respect your child's wish to not talk.** Do share basic information, as well as anything that may directly affect your child, to avoid confusion and surprises. Check in with your child from time to time and ask if he is hearing too much, too little, or the right amount about the deployment or other changes at home.

A Dozen Lessons Learned From the Parenting at a Challenging Time Program, *continued*

7. **Don't let your child worry alone.** Encourage your child to share her worries with you. Sometimes people outside the family say unhelpful things with the kindest intentions. Ask your child to share with you what others may have said about war in general or about your family's situation in particular. Tell your child how varied military and family experiences can be and how someone else's experience may not be the same as yours.

8. **Keep the channels of communication open with key caregivers.** This includes grandparents, teachers, babysitters, coaches, and parents of close friends. Ask your child to help you identify who the key point people should be. By keeping them in the communication loop, you make it easier for these caring adults to provide the appropriate emotional support and stable routine your child needs pre-deployment, during times away, and during reintegration.

9. **Try to maintain your child's usual schedule.** To help keep the routine as normal as possible, assign a point person for each child. Post schedules, make lists, and use calendars to help your child and caregivers know what each day holds. Talk with each child's teacher and let your children know whom they can go to if they have a hard time at school.

10. **Carve out protected family time.** Turn off the telephone and ask your friends and extended family not to visit at these times. Designate time when your child has your full attention without distractions. Use these moments to check in on the specific details of your child's day. Listen carefully to hear his successes, frustrations, or concerns about the future.

11. **Create special family time in preparation for the deployment.** Taking photographs, making videos, and creating shared memories helps a child cope with the separation of a parent during deployment. Explore new ways to communicate across the distance such as special Web sites and Web-based telephone services.

12. **Take care of yourself.** Parents need to be mindful of their own well-being and its effect on children. Be sure you get the help you need to feel confident. It is normal to feel worried, but if you are overwhelmed, turn to your support network of family members, friends, clergy, and others who can help you with your emotional health.

Talking With Children About Upsetting News Events

The following thoughts are from Paula K. Rauch, MD, and colleagues at the Mass General Hospital for *Children and the Home Base Program.*

All children are exposed to news via newspapers, radio, the Internet, and especially television. And they naturally turn to their parents with questions about what they have seen and heard. For a child whose parent is deployed, news about the wars can raise concerns about their parent's safety. This poses a special challenge for the parent who is at home to listen, understand, and answer their children's questions in a manner that is honest and reassuring. Meeting this challenge successfully strengthens your child's inner strength, sense of security, and trust in you.

First, you know your child best. You have likely been through good times and stressful times before. How your child has reacted in the past is often a good predictor for how he will cope with new challenges. Think about what has been helpful for your child previously, and use these successful strategies from the past. Most children will benefit from maintaining regular routines, including daily schedules and normal expectations for schoolwork. Children will take their emotional cues from the adults in their world. If we are calm, usually they will feel secure; however, it is important to talk to your child about his specific concerns.

Second, check in with your child. Find out what she has been hearing, seeing, and thinking about a new event or whether it has not yet come to her attention. Questions such as, "Are kids at school talking about _____?" or "What have you heard about _____?" are good ways to open such a conversation. If your child is younger and is not aware of the news, you may elect to go no further with this conversation. If your child has heard about the news event, encourage her to tell you about what she has heard or what she thinks about what others are saying. Ask if she has any specific worries. To answer questions and allay fears, it is important to really understand what your child is struggling with before you move to answer or reassure her.

Third, TV images can be upsetting. Turn off the TV around young children or those who may have been upset by TV news in the past. Be mindful that coverage of the same violent event over and over again can be misinterpreted as something that is happening repeatedly. Watch television with older children so you can answer questions and be aware of their feelings. Some older children need to be reminded that the TV images can be overwhelming and that it's okay not to watch. This is true for many

Talking With Children About Upsetting News Events, *continued*

adults, who may feel better listening to radio reports or reading newspaper coverage rather than watching disturbing TV images.

Fourth, make the most of family time. Spend extra time with your children. Turn off the telephone and the TV during meals so you can talk together. Often parents can identify times in the day or activities that facilitate thoughtful conversations. Sometimes, it is while driving in the car or when a child sits with a parent who is working in the kitchen. Those are great times to check in with your child and talk.

Finally, when a child feels the world in general is a little less safe, it is important to underscore the active things we do to increase our personal safety. These may include wearing seat belts or bike helmets, eating healthy foods and exercising, looking both ways before crossing the street, and identifying who the supervising adults are in different settings so a child knows who to go to for help. When a child is feeling worried specifically about the safety of the parent overseas, support the child's connection to the parent overseas by using whatever avenues of communication are available. Remaining confident yourself, and reminding your child of the security that comes from the deployed parent's preparation, training, skills, and those of the military leadership, can go a long way to reestablish a child's sense of safety.

The following tips may be helpful at any challenging time:

Infants
* Infants pick up on the anxieties and actions of those around them, so remain calm when interacting with your infant. Keep routines and environment consistent.
* Infants may be fussy in reaction to anxieties around them.

Toddlers
* Keep routines consistent.
* TV and radio news exposure should be limited and only in the presence of an adult.
* Offer videos to watch, read books, and play with your child.
* If a toddler asks questions about what is going on, answer in simple terms. Make sure your child knows that you are there to keep him safe.

Talking With Children About Upsetting News Events, *continued*

Preschoolers

- TV and radio news exposure should be limited and only in the presence of an adult.
- If your preschooler asks questions about what is going on, answer in simple terms. Make sure your child knows that you are there to keep her safe.
- Spend extra time hugging and cuddling your child.
- Play with your child. Connect with friends or organize a playgroup.
- Do some type of special activity together. Watch a movie, play a game, or bake cookies.

School-aged Children

- TV and radio news exposure should be in the presence of an adult.
- Give children plenty of opportunities to talk about what they think is going on, and clear up misconceptions.
- Encourage children to share their feelings and concerns with you. Let them know it's all right to be afraid and that you will do everything you can to keep them safe.
- Be available, as this age group may be more interested than younger children in the events but less capable than older children of coping and communicating.
- Reassure kids that many people are keeping them safe and that your family is safe.
- Offer special activities or games to them.

Adolescents

- Listen, listen, listen.
- Watch TV news with them.
- Engage your adolescent in healthy conversation. "What do you think about the events that are taking place in our world today?" "How did you feel when you first heard about this?"
- Share your feelings with them honestly.
- Encourage them to express feelings of anger and brainstorm with them about how they can deal with those feelings.

Talking With Children About Upsetting News Events, *continued*

All Children

- Be with your children as much as possible.
- Ask about their understanding of events reported in the news—don't assume you know.
- Validate feelings that your children share with you as real, ensure they understand that there are no wrong feelings, and tell them that you have similar feelings.
- When they ask about their safety, explain that you as a parent will do everything you can to keep them safe. Address their specific concerns.
- If children have questions about the safety of their school, explain that parents, teachers, and school officials are doing everything possible to keep them safe. Address their specific concerns.
- Children may exhibit some of the following behaviors during stressful times:
  - Regression—acting younger and seeking attention
  - Becoming more clingy
  - Having difficulty sleeping
  - Being more temperamental or making angry comments
  - Talking about acts of violence
  - Playing or acting more aggressively

All of these reactions are normal. It is important to keep talking to your children and allow them to express all of their feelings.

Character

A child can be very competent, confident, and deeply connected, but still not be prepared to thrive. Renee is a good example. She is intelligent and highly competent. She has great problem-solving skills. She knows how to stand up for herself. She is not intimidated by peer pressure. Her confidence has often helped her get out of a jam.

Renee has strong connections—she is a member of a girl gang to whom she is extremely loyal and which serves as a surrogate family. She may be able to survive in a world that is too tough for most to comprehend. But despite all her competence, confidence, and connection, Renee will not rise above all the challenges in her life to be a positive, contributing member of society without another vital ingredient of resilience.

Character is the component that's missing for Renee. Her family members have been a passive influence in her life, perhaps because of their own struggles. Her parents didn't instill values such as responsibility to the broader community or the value of each and every life. Perhaps her school failed her and didn't allow her to grasp that she had other competencies that were far more valuable to society than those she learned on the streets. Her community failed her by not ensuring that she grew up in a safe enough environment, so survival alone had to become her core value.

Renee's connections were formed with a dangerous peer group that offered the allure of family. But these connections have been negative for the most part. Renee has not been supported by relationships with positive role models or caring relatives and community. It is these positive role models and loving relatives who would have instilled that basic sense of right and wrong—character.

❖❖❖❖

Every family has its own recipe for what constitutes good character. We may prioritize these character traits differently. Some families may value humility, while others more avidly nurture the ability to present oneself aggressively. Some parents' highest priority is that their children are civil, polite, and respectful of others. Other families most highly value generosity, while others value individuality.

We can probably agree about traits that we *don't* want in our children— hatred, bigotry, self-righteousness, and insensitivity. If we all took a deep breath, I believe we would agree that we want children to be moral, responsible, decent, and kind. The deep breath is necessary because sometimes— after we become overwhelmed with all the messages about what good parents do, the magical opportunities they create for their kids, and the fabled head starts they make sure their children receive—we forget about what matters to *us* and *our* children.

I have no right to tell you which character traits to instill in your child. Only you know what is best for your child, family, and community. Although I will not tell you which traits to emphasize, I will tell you that all parents need to be active about developing character. Children hear so many messages about what kind of people they should be. The media tell them what they should look like and which items they need to be happy. Peers tell them how to behave, and those suggested behaviors shift like the wind. Teachers have one set of expectations, clergy another, coaches still another. It isn't surprising that young people are confused by all these mixed messages.

My point is that character development responds to feedback and direction. Parents want to make very certain that direction comes from them and people who they believe will help their children build strong character. In short, we cannot leave character development to chance. In Chapter 5, I addressed getting out of the way so that parents don't stifle a child's natural resilience or inhibit competency by interfering too quickly. When it comes to character development, however, parents must be active.

There is nothing purer and with greater potential than a small child, but children are also inherently selfish. They have needs and will do what it takes to get their needs met. Usually their charm and innocence draw in adults to help them. When they resort to tantrums or pull out every play in the book to get what they need, we adults have to modify their behavior. We have to take action. We need to make them understand that cooperation is a greater value than fighting, waiting your turn is better than shoving, and talking gets better results than tossing tantrums. It's up to us to ensure that those lovable but self-centered youngsters become fine human beings capable of loving the next generation.

Challenges to Character

In our fast-paced society, we face many challenges when we try to raise young people with character. Our culture values personal success, so how do we make sure that our children are hard workers but still value kindness, cooperation, sharing, and compassion for other people? In a society that fosters winning the prize, how do we reinforce that it is how we play the game that defines us as humans? In a world in which independence is a hallmark of success, how do we convey that the finest people are those who can admit they need others to achieve contentment?

I wish I had brilliant answers for those rhetorical questions. They pose some of the heftiest challenges of our times. I invite you to struggle along with me here. I do know this—character development does not come in a bottle, nor will it come through a lecture. Telling kids how to act ("Be nice to your sister."), how to care ("You should be kinder to the new kid in your class."), and what to value ("Honesty is important.") is simply not enough and usually doesn't work.

Children learn character by the values you teach, your words of praise, or the way you correct them. They learn character by observing your values and behavior in daily interactions outside your home and watching how adults treat each other in your home. While I don't pretend to have all the answers, I can offer some suggestions designed to spark conversations. They are not intended as a definitive list of everything you have to do to build character, but I hope you will use this section to trigger a conversation with other adults who care about your child's developing character. I'm taking the liberty here of listing 15 categories that my wife Celia and I have discussed in terms of raising our daughters. Please use this as a tool to make a list that works for you.

1. **Notice children's acts of kindness.** How often do we praise children for accomplishing a new task or achieving a good grade? Probably a lot. They get the most adult recognition when they produce. We also need to catch them when they are kind, generous, and thoughtful and tell them how pleased we are.

2. **Notice acts of kindness and decent behavior in others.** Think about what makes news. What do we choose to talk about around the office water cooler? What do we gossip about with our neighbors? What kind of human interactions are written into sitcoms? Isn't it usually the appalling behaviors that get our attention? Children are watching and listening too, but they don't know that we edit out all of the normal behaviors and most of the decent deeds that people do. If we aren't careful, we expose children to a world much worse than reality. Let's begin talking to each other about the positive things our friends and neighbors do every day that go unnoticed. Let's talk about the coworker who visits her mother every day, the

grandson who takes meals to his elderly grandmother, and the block captain who makes sure there are activities for children in the neighborhood. In other words, let's redefine our heroes and minimize our scandals, and let's do it in front of the kids.

3. **Treat each other well.** Children pay close attention to how adults treat each other. Whether their parents are married, separated, divorced, or never married, children notice how the adults around them relate to each other. The best marriages include disagreements, sometimes about parenting styles. Divorces, of course, are likely to produce even more conflicts. While younger children may become frightened by disagreements, older children worry less about them and more about how they are resolved. When partners treat each other fairly and with respect, young people observe and remember. When problems are discussed and resolved honestly and openly, without hostility, children learn it's safe to voice opinions.

4. **Treat strangers well.** Children learn to value qualities like compassion when they see their parents consistently acting compassionately toward others. No words we say to children will ever be as influential as our own demonstrated behavior and acts of kindness and understanding.

   For example, my wife's father, Eli Pretter, was a *mensch* (a real man) if there ever was one. At his eulogy, I retold the story that Celia says defined her childhood. On a bitingly cold winter day, a shabbily dressed man was walking along a nearly deserted road. Celia, then 6 or 7 years old, and her father were driving toward him. Celia asked her father to give the man a ride, but Eli explained that it was not safe to pick up strangers and drove past. Celia wept. Eli then turned the car around and drove the stranger to his destination. Eli later told Celia, "Sometimes, a grown man has to learn from a little girl. Thank you for being so kind." It may not have been wise to pick up that man, but I know it had a lasting effect on my wife.

5. **Reinforce the importance of including all children.** Childhood seems innocent enough, but it sometimes centers on *in*-groups and *out*-groups. Those cliques shift so frequently that they are difficult to define. Often the best way to ensure that a child is welcome in the in-group is to reject other kids, the "outs." Help your child realize the importance of other children's feelings, while still maintaining his best friendships. This means knowing who is invited to his parties and who is not. It also means reinforcing his acts of kindness when he befriends a less popular child. It means asking what's going on when your daughter suddenly bursts out, "Julia is weird. I don't like her anymore." It means going out of your way to enable your child to play with others who may have a physical disability and not travel as easily as others in the group. The friendships your child makes with

others who have differences are likely to expose him to peers with strong character traits. Children who are physically disadvantaged are often greatly advantaged spiritually and emotionally.

Having a wide variety of friends is a great asset, but it's even better when children choose friends for themselves rather than based on what others say or think. That is a priceless quality that your child will carry over into the adult world. Don't be surprised when those peers your child has befriended and supported during tough times will support him when they are needed.

6. **Promote responsibility.** A key trait of resilient people is taking responsibility for their behaviors, including failures, and taking action to improve them. This important character trait will make a large difference in how a young person performs later in work and personal life. Parents can do a great deal to teach children to accept responsibility. (This will be addressed further in Part 5.)

7. **Don't spoil your children.** How we'd love to give our children everything they want—they're so darned cute! But adults who expect everything instantly and on their terms, who feel that they're entitled to anything they desire, are not so cute—may I say detestable? If you follow the other suggestions in this chapter, it is unlikely that your child will be spoiled, but here are some thoughts to consider.

   – Don't worry about spoiling infants when you meet their every need!
   – If children realize that some people are less fortunate, they are less likely to be demanding. It's important for children to know that they aren't the center of the world. If they are taught to take responsibility for their actions, they will understand the causes and effects of good behavior and good works. They will not feel entitled to what they have not earned.
   – Parents who listen to their children carefully and give them undivided attention are less likely to feel the compulsion to shower children with material objects or grant all their wishes.
   – Help children learn patience. If they want something, they may have to wait. This is a major reason we have birthdays only once a year!
   – It is perfectly okay to explain that something costs too much money to buy.
   – Offer your child a safe home, adequate clothing, nutritious food, and lots of love. Sure, he needs some toys, but he doesn't need every toy-of-the-week. Help him develop his imagination by using old toys for new purposes or making playthings out of natural or found objects. Even if you are affluent, make your child work for special objects. Teach him that things cost money. Let him earn certain items he craves. By doing extra

little jobs around the house, children as young as 4 or 5 years can earn something special. Older children can do jobs that you would pay someone else to do (like painting a fence or mowing the lawn) so they grasp the clear connection that money buys things.

- When children learn to win at parents' expense, they absorb a dangerous lesson that their needs are more important than others' needs. This is why giving in to a tantrum does children a great disservice.

- Don't ever worry about spoiling your child with love. Love doesn't spoil children, it only makes them sweeter.

8. **Watch television and listen to music—be there when they receive unfiltered messages.** Because most children spend about as much time with media as they do in school, they may be heavily influenced by what they see and hear. They may come to believe what they see on television is normal and acceptable. Music has wonderful potential to stir or soothe emotions, but some lyrics contains violent or hateful messages. Whenever you can, try to screen the material before your child is exposed. It's not uncommon for sexist, homophobic, antireligious, or intolerant words to be inserted into songs. Adults who don't pay attention to the lyrics will not be aware of the words creeping into their children's perceptions of the world.

    Don't allow children to buy material you think is inappropriate. When your child gets older, he will probably reject your screening of what he listens to and watches, so be specific. If you say, "Turn that awful music down. That stuff is trash!" you are only widening the generational divide. Instead, voice your precise concerns. "Are you listening to the words? Do you hear how hateful they are toward women?"

    Enjoy entertainment with your children. Watch programs along with them, but don't try to turn entertainment into education. Use fictional characters' choices and behaviors as starting points to have family discussions. Do this rarely and keep the tone casual, or you will be banned from the family room (as discussed in Chapter 11).

9. **Work toward a better world.** The next chapter is framed around children's contributions to the world, but what about yours? You may or may not have time to volunteer for a good cause, but certainly you have a moment to pick up trash instead of walking by it. You can give your seat to an elderly person on a bus. You can make time to call your relatives. Your children are watching and learning from you. Talk to them about the injustices in our nation and world. You cannot fix all the problems, but you needn't remain silent either.

10. **Give charity in the name of justice.** If your child is to count his blessings, he must know that many people are less fortunate. In a world driven by accomplishment and individual success, do you want your child to be aware that he has a responsibility to others? If so, make charity a central theme of your household. The amount is not important. Younger children don't even understand the difference between a $10 and $1,000 donation. When you talk with your child about giving to charity, let him know you aren't doing it out of the goodness of your heart but because it is the right thing to do.

   For example, we have a tzedakah (justice) box in our house as a center piece in the living room. Our children have no idea what amount we give, but they know we do give. When they are feeling fortunate, they put something in the box so others might have better fortunes. As they have grown older, we've allowed them to help decide where our contributions are made. We narrow our choices down, they research the charities, and we donate to their selection.

11. **Honor plurality.** We are a nation that draws strength from our differences. Within our pluralistic society, we may feel connected to certain familiar groups—ethnic, political, or religious. We may want our children to be tightly connected to these groups (as discussed in Chapter 20) because they share our values. This desire for connection should *never* be an excuse for not teaching children tolerance or for allowing prejudice. It is highly destructive to turn people who do not belong to our group into "the other."

   Honoring plurality doesn't mean, however, that you have to buy into an "I'm okay, you're okay" ethic that says everything is fine as long as no one gets hurt. It's good to have strong values and stick to them tenaciously. Honoring plurality means that we respect the fact that others can also have strong value systems, and we remain open to rich discussions. Character develops when ideas grow and thoughts are honored, and nations are built by individuals with this strength of character.

12. **Avoid prejudice.** An unfortunate, sometimes deadly human trait is the tendency to divide into *us* and *them*. We may feel safer among those we call "us," and that's not necessarily a bad thing. It becomes worrisome, though, when people define themselves by saying they are glad they are "not them." It becomes dangerous when they need or want others to fail so that they can succeed.

   Prejudice is not always intentionally malicious and is often unconscious. Prejudgments we make based on limited information, however, come in many flavors and have some very troublesome consequences, including justification for discrimination. In the least, prejudice prevents us from getting to know each other better.

On a summer day several years ago when I was working on the first edition of this book, my 10-year-old daughters were with me at a swimming pool. My eyes were burning from chlorine as I tried to review a book that could inform this section. Talia offered to read it to me. After a few pages, I wasn't sure she understood the meaning, so I asked her to explain it. "It's about racism," she said. I asked her what the word meant (though we have discussed it in the past). "It's when people don't like other people just because of their color." I asked her what that meant to her. "It means if I was a racist, I wouldn't be able to have some of my very good friends. That would be really sad."

The United States is becoming more diverse by the day, and the world is becoming more connected by the hour. Children need to be raised free of prejudice if they are to thrive in this world. Prejudice rears its head in many places, often very subtly. No matter how subtle, even preschoolers pick up on the building blocks of intolerance and racism.

Children are like sponges, absorbing ideas and attitudes from everyone around them. They notice parents' words and unspoken language. Assuming we parents do everything perfectly, we can't overlook other influences like the media, music, children's books, and our children's friends. Overtly prejudiced statements may be rare and screened by parents, but subtle, pervasive messages are everywhere. If we don't want our children to be socialized by these worrisome stereotypes, we must closely examine the messages they receive and look for materials that do not contain harmful hidden stereotypes. The Anti-Defamation League book, *Hate Hurts,* by Caryl Stern-LaRosa and Ellen Hofheimer Bettmann, proposes an exercise to alert parents to biased messages. I draw on this exercise and add some thoughts of my own to summarize it here.

When looking at children's books, listening to their music, or considering whether they should see a movie, for example, examine how many characters are of different races and consider who are heroes and heroines and who are villains. Who's smart and capable? Who solves problems? On the other hand, who creates problems and who is unable to solve them without the help of others? Are minority characters only able to perform heroic acts because they've been helped by a white hero? Who is brave? Who is weak or scared? Who fights? Who resolves conflict? Who is successful or rich? Who are passive and unable to help themselves? Who is poor? Who are the criminals? Who leads? Who follows?

We wouldn't be honest with ourselves if we didn't acknowledge that certain minorities are portrayed more often in an unflattering, unrealistic manner. Here's my mantra again—children live up or down to our expectations of them. Imagine you are an African American or Latino child—what would it feel like to see yourself, or an image you relate to, portrayed in this manner repeatedly? If you are raising children who are in a racial minority, point out the distorted message. Tell them with pride about what it really means to be an African American or Latino member of this society. If you are raising a white child, point out that these messages are unfair and untrue. Talk about the fact that some groups, like Native Americans and Asian Americans, rarely appear in the media, but when they do, they are frequently cast as stereotypes. In the post-9/11 world, we need to prevent children from developing distorted images of Muslims. It's very easy for them to watch the news and pick up misconceptions of Islam. We can explain that there is a great difference between a minority of fanatical terrorists and the vast majority of Muslims who make our country stronger and richer.

Don't simply tell children that prejudiced messages are untrue; show them by exposing them to positive images of diverse groups. Multicultural books, media, dolls, and museum visits can help children understand the history and culture of other people, including the history of their painful oppression. Equally important is the opportunity to make friends with other children of diverse backgrounds.

Talk about why members of minority groups may be poor. Don't be afraid to talk about some ugly truths like economic disparities, racism, and failing schools. If our children don't know about them, who is going to invest in fixing them? Point out that poverty and wealth come in every color and that what matters most is that we strive for a world in which everyone has enough. Mention all the wonderful contributions made to this country and world by people of every ethnic group and color. Make certain that children understand that we're stronger and wiser because we are diverse. Help them realize that people with different experiences, perspectives, and backgrounds challenge us to think outside of our own boxes and make each of us richer.

It is not just the media that molds biased images. Children hear our words and pick up our subtle body language when we become angry or apprehensive. The words we say hold great weight with them. What may seem like a casual ethnic or sexist joke to a parent can mistakenly become a child's image of that ethnicity or gender. If we travel in unsafe neighborhoods and automatically lock the car doors or become apprehensive if a shady-looking character walks into the mini-market, children will notice our unspoken biases. In certain circumstances, it may be wise and justified to become protective. Be aware that children who are not exposed to a wide variety of people may make quick judgments that sear into their subconscious and last a lifetime. I am not advising you against trusting your instincts, but I am suggesting that you discuss your anxiety with your child and make clear how targeted your action was. For example, "That man made me nervous because [for whatever specific reasons] and that's why we left the store." This will help your child understand that you did not react because of the man's race.

Prejudice and racism are not just a black-white or Latino–non-Latino issue. Harmful prejudgments are made about gender, sexual orientation, religion, ethnic groups, and every race. A group of Asian American youth shared with me how they continually deal with many people's assumptions that they are "foreign." Native Americans still face assumptions that they are "uncivilized." Girls sometimes receive messages that they are less capable at sports or math and science. Gay youth find themselves amid a culture war. The list goes on for every group. Each shares a common experience of having other people make quick, hurtful, untrue assumptions about them. All share the desire to be seen as individuals who are enriched by being members of a group that gives them strength and identity.

Many parents are deeply committed to raising children who see no difference between groups, essentially to be color-blind. When children ask about race, these parents tell them, "There's no difference; all people are the same." This is a lovely, well-intentioned answer, but it is not true. It may be correct to teach that on a spiritual level, people are the same, but here on Earth, a wide variety of differences exist between groups and individuals. That is what makes us strong. That is what makes us interesting. This is why it is so important to broaden our horizons by knowing others. Rather than raising children to be color-blind, we can raise them to honor, respect, and deeply appreciate differences.

Not being color-blind unfortunately means becoming aware of prejudice and unfair treatment of ourselves and others. No matter how we want to make life fair in our children's world, life is not fair for everyone. Regardless of children's backgrounds, at some point in their lives, they will be treated unfairly. This will happen to some more than others. Denying this truth robs children of the tools to advocate for themselves and others. Don't wait for your child's school to teach lessons about discrimination. We need to talk to our children about issues such as slavery, the Holocaust, present-day genocide, and other injustices. If we choose to be silent about these matters, our children will have to navigate this road independently, which can be harrowing and hurtful.

Remember, our children hear our silence loudly and clearly.

The struggle for every parent is how to expose children to these painful issues in a developmentally appropriate way. Too much, too soon can be harmful. Thankfully, many books are designed for children of different ages (see Resources).

In covering numerous topics in this book, I have tried to make them user-friendly, often by translating scientific information or expert opinion into practical ways parents can put resilience-building strategies into place. I admit to being uncomfortable about attempting to take on as complex, volatile, and urgent a subject as prejudice and simplifying it in a few brief pages. I feel committed, however, to acknowledging the importance of tolerance as a crucial character trait children need to thrive in this world.

13. **Care about nature.** What child doesn't love to climb a tree, hike in the woods, or wade into a stream? Children relate easily to efforts to save the environment. They can get almost immediate satisfaction by planting tree saplings or clearing trash from a creek. Because most children love animals, they easily relate to saving endangered species. Getting involved with environmental efforts carries great social good and is less heavy and burdensome than working to relieve human suffering on a grand scale. Let children know how much you care about nature and that there is only one planet where we all live, so we must preserve it.

14. **Believe in something bigger.** I wouldn't venture to tell you what to believe in, but people who believe in a higher power or the interrelatedness of humanity have something greater than themselves to turn to on a daily basis and especially in times of crisis. Your connection with a group of people with similar beliefs can ensure that your children can draw character-building lessons from many people in addition to you.

15. **Be human.** Enough already with kindness, generosity, decency, and altruism—let's get real. Every human, even those with children and perhaps especially those with children, has a full range of emotions and traits, including selfishness, impatience, anger, and greed. Our challenge is to ensure that our better selves prevail and control our unattractive, even destructive impulses. Children have the same struggles. Anyone who has ever spent time with 2- to 4-year-olds has witnessed the mighty battle between wanting things ("Mine!") and the desire to please adults who extol sharing and cooperation. We do children an injustice by pretending to be perfect. Let them know that we adults also struggle to be good people. We can give them permission to struggle themselves; this

will help alleviate guilt and the catastrophic fears that they sometimes have when their all-too-human emotions surface. When we talk aloud and share how we strive to make sure our better sides prevail, even after an outburst, we model how to do the same. We remind children that the world does not come to an end when we have uncontrollable feelings.

◈◈◈◈

When people have strong character, they have the ability to return to a set of core values during times of crisis, which makes them more resilient in the most trying of times. But it's about more than adaptability and recovery; children need to develop character so that we can build a society with lower crime rates, greater attention to the planet's needs, and a firmer resolve to treat each other with integrity, honesty, and fairness. We need the next generation to tell us old folks what we're doing wrong, question our decisions, and poke at our hypocrisies. Youth are our resource, and they need strong character to make the greatest contribution.

Contribution

Confident young people who recognize their competencies, who feel connected to people, and who have a strongly rooted character are poised to contribute to the world. Contribution may flow from the other Cs, but children and teens who take active steps to contribute will receive ongoing feedback and gain experiences that prepare them to thrive. Parents and communities who ensure ample opportunities for children to contribute will build the next generation of leaders.

When young people work to improve their communities, they develop a meaningful sense of purpose. They receive positive feedback that protects them from some of the negative, destructive messages about youth. They hear from numerous people besides their parents, "I think you are wonderful," and absorb the important belief, "I have high expectations for you." They are surrounded by thank-yous rather than condemnation. Because kids live up or down to expectations set for them, these thank-yous can be highly protective.

My wife and I wanted to teach our daughters from a very early age that contributing to others is an important value. We wanted them to know that the world could be a better place because they are in it, so our girls began contributing as pass-around babies at a nursing home when they were 3 months old. They don't remember how their smiles brightened the days of elderly residents, but that experience was the beginning of many volunteer efforts.

When they saw famished children on the front page of a newspaper and asked me about it, I gave them an explanation tailored to 4-year-olds—"They don't have enough food." My girls asked, "Can we send food?" I told them how difficult that was, but we could send money. At their prompting, I then spent $40 and an entire day building a lemonade stand (and building is not one of my competencies!) so they could earn $3.75. Of course it was worth it! The girls felt their efforts mattered and they could make a difference for a hungry child on the other side of the globe.

Throughout childhood, they continued to explore ways to repair the world. Sure, they knew it pleased me, but it seemed to bubble up from within them and was continuously reinforced by feedback from neighbors who viewed them as idealists. When times are difficult for them, I trust they'll be soothed by knowing they can immerse themselves in a project that demonstrates how important and valued they are.

They still care deeply about the world, but their contribution has changed now that they are teens. They are role models to many of our neighborhood's younger children. They are the athletic girls whose attention is valued and whose values are noticed. They are sought-after babysitters. They consistently receive the messages that the children are watching them and that parents are pleased with the model of teens they portray. I also know that neighborhood parents noticing my daughters adds an extra layer of protection for them. Perhaps most importantly, when they are held as good examples, they'll be less likely to adopt behaviors not befitting role models.

Seeing Beyond Themselves

Contemporary culture is so focused on material things like electronic equipment, expensive shoes and clothes, cosmetics, and cars. Children naturally get swept up in this tide because they see it all around them. To counter this influence or put it in perspective, parents can support opportunities for children to give rather than receive. Children will learn that the universe doesn't revolve around them or owe them everything they desire. When they raise money for earthquake relief, collect recyclables, or tutor younger children, they gain a more realistic perspective of the world and their places in it. They begin to see beyond their isolated, self-oriented circles. They recognize themselves as part of larger communities in which they can make a difference.

Children can contribute to society in a multitude of ways—collecting coins to feed the hungry, cleaning up the environment, volunteering with children who have physical disabilities, and even simple, spontaneous acts of generosity and courtesy such as holding open heavy doors for a parent pushing a baby stroller or someone carrying heavy bags.

Contribution directly fosters resilience because it helps children gain a sense of purpose, something positive to strive toward and achieve. When I met with young people at Barrington High School in Illinois, I learned that Ray Piagentini, a guidance counselor, had been taking students on a service project for the last 25 years to the Crow Creek Reservation, very near the Cheyenne River in South Dakota, which had so powerfully influenced my perspective on the inherent strength of people. The students and I spent 2 hours after school talking about the meaning of serving others and the lessons they absorbed about the resilience of the human spirit. They learned that although they went to "help," they received so much more than they ever gave. They understood that experience was the greatest teacher and that they could learn life's most valued lessons by listening to those who shared their stories. They learned that even challenged communities with a strong connection to their culture could find most solutions from within their own timeless wisdom. And they gained a deep respect for people from a different culture and knew that this lesson in diversity would serve them throughout their lives.

These young people, who were not even sure why they were drawn to this service project, felt that it would flavor their perspectives forever. They wanted to be active participants in efforts to repair the world.

I came to Barrington to inspire youth and left the one inspired.

Contribution is interwoven with competence, confidence, connection, and character as an integral thread in the web of resilience. Let's take a quick look at how contribution ties into the other components of resilience.

Competence. When children actively participate in volunteer activities, they develop new competencies by giving and doing. They discover new interests and talents they may not know they have. If a project involves raising money for a good cause, for example, kids learn that they are capable of knocking on doors, talking to adults in a polite and convincing way, counting up their collection, and sending it in. They learn individual skills such as organization and responsibility, as well as the bigger lesson—they have accomplished something meaningful.

By contributing to someone else or efforts greater than themselves, children increase their life experiences and thus become more competent—"I can do this!" They gain a solid sense of their own abilities and worth.

Confidence. When children carry out these efforts, they become more confident about themselves because they have demonstrated their abilities. They can see actual results—a collection of dollars or canned goods, smiles and applause from grateful nursing home residents, 20 stacks of sandwiches made for a homeless shelter, or 10 bags of garbage cleaned up from a polluted creek or park. When young people contribute and make a difference in the world or others' lives, they usually get positive feedback for their efforts, which further adds to their confidence and resilience.

Children who volunteer and contribute to worthy causes not only gain confidence, but they also avoid problems. The Minneapolis, MN–based Search Institute, a nonprofit organization whose aim is to promote healthy children, youth, and communities, has reported that children and teens who volunteer just 1 hour a week are 50% less likely to abuse drugs and alcohol, smoke cigarettes, or engage in harmful behaviors. Of course, this may mean that the type of children who volunteer are not as likely to do drugs in the first place, but who cares? Don't we want our children to be that type of person?

Connection. Contribution also helps young people forge connections with their neighborhoods, schools, and world. From participating in local community service projects or drives that provide food, medicine, pencils, and paper to schools across the world, children gain a sense of purpose. They can see beyond their near horizons and recognize their place in the human family and on our common planet. The more strongly they feel connected, the more resilient they become. They learn that someone else is always poorer, hungrier, or less cared for than they are. They come to appreciate their blessings and with gratitude, learn to give something back. They will also learn that giving and receiving, sharing during times of plenty, and asking for help during difficult times are normal, healthy things for humans to do. We want our children to know that just as they give, they will receive if misfortune hits. If they are to be resilient in the face of an unforeseen tragedy, this is a vital lesson.

When looking for volunteer opportunities, talk with children about their interests and try to match them with appropriate community resources. Don't do all this for them, but guide them along. Encourage them to ask at school or a local library where they can find volunteer openings. If children are interested in animals, for example, they might look for local animal or bird sanctuaries.

When children become involved in volunteer activities, they will likely work with adults who are good role models. As they work alongside adults who contribute to worthwhile causes, children not only learn specific skills but also connect with adults who are working to make a difference, and that will have a positive influence on your children.

Character. Contribution strengthens character because it develops desirable traits such as responsibility, generosity, and caring. Children learn responsibility when they volunteer for a community project, for example. They know they have to follow through because others are depending on them; they have to show up on time and do their part.

The positive feedback they receive for their efforts and their own sense of accomplishment also enhance character. The more their generosity and caring are acknowledged, the more generous and caring they are likely to become.

Contribution is a 2-way street. When kids raise funds for cancer research or collect toys and books for disadvantaged children, they not only give something, but they also get something. They realize that they have purpose and value, and the world is better because they are in it. We need to remember, too, that we adults *need* young people to contribute. They are our greatest resource for the future, so we need their contributions.

Words of Caution

Parents, scout leaders, teachers, and other adults sometimes take over youngsters' volunteer projects. We adults can be supportive from the sidelines, but children should choose and carry out these activities as independently as possible if they are to become more competent and confident. Nothing discourages their efforts more than an adult who steps in and says, "Let me do that for you," when children can do it themselves. Even if they don't run the project as efficiently as they might with adult help, let them do it and learn from their experiences.

Contribution builds a child's life résumé. It should not be encouraged primarily to have another asset on their college applications or impress scholarship committees. It should feel like a wonderful thing to do that also happens to build a résumé.

Some organizations offer cash prizes or scholarships to children who have made outstanding contributions to their communities or have demonstrated selfless acts of kindness. Those are wonderful rewards, but children shouldn't be encouraged to volunteer predominantly in the hope of winning a scholarship or prize. They should be encouraged and supported because it is a worthy thing to do for others and themselves.

Beyond Charitable Deeds

Contribution isn't only about good deeds and noble actions. Children also need to know that they can contribute ideas that will be taken seriously and respected. When adults invite children's suggestions and opinions, especially about matters that concern them, we increase their sense of control, which in turn enhances their resilience. For example, when planning a neighborhood playground, who knows better what type of equipment to install than the children who will use it? Who knows better what it would take to keep community children away from drugs than the kids living in that community? Whenever adults design programs for children, the best ideas usually come from the young consumers themselves. As a qualitative researcher, I have asked adolescents some of these very questions and have found that they consistently arrive at wise answers that adults never would have considered.

In terms of our individual families, we can include children in family meetings and really listen to their ideas about how to resolve conflict and what kinds of specific supports or actions they need from us to help them reach their goals. When their ideas are heard and respected, kids learn skills, gain confidence, and come to understand that they can contribute to the well-being of themselves and their families—all immeasurable gifts.

Speaking of family contribution, children can also contribute to families by doing their fair share of chores. The word *chores* may have an unpleasant ring from your own childhood. You may remember your parents nagging you to take out the garbage or mow the lawn. Today's families don't delegate many chores to children because we have so many labor-saving devices or because some parents believe kids should spend their limited time at home on homework or computers. Chores do have a place in developing several ingredients of resilience. They teach children that they are an integral part of the family and are expected to contribute to it. Chores develop skills and responsibility that translate into new competencies and then confidence in their abilities to do these jobs.

Very young children can be given simple chores, such as collecting their toys and putting them in baskets or boxes when they finish playing. Preschoolers can learn to put dirty clothes in a hamper and carry their dishes to the sink counter. As children grow, chores should reflect more responsibility and skill around the house.

To make chores more tolerable, make sure that your child understands the steps required. Rather than saying, "It's your job to take care of the cat," give clear, specific instructions that will be understood—"Pour out the dry food, empty the litter box." If your child is old enough to read, written descriptions of chores and a schedule to check off when she completes them will help avoid excuses. ("I didn't know that was my job. I thought it was Kayla's turn.") Many children love to check sheets or stick stars on charts because they show visible proof for all they've accomplished.

Be flexible and don't expect perfection. So your child missed some fingerprints when she sponged off the door frames—don't grab the sponge from her hands and do the job over again in front of her. This only deflates her confidence and doesn't enable her to become increasingly competent as she improves her skills.

Don't delegate chores that are too difficult or daunting. Try to make them fit each child's age, ability, and time. If it's examination week, for example, be flexible enough to say, "I know you're really studying hard this week, so I'll do that one for you today." Statements and generous gestures like this will model cooperation for your child. The next time you're extremely busy, she may offer to help you!

Doing chores along with your child also promotes connection. Washing the car together on a weekend morning can be a fun family activity, as can washing dishes, watering the garden, raking leaves, or shoveling snow. Even daily duties like walking the dog can be opportunities for togetherness. Rather than handing your daughter the dog's leash and sending her out the door, go along with her. It's a chance for both of you to get some exercise as well as talk and listen to each other.

A special note about chores—don't take your child's efforts for granted. When she completes her chores, acknowledge that fact and express your appreciation. Gratitude is a powerful connection and confidence booster. Let her know how much you appreciate her contribution to the family.

Resilience in Times of Great Need

The ultimate act of resilience is to turn to another human being in times of extreme need and say, "Brother or sister, I need a hand." This is never easy, but it may be necessary. We want children to become adults who can seek help without shame. If they have the experience of service, they will have learned a vital life lesson: It feels good to give; it is deeply rewarding to help other human beings. People who contribute to others' well-being don't feel burdened or put upon; they feel honored, even blessed, to have been in the right place at the right time, perhaps with the right training. They often get more than they give. People with this experience can turn to others more freely because they're equipped with the understanding that the person guiding them through troubled times is there because she wants to be there. Children deserve to learn this lesson through the opportunity of making a genuine contribution to another person's life. They will learn there is no shame in reaching out, only a moment of authentic humanity.

PART 4

Coping

Getting a Grip on Stress

No matter how competent and confident children are, no matter how secure their connections, how sterling their characters, or how generously they contribute to the world, resilience requires a wide repertoire of skills to cope with stress and challenge. Here's the bottom line—life is stressful, so we need to prepare children to handle it effectively. In other words, they need to become competent at *coping* if they are to be resilient.

While we'd like to think that childhood is idyllic, children are not as shielded from stress as we might imagine. They worry about school, their peers, the future, their identity, and their appearance. They want to please us, and sometimes they worry about us. They sense parents' stress even when they're small. Children pick up on all our spoken and unspoken words. When we seem unnerved, they feel anxious. Older children worry about things beyond their immediate circles that we may presume they don't notice—war, violence, even the economy. They don't have the benefit of having lived through cycles of such events and haven't adopted the "this too shall pass" protective beliefs that adults use to move on.

How Do I Know if My Child Is Too Stressed, and What Do I Do?

Stress makes us terribly uncomfortable. We feel nervous, unsafe, insecure, and ungrounded. We can't think clearly. We become restless, lose sleep, become tired, and maybe get headaches. Our muscles ache, our bellies feel bloated, and our hearts throb. We grow irritable, less patient, and much less understanding of others.

Children experience many of the same feelings, but they usually don't understand the connections between how underlying stress drives their moodiness or irritability. That's why parents need to always consider whether their child's moods, isolation, tantrums, hostility, or even rage may be signs of stress or even depression. This can sometimes be difficult because it's normal for children to have occasional tantrums and for teenagers to be moody.

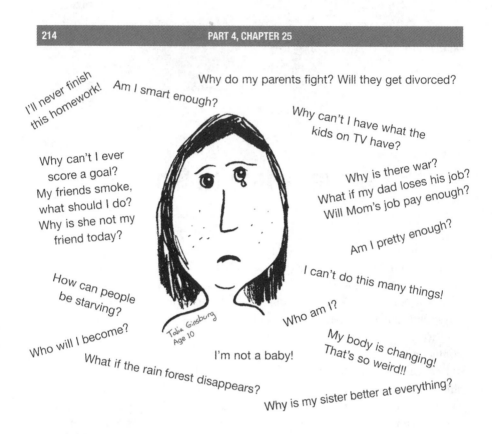

Children's bodies can accumulate stress just as adult bodies do. Frequent patterns of headache, belly pain, and fatigue tend to point to the possibility that stress is driving those uncomfortable feelings. This is especially true when there is no medical explanation. Tell your pediatrician if you've noticed that physical symptoms seem to be tied to stressful events. The health professional will still consider medical concerns but will be better able to get to the bottom of stress-related symptoms. (See Chapter 36.)

Many of the stress-reduction strategies offered in this book can be useful in helping children and teens manage existing stress. These strategies are also designed to be preventive. We hope that children who are well equipped to deal with stress will experience less of it in the first place. If you're worried about your child's ability to cope or just know that she has been under recent stress, please use your child's teacher, counselor, pediatrician, or clergy to help you decide the level of support your child needs.

Dealing With Stress

Children, adolescents, and adults all hate discomfort, whether it's emotional or physical. To avoid it, we figure out some way to cope and make ourselves feel comfortable again. Anything that will banish those disquieting feelings will make us feel more settled, at least for the moment.

We have positive and negative ways of coping. It's not that positive ways always work and negative ones always fail. On the contrary, some negative ways offer immediate relief. The difference is that positive coping strategies enhance well-being and ultimately lead to at least partial relief. Negative strategies might feel great and offer quick relief, but they end up causing harm to the individual or community and ultimately perpetuate and intensify the cycle of stress.

Virtually all the behaviors we fear in children and teenagers are misguided attempts to diminish their stress. Procrastination, feigned laziness, and boredom are methods of dealing with school-related stress. They temporarily push stress out of sight and mind for a while. Bullying, smoking, drugs, gangs, sex, disordered eating, and self-mutilation are also efforts to deal with stress. Our challenge is to raise children who have a variety of positive coping strategies that will enhance their strengths (see diagram on page 217). We may have our greatest effect in helping children and teens avoid negativity and dangerous behaviors by equipping them with a wide range of alternative, effective, and safe coping strategies.

Unfortunately, I can't guarantee that your child will never try a worrisome behavior, even if he is emotionally intelligent and equipped with good coping strategies, because some of those feared behaviors are fun or feel good. A young teen may try drugs to test his limits, rebel, or have fun with friends. We hope he will move beyond this phase quickly. But a young person who seeks solace through drugs, who uses an altered state of consciousness to mask his feelings, is destined for addiction. Children with better, safer, and healthier means of coping with stress don't need to blur their consciousness with drugs.

Coping Styles

Everyone has an individual style in response to challenge. A great deal of research has looked at how different people cope and what styles help them cope most effectively. Experts have identified key differences in coping styles. Some people cope by tackling a problem head-on and trying to fix it as best they can. Other people focus more on the emotions that those problems create; they tend to do what makes them feel better to decrease their discomfort. Both styles, *problem-focused* and *emotion-focused,* are active styles that attempt to engage the problem. Other people choose to avoid the problem; they use full-blown *denial* or its close cousin, *withdrawal.*

People who choose to engage a problem actively tend to choose 1 of 2 approaches—they try to change the stressor itself to make themselves feel more comfortable, or they change themselves just enough to adapt to the stressor.

Children have the same styles, though they may not be aware of them. Ruby feels overwhelmed by all the homework in her 20-lb backpack. When she decides to break her assignments into segments that she can handle one at a time, Ruby uses a problem-focused strategy. When Amit's friends challenge him to smoke cigarettes and he talks with his best friend Kyle about why he doesn't want to smoke, Amit attacks the problem. When Maria feels frustrated with her parents' "old-fashioned, ridiculous rules" and chooses to sit down and negotiate compromises with them, she goes right to the source of her stress to solve the problem.

Some children who use emotion-focused strategies want to escape stressful feelings and may choose to deny the problem exists. What works for them? Drinking beer to cloud their awareness of the problem or bullying others to feel in control may make them feel better in the short term. But not all emotion-focused styles are negative. Many can be positive if they help a child deal with feelings in ways that are healthy, like exercise or meditation, or release pent-up stress, like journaling, crying, or laughing (see Chapter 28).

Stress and Coping Styles

As children and adults think about dealing with challenges, a fundamental decision must be made—how much am I willing to change? Sometimes we try to change the environment. For example, if Amit's conversation with Kyle ended with Kyle's decision not to smoke, Amit would have created a safer, more problem-free environment. It would be less stressful because he could hang out with at least one friend, Kyle, who also doesn't smoke. Amit has changed his environment without compromising. But suppose Kyle convinced Amit to "just try one" cigarette. Amit may decide that the best way of managing his stress is to smoke just a little, just to get Kyle off his back. As parents, we fear where this is leading, but it's worth recognizing that some compromise may be the wisest decision for a kid in certain situations. After a hurricane, a person can't choose to make the storm reverse and "unflood" his house. He needs to cope by finding himself a makeshift shelter.

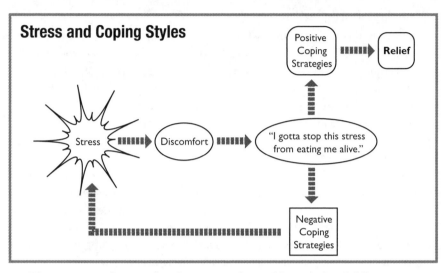

Stress and Coping Styles

The strategies discussed so far engage the problem or the child's reaction to the problem. Other coping strategies do not engage at all. Younger children often use denial or avoidance. They don't notice the problem because their cognitive abilities are limited or they find it safest to enter a fantasy world. Fantasy is great fun and builds creativity, but when it's used as a response to a stressful problem, it may be a route to denial. Older children and adults also use denial to convince themselves and others that no problem exists. (How many times a day do we hear, "No problem"?) Sometimes we're aware of a problem and aren't truly in denial, but we choose to ignore it, play down its significance, or withdraw from the people or circumstances that cause our discomfort. In the worst-case scenario, withdrawal can lead to isolation or depression. Substance use can also be included among avoidance or disengagement strategies because users withdraw from reality.

A word about denial and withdrawal—it would be a mistake to believe that we *should* rise to every challenge and face it head-on. Certainly long-term avoidance of a situation will never overcome the obstacle. But sometimes a problem is so overwhelming or frightening that it is temporarily wise to say, "I really don't care; it doesn't bother me." I have learned time and again from patients who have every reason to be furious at their circumstances that they take the position of not caring because it is all they can handle. I urge parents to raise children who can deal with emotions and confront problems, but I caution against pushing children to show they care just because we know they ought to care. We shouldn't force all children to face every struggle or dilemma. Give them time and space and allow for the skills to be developed that will enable them to react appropriately.

Although it's a mistake to state with certainty how anyone *should* cope, it is generally agreed that people who engage a problem do better than those who deny or withdraw from it. Children and adolescents who use problem-focused coping strategies to address stressors, rather than the uncomfortable emotions they produce, usually fare better because the problem's intensity is reduced. When only emotions are dealt with, the problem remains to strike again. But positively oriented emotion-focused strategies are also useful because they help us feel better in the short term and may foster interpersonal connections as we seek support.

Resilient children are able to address problems competently *and* manage the physical and emotional discomfort that stress creates. They also need to feel comfortable withdrawing from or avoiding problems so they can conserve energy to address those problems they are prepared to change or solve. The challenge is to raise a child with effective problem-focused coping strategies, healthy emotion-focused strategies, and safe, thoughtful avoidance strategies.

Changing Coping Skills as Your Child Grows

A growing body of research explores which coping strategies work best in varied situations for children at different developmental levels. The findings are beyond the scope of this chapter, but I want to emphasize that coping skills change over time. It would be a mistake to think that a 3-year-old requires the same approach as an older child or adolescent.

Even infants experience stress and have their own strategies to address it. They cry to get an adult to meet their needs. Then they calm as they suckle. An adult's very presence is enough to return them to a lulled calm. This is also true for small children who can calm themselves with a snuggle and draw their sense of security and normalcy from parents. Other children keep a security blanket or toy with them everywhere to comfort them with something familiar in a world full of unfamiliar objects and strangers.

Preschool children begin to develop fantasies to soothe upsetting emotions and reassure themselves. Think about how many fables and fairy tales involve vulnerable children being rescued by a superhero or fantasy figure. (I remember that a shadow in my room always made me feel safe. Okay, so I was a little strange, but the night-light cast a shadow from the moldings along the ceiling. My shadow looked exactly like Superman flying with his cape open. If I felt unsafe, I always reminded myself that Superman could fly to rescue me if I called him. Sadly, the Dean didn't let me take my molding with me, making this coping strategy harder to access when I went to college.)

Another common coping strategy for young children is avoidance—don't see it, run away from it, and the problem ceases to exist. As children reach school age, they begin to grasp how stress affects their emotions and become better able to begin calming those emotions. They start to problem-solve and take active steps to address their concerns as they get older. They learn to relax without thinking about a fantasy figure to solve their problems. They may reassure themselves that parents will become available if they are not present at the moment. They learn to reframe situations and soothe their emotions by reassuring themselves with positive self-talk. As children approach adolescence, their coping strategies become increasingly sophisticated.

My point here is not to make you obsess about which strategies your child uses at different ages, but help you realize that your child's repertoire evolves over time. If you deliberately or actively focus on coping with a younger child, you may only add to his worries by making him wonder whether he is doing a good-enough job in dealing with his fears. Focus your energies instead on modeling appropriate coping strategies. Help preschool-aged and older children know that most of their worries represent a problem, and they can take steps to address that problem. Expose children to the kind of things they'll be able to draw from later as they widen their repertoire.

When you expose them to exercise, the creative arts, and reading, for example, you needn't say, "This will help you deal with problems that may arise." Instead, expose them to these wonderful things for the sheer sake of enjoyment. Trust their own natural resilience to draw on them when they are needed as coping strategies.

CHAPTER 26

Taking Action

I have met remarkable young people who've thrived despite enormous stresses. I've asked them why and how they have managed to survive and succeed. By listening to what works for my patients and their families and by synthesizing their wisdom with the scientific literature on effective coping, I have developed a 10-part stress-reduction plan. It is not a 10-step plan; there is no designated order to approach stress. Instead it offers a repertoire to draw from at appropriate times. For example, some strategies involve thinking, but during times of extreme stress, it makes more sense to work out the stress through exercise before even attempting to resolve an issue with thought.

These 10 parts will be addressed in chapters 26, 27, and 28. Here's a preview.

1. Identify and then address the problem.
2. Avoid stress when possible.
3. Let some things go.
4. Contribute to the world.
5. The power of exercise.
6. Active relaxation.
7. Eat well.
8. Sleep well.
9. Take instant vacations.
10. Release emotional tension.

Each of the points includes a variety of activities and actions to handle stress. My goal is to offer you and your family as wide a range of useful coping strategies as possible. While this plan is quite comprehensive, no one should expect to use all the techniques. I suggest picking an item or two from each category to see which ones fit best. For example, the creative arts offer vital outlets for expression, but not everyone needs to excel at art, music, dance, and photography. As you tailor a stress-reduction plan to your needs, keep in mind that approaches can change over time. I'm trying to say gently, "Don't stress about the stress plan." It has too many ideas for anyone to do them all. It has to be individually tailored and fluid, changing with a child's development and circumstances.

You'll notice that nothing in this 10-part plan specifically addresses childhood. The plan can help adults and children cope with a stressful world, which brings me to an essential point—parents who use and actively model this approach not only help themselves reduce stress, but they also influence their children far more effectively than any words they say or activities in which they enroll their kids.

Even the youngest children pick up ambivalent messages. They know the difference between what parents say and what they actually do. Adolescents pounce on hypocrisy, point it out mercilessly, and use it to explain why parents shouldn't have the authority to set rules of behavior. So if we don't want our children to use negative strategies to cope with stress, such as fighting, smoking, or using drugs, we have to use healthy strategies ourselves. We can't model problem-solving if we take a nap to avoid our discomfort each time we get stressed. We can't tell kids it's good to talk about their feelings if we bottle up our own emotions. We can't teach the danger of drugs while using alcohol to treat those emotions. We can't talk about the importance of balancing our lives if we haven't taken a day off in a month.

I want to give you a prescription to take care of yourself. Don't think it's selfish to have a hobby, take time to relax, or have creative outlets. When you take care of yourself, you show your children how to be emotionally healthier. You are the model they will follow as they learn to manage stress. Role modeling is most effective when you talk aloud about what you're doing. Some of the following self-talk suggestions give you a glimpse of ideas in the stress-reduction plan:

"This is a gigantic work assignment to finish in just a week. I'm going to break it down into smaller parts that I can handle." Then later say, "I feel so much better. I really got a lot done."

"I'm so stressed out that I can't even think. I'm going for a run. That always makes me feel better."

"I really need to clear my head. I'm going to take some slow, deep breaths and imagine I'm on that beautiful beach we visited last summer. Remember that sunset?"

"I really need a few minutes to myself after the day I've had. I'm going to soak in the bathtub for a half hour."

"I'm so angry that I can't think straight. If I make a decision now about how to deal with your behavior, you won't like it one bit. Right now I need some time to myself to cool off. I'm going for a long walk to relax. Then we're going to deal with this problem."

"You see, darling, when I paint this picture, it tells a story of how I feel. That way, I don't have to keep all my feelings inside."

"Oh, I had such a hard time today. Come and give me hugs. I always feel better when I'm with people I love."

"I need to figure out how to handle this situation with the neighbors. I'm going to call Aunt Mattie. Just talking makes me calmer, and sometimes she helps me find a totally different way of looking at things."

"I'm not even going near that casino. Just being near it makes me want to spend money. If I'm not there, I don't miss it a bit."

"You know, I feel lousy today. I ate a bunch of junk food instead of lunch and I always feel sluggish after doing that."

"I'm exhausted. I broke my rule and fell asleep while I was still worried about work. I sleep so much better whenever I relax before bed or at least make a list of things I have to do the next day so they don't keep spinning in my head."

Before we plunge into the details of the stress-management plan, I want to make some suggestions about how to use it. At first it may seem that this set of strategies is a résumé for life. In fact, if children learn some of these techniques, they will build a balanced résumé that prepares them for college and adulthood. As you guide children in developing these approaches, here are the basic points to remember.

- When you choose strategies from this plan, select those you think will work for your child, not those that will impress someone else. For example, if you focus on the musical expression part of the plan because your child loves playing the guitar, just let her play the guitar; don't make her take bassoon lessons because you think that will impress a college admissions committee.
- The plan cannot be imposed on a child; it has to be welcomed to be effective. If your child doesn't take to one strategy, try another.
- Really, don't stress about the stress-management plan! Don't feel that your child must be exposed to everything in the plan to cope with stress successfully.

As children learn to manage stress, they need to find that fine balance between living in the moment and working for the future. One strategy is to enjoy the little pleasures surrounding us, but it's difficult to do if we are always thinking about it. So as you guide your child through these wide choices of coping strategies, take it casually. Let your child's individualized plan develop over time, and don't worry about every detail. Enjoy your child and your life right now. By your actions and attitudes, you'll be modeling a far more effective approach than any written plan. Keep in mind that children at different developmental levels naturally need different coping strategies. Don't expect a 3-year-old to problem-solve. At that age, escaping through fantasy (perhaps by acting out a situation with action figures, dolls, or puppets) is normal and healthy.

Chapter 39 is designed for tweens and teens to build their own coping strategy. Children younger than 10 years will need more direct guidance from adults. I encourage you to share this plan with as many young people as you can reach. You can also find it at www.fosteringresilience.com and on the American Academy of Pediatrics Web site for parents, www.HealthyChildren. org. The plans in Chapter 39 and on the Web, however, do not offer the detailed explanation that this chapter does. The remainder of this chapter and the following 2 chapters are intended for parents or child professionals as a guide for helping children learn to manage stress. Many of the techniques are explained so that you will be able to follow the techniques yourself. This is intentional, done so you can more easily be a role model.

1. Identify and Then Address the Problem.

Problem-solving is the most effective and basic way to begin coping with stress. Any effective approach to managing stress begins by identifying the concern and determining what can be done to solve it. Without this attack-the-problem-first strategy, we chase our tail. We react and feel better, only to need to react again because the problem persists.

Two important steps are necessary to problem-solving. The first is to make a realistic assessment of the magnitude of the problem; the second is to break it into manageable steps.

It's inefficient to tackle problems until we first remove the barriers of anxiety, fear, and frustration that get in the way of solving them. As a starting point, learn to assess a situation realistically. We may be able to teach children to be problem-solvers, but those lessons are useless if kids cannot manage the emotions and discomfort caused by stress. Clear thought and steady nerves are required to assess and solve most problems. We can't think clearly if we're running from our modern-day tigers; we cannot sit down and serenely resolve our differences with a tiger who's charging at us. Nor can we politely ask the tiger for a time-out so we can plan our escape route. Problem-solving is our escape route here, and we simply can't do it while fleeing. The strategies in the next 2 chapters clear our minds; and sometimes exercise or relaxation techniques alone are enough to regain our rational thought and allow us to downgrade situations from crises to manageable events. You may find that these techniques to clear the mind, when combined with strategies that break problems into small pieces, are enough to help your child manage problems.

A problem sometimes feels so overwhelming that until a young person thinks differently about it, she can't possibly begin to deal with it. In effect, she is paralyzed by anxiety or catastrophic thoughts. When this happens, she feels powerless and can't imagine any strategy will work. The thinking clearly skills discussed in Chapter 9 help manage emotional responses by reframing catastrophic thoughts into more realistic appraisals. These cognitive or thinking strategies help young people calm themselves and use their intellectual abilities to solve problems. It may be that the strategies shared in Chapter 9, drawn from Drs Reivich and Seligman's work, are needed to further guide a child to think clearly. It's also possible that children experience so much anxiety or fear that professional guidance is needed to help them more clearly differentiate real tragedies from those manageable bumps in the road. Even if you determine your child's starting point should be to seek professional guidance to teach her to rethink how she interprets stressful events, the other coping strategies offered in this plan will likely still be helpful.

Once someone has a realistic appraisal of the nature of the problem and whether it poses a real immediate danger or one that just needs to be addressed, the next step is to break it into manageable pieces. As long as we visualize a problem as huge, it will overwhelm us. If we view it as a mountain, we cannot imagine navigating around it and certainly cannot imagine scaling it. On the other hand, if we understand that a mountain is really just a series of hills piled on top of each other, it feels less foreboding. If we imagine climbing the hills one at a time, the top of the mountain feels less overwhelming—even better if we understand that hills are just made up of rocks and dirt and that with shovels we have the ability to move these hills.

The way we break the mountains into hills is by taking a problem and breaking it into its component parts. This includes creating lists and timelines to make work manageable. It also includes looking at an overwhelming social problem and considering which inroads will solve it. For example, when a 13-year-old girl has been rejected by her group of friends, she may become emotionally overwhelmed and never imagine having another friend again, let alone reconnecting with this group. If she can get past her catastrophic thoughts, she might be able to think the problem through and realize that one of the friends may be able to create an avenue for her to reconnect with the others. As we tackle each step, it becomes easier to take on the next.

It becomes easier to move the hills when we have the figurative shovels (or skills) to move the dirt. If the problem feels catastrophic, turn first to the skills taught in Chapter 9 on thinking clearly. If the problem is homework, the shovels are confidence, knowledge, academic preparation, and an organizational plan. If the problem is social, the shovels are emotional and social intelligence coupled with some of the peer navigation strategies discussed in Chapter 13. If the problem creates emotional pain, even to the point that one feels incapable of feeling the pain for fear of opening Pandora's box, the shovels are strategies to safely release emotions (as will be discussed in Chapter 28).

2. Avoid Stress When Possible.

We know we can reframe situations by changing negative thinking patterns such as, "Why does this always happen to me?" and looking instead for other, more effective ways to figure out solutions. Along related lines, we can avoid negative situations to reduce stress. This technique involves a little analysis. What brings you down? What makes you tense or upset? What always gets to you?

I teach my patients to think about which situations have gotten them in trouble in the past, then pay attention to the subtle signals their bodies send out to warn of a similar potential problem. If they learn to pay attention to those sensations (like butterflies, anxiety, and heart racing), they can recognize what might get them into trouble before they actually find themselves in a crisis.

The answer to "What brings you down or always gets to you?" can usually be found in these categories—people, places, and things. If we teach kids to identify the people who frustrate or bother them, places where stress usually rises, and things that provoke or intensify stress, they can learn when and how to avoid those stressors. They cannot always avoid them, of course. If a child must sit next to an annoying classmate and the teacher refuses to change the seating arrangement, the child can't completely avoid the people (in this case, the classmate) or place (the classroom). But the simple act of identifying the situation helps children recognize potential stress so they can try to ignore the pesky classmate. In other cases, they can avoid negativity by staying away from the corner of the playground where the mean kids hang out or going to the mall at a different time than the friends who dumped them last week. If scary stories or movies make children nervous, they can learn to choose more upbeat books or movies.

In the case of teenagers, the key to staying out of trouble is recognizing which people, places, and things have brought them down in the past and are likely to pull them down again. People, places, and things are a central theme in many recovery programs. The concept is used to prepare people with addictions to return home. To succeed they must learn to stay as far away as possible from the triggers of their old behavior and the forces that pressure them to relive old habits. It's particularly important to avoid friends with whom kids have shared bad habits. Those friends have a great deal invested in making sure that others don't rise above them.

Marc, for example, used to get high with a trio of friends, Andrew, Jorge, and Jacob. Marc found his life seriously affected by drugs. His grades plunged and he had a near-death experience. He realized that he had no choice but to quit drugs. Jorge, his pal since kindergarten, also wanted to stop clouding his own mind and supported Marc's decision. But Andrew and Jacob weren't ready to quit. Every time they thought about quitting, they pushed the thought away. Facing their own stress was too overwhelming. "Everybody does it," they told themselves. "This is just what you gotta do to survive." When Marc found the motivation and resolve to quit, their fallacy of "everybody does it" fell apart. They became motivated to find ways to ensure Marc's recovery failed—to pull him back down again—which allowed them to avoid guilt and their own demons. People, places, and things—kids who understand the negative influences in their lives are prepared to avoid major sources of stress and move beyond negative behaviors. For Marc and Jorge to continue to stay away from drugs, they learned that they had to stop hanging out with Andrew and Jacob.

Why wait for a problem? There is no reason to have to pick up the pieces if the problem is avoided at the outset. The old adage, "The strongest man is the man who does not need to fight," applies here. It is much easier to avoid problems from a distance than up close. Teach your child that many problems do not have to be confronted—they are best managed by avoiding them in the first place.

3. Let Some Things Go.

We want to tackle problems, but we need to acknowledge that not every problem is worth attacking. Some problems may upset us but are of no real consequence. Problems (like bad weather) may bother us, but we are powerless to change them—that game we were looking forward to is simply rained out. To conserve our energy for the things we can change, we need to learn to let go of problems we can't fix. It's important for parents to model for children that we sometimes advocate strongly for change but at other times, we just need to move on.

Optimism is an important trait for many situations. That can-do spirit sometimes gives you that extra push to try a little harder because you believe the effort will pay off. On the other hand, not every problem can be tackled.

Even though we want to raise children with that "I can handle it" attitude, it's important to have the ability to realistically assess a situation to see whether it should be handled or if the better way to go is to conserve your energy for an issue you can handle. This idea is best summarized with the well-known Serenity Prayer.

> G-d grant me the serenity
> to accept the things I cannot change;
> the courage to change the things I can;
> and the wisdom to know the difference.

4. Contribute to the World.

Chapter 24 is devoted to the importance of contribution as one of the critical 7 Cs of resilience. It merits a recap to earn its place in the stress-reduction plan. Contribution helps people cope for 2 major reasons.

First, when we contribute to our communities or attempt to repair the world in any small way, we put aside our own troubles. Whether we volunteer on a regular basis or only occasionally, we contribute to an effort bigger than ourselves and gain some perspective on our own stressful situations. The thank-yous we receive remind us of our own value even if we are not feeling good about ourselves.

People who have faced major misfortunes often turn to activities that allow them to give something back or heal their own traumas. At the adult level, for example, mothers of children killed by drunk drivers are committed to Mothers Against Drunk Driving (MADD). Teenagers who have lost relatives or friends are active in Students Against Destructive Decisions (SADD). Even young children benefit by contributing to causes like Alex's Lemonade Stand, the nationwide effort to raise funds for cancer research that was started by Alex Scott of suburban Philadelphia before she died at the age of 8 years. She used this mission to give back even while bravely fighting cancer. Her parents and community are aided in their healing process by helping other children and their families.

Second, remember the ultimate act of resilience is to turn to another and request assistance without humiliation or shame. When your child makes a real contribution to another person's life, he will learn that it feels good to give. And at a time of unimagined stress, he will more easily seek help from another person because he will not feel like a burden. He may feel instead as if he has given, and it is now his turn to receive.

Taking Care of Your Body

The following 4 parts of the plan can help children and adults manage stress more effectively by nurturing minds that are better prepared to meet and overcome emotional challenges by being calm and focused and bodies that are prepared to remain healthy and responsive to physical challenges. This chapter discusses exercise, relaxation, nutrition, and sleep. Each benefits the body and the mind. The lessons learned here will contribute to a child's resilience now and—more importantly—will promote healthy habits for a lifetime.

5. The Power of Exercise.

If I had only a few moments with every young person to teach how to manage or reduce stress, I would focus on the transformative power of exercise. Exercise can change the body and make it stronger and better able to withstand all kinds of challenges. In moments, it can transform moods like nervousness, frustration, and anger, and it can have an ongoing effect on anxiety, attention-deficit/hyperactivity disorder (ADHD), and even depression. Appropriate exercise can help alertness, focus, and concentration and can even contribute to a good night's sleep, which has its own stress-management benefits. Finally, people who exercise may be more likely to choose more healthful foods.

Whenever I talk to young patients about stress, I start by explaining that stress is not our enemy. In fact, when well managed, it is quite useful. Some experts have compared well-managed stress to the strings of a guitar. If there is no tension, the strings will not make a sound, Yet when there is too much tension, the sound is harsh and unpredictable, and the strings may even break. An appropriate amount of stress is the key to making music. Likewise, our bodies contain many different hormones that sometimes help us respond rapidly to danger and other times calm us. Fear causes the release of adrenaline, but exercise and relaxation release endorphins and other brain chemicals that are calming. Being aware of this dynamic is one of the secrets to finding the right personal balance that works for you or your child.

A rush of adrenaline is harmless in certain situations, like taking a scary amusement park ride. It puts us on alert at other times, such as when we're walking along a dark, deserted road. Or it prepares us to run from tigers or modern dangers. When I tell young people about our ancestor Sam, I explain a few choice details, depending on the child's age. Even a 6- or 7-year-old can understand that blood had to rush to Sam's legs so he could sprint from a tiger in the jungle. I then explain that the reason kids feel butterflies in their tummies when they're anxious or afraid is because blood leaves their gut to rush to their legs to prepare them for running. Kids also understand that their hearts beat faster and their breathing is more rapid to help them run. They particularly like learning about how their pupils dilate to let in more light so they can see well while running.

Few kids today have to run from wild tigers, but they certainly have other tigers in their lives that provoke the same physical responses to stress. When young people learn to listen to their bodies and read their stress responses, they become better able to cope. This is especially true when those stress responses are overly strong and instead of helping, actually get in the way of meeting a challenge. If a bully starts to chase them, the shift from a calm state to an aroused state makes kids ready to run and is an appropriate response. But it's counterproductive when the "tiger" is a history examination. They can't focus on studying if they're only focused on fleeing. Remember that you're not supposed to turn to a charging animal and request a time-out. "Excuse me a moment, I am taking a history exam. Could you attack me a bit later?"

Move It!

The most direct way to listen to your body when you're stressed is to exercise. Your body is shouting, "A tiger is gaining on me fast; I don't want to get eaten! Hey, legs, get moving!" If you don't move, the stress hormones keep circulating, unused and confused about why you aren't paying attention. In fact, these recirculating unused hormones explain much of chronic disease. The hormone that replenishes our bodies after bursts of adrenaline is cortisol. Excess cortisol leads to weight gain, high blood pressure, and heart disease.

This body confusion occurs because our stress hormones are saying "run" and we are sitting still. The solution to stress therefore lies largely in listening to our bodies. It makes biological sense for exercise to be the starting point of stress management. Unfortunately, it's often the first thing to go when people think about time management because they fail to realize that most tasks are performed more efficiently *after* they exercise.

When one of my patients is cramming for a test and feeling tense or nervous, I tell him to go outside and run, jump rope, play some basketball, or kick around a soccer ball. This physical activity simulates running from the tiger and relieves stress by using up that surging adrenaline. Once the body thinks it has survived the challenge, it can kick back, chill, and prepare for the next adventure—in this case, to study better. When kids tell me, "I can't exercise. I have no time because I've got to study," I tell them, "You have no time *not* to exercise. You'll think better, be more alert, and be able to remember what you study."

How Much Exercise and What Kind?

Exercise reduces stress even when no figurative tigers are chasing us. We should exercise regularly when all is going well because it keeps our bodies healthy. Healthy people manage stress better. If we raise children to be active, they'll enjoy lifelong physical and emotional health benefits. We now know that people who exercise regularly protect their brains and keep them developing well into advanced age. John Ratey, MD, summarizes exciting new evidence behind the power of exercise to help people think more clearly and manage a range of behavioral concerns, including ADHD, anxiety, and depression, in *Spark: The Revolutionary New Science of Exercise and the Brain.*

Exercise is key to successful stress management. It should not be the source of stress. As with all things, we seek balance, not compulsive but healthy exercise. It doesn't have to include competition; movement itself offers benefits.

Parents sometimes tell me, "My kids get plenty of exercise. Tonya plays soccer 4 times a week and does gymnastics year-round. Eriq is on the swim team and plays floor hockey." Participating in organized athletics is wonderful, but I worry that some children are pushed too hard to become little superstars, which simply is not healthy if they focus on one sport intently and year-round.

Traditionally, youth sports seasons lasted 3 to 5 months. Kids trained, played hard, and then went out for a different sport the following season. Each sport used different sets of muscles, bones, joints, and parts of the mind, so the body had an opportunity to alternate movement and thought patterns from season to season. In recent years, though, a trend has appeared to breed young athletes to focus on the same sport all year long. This causes more repetitive wear and tear on the developing muscles, bones, and joints, which leads to an increase in sports-related injuries and, potentially, single-patterned strategic thinking.

Athletic pursuits offer children a chance to be at their most competent and confident, but I urge parents to make sure that they are well managed by coaches who understand young athletic bodies. If children love a sport and enjoy playing, that's terrific. But if they are pushed to excel for the primary purpose of getting into college or winning an athletic scholarship, that is not always healthy and can produce unnecessary stress. A better solution is to encourage them to exercise and participate in a variety of athletic activities.

Needless to say, parents shouldn't select sports for children or make them sign up for certain leagues if they aren't really interested. Encourage them to play sports, but let them pick their own activities based on what they enjoy with their friends around the neighborhood or at school. Some children shy away from competitive team sports. That's okay, as long as they remain active through play or individual sports. Whether or not they enjoy team sports, all kids should be exposed to individual sports like track, swimming, bicycling, or skating and some 2-player sports like tennis, golf, or racquetball because they'll be able to do these activities and reap the health benefits throughout adulthood. By the time many kids reach high school, it is harder to gather a whole team together, but they can usually find one other person to play with.

Most importantly, exercise should be fun. When your children are young, just let them play without worrying about scores and rigid rules. As they get older, let them choose their athletic activities. If they feel that participating in sports is a chore or another kind of pressure, they may give up on exercise as soon as they're old enough to make their own decisions. Walking, riding bikes, hiking, and swimming are lifelong activities that make a difference in adult health and are great for family togetherness. You don't have to push any of these on your children, but if you offer them as healthful, fun ways for the family to connect with each other, your children may enjoy these same activities with their children. In this way, healthy living is a multigenerational investment in your family. Paul Stricker, MD, FAAP, speaks about all these issues and more in *Sports Success R$_x$! Your Child's Prescription for the Best Experience: How to Maximize Potential AND Minimize Pressure.*

Releasing Stress and Conquering Anger

Stress hormones generate a fight-or-flight response. Fear or nervousness makes us want to flee. So it makes sense that any exercise that involves running (including most sports) or moving your legs (like swimming, dancing, or jumping rope) will help relieve that anxiety. On the other hand, raw anger drives us toward fighting, a behavior we certainly want to discourage. When children and teens are angry, I urge them to recognize what that rage is doing to their bodies and to release it by screaming, ripping up papers, or hitting pillows or punching bags. I call this *sham fighting.* These are excellent ways to release anger-induced stress. When they're irate and "want to get something off my chest," I tell them, "Then lie down on your back and lift weights to get it off your chest, or do push-ups." Anaerobic exercise, such as weight lifting, can give young people a sense of control and power. Just as they think they can't do one more rep, they somehow find the strength from within themselves to push it out. This also engages the mind, allowing whatever made them angry to seem less important, even lost in the full-on focus required for such activities.

6. Active Relaxation.

Relaxation is often thought of as the absence of activity. Certainly, to relax you need some downtime just to be. But by *active* relaxation, I mean you can take active steps to transform your body into a relaxed state. If you are really busy, you might even have to schedule time to achieve a relaxed state, but the health benefits and efficiency you will gain in other areas of your life are well worth the investment. With a little practice, we can train the body to have a relaxation response that will help us be more efficient and feel better, and contribute to our health. *Guided meditation, visualization,* and *progressive relaxation* are some useful techniques that I will discuss throughout this chapter. While each of them sounds very different or even exotic, they are actually quite simple and similar; each has particular strengths that might be tailored to appeal to the uniqueness of your child's strengths.

By exercising or being physically active, kids use up all those stress hormones that tell their bodies to flee the tiger. After they use them up, or if they are unable to exercise them away, children can still learn to fool their bodies into thinking they aren't stressed, which translates to more peace of mind. To see how this is possible, it's necessary to understand the power of the mind over the body. There is still much that we don't understand about the mind-body connection, but we do know that certain techniques can be powerful aids on the road to wellness—the oil, you might say, that helps all your child's other skills run more smoothly.

For starters, we have 2 nervous systems. The *voluntary* nervous system makes our muscles do what we want, like stand up, walk, lift a heavy box, or climb stairs. The *involuntary* nervous system controls the functions that happen automatically without thought or planning, like heart beating, swallowing, breathing, and digestion. Interestingly, it actually has 2 contrasting components. One fine-tunes our body for relaxation, thinking, and digestion. The other rapidly adjusts to prepare us for a sprint or battle. Here's the really cool part that science is only beginning to understand: We can take control of our involuntary nervous system if we use our brains to trick the system. By definition, stress is tense and relaxation is supple. Our bodies cannot be calm and in crisis simultaneously. That simple fact is the key to our mind's ability to relax the body. If we learn to fool our bodies into sending out signals to our relaxed, involuntary nervous system, we can flip a figurative switch and our stress hormones stop firing. Our relaxation response then takes over. This is one of the key secrets to many ancient methods of healing.

Because the 2 components of the involuntary nervous system cannot work together at once, we can fool our bodies by making them do the opposite of what they'd do under stress. This isn't always easy. We can't reroute our blood back to our bellies after it has shifted to our legs in preparation for running away. We can't shrink our pupils, reverse our sweating, or stop our faces from flushing. It's extremely difficult to calm our thinking and slow our heart rates. Breathing, however, can be consciously influenced and therefore is the most direct way to flip that switch. In the next few pages, I'll give you a brief overview of techniques to calm the body. Some people who spend a lifetime learning to achieve a state of calm present these approaches in a much more comprehensive way. I wish only to help you consider techniques to choose and explore further if you choose.

Breathe to Relax

Controlled breathing is at the core of almost every relaxation technique. Slow, deep breathing is a highly effective way to fool a stressed body, and breathing exercises can be done at any time—while lying down, sitting, standing, walking, or even engaged in activities. Here's one simple method to get you started: Just sit comfortably with your back upright but not rigid. Put your feet flat on the floor if you're sitting in a chair or sit cross-legged on the floor. Let your hands rest halfway between your knees and hips and gently close your eyes. Begin by inhaling slowly and concentrating on your breath as it flows deep into your abdomen. Let your belly expand with air. As you inhale, notice whatever comes to mind, perhaps that the air is cool. Don't hold your breath; allow your lungs to empty slowly and naturally, and allow your mind to empty along with your lungs. You might notice that the outflowing air is warm. The key is to take it easy and fully engage your awareness in the repetition. Continue to breathe in and out in a relaxed, steady rhythm. Fill your lungs fully and exhale slowly, with no force or strain. When your attention wanders, as it likely will, focus on your breathing again. Remember, this is a technique to relieve stress, and being overly strict and performance-oriented can defeat the purpose. Congratulate yourself for noticing when your mind may have strayed some, and then gently return to the practice.

Interestingly this mind-body thing is a 2-way street, and sometimes how your body feels will affect your mind's ability to focus. Luckily the solution is the same. The breathing exercise you just learned is one of the most basic yet profound meditations—constantly returning your attention to the breath, truly marrying mind and body. For our purposes, we can define *meditation* as any method that helps free you of your thoughts' tendency to snowball and gain power over your body. With practice, many people discover greater levels of self-control.

Later, with a little practice, you can add in a slight pause at the end of each inhalation and exhalation. This opens the door to a deeper practice. Here's the breakdown. The in-breath is the opportunity to notice. Anything that comes up is fair game; it may be a thought, a feeling, or maybe just the sounds around you. Just notice it as you inhale. Then there is a slight, comfortable pause to simply recognize whatever may have come up. Hold no judgment and know that at least for now, you don't have to do anything with it. Just "be" with it. Finally, allow your body's natural elasticity to release the breath and with it, everything you just noticed, felt, heard, or thought about, allowing your mind to become as empty as your lungs and aware, prepared, open to the next breath, the next moment. Allow for a slight, comfortable pause, and then your body will naturally begin the process again.

This is my favorite method because it mirrors what the body's wisdom does when surprised in a healthy state (which is what our stress system is for). First, there's a stimulus (like a "tiger," a fancy car, or surprising news) that "takes your breath away" or causes you to "wait with baited breath." Often this is accompanied by common expressions, such as "Whoa." Then there is a brief pause for evaluation. As you get better at paying attention in moments like this, you will find that all your breathing muscles are briefly inactive while your mind is deciding what to do with the new information. This is a moment of evaluation, where in a split second you figure out what to do, usually by asking questions like, "Am I in trouble?" "Did you see that ride?" or "How am I going to deal with this?" Finally there is a "breath of fresh air" that readies you for action. "Whew, that sure got my attention! Next moment, please." To recap, breathing in, you notice; pausing for a moment, you "be with"; and letting the out-breath go naturally, you make yourself available to the next thing (in the case of meditation, the breath).

You might decide that a more proactive approach is better for you; in this case, visualization can help a lot. You can get really creative here. In your mind, picture your breath flowing in and out of your lungs and through your body. Imagine breathing in colors that you enjoy or that make you feel peaceful, and breathing out colors that remind you of the stress you wish to release. For example, breathing in "sky blue" and letting it flow through your body, then washing away all the "icky green" that is then exhaled might work for some. For others, the opposite may be true—breathing in "spring green" and breathing out "sad blue." Getting creative in this way not only personalizes your relaxation time but helps to make it more engaging.

Deep, slow breathing is the simplest way to begin calming your racing mind and is the foundation to the various techniques I mentioned previously. Outside thoughts will probably intrude ("I have to remember to…"), but keep refocusing on your breath. Meditate. Visualize. Breathing exercises can be used whenever you feel tension rising, but in the same way an athlete prepares for an event before it happens or a good student studies before finals, it's beneficial to make it a regular routine even when you're not stressed. Five or 10 deep breaths when sitting down at the work desk is beneficial and helps to focus on the task at hand, but try to breathe this way for about 15 minutes a day and make it as much a daily habit as brushing your teeth.

Even young children can learn controlled breathing. When teaching them this technique, sit with them quietly and talk them through the process. ("Breathe in slowly. Puff out your tummy with air. Sloooooowly let your breath out through your nose.") Do the breathing with them and leave long, silent pauses between instructions. When I work with older teens and young children alike, everyone has a relatively easy time imagining breathing like a balloon. Generally, I'll have them sit or lie down, and say, "Imagine that you are a balloon, just the same shape and size as you are. What color is it?" The color question is a trick from hypnosis and basically serves to engage the imagination more fully through visualization. Let's say the child picks red. I then say, "You know how a balloon blows up, right? It just gets bigger all at once. When you breathe in, imagine this big red balloon that is you getting blown up. How would that feel? Balloons don't blow themselves up, right? So imagine your whole body making room for the air. Let's try this a few times."

The goal is not to move so much air that one coughs or gets light-headed but to relax every abdominal muscle so that the real workhorse of breathing, the diaphragm muscle, can move more freely. Once I see the belly moving freely with the breath, I continue, "Now, while balloons don't blow themselves up, they do empty themselves, right? So just let yourself become empty. Now let's put them together. Blow yourself up…hold for just a second and whew… let it all out." After several practice sessions, kids will be able to do it on their own. This is a highly effective and simple technique. You can try it right now.

Blowing bubbles is another simple, effective way to show young children how to relax through breath control. When they are tense, pull out a jar of bubble liquid with a wand and give your child the opportunity to blow. He may be too young to be aware of exactly what he's doing, so talk him through it. The focus isn't on blowing the biggest bubble or chasing after a stream of bubbles. Instead, have your child sit quietly and guide him along this relaxation route. "Take in a slow, deep breath. Pull the air way in to your belly." (Demonstrate it as your child follows your example.) "Now blow out slowly, slowly through your lips. Watch the bubbles float away. Let's do it again. Pull the air into your belly slooooowly, pucker your lips, and blow out through a little hole between your lips." Keep doing it as long as it takes for your child to become calmer.

Swimming laps is another great way for children, teens, and adults to use breathing as a stress reliever. It is not just good exercise; swimming laps also requires rhythmic breathing that helps people relax and even meditate.

If teenagers struggle with the idea of deep, meditative breathing, I make the analogy to smoking. If they are smokers or have tried cigarettes or marijuana, they catch on right away. "Just try this," I say. "Pull a breath, pull it deep, hold it, and...aah...." If they are regular smokers, this is a way to help them quit. I teach them that part of the relaxation they get from smoking comes from choosing to take a break and then, once outside, from the pull. If they try deep breathing as a regular stress-reduction strategy, they can enjoy the drag without the poison and it won't cost them $6 or $7 a pack, risk a drug bust, make them smell, or pollute their lungs. And taking a break is always a great idea as well. For many, it may be the most important aspect.

Body Position

Some simple physical postures can fool a tense body and reduce stress. If someone confronts you in an aggressive way and moves in close ("gets in your face," as kids say), don't stand chest-to-chest. That's a hostile posture and makes you want to fight back. Instead, turn slightly to one side and drop your shoulders into a more relaxed position. This simple postural shift can be compared to the 3-second rule in defensive driving, which says that there should be enough room between cars that it takes 3 to 5 seconds for your car to pass the same utility pole, sign, or inanimate object as the car in front of you. Being aware in this way buys you time to evaluate, brake, and evade hazards, and so it is with the nonconfrontational posture. Martial artists know that this is not just a superior position for diffusing a potentially hostile situation. It is also a better position should things get ugly, as they sometimes do, because it narrows the aggressor's selection of potential targets and offers more angles for blocking, countering, and escape. I have found that such analogies appeal to the young people who find themselves in these situations, as it is empowering and appeals to their aggressive side without encouraging violence. It also ties in somewhat with the fast-rising sport of mixed martial arts. As parents and educators, it is important to realize that if this is the stuff network television is using to reach our kids, it is our responsibility to capitalize on it as well. Tense situations can be neutralized by sitting down, angling your body, and taking deep breaths to control your thoughts, then problem-solving through negotiation. It is likely that a skillful navigation of adversities and other stressors will yield better results than non-skillful means, and that is exactly the toolbox we are trying to build and encourage.

The study posture is a common position that makes the body tense. How often have you seen kids hunch over a desk or table, compressing their breathing apparatus with tight, rounded shoulders; bent heads; and curved spines? Their legs and hips are bent in a position as if they're preparing to leap up from the desk and sprint. Often their legs are shaking to work out their nervous energy. Their entire posture seems to say, "Why am I doing homework when I should be running from this tiger that's chasing my butt?"

If they want to be calmer while doing homework or taking a test, suggest that this posture and leg shaking make them even more tense. Instead, they can take control of what their bodies are feeling by sitting up straighter, with shoulders back and relaxed, and legs stretched out comfortably, without shaking. They can take some deep breaths to remind themselves that they can be calm and aren't about to run from a tiger. Now they are physically prepared to problem-solve while taking an examination or finishing homework. Simply knowing these easy tricks makes kids feel more in control of their situations and thus, less anxious.

Yoga

Yoga is sometimes described as meditation through movement. It has been practiced around the world for many years. While there are many variations, the core intention of yoga is to become healthy and free of anxieties and worry. Often this is done by combining breathing, visualization, and movement or posture. Concentrating on slow, deep breathing, people who practice yoga relax while moving through poses that build bones and stretch muscles and tendons. In modern terms, you might call it the art of chilling out by freeing oneself from the hang-ups that habitually get in our way. We know that there is an intimate relationship between how the body and mind feel, so it makes sense that broadening the range of motion in the body can help to broaden the mind's range of motion as well. Although originally intended as a way of life, we can still benefit greatly from the wisdom that has been passed down and built on through the ages.

For children and teens, yoga offers a counterweight in their stressful world of school demands, hurry-up home lives, competitive sports, and peer pressure. Yoga develops concentration and stillness that promote relaxation of body and mind. It fosters physical competencies because children master balance, breath control, and flexibility. They gain confidence, strength, and body awareness in a noncompetitive, cooperative setting.

Children learn yoga postures in familiar terms—they pose like trees and flowers, sit twisted like a pretzel, stretch like a cat, and take a warrior's stance. They balance like a flamingo and breathe like a bunny rabbit. Few young children like to remain silent for long, and yoga allows them to make noise. They can meow while in the cat pose, hiss like a cobra as they stretch their spines, and bark during the downward dog pose. Some yoga instructors encourage kids to count or recite their ABCs while holding different poses.

Learning to do yoga is probably best accomplished in a class setting where a qualified instructor makes certain that poses and breathing are done correctly. Once those are learned, you and your child may want to continue them at home with a videotape, a DVD, an online resource, or an illustrated book for guidance. Yoga can be practiced on a regular basis, several times a week. Also teach your child that whenever he feels tense or upset, he can cope better if he does some yoga breathing and poses during stressful times, literally relieving the tension he feels. In practice, yoga is a cat-and-mouse game of discovering and releasing tension in its many forms. At the least, it will help him feel better. At the most, it will offer access to a feeling of calm, helping him navigate an often confusing world.

Yoga is not only a great de-stressing technique for children, but when learned and practiced with parents, it also can become another enjoyable way to promote family connection. As I've frequently said, parents who practice effective coping strategies model excellent examples for their children, so give yourself and your child a gift that will benefit both of you.

Meditation

Meditation comes in many forms and has been practiced all over the world for thousands of years. The core of meditation is breathing awareness, often combined with movement and visualization. We have already discussed guided deep breathing; now let's go a step further to get the full benefit of meditative breathing.

Meditation is sometimes called *mindfulness*, which means being in the moment and shutting out distractions and surrounding noises. The goal of meditation is to turn off mental activity, to calm the thoughts racing wildly through your mind. While meditating, you turn off your thinking process but remain in a clear state of awareness. This gives your mind a rest and lets your body relax.

People who have learned to meditate often discover that meditation helps them focus better when doing daily tasks in times of high stress. If you're multitasking under a lot of pressure (the boss is demanding a report by tomorrow morning; coworkers are pushing extra work on you; you need to leave work on time to make your child's ball game), you can use meditation to concentrate on getting through the tasks step-by-step without letting them overwhelm you with anxiety.

Meditation techniques take the power from those thoughts that run away with you and put it back in your hands. It can help disengage the identity from problems. For example, rather than thinking, "I am angry," which makes us feel as if this were so, meditation gives us the power to realize, "I am experiencing anger." The difference seems small but gives us the freedom to experience other things at the same time. When we *are* angry is when we do things we might later regret. When we *experience* anger, we retain full self-control. The same goes for any "I am" statement. We are so much more than any one thing, like depressed, mad, or sad, and meditation helps us realize that.

One example is to imagine that your thoughts are clouds. Scary thoughts become big, dark, scary clouds, and happy thoughts become bright, airy, poofy clouds. Just imagine that each thought, as it crosses your mind, is a cloud crossing the sky. Simply recognize and watch. Imagine that your breath is the wind blowing the clouds across the sky. Do this for 10 minutes and notice how you feel.

Another method is to simply notice whatever comes to mind as you inhale. It could be a noise, feeling, or thought, but be with whatever you notice as you hold your breath momentarily. As you release your breath, let it all go—the breath, the thing you noticed, everything. Make yourself available to the next breath, the next moment. Repeat.

Even young children can meditate if we show them how to do so in age-appropriate ways. The following example is not technically meditation, but it suggests a way to teach a meditation or relaxation method to very young children. An experienced Montessori teacher in a Philadelphia suburb, Ellen Sheehan, has used a book called *Play with Me* by Marie Hall Ets to introduce the concept of silence to 2- to 5-year-olds. In the story, a little girl goes into a meadow where she meets a frog, turtle, grasshopper, bird, rabbit, and snake. She runs after each one and says, "Play with me." But they all hop, slither, swim, or fly away. The unhappy little girl sits on a big log and sadly contemplates why no one will play with her. As she sits motionless and quiet, all the creatures return and sit with her. A little fawn comes close to lick her face.

Children love this story, Ms Sheehan reports, and listen in rapt attention. When the story ends, teacher and children talk about what it means to be silent like the girl sitting on the log—no movement of hands, feet, body, and face; no talking. The children close their eyes and listen. Gradually, voices from the hallway, the hum of a ceiling fan, the sound of an airplane, and the chirp of birds outside all drift into the quietness.

The group listens silently for a full minute. Then Ms Sheehan tells them in a gentle voice, "Boys and girls, you made beautiful silence," and asks them if they have anything to share. One by one, they open their eyes and respond. "Silence is viewed as a positive act," Ms Sheehan explains. "It is something the child makes, and the child feels a sense of accomplishment, satisfaction, and peace."

Progressive Relaxation

For this very simple and effective method of active relaxation, basically all you do is systematically move your awareness through your body. Where your awareness goes, relaxation follows. For many, practicing progressive relaxation from scalp to toe is very sedating, as the awareness gradually moves away from the head, where a lot of tension starts as self-conflict or frustration. Moving from feet to head is also relaxing but often has a more energizing effect because the awareness that is relaxing the body ends its journey in the body's control tower, the head.

There are a number of simple ways to do this. First, become fully aware of your scalp and any sensations at all, then allow it to relax completely, including your mind's effort to notice. Next, become aware of all the little muscles around your ears and any sensations, then allow them to relax completely as well. Next, work with your eyes and forehead, then your neck, then your throat, and so on. Continue in this way, working through your body, bit by bit, all the way to your fingertips and toes, being sure to address every area of your body.

A useful variation is to tense and release each body part as you go, using muscle energy to encourage results. Muscle energy also helps to maintain focus, as does visualization. You can even combine all 3—progressive tense and release while visualizing, imagining, for example, that your muscles are "milking" the tension or "bad energy" right down and out of your body.

Remember that you can also work from feet to scalp; once you're well practiced, you can even work part-specific. If your shoulders are tense, you can just focus on them, but be sure to take care of all your parts regularly to maximize your results.

Aromatherapy

Combining aromatherapy with deep breathing is an excellent method for stress reduction. Simply place a drop of fragrant oil on a cotton ball and breathe it in as you practice deep breathing. To ensure you get good quality oils, be sure the bottle says "organic" or "therapeutic grade." If it is difficult to obtain pure essential oils, you can use the ones nature provides—flowers, citrus peels, and pine needles are all rich in therapeutic fragrance. If nothing else, it makes the experience of deep meditative breathing varied and more pleasant.

A Note on Very Young Children

When working with very young children, visualization is usually the way to go. You can simply ask them to imagine situations that will provoke the desired results. Be sure to use familiar terms that they understand and will enjoy. As you give them direction, asking them to describe their imaginings helps to solidify their experience and creates an opportunity for you to join them in their land of make-believe. Visualization is further described in the next chapter as a way of taking an "instant vacation."

Here are some scripts you might use to get young children started as they learn to actively relax.

For progressive relaxation

❉ "Imagine your whole body is loose and wiggly like spaghetti, wiggling from head to toe."

❉ "Imagine that the whole ocean is inside you and the waves are washing from head to toe, cleaning you out on the inside, and making you feel better and better."

❉ "Imagine all your good feelings are your favorite color and all your bad feelings are your least favorite color. Imagine all that favorite color filling you up from the top and washing the other color right out through your feet."

❉ "Imagine there are bunches of little garbagemen going through your head, back, belly, arms, and legs, taking away all the garbage and leaving you squeaky clean inside."

For visualization

❉ "Imagine that you are in the most beautiful place you have ever been. What is it like?" (After this opener, you can discuss the place, the details, and how it makes the child feel.)

❉ "Imagine you're in a beautiful field of flowers, relaxing in the sunlight. Do you see any animals? Do they have a name?" (Discussing what comes naturally might be a clue to the child's overall well-being. Perhaps frogs and birds are happy signs, but scary animals like bears deserve a conversation to find out what is wrong and how to make it better.)

❉ "Imagine you are at the zoo. What animals do you want to see?" (While discussing the animals, imitate their qualities. Cats know how to relax, elephants are strong, monkeys know how to play nice with each other.)

Maximizing the Effects of Exercise and Relaxation Strategies

To maximize the stress-reduction benefits of exercise and relaxation, it is important to know how to coordinate these tools. Here are some key points.

* Morning exercise can increase alertness and have a powerful effect on mood for the rest of the day. This may be particularly true for people with concentration difficulties.

* Exercise is a good first strategy to use when stress feels overwhelming. In fact, you may not be ready to use the other strategies, especially those that involve calm thought and planning, until you've worked out those overwhelming feelings by exercising.

* When exercise isn't possible—like the moment your boss delivers bad news or during a pop quiz—the best first step can be to control your thinking pattern. Divert it away from moving toward catastrophic thoughts (see Chapter 9) by sitting in a comfortable position that tells your body there's no emergency worth running from. Then draw in slow, deep breaths to flip the switch that turns on your calm nervous system.

* The ideal combination is first working out your stress physically and then taking active steps toward relaxation.

Let's use a child's tantrum to illustrate an appropriate sequence of exercise and relaxation through breathing. When a 4-year-old has a tantrum in pre-school, the teacher could send him into the corner and tell him to calm down. The problem is that his frustration or anger is so intense that he simply can't calm himself. He shakes, cries, and feels he's even more of a failure because he can't follow the teacher's instructions. All of this will be worse if done in front of classmates because he will also be embarrassed, and embarrassed people feel as if they are being attacked and may lash out protectively.

Alternately, the teacher could remove him from the peer audience and then tell him that she understands he's feeling angry and frustrated, but until he can explain his feelings, she can't help him as much as she wants to. She could tell him to run in place for a minute or two and really work out his feelings. After the energy is released, she could have him blow bubbles with slow, controlled breathing. In this way, his tantrum can serve as a valuable life lesson about how the choices he makes can control his uncomfortable feelings instead of reinforcing his feelings that he is out of control.

7. Eat Well.

Nutrition is vitally important to children's physical growth and development, but it must also be seen as part of an overall stress-reduction plan because a healthy body helps us manage stress.

A particularly valuable resource is MyPyramid.gov, an interactive site that allows children, teens, and adults to plug in their gender, weight, and height and receive personalized guidance for healthy nutrition balanced with exercise. It has been changed from the food pyramid that many of us were accustomed to in the past. Perhaps most importantly, it now includes steps on the side of the pyramid that represent the crucial balance between exercise and nutrition.

But before we look for external sources, I would like to repeat that parents' modeling is more important than any words they say or resources they guide their children to use. If parents drink cases of soda but tell their children it's forbidden or only an occasional treat, soda will quickly acquire a special allure. Keep in mind, we parents buy the food and model eating habits.

Some General Guidelines

- Treat soda and other sugary drinks for what they are—candy water. Sodas should be highly restricted or drunk only occasionally. Soda can be harmful to tooth enamel. When children drink a lot of soda, they tend to drink fewer nutritious beverages like milk. Even many juice drinks are packed with high-fructose corn syrup, so they are not as nutritious as the term *fruit drink* might imply.

- Make sure children drink lots of water. Water is a healthy drink that gives the body exactly what it needs without all those empty calories. If kids find water boring, give it to them in a cool sports bottle. Show them how to flavor water to give it a twist (with a squirt of lemon juice, for example) but without added calories.

- Offer lots of milk and dairy products, or high-calcium beverages like soy milk if your children are intolerant of milk. Some brands of almond and rice milks are also enriched with calcium. Generally, children younger than 2 years should drink whole milk from the time they stop breastfeeding or using formula. New American Academy of Pediatrics (AAP) recommendations, however, state that children at risk of being overweight or with a family history of heart disease, obesity, or high cholesterol can switch to low-fat milk between 12 months and 2 years of age. After 2 years of age, all children should drink reduced-fat milk.

- Make plenty of fresh fruits and vegetables available. Put out bowls of fruit or cut-up vegetables as snacks. Recommended amounts of fruits and vegetables—8 or 9 servings a day—may seem nearly impossible, but numerous studies extol their nutritional benefits. Many kids reject certain fruits and vegetables; try to experiment until you find some they like. Just because they reject steamed broccoli one day doesn't mean they won't like munching on raw broccoli dipped in yogurt next week. Keep reintroducing these foods while also offering new varieties.

- Avoid linking food to punishments ("If you don't finish your spinach, you can't go out and play.") and don't use snacks and desserts as bribes or rewards ("You've been so good, you deserve a bag of chips.").

- If you want to be certain that children get adequate vitamins and minerals, be sure they eat lots of different-colored fruits and vegetables that supply a healthy variety of nutrients.

- If you want kids to maintain an even-keeled temperament and therefore be better prepared to manage stress, teach them how to have a *steady* supply of energy. This means avoiding foods that cause quick peaks and crashes of energy to the brain. A little background: Glucose is the source of energy to the brain. It is found in simple and complex sugars *(carbohydrates).* Simple sugars are those that taste sweet and are found in candy and soft drinks. They get quickly absorbed and deliver a burst of energy but then are followed by a crash. Complex carbohydrates don't taste as sweet and deliver a slower, more steady supply of energy to the brain. Complex carbohydrates are found in fruits, vegetables, and whole grains.

- Help your children distinguish between healthy and non-healthy snacks. I simplify this idea for my patients by asking them to imagine 2 kinds of snacks, *soap* and *no-soap,* that they eat only with their hands. After eating those snacks, do they need soap to wash their hands or just water? This is an easy way for kids to recognize greasy foods that are less healthy than most alternatives.

- Snacking is an important part of childhood. Children are growing and burn a lot of energy. They're hungry after school. They may need a snack while studying at night. They're hungry and thirsty after playing vigorously. Don't eliminate snacking entirely. Instead, provide a variety of healthy snacks. Everyone knows that fruits and vegetables are the healthiest snacks, but many people don't realize that there are large differences among all the salty, crunchy snack foods available today. The greasier they are, the less healthy they are. Some examples are included in the Table on the next page.

Snacking Can Be Healthy!		
Unhealthy *Soap* Snacks	**Healthier *No-soap* Snacks**	**Healthy Snacks**
Potato chips	Pretzels	Fruits
Corn chips	Salted unbuttered popcorn	Vegetables
Cheese puffs		Low-fat yogurt
Buttered popcorn	Baked crackers	Unbuttered popcorn with fat-free spices

Why Do You Eat?

A major difference between people who eat healthily and those who don't is found in their answers to the question, "Why do you eat?" Healthy eaters tend to eat when they are hungry. Unhealthy eaters often eat when they are hungry *and* when they are sad, excited, or bored. Sometimes they eat without thinking, just to give themselves something to do while they are watching television.

Try to make mealtime an event that your family enjoys together in the kitchen or dining room and not in the family or recreation room. As difficult as it seems, I suggest that you ban junk food snacks from the room where you watch television, but munching fruits and vegetables, or even spiced air-popped popcorn, is okay.

How Much?

We live in a super-size-me nation. The 4-oz hamburgers that our mothers made a generation ago have morphed into 8-oz patties or larger. A small-sized ice cream cone is now 2 or 3 scoops. And popcorn and soda at the movies? Medium sizes are enough to stuff an elephant and float an aircraft carrier.

Portion size does matter. Several studies show that portion size is the most significant factor in weight control. Most people eat what is in front of them. If the all-you-can-eat buffet table overflows with tempting foods, we load our plates and go back for more—not because we're still hungry, but because the food is within view. The more we see, the more we eat.

Parents can dish out reasonably sized portions on each child's plate or place bowls and platters on the table for family members to serve themselves. Don't offer second helpings unless children say they're still hungry. It takes about 20 minutes for the body to register whether it is satisfied or still hungry, so encourage your family to eat slowly. And having a relaxed conversation during meals will slow their pace.

Parents should also control children's portions when eating out. Give them a choice between one item or another, but not both. They can share a tub of popcorn or cut a pizza into smaller slices.

No Fighting Over Food

Don't make food a battleground. Model good nutrition yourself, and make sure your child has healthy foods to select, but don't take away the pleasure of eating. Mealtime is a great opportunity to enhance family connection and check in with your child. The atmosphere should be relaxed. But if you turn "Eat all your rice" into a battleground command, tensions rise and your child may turn food against you and refuse to eat the foods you offer.

When we talk with children about good nutrition and healthy bodies, we should be careful not to send the wrong messages. This isn't about how kids *look*. So many destructive media messages exist about what we should look like. Men are supposed to have six-pack abs and women should be skinny. Please be careful not to encourage those images. Never tell children that they don't look right. If they eat well and get regular exercise through play or sports, they will be fine. Be cautious, too, of the overuse of body mass index (BMI). It is a useful tool that is more accurate than simple weight and height, but never forget to look at your child and consider her body type. For example, a girl may have a high BMI even though she is in excellent shape because her muscles weigh more than fat. Use BMI as a screening tool, not a label.

If you think your child is overweight or obese, yet you're modeling healthy eating habits and providing good food choices at home, let a health professional counsel your child. When food becomes a battleground within families, not only does it add extra stress, but serious consequences may result during adolescence if teens choose to control their anxieties—or you—by limiting what they eat or by overeating.

Meals as a Bonding Time

A significant amount of research demonstrates that family meals are highly protective for young people. It's not about food on the plate; it's much more about the connection that occurs when families spend time together. An added benefit of these meals is that healthy family time becomes associated with nutritious leisurely meals. When people take time to eat and associate it with pleasant times, they may be more likely to develop lifelong healthy eating habits.

8. Sleep Well.

Sleep affects everything. Stressful situations that could be easily managed when you're well rested can put young people (or you) over the edge when you're tired. Inadequate sleep can have a profoundly negative effect on health, the ability to think, and mood. Adequate sleep is necessary to solidify newly gained memories or skills, so it isn't surprising that school performance declines with lack of sleep. Sleeplessness has also been associated with other serious consequences such as an increased incidence of automobile crashes and even depression.

We know from our adult experiences as well as from parenting our children that sleep really matters, but getting children to bed on time and up at 6:00 am can be nearly impossible. For teenagers, it's even more challenging. Sleep research data indicate that adolescents require 9 to 10 hours of sleep each night. But the majority of them aren't getting nearly that much, which is why excessive daytime sleepiness has become a widespread problem among teenagers.

What's Interfering With Sleep?

Most cases of sleepiness result from insufficient time in bed, often caused by external pressures (like studying) to go to bed later and wake up earlier. Worrying in bed can also keep us from falling asleep and wake us throughout the night. Stimulants like caffeine can impair sleep quality and cause daytime sleepiness. Finally, the sleep-wake cycle changes dramatically during adolescence, making a teen's time clock quite different than an adult's.

Although medical conditions are not the most likely cause of sleepiness, it's important to consider them as a possible cause of a child's lack of sleep. The AAP and the National Center on Sleep Disorders Research (National Heart, Lung, and Blood Institute; National Institutes of Health) say that we should pay special attention to young people who have excessive sleepiness because they are most likely to have an underlying medical or mental health condition. According to their report, "Excessive Sleepiness in Adolescents and Young Adults: Causes, Consequences, and Treatment Strategies" *(Pediatrics.* 2005;115:1774–1786), we need to consider depression, obstructive sleep apnea, insomnia, narcolepsy, and other sleep disorders in adolescents with ongoing sleepiness. If your child often has trouble sleeping or is unusually sleepy during the day, talk with your pediatrician, who can help determine whether your child may be suffering from chronic sleep deprivation or an underlying sleep disorder.

A health professional may ask your child the following questions, so you may wish to think about how they relate to your child:

❋ Do you have trouble falling asleep at bedtime?

❋ Do you feel sleepy a lot during the day? In school? While driving?

❋ Do you wake up a lot at night?

❋ What time do you usually go to bed on school nights? Weekends?

❋ How much sleep do you usually get?

❋ Has anyone ever told you that you snore loudly at night?

❋ Do you have repeated dreams that disturb you?

In addition, your child should be asked about mood and stress to consider the possibility of depression. The next thing to consider, and possibly the easiest to address, is the use of stimulants. It takes 6 to 8 hours for caffeine to get out of our systems. Caffeine is found in coffee, tea, colas and other soft drinks, and chocolate, and at very high levels in newer energy and power drinks. Research finds that teens who drink caffeine in the afternoon and evening have more difficulty sleeping and are more tired during the day. Although caffeine does keep us awake for a short time, it won't overcome excessive sleepiness and does not overcome a sleep debt. In other words, it works in the short term but really adds to the bigger problem of sleepiness. I am not prepared to make a global statement about the use of caffeine, only to state that we need to understand that it is a real drug and should be used wisely and sparingly.

Most of us can relate to another major cause of sleeplessness—using the bed to do some of our best and often our toughest thinking. Sometimes we're so overstretched and busy that there is no downtime in our lives, no time for processing our thoughts and feelings or even for planning for tomorrow. The first chance to really be alone with your thoughts is when your head hits the pillow. Although it can be a relief to finally have some alone time, when the bed becomes the place to deal with important issues, it becomes a friend, even a counselor.

No wonder it becomes difficult to fall asleep. And then we wake up in the middle of the night for another opportunity to think through our problems. We all deserve a space to work through our feelings and develop solutions; it just shouldn't be the place where we sleep.

It is not just worrying that prevents the bed from becoming the place our bodies naturally associate with sleep. Anything that creates too much stimulation keeps our minds revved up and prevents us from falling smoothly into sleep. If young people move from activity to activity, they sometimes lack time to wind down. Wonderful thoughts may fill their heads, but they're still spinning from the day's activities.

Any activity done in bed increases the possibility of sleep problems. When homework is done in bed, the bed can become associated with anxiety about grades and tests. And nighttime awakening may increase in frequency because teens wake up to get the work done. When kids sprawl in bed while texting or talking to friends, the bed can become associated with excitement and social pressures. I explain to my patients that the brain doesn't turn off when we fall asleep. It's just dialed down, like when your computer goes into sleep mode, and it's easily revved up when subconscious concerns come close to the surface. When the bed is used for purposes other than sleep, the brain is more likely to do its low-level thinking when you're asleep. As sleep naturally cycles from deep to light sleep throughout the night, we wake up in light sleep when our brains suggest we can finish our "work" if only we wake up. (Remember, work can be emotional work, schoolwork, or a progress report.) We are much more likely to wake at night if the bed is our work space. I don't tell kids not to worry, not to communicate with their friends, or to skip homework. I just want them to learn to do all of those things somewhere other than in bed.

If you think that your teen has become a night owl, you may be right. Adolescents' biological clocks actually shift during puberty. They naturally want to stay up later because as puberty progresses, the brain's sleep-timing system switches on later at night. This sleep-timing system is controlled by *melatonin*, a naturally occurring chemical that regulates biological rhythms; one of those is the circadian rhythm of wakefulness and sleep. Because high schools have generally not shifted away from early morning start times, most teenagers lack adequate sleep. Some school districts acknowledge this and are moving toward later start times for teens and earlier ones for younger children, but that is not yet a widespread practice.

Sleep 101

Before we put together a plan for adequate sleep, it's important to review some basics of sleep.

We fall asleep when we allow our minds to turn off. We stay asleep when we believe that the bed is just for sleeping. We have a natural circadian rhythm that regulates our patterns of wakefulness and sleep. We are naturally diurnal, meaning that we are designed to be awake during the day and asleep at night. Anything that interferes with allowing our bodies to stick to that rhythm may interfere with sleep.

As diurnal creatures, we tend to become awakened with light and sleepy in the dark. This is critical to understand because artificial light has affected this natural design, and we can partially restore it by using light and darkness appropriately.

As diurnal beings, we awaken when our bodies become heated, as they do in the sunlight of day, and become tired as they cool down. It is important to recognize that our bodies become heated with exercise and bathing. It takes 5 to 6 hours after exercise and 1 hour after a bath or shower to cool down.

Digestion takes work. Large meals before bedtime can cause indigestion. A lot of liquid before bed can necessitate nighttime bathroom visits.

When we wake in the middle of the night, we sometimes worry about getting back to sleep. As our anxiety builds, the chance of getting back to sleep lessens. It is better to get out of bed, sit in a chair, and return to bed when really drowsy.

Dos and Don'ts

If we combine everything we know about sleep patterns with what we know about actions that interfere with sleep, a list of dos and don'ts becomes apparent. Remember, the reason to help your child (and maybe even you) follow these rules is not to take away late-night fun or become rigid; it is to help manage the stressors of daily life while remaining alert and healthy.

Dos	Don'ts
Drink soothing beverages like herbal teas or warm milk before bed.	Consume caffeine 6 to 8 hours before bed.
Keep the cell phone recharging dock in the kitchen or living room, and insist all electronic devices get recharged there overnight.	Have TVs, computers, or cell phones in the bedroom. (If they're already in the bedroom, they must be turned off at bedtime.)
Have a place to release emotions and express feelings, not in bed.	Worry in bed.
Complete homework before bedtime and feel satisfied that it is done.	Do homework in bed.
Make a list of things that need to be done before going to bed and feel secure that the day is strategically planned.	Plan tomorrow in bed.
If you awaken at night and can't fall back asleep easily, get up, stay in a dark room, and return to bed when drowsy.	Stay in bed worrying about getting to sleep.

Dos	Don'ts
Maintain a regular (but not rigid) sleep pattern.	Take long naps. (They interfere with developing a steady sleep pattern.)
Take power naps, limited to 20 minutes and not remotely close to bedtime.	Stay in bed very late on weekend mornings. (This also prevents a sleep pattern from developing.)
Eat healthy.	Eat heavy meals or large drinks before bed.
Exercise 5 to 6 hours before bedtime.	Do a heavy workout before bed.
Take a relaxing bath or shower an hour before bed.	Go to bed overheated.
Dim the lights an hour or so before bed; open the shades or turn on the lights in the morning.	Stay in bright lights late at night.
Create a dark, quiet, comfortable sleep environment.	

A Plan for Young People Who Are Struggling With Sleep

First, a recap. When I talk with young patients about the importance of sleep, I suggest that they make their bed a special, almost sacred place. It should only be used for sleeping. Bed should *not* be a place to eat, read, listen to music, play games, veg out, talk on the phone, watch television, or play videos. Kids who treat their beds as sacred will get in the habit of relaxing and falling asleep more easily.

A leisurely bath an hour or so before bed helps relax the body and prepare it for sleep. I urge young people, as they are falling asleep, to unwind from the day and put aside worrisome thoughts. It's easier to do this if they have followed one of the strategies for releasing emotions (more in the next chapter and the ninth point of this stress-reduction plan). They must release their emotions somewhere other than in bed—perhaps sitting at a table or in a comfortable chair. Their bed should be a special place, not a place to worry, just to sleep. If it becomes a place to worry, it will become their counselor. They will want to talk for at least 50 minutes and will wake up through the night for another appointment.

Then I help them to develop a pattern to teach their bodies to sleep. This lesson starts with determining a reasonable bedtime. My intention isn't to create a rigid bedtime or for them to feel that it's a punishment; rather, I want their bodies to develop a healthy sleep-wake pattern. They set a time that they think will allow them to complete their homework and still get at least 8 hours of sleep. We then call this *time zero* (T0) and work backward, like this.

* **T0-6 hours:** Work out. Exercise will help them manage stress and get their brains ready to be productive for homework.
* **T0-5 hours:** Do homework until it's finished. When homework is done, relax, play, or hang out. This is well-deserved downtime.
* **T0-1 hour:** Take a warm relaxing shower or bath in dim lights.
* **T0-30 minutes:** Release emotions through prayer or written, artistic, or verbal expression. (See stress-reduction point 10.) Plan for tomorrow by keeping a list or creating a timeline. The point is that all this work should be *done* before bedtime. It should be completed in dim light and, if desired, while sipping a calming drink. A note of warning: For young people who are particularly stressed, this wind-down emotional work may bring up anxieties too close to bedtime. If this is the case, the time for expression can be moved earlier and this time can just be used for emotional vacations (see stress-reduction point 9), like listening to music, meditating, or reading a book.

Some young people still struggle to wind down even after following this routine. At Covenant House Pennsylvania, we work with young people who have endured very difficult lives. Many of them have a great deal of difficulty falling asleep and ask me for medication. Instead, I have them work with Jed Michael, our stress-reduction specialist who has been trained in Eastern Medicine healing practices. As I have learned from him, a person needs to have the opportunity to slip away into sleep and can do this best when they're distracted from their thinking. The old technique of counting sheep is designed to distract people from their thoughts. But that technique does not take full advantage of the relaxing tonic of controlled breathing. Jed teaches our patients the 4–8 breathing technique. First, he teaches them that full breaths are belly/balloon breaths. They learn to lie on their backs and place their hands on their bellies with their fingers loosely interlocking. Normal breathing does not distend the abdomen and therefore does not cause the hands to rise or fingers to separate. Deep, cleansing breaths first fill the belly, then the chest, then the mouth; the breath expands the belly and the hands pull gently apart. Our patients are taught to take a full breath while counting to 4. Then they hold that breath for about twice as long, or an 8 count. Finally, they slowly exhale to the count of 8 or even longer, if that's comfortable. This meditative breathing relaxes the body after a few cycles, but just as importantly, it requires full concentration. The mind is too preoccupied on the cycle of breathing to also focus on worries. We have found that with dedicated practice, even young people with a long history of insomnia slip away into a peaceful sleep. In most cases, results are obtained the first night. In time, many return to tell us that with greater sleep at night, they can better manage the stresses of their daily lives.

Expect Resistance

When I speak to families or audiences, I probably get more resistance on the topic of sleep than any other guidance I offer. Everyone knows that sleep is important, but they just don't feel it is practical to get even close to the recommended amount of sleep. Adolescents worry they won't have time for homework or with friends. They cherish sleeping into the afternoon on Sundays, so they especially reject sticking to the same number of sleep hours on weekends as weeknights. Parents worry most about homework; they just don't think there will be enough time for exercise, relaxation, and emotional releases as well. Many teens and parents think that life will become cloudy without that late-afternoon jolt of caffeine.

I have not been hiding under a rock. I witness how many directions children are pulled in, and I also want them to succeed. I challenge them to endure a trial period in which a healthy amount of exercise, good nutrition, and adequate sleep comprise their main medicine. I feel certain that their increased efficiency, their lighter mood, and their newfound ability to concentrate will more than make up for all that time they "wasted" taking care of themselves. This is a lesson I hope will last them for a lifetime. I end with one more reminder—when parents model taking care of themselves, kids follow.

Taking Care of Your Emotions

The next 2 parts of the stress-reduction plan suggest numerous ways to cope with the effect stress has on our emotions and well-being. These strategies include some that calm emotional reactions (to be used with exercise that fools our bodies into thinking we've dealt with the stress) and others that engage us in healing activities or use the power of distraction.

9. Take Instant Vacations.

We don't always have to travel for miles or spend a lot of money to take a vacation. There are several ways to reap the benefits of a vacation and de-stress wherever we find ourselves. Remember, some people cope by avoidance, withdrawal, disengagement, or running away. Most of these techniques are counterproductive and some, like drugs, are dangerous. But there are healthy ways to disengage too. One of the best ways to conserve energy, especially when your subconscious mind needs time to mull over solutions, is to healthfully and temporarily disengage.

If we use the following techniques and teach them to children, we can escape stress for a while, find a safe refuge, and reenergize ourselves:

Visualization. When my daughters were 5 years old, I was able to take my family to Hawaii where I did a visiting professorship. We found an out-of-the-way beach with black sands, crashing turquoise waves, and salt spray in the air—one of the most beautiful places I have ever visited. I wanted my daughters to remember this place so that they could return there if they ever needed to get away from anything, a place of extreme calm whose memory would be bathed in love. First, I wanted to help them imprint the spot into a deep memory, so we used each of our senses one by one. I asked the girls to close their eyes and pay attention to everything else.

"What do you feel? The warmth of the sun on one side of your body and a cool breeze on the other; the wetness of the ocean spray against your skin.

What do you hear? The sound of crashing waves, the softer sounds of birds singing. What do you smell? The salt in the air. Now open your eyes, look around you, and tell me everything you see. Now close your eyes and describe it to me again."

Finally, I told them how much I loved them and why, and my wife did the same. I told them this would be our special place and anytime they needed to be calm and quiet, they could take an instant vacation by closing their eyes and recalling this place, which we named our Hawaii family spot. Whenever they have been stressed, this has been a very effective way to de-stress. I went through the same process on a beach in Quebec when the girls were 9. This time, I asked them to lead my wife and me through the sensory imaging. I was amazed by how well they did.

I urge you to show your children how to visualize. There are many ways to do this, and it's so simple. Visit a serene, beautiful place, or go outside on a quiet, clear night and gaze at the stars and moon. Ask your child to imagine her own special place and make it a memorable mental snapshot that she can pull out whenever it is needed. It doesn't have to be on a vacation or even a visually astounding place; it could also be a place of profound warmth and safety, such as a grandmother's kitchen. The key here is to take the step beyond the visual or sensory memory and bathe the place in the security of your love for your child.

Think of your instant vacation spot as a screen saver on your computer— a spectacular view of sparkling blue water or a few gauzy clouds drifting across the sky. You can click on this tranquil picture in your mind's eye whenever you need to escape the stress of the moment. Simply close your eyes, picture this special tranquil location, and be in the moment. Do nothing else, be still, and think of nothing else.

Hobbies. Hobbies provide another way to escape for a little while. A hobby may be something you choose for your child, such as a model-building kit for a birthday present. It may start with casual play and become such an interesting activity that it takes on a focus, even a fervor, for your child.

It's terrific if children have a wide variety of interests. When they develop a real love and passion for hobbies, it can be more than a good way to spend a rainy day; it can become something they turn to for an instant vacation when they're feeling stressed or upset.

Reading. Instant vacations can come in many forms—listening to music, watching television, or going to a movie can provide entertaining, relaxing escapes. But there's nothing quite like reading as a full-immersion experience for a true, full escape. A reader has to visualize the panorama, hear the dialogue, and smell the aromas. Unlike television, which hands the sound and visuals to you, reading requires several senses to kick in actively so you get a fuller, more engaging escape.

There's no question that reading is one of the most important things parents can do with children. Read aloud to them when they're babies and preschoolers and have them read to you when they're in school or take turns reading chapters aloud. Reading together is a wonderful way of fully engaging with children. They will associate it with your time and attention and develop a lifelong love of reading. While this has beneficial implications for their schooling, it will also provide a useful escape, a real instant vacation—a full immersion in another world or time.

Baths. Soaking in a warm bath is a great way to relax. A bath is also like a mini-vacation—a private time and a protected, safe space. You deserve 30 minutes a day to decompress with no disturbances allowed. You may want to light candles or scents or play soothing music.

"Is he crazy?" you're thinking. "He doesn't know my family. Thirty minutes without interruptions? Must be a fantasy." I urge you to protect this time for yourself. Think of it as a selfless act because you'll be modeling for your child the importance of a daily, private relaxation zone.

Young children won't use the bath in this leisurely way. You'll be lucky if they bathe long enough to scrub the mud off their knees. In the early years, a bath is usually a time of play and connection with parents as you splash, rinse, and perhaps sing to them. As they get older, preteens and teens crave a private space of their own. If you've modeled the soothing bath routine, they may find it's a useful tool for them too. Even if they don't use a bath, they will understand that their parents have private time to replenish themselves at the end of a long day—an important lesson that they can use to give themselves permission to refuel throughout their lives.

A bath an hour before bedtime is a particularly good way for adolescents and adults to cleanse away the day's stress and get a better night's sleep. Baths can have a certain meditative quality. As you take deep breaths, your lungs act like balloons, and your body gently rises and falls in the water if you allow your upper body to float. If you submerge your ears under water, leaving only your face above the surface, you can draw those deep cleansing breaths and listen to your rhythmic breathing. If you take your pulse, you will notice it slow as you fool your body. The bath becomes an effective biofeedback machine to help achieve relaxation. One man told me that he bathes nightly to replenish himself as well as to visualize his problems and concerns disappearing. After he soaks and unwinds, he lets the water drain slowly and visualizes his concerns swirling away and, whoosh, they're gone.

Vacation from conflict and worries. When the bills are piling up, taxes are due, and work is overwhelming, we get caught in a cycle of worry, stress, and conflict. We may act out our stress at home on the people we love the most. It feels safer to do this at home than outside the home, so we find ourselves in fights over money or other matters. The arguments feed on themselves, and everything seems to spin like a tornado—the cycle has to be stopped, but how? A break or brief vacation from worries can interrupt the cycle. It may not solve the underlying problems, but it can keep the spiral from spinning out of control.

We can't hop on a plane to a tropical island, but we can try to make our homes peaceful, safe islands. We can structure an hour every day or two—or, let's be crazy here, even a week—when we take time off. We put aside the list of home improvement projects, we let the grass grow another inch—we forbid outside worries from encroaching on family life. Ongoing conflict is suspended because our love for our family remains solid. Then we can enjoy the love and safety within our homes that sometimes gets dwarfed by worries or conflicts.

This kind of break helps everyone. Children don't have bills to pay and they don't go to work (though school is certainly work), but they have their own tensions and, if there's more than one child in the family, some conflicts on the home front. Children can thoroughly enjoy a break, too, when conflicts are suspended and none of the touchy subjects are broached, when family members just enjoy each other. This can be a time for reading, hobbies, or laughter.

You may think I'm suggesting that you say to your family, "I declare a brief holiday from conflict," but I'm not. This technique isn't one that you explain to children or teach them. Rather, simply do it. Your child will learn that just as we have the ability to escalate tension, we also have the ability to turn to the people we most cherish, in the place where we feel most secure, and say, "Time-out. Let's enjoy each other." If you do this, you will help your family thrive even during stressful times, and you will expose your child to a lifelong stress-reduction tool.

Smelling local flowers. People who are able to take pleasure in the simple things can find instant vacations everywhere—in the scenery they drive by, the glow of buttercups under their child's chin, or another person's smile. Even during times of extreme stress, they are able to see a little beauty and restore their energy. So many of us, including our children, live hurried lives, always rushing from one activity to the next. We are so immersed in work that we don't notice what is all around us.

Children benefit if they learn from us (forgive a twist on the cliché) to take time to smell the local flowers. When we take time to be refreshed by the beauty in our yard, trees in the park, a visit with dear friends, or a baby gurgling in delight when adults make silly faces, children notice parents' small pleasures and learn that it takes little to please us.

Even when they are very young, take them on walks, watch the birds, help them see all the mini-vacations that surround them. This is yet another reason to encourage unstructured play. Children who are rushed from activity to activity never learn to explore their immediate environment. They don't learn to discover pleasure and fun exactly where they are, without needing bells and whistles or older people to tell them how to enjoy the experience.

10. Release Emotional Tension.

So many young people tell me that their biggest problem is anger, and they don't know where it comes from. Others tell me that they cannot sleep because their heads spin with the day's worries or excitement and their anticipation of the next day. I worry most, though, when they tell me that they feel numb and have nothing worthwhile at all in their thoughts. What these youngsters have in common are disorganized, overwhelming thoughts. In some cases, they have been exposed to emotional, even physical, traumas that overwhelm their capacity to deal with or even feel their emotions.

Many of my teenaged patients lead what would seem to be charmed lives—a wealth of material goods, good schools, and intact families—but they feel pressures coming at them from every direction. They can't figure out how to diffuse those pressures. (Of course, kids with charmed lives are also exposed to the world's complexities and the struggles that exist even in well-functioning homes.) While these teenagers might not have anger, they do have frustrations and are overwhelmed by all the expectations placed on them or numerous commitments they have made.

I visualize these overwhelming feelings as a chaotic maelstrom of emotion. Each thought, concern, or painful memory seems to be shooting from a different direction. To maintain our sanity, we build a container to enclose and control what would otherwise be chaos.

Those of us with healthy outlets have release valves attached to our containers that prevent the pressure from blowing in a dangerous way. Many of us, however, become afraid of opening our containers because the emotions within feel too painful, scary, or totally unmanageable to face. Instead, we keep squeezing our day-to-day troubles into the container for safekeeping so we can avoid dealing with them—we fantasize that we will deal with the contents later. Over time, the walls of the container have to become thicker and thicker to keep all our stresses inside. It becomes a figurative leaden box—too heavy to lift, impossible to see through, and indeed toxic.

What happens when we have so many important, though painful, thoughts and emotions trapped inside our self-created leaden box? Occasionally someone will push our buttons and cause the lid to pop open. Inexplicable, uncontrollable rage pours out.

I visualize the anger described by many of my young patients as the lid cracking open from a crammed leaden box. The adults in their lives see only the anger and problem behaviors without understanding the maelstrom of emotions and experiences beneath the rage.

Some kids describe the sensation of having overwhelming, boxed-in emotions as head spinning. One young man said it feels like a tornado. Another visualizes his head squeezed like a tennis ball by a powerful man intent on making it explode.

Many of my patients agree that drugs do a great job of stopping the spinning and releasing some of the pressure. They may be correct for the moment, but we know that drugs create bigger problems that will accelerate the spinning out of control. Hence the cycle of abuse—more spinning, more drugs, more spinning, and so on.

The leaden box can create something arguably worse than anger. It can create a sense of numbness. It can stop us from caring. It can make us lose what we value the most—our humanity. When we expend so much energy squeezing those painful, passionate, but real experiences inside our box, it becomes too difficult to care about the little things that make life worthwhile.

When a 7-year-old worries about being bullied and doesn't feel safe at school, how can he experience the thrill of reading a story that takes him to limitless fantasy worlds? When a 14-year-old is struggling over her burgeoning sexuality, her parents' divorce, pressure to earn high grades, and peer pressure from cruel classmates, how can she possibly savor the smell of spring flowers or recognize the unconditional love of her parents? How can she engage in polite conversation when she is working so hard to suppress intense emotions?

Numbness is a lost opportunity for cherishing every moment. When the present isn't cherished and small things aren't appreciated, it is hard to be resilient. We don't want this for our children. Although they will be exposed to challenges and pressures, we desperately want them to thrive, live life to the fullest, and have the resilience to survive no matter what curveballs are thrown at them. We have to raise children who can be exposed to stressors without locking their thoughts into emotionally toxic leaden containers.

Our children need to be secure about accessing their emotions rather than fearing them. To do this, they need a strategy for feeling and dealing with their experiences and concerns in manageable doses.

Containment is a good thing. People who feel everything fully in the moment can become dysfunctional. You probably know people who share every thought, feel every experience intensely, spout off reflexively, and send group e-mails in response to every perceived slight. While these people do not have a leaden box, they are rarely happy and find it difficult to maintain relationships because they exhaust themselves and others.

Building a Better Box

I propose a different kind of container—a Tupperware-type box. In contrast to a leaden box, it is made of light, flexible, nontoxic material. The container may be transparent so the contents can be seen and are safely stored in neat portions, but the contents don't stink. More importantly, you can lift the lid, remove one portion at a time, burp the box, and tightly reseal it.

People who know the contents of their boxes are emotionally intelligent and aware of issues that challenge them and experiences and memories that haunt them. Rather than letting tornados swirl in their heads, they can choose to release a bit of pressure by selecting one issue to deal with at a time.

When I work with troubled young people who tell me that they have unpredictable, uncontrollable anger, I help them build a Tupperware box. We talk about how this type of container allows them to name the issues in their lives that overpower them. This is an important initial step because once they can name those troubling issues, they can begin the healing process by choosing one at a time to process while safely storing the others for a while.

The parallel process of naming their *strengths* is vitally important. Not only would it be inefficient to make someone categorize all their problems before they're equipped to deal with them, it might even be dangerously frustrating. So before going through the process of identifying their stressors, it's equally important to be aware of their strengths and feel confident about having strategies to deal with feeling overwhelmed.

I use the Tupperware box technique with troubled youth, but it is also a preventive strategy. You don't need to discuss leaden or Tupperware boxes with young children. Instead, just help them learn to identify and name their problems. Help them understand that when they feel overwhelmed or confused, they can identify a few manageable problems and work on them one at a time. If they are equipped with some of the following techniques, they can manage the swirling emotions that are paralyzing them from taking action. I'd like to return to the mountain metaphor for a moment. Remember that when our problems feel like overwhelming mountains, we become frustrated and feel powerless to address them. This Tupperware box technique is a way of breaking these mountains into smaller hills. Through the process of emotional intelligence, we decide which hill to climb first. The following techniques are the figurative release valves for the Tupperware box—the shovels to move the dirt from mountains into hills.

Using Our Creative Energy

Creativity is more than a component of coping; it is a facet of ourselves that enables us to develop perspective and flexibility, both of which help us to be more resilient. As I have watched my children grow, I've seen firsthand how creative expression can give kids a voice to articulate their emotions, as well as a way to lose themselves in the act of creation. I am grateful for 2 teachers in particular, Maryanne Yoshida and Debbie Pollak, who have fostered creativity in my children. I wanted to learn more from them about how to engage children in art and nurture their creative sides. I thank them for their thoughtful contributions to this section, which I've added to the wisdom that my patients have shown me over the years.

People with creative energies have a built-in antidote to perfectionism. It may take years to develop the skill to paint a perfect picture or sculpt a flawless statue, but the process itself is rejuvenating. Learning a new process and making many messy attempts can be more exciting than the end product. Those of us who appreciate the creation may assume that it flowed effortlessly from the artist, but most artists know that their best results usually come after many attempts, much practice, and hard work. They enjoy the process of creating and despite frustrating fits and starts, keep trying to improve their creative works.

Take photography, for example. We may see a magnificent panorama or a portrait that captures the subject's emotions and marvel at the photographer's talent. Dozens or hundreds of rolls of film have been shot and developed, but the picture we're looking at is the only one that satisfied the photographer fully enough to print. A perfectionist would never take the chance to fail so often, by shooting roll after roll, before producing the desired result. Artists strive for the perfect picture but know they can never achieve it without many attempts, learning each time how to do better. This flexibility to keep trying, to do better, enhances resilience.

Creative expression also draws on our ability to look at situations from different angles and approach a problem from various perspectives. It's like a photographer who changes vantage point, lenses, and lighting many times to capture totally different images, while most people would have just snapped a shot. People with only one perspective, who see life through a single lens, are limited in their approach to problems. People who shift perspectives can reframe or paint an entirely new picture and make changes. They understand how to focus on a problem and attack it from different angles, as well as see other people's perspectives. These benefits of creative expression make us more flexible and resilient in confronting challenges. Children who develop their creative selves enhance their resilience by learning to see problems from many angles and meet challenges by using varied techniques and perspectives.

The Joy of Artistic Expression

Artistic ventures can be instant vacations. The processes of singing, acting, drawing, painting, sculpting, writing, dancing, composing, or playing music can be joyful releases. For some, artistic expression is a solitary event that allows time for reflection, introspection, or simply quiet private time. For many others, participating in a group effort, such as a class performance, offers an opportunity to express themselves while connecting with other people.

Ms Yoshida and Ms Pollak have taught children and adults for years. They told me that in their early years of teaching, they were very disappointed whenever students left their work behind, seemingly forgotten. The teachers later learned that the students' joy lay more in learning to be creative and practicing their new skills than in their completed masterpieces.

If you have ever taken a pottery or woodworking class, for example, you probably didn't set out to create a 60-piece set of dinnerware or rolltop desk. Instead, your greatest enjoyment no doubt came from the process itself of centering wet clay on the wheel or sanding wood to a smooth finish.

We want to educate children by fostering their creativity and expanding their minds. By the middle of elementary school, many kids regurgitate facts and figures; their success is defined by how well they can recall those facts and figures. Art as a steady presence in children's lives allows them to continue having open-ended opportunities to express themselves with less emphasis on the final product.

Creativity as a Release

I have seen many young people tap into their creativity as a means of coping with their problems. They use music, art, dance, poetry, or prose to express their feelings vividly and intensely. These outlets allow a degree of privacy; whether to show them is the artist's choice. Each creative work is subject to interpretation, but only the artist or creator needs to have a full understanding of what the piece means to her.

Rather than containing emotions to fester within, artists are essentially able to say to themselves, "I know how I feel, there it is!" Rather than bottling up their emotions, creative people express them and literally place them outside their bodies.

I am amazed by how many poets and artists I find among my young patients who have lived the toughest lives. I have no doubt that their creative expression has helped them survive. When words fail them or don't come easily, it isn't uncommon for them to rap, sing, write poetry, or draw to express themselves. As I explore with them how they have survived difficulties that I couldn't imagine, they frequently tell me, "I draw," or "I write music." These are powerful survival tools that soothe their souls. In my work with homeless youth, I sometimes create a simple book for them, a place for them to place their creative work. For many, this small gift of a folder and stapled-together paper is quite precious because it gives them an important outlet for their feelings.

Some young people look at their picture and can describe what it means, using their verbal skills to magnify their emotional release. Others could never describe out loud what the picture means, but their subconscious pent-up emotions may still be released. Don't assume because children can't always put into words what their art means to them that we should help them tell the story. The art does the work itself.

Can We Foster Creativity?

Every child is creative. Each is not a Rembrandt or Mozart, but all children express themselves through some form of art. When they are young, we encourage this creative outlet in a few kids and stifle it in many, who then decide they have no talent. I am totally uninterested in whether their artistic product pleases the masses. I am not talking about training the next generation of cutting-edge artists. I simply want all children to be able to draw on their creative side because this gives them an avenue to release their tensions, fears, hopes, and dreams. It gives them an opportunity to experience the joy of creating, and it trains them to see other perspectives. It gives them another way to cope.

Parents can do any number of basic, inexpensive things to nurture children's creative expression. You don't have to enroll them in classes or buy expensive equipment. The following ideas apply primarily to the visual arts, but if your child is more inclined toward the musical or dramatic arts, you can adapt the same principles:

1. Make a wide variety of art supplies available. Some of the least expensive creations are made from sticks, stones, and scraps of cloth. Socks and mittens can become hand puppets by decorating them with buttons, yarn, and colorful laundry pens.

2. Expose children to tactile stimulation so they can discover the joy of working with their hands. Nothing fancy is needed—try clay, wood, sandpaper, or various textured fabrics. With young children, have them guess what the different textures are with their eyes closed.

3. Have some turn-off-the-screen time. Many kids turn to television, hand-held devices, or the computer when they have "nothing to do." Without pushing art per se, simply make art supplies available and limit time wasted in front of a screen.

4. As they produce their artistic masterpieces, make open-ended comments like, "Tell me about that," or "It's beautiful! Explain it to me, please." This will avoid the embarrassing and belittling exchange we have all heard ("What a darling little elf you've drawn." "No, that's you, Grandma."). Exchanges like that embarrass children and convince them that they have no talent, so they stop creating. More importantly, open-ended questions and comments give children an opportunity to explain the content of their pictures or meaning of their poems or songs, and that is good practice for self-expression too. Occasionally, you might add, "What were you feeling when you created this?" If a child doesn't choose to answer, just drop the subject.

5. Look for beauty in their creations. Not all their works will be gorgeous, but all have something special. Be genuine when you point out something noteworthy. A boat floating on an ocean might not look at all seaworthy, but the ocean may be inviting. "Look how well you used the blue paint. I want to dive in and go swimming."

6. Display their art, listen to their poetry, watch their dances, and applaud their music to show them that you're paying attention. You are genuinely interested in them, proud of them, and appreciate their creative efforts.

7. Look for art everywhere. You can go to a museum or concert, but you can also notice designs in cloud formations or point out how junk can be turned into beautiful or whimsical objects. It's simply a matter of keeping our eyes open. Public art and unintentional art are all around us. Give a child a camera and let her see how many perspectives exist in each picture.

Here are some steps to avoid when thinking about children's creative expression.

❖ Don't supervise or direct their art making (poetry writing, singing, dancing). It's about their expression, not yours.

❖ Don't rave so much and so often that they think you expect them to create masterpieces every time. This only adds stress. Do show appreciation for creations that they present to you.

❖ Don't sign children up for lessons in an effort to make them the best in the field. Again, that produces stress; it may take away their joy in the creative process and could negate any benefits of the lessons. On the other hand, if they want to develop a talent or expressive art, lessons can be a gift.

❖ Don't automatically display their creative works without their permission. Some works may be deeply personal items, as they should be. Encourage children to keep it personal and only display it at their discretion.

Spirituality

People with strong faith or a deep sense of spirituality find comfort in prayer or meditation. While parents certainly can expose their children to religious practices and beliefs, ultimately each child will decide what role religion has in her life. She may see it as a community institution, cherished family institution or tradition, or personal means of managing her life, or she may reject it entirely.

In the context of resilience, I am interested in how young people can use spirituality as a moral compass, as a means to reduce daily stress, as solace in times of crisis, and as a means to solidify a sense of purpose in their lives. Spirituality is a way for young people to grasp the interrelatedness of life on Earth and strengthen their sense of connection and responsibility to others. I advise parents for whom spirituality is important to speak with their own spiritual leaders about how to encourage children to use their religious beliefs as a personal, portable tool to manage life's stresses and disappointments and draw inspiration.

Journaling

Journaling, or keeping a diary, can be a powerful tool for releasing emotions. It's another technique that says, "You want to know how I feel? Here it is, tucked away securely. My emotions are in a safe place where I can access them when I want to. I am in control of them. They aren't swirling around inside and taking control of me."

Younger children can be encouraged to begin journaling by buying them a simple diary or having them make one for themselves. Tell them that this is a special book that is very private, a place to draw or write anything they want, and no one will ever look at.

It can be tempting to gain insight into a child's secret world and innermost thoughts whether they are 6 or 16 years old, but I strongly urge parents against looking at a child's diary. That would be a deeply felt violation that takes away this important tool from children and teens—"If it's no longer private, why keep it?" they would conclude. Violating this trust can harm their relationships with parents. I have seen this happen many times, and though parents explain that they looked at the journal out of love and concern, kids never accept this argument. I always tell parents that the journal is a place to write absolutely everything, true or untrue, real or imagined. If it's to be effective as a way to release emotional baggage, it must be a place where young people can play out their fantasies, darkest thoughts, or most romantic dreams. If parents read a journal, they might get an unnecessary scare. In other words, their yield will be low and they'll have taken away their child's release valve.

If parents become so worried about a child's behavior or emotions that they feel the need to check the journal, it is far better to open up communication instead of the journal. If the child shuts her parents out, get professional help.

As much as privacy should be respected, parents should be aware of the Web log or *blog*. Many young people who may not take to a journal, perhaps because pen and paper are so old-fashioned, prefer blogging. These online journals can become very public. Anyone can check in on a child's most private thoughts or at least those she chooses to make known through the blog. Some blogs can be made more private if children give passwords to friends they want to keep in the loop. If your child does blog, talk to her (perhaps through a choreographed conversation) about the possibility that some of the things she reveals online may find their way to people who don't respect her privacy even if they do use passwords. Perhaps an old-fashioned paper journal would be more secure for her innermost thoughts and feelings. (See Resources to find National Center for Missing & Exploited Children advice on Internet safety.)

Young people who don't blog may use social networking sites where they much more casually express their feelings. Once the send button is pushed, those feelings spread like wildfire among "friends" and can't be taken back. Rapidly developing technology has had many benefits, but it also allows alarming, even dangerous situations for young people. Talk with your children about *cyberbullying* and *sexting* (sex + texting), which have become all too common. National surveys report that 1 in 5 teenagers has sent or received sexual images electronically. Sending risqué or nude photos via cell phone or videos over the Internet, and harassing classmates electronically with cruel notes or pictures, have serious consequences.

Talking With People Who Have Earned Trust

The greatest release of emotion for many people occurs when they share their thoughts, fears, and frustrations with others. It is a way of letting it go while getting needed attention. Sometimes talking is also a way to problem-solve, because it helps the talker focus ideas and develop strategies to deal with the problem or because the listener has a different perspective or experience with a similar challenge. Someone else's viewpoint can throw new light on a problem and shed wisdom on another set of choices.

Talking to another person also provides a chance to decompress, to let it all go. Sometimes we feel better when someone else knows all the things we're trying to handle—it somehow validates our feeling overwhelmed. But no one can resolve all stresses at one time. Talking can be more effective in 2 phases. First, get it off your chest. Use the opportunity to talk about what's bothering you as an escape valve to prevent all your emotions from swirling inside your leaden box. Then focus. Pick one issue to make it manageable. Talk about that one issue. Just talking about it may be all that's needed for you to begin bringing it under control. Talking about that issue may be the catalyst for solving the problem. Either way, the Tupperware box is burped and less chaos spins inside.

Young people need to be exposed to different perspectives, so it's important that they can talk to a variety of people. Parents often become frustrated when children are so eager to talk with their friends (in person, on the phone, through incessant texting, and on the computer for hours), yet they're so monosyllabic at home. When we ask them, "How was your day?" they're likely to reply, "Okay." We make another attempt. "What did you do?" The answer is, "You know, stuff."

We acknowledge that they talk more with friends who, after all, do share more of their time and experiences. We hope those friends care enough about our children and have the good sense to steer them in the right direction. Friends can be ideal sounding boards, or they can be poor influences.

Other people can also offer children varying perspectives—older, mature adolescents; teachers; relatives; clergy; and coaches. Some parents feel guilty or insecure when children confide in another adult, but they should know it's more beneficial for their child to talk with someone than to talk to nobody at all. During mid-adolescence in particular, when teenagers' struggle for independent thinking is at its height, it's vital for them to know people other than parents who will listen and talk.

Most parents naturally want to be their child's favorite listener. When I first meet families, parents often tell me, "Oh, yes, we can talk about anything. My kids tell me everything." Sadly, teenagers tell me a different story. Many say that they stop talking to their parents because their parents "just don't listen." This is partly developmental, a distorted perception that's a side effect of kids' need to trust their own decision-making skills. They reject out of hand their parents' potential for good advice. But the statement is often the truth, as well. When parents don't listen, kids stop talking. Volumes have been written on this subject (see Resources) and we discussed the importance of listening in Chapter

18. The good news is that parents who learn to listen better find that their children do talk to them more readily. Parents earn their children's trust when they make themselves worthy of talking to by responding less and listening more carefully.

Some kids' stress levels can become so high that they need to talk to a professional. It's an act of great strength and resilience to seek help when burdened. Never feel as if you have failed because your child needs someone more objective and trained to help her through critical times. Sometimes a parent's job is just to love the child unconditionally while another trusted adult helps her resolve an important struggle. As parents let this other adult do much of the talking, they should remember that the security of their love remains the bedrock of any solution. Seeking professional help is discussed in Chapter 36.

Laughter—It's No Joke

Laughter is good for all of us, and we probably don't get enough of it. If you think about it, laughter is such a silly-looking thing. We snort, we grunt, and we make ridiculous sounds. There must be a biological reason that we're given this gift. Did you know that laughing releases stress? Researchers at the University of Maryland Medical Center measured people's blood vessel dilation (how wide open the vessels were) before they watched 15-minute clips of movies that were tense, disturbing drama (the opening of *Saving Private Ryan*) or laugh-inducing comedy *(Kingpin)*. As reported by Michael Miller, MD, author of a study presented at a scientific session of the American College of Cardiology, the study participants' blood vessels were measured again after the movies. The results? The blood vessels of the people who'd watched the comedy were more open, and the blood vessels of people who'd watched the drama were more constricted. This makes sense because blood vessels must narrow quickly to speed up blood flow in an emergency. Every once in a while, science proves what our grandmothers told us. My grandmother, Belle Moore, used to say, "With a sense of humor, you can get through anything." How true.

I see laughter as a refresh button. Let's say you're listening to a boring presentation at work. You can't pay attention for another minute—and then a well-timed joke wakes you up. Or you're feeling down and someone tells a story that evokes a huge belly laugh. Afterward, your mood is completely changed. You're refreshed. You feel you can start over.

So whenever you feel tense or worried, laughter can be a quick release. Make a point of reading humorous stories, telling jokes, or even making yourself laugh for no particular reason. Just start laughing as an exercise. Do you know the ha-ha game? Someone begins by saying, "Ha"; the next person says, "Ha-ha"; the next says, "Ha-ha-ha"; and so on until someone breaks down and laughs. Yes, you'll sound silly, but laughter cascades. You'll relieve tension and feel lighter.

Most kids are born comics. They make us laugh at their antics. We may get tired of their making silly faces or telling poop and knock-knock jokes after a while, but encouraging children to have a sense of humor is certainly worthwhile. If we are always too serious, kids may stifle their natural ability to make us laugh. Trust me—trust my grandmother—laughter can help us rebound during difficult times.

Crying

Crying is another of those biological oddballs. People look so vulnerable and unattractive when they cry. It simply must have a purpose. Perhaps vulnerability is the point. Perhaps our need to get others to pay attention to our grief is the reason that crying is so entrenched in our social repertoire. Perhaps we need the attention to gain the sense of security that reminds us we remain connected to others.

Certainly, crying is a powerful tool for releasing pent-up emotions. The old saying, "Have a good cry," is on target when we're sorrowful or consumed with stress. Think of how we comfort someone who's in tears—"That's okay, let it out." Letting it out is the goal. People feel lighter after they've released those pent-up feelings. Crying doesn't solve the basic problem, but it cleanses the emotions and prepares us to move toward a solution.

When little children fall down or feel frustrated and cry, why do we instinctively say, "Don't cry. It's okay. You're all right," or worse, "Big boys don't cry"? How can we deny half our population such an important inborn tool to release emotions?

Of course it's okay to cry. Tears are a normal reaction to sadness and pain. We may want to comfort a child or discourage crying whenever a child doesn't get what she wants, but saying, "Don't cry," is not the best way to comfort children or build resilience. It forces them to create a disconnection between their feelings and their abilities to express them. It makes children ashamed of those very real emotions, and therefore may prevent them from seeking the support they need and reaching out in whatever way they can.

When children are genuinely hurt or upset, it's more empathetic to say something like, "I see you're sad. Would you like to tell me what's bothering you?" and then listen and encourage them to talk about it. Oftentimes no words are necessary. A hug and a shoulder to cry on silently communicate, "I'm here for you; this is your secure base. Lean on me." Children who have a place to recoup from sadness are better prepared to move ahead.

Making Lists

Getting organized is a key problem-focused strategy, but I mention it here because it can also help release emotional frustration. You know the feeling of being pulled in a hundred different directions—too many demands, too much responsibility. The stress seems overwhelming and chaotic. You can't enjoy anything because your head is spinning with thoughts about everything you must accomplish and all the work you aren't doing at the moment. You can't focus, you're inefficient, you can't fall asleep because you're making tomorrow's plans. You need an escape valve.

This isn't an adults-only phenomenon. Children's heads also spin with worries about homework, after-school activities, friends, and chores. Like adults when they feel snowed under, kids make excuses and procrastinate. Sometimes it seems so impossible that they freeze and do nothing.

It's quite helpful for children and adolescents to understand that getting organized can remove a lot of their stress. They don't have to accomplish everything at once; they simply can begin by breaking a big job into smaller, manageable steps.

With young children, a task like "clean up your room" seems gargantuan because toys, books, and clothes are scattered all over the place. They may think it will take a week, and they'd certainly rather play elsewhere at the moment. Parents can help them organize the task by suggesting, "Just start in this corner. First, put all the clothes in the hamper, or begin by putting the books on the shelf."

Older kids and teenagers can break down jobs and to-do schedules by making lists on paper or computer. "What I need to do today. What I need to do tomorrow. What has to be finished by Friday." When their lists are written down, there's a strategy in sight. They begin to feel they've taken some measure of control over the chaos by organizing it, and the pressure is diminished. Their mental and emotional energy can then be directed toward tackling problems one by one.

Two tricks make list making more effective. First, make sure something on the list is pleasurable. When a school-aged child comes home with a book bag full of homework, breaking it down into manageable pieces is important, but there should be some balance too. After she's organized her science, math, and reading work, for example, suggest she also list a fun break somewhere in the middle—a half hour to play outside, enjoy her favorite hobby, or play a game with a parent or sibling.

The second trick is meant to keep anxiety low. Lists should be realistically designed. It's okay to have a long-term plan that includes goals that may not be accomplished for weeks, but it's also important for daily lists to be constructed in ways that assure children they're moving forward each day. For example, a child may be worried that his group science project can't be finished by the deadline 3 weeks from today. So several items on his list can be broken down into doable segments like, "Look up Saturn's rings," "Sketch my model of the solar system on big paper," and "Make sure Owen gets the wire to connect the planets." As each segment is completed, he can check off that item on his list, see that he's making progress, and diminish his anxiety about completing the entire project.

Once again, parents can show the effectiveness of list making as a stress reducer by modeling the technique. When your child sees you making your own to-do lists, she'll pick up the lesson more easily than if you simply say, "Get organized." When you do so, talk aloud about the fact that you make lists not just to organize all your responsibilities but because it helps you reduce stress, preserve your energy, and enjoy the rest of your time.

One caution—list making can be overdone. If you become compulsive about it or notice that your child is doing it to excess, pull back. This is meant to reduce stress, not add to it. You might say, "I have so many things on my mind and this list is getting too long. I'm going to put my list on the table and take a well-deserved break," or "Right now, I'm going to work on just one thing and not look at the other things on my list until tomorrow."

❖❖❖❖

Now that you have read through this comprehensive stress-reduction plan, I want to remind you again that these points are suggestions that you can adapt for your child and yourself. No one is expected to use all of them all the time. You're probably familiar with many of these techniques but may not have tried them, or you may have other techniques that I've omitted.

I hope you expose your children to a wide selection of stress-management techniques so they're better prepared to deal with stress when they feel challenged. When I say *deal with,* I have a specific point—children can be helped to cope with stress and somehow get past it, but nothing in this plan can make them immune to stress or make stressors disappear entirely. Everyone has times when they feel they simply cannot take any more stress. I believe that the tools in this plan can equip children to bounce back faster and stronger. I don't want to leave you with the false sense that this plan is an answer to every problem or that you (and your child) should be able to handle everything just because you have a plan. It's okay to go through periods of absolute rage or profound sadness. Don't deny your own emotions. Give your child the comfort zone to acknowledge her own feelings. We're all human; if we deny emotion, we deny the most complex, perhaps most valuable part of being human.

Above all, take care of yourself first. Model for children that there are healthy ways to manage life's bumps and bruises. It is the best lesson you can offer.

PART 5

Control

Styles of Discipline

Let's get off on the right foot. By *control*, I do *not* mean inflexible parental control, the "Do as I say because I'm the parent" style. We cannot and should not attempt rigid control of our children's actions, emotions, thoughts, or choices if we want them to become more resilient. When I discuss control in the context of building children's resilience, I mean *their* controlling their actions and therefore the outcomes.

Children who learn inner control by making decisions and facing the consequences gradually become more independent and ultimately more resilient. Children who understand that they have control over their lives take responsibility rather than blame others for problems and failures. Look at it from the opposite side—children who routinely blame someone or something else for adversity ("Why does that always happen to me? It's never my fault.") will see themselves as victims and will be passive in the face of difficulty because they do not believe an action they may take will make a difference. Resilient children understand that things don't just happen to them. They can be decision-makers and problem-solvers who control outcomes. They learn that delaying immediate gratification often leads to success at a long-term goal.

The development of resilience depends on parents' relinquishing tight control in favor of guidance, attention, and support so that children have opportunities to test their inner control. That is not to say that parents take a completely hands-off approach, of course. Parents can enhance children's growing sense of self-control by observing, offering a steadying hand, and guiding children rather than controlling their every action.

This discussion about ways parents can contribute to a child's having control will be divided into the following 4 basic categories:
1. Considering how controlling we should be as parents
2. Disciplining in a manner that teaches self-control and delayed gratification
3. Helping children trust their own decision-making skills
4. Knowing when we need to take control and when to conserve our energy

How Controlling Should We Be?

Before I suggest various ways to help your child develop control, I ask you to consider your own parenting style. Of the following 4 general styles of parenting, which best describes you?

Authoritarian. This parent's attitude is, "Do as I say. Why? Because I said so. Don't question my authority. Until you're 18, I'm the boss in this house!"

Permissive. This parent may teach sterling values and give terrific support and love, but ultimately says, "I trust you," instead of setting appropriate boundaries. Permissive parents often treat a child like a pal and fear the child won't like or love them if they clash. They hope that their children will do the right think because they do not want to disappoint their parents.

Disengaged. This parent is too busy or otherwise occupied to monitor a child's activities and behaviors closely or set limits unless the child is in trouble or imminent danger. This parent says nothing or says, "Do what you want." This parenting philosophy is "kids will be kids." Disengaged parents don't believe that they have much influence anyway. But when major problems erupt, they may come down hard on a child, leading to inconsistency and mixed messages.

Authoritative. This parent sets the tone and reasonable limits, expects good behavior, offers a lot of love, and encourages kids to make choices and be independent, but when it comes to the big issues, it's, "Do as I say." Authoritative parents balance warmth and support with control when necessary.

Children raised with authoritarian parents heed the line to a certain point, but then may rebel fiercely. Even if they remain obedient, they may become unwilling or unable to make their own decisions and instead seek authority figures to control them even into adulthood. Barring this scenario, what happens after age 18? There's nothing magical about an 18th birthday. I want my children to come to me for guidance and comfort throughout their adult years, though I hope the guidance will become more mutual as they gain greater wisdom.

Children raised with permissive parents know how loved they are, but they sometimes crave boundaries because it may be their conscience (guilt) that sets boundaries. They are terrified of the D word. The thought of disappointing their parents can paralyze them or force them to weave a web of lies. Children with disengaged parents fare the worst because there is nothing more painful to children than being ignored by people who are supposed to care for them. They sometimes need to push their behavior to the extreme to get the attention they crave from parents.

If you find your parenting style leans toward the authoritarian, permissive, or disengaged models, I would suggest you consider how to become more authoritative. Ample evidence suggests that children raised with authoritative parents are less likely to engage in worrisome behaviors and more likely to be resilient. The balanced, authoritative model requires lots of love and attention and opportunities to gain increasing independence, with close supervision and clear boundaries. This parenting style has been shown to delay sexual initiation, lower drug use, improve school performance, and decrease delinquency. My own research at the Center for Injury Research and Prevention has demonstrated that teens who describe their parents as caring and supportive individuals, who also monitor them and have clear rules and boundaries, are half as likely to crash cars, twice as likely to wear a seatbelt, and 70% less likely to drink and drive.

Before you convince yourself that this will be easy, I ask you to reflect on which of the 4 styles best describes your own parents. Did both parents have the same style? If not, how did their conflicting styles confuse you? How did you manipulate them if their parenting styles didn't match? Most importantly, how did you respond to their styles? Chances are that you have copied their styles or moved in a clearly opposite direction. Parents who give no thought to this may be destined to react according to their own childhood experiences rather than arrive at a parenting style that's best for their children. Even with deep, reflective thought and the best of intentions, don't be surprised or come down hard on yourself when your child misbehaves and your father or mother's words leap from your mouth.

Overcoming Your Authoritarian Side

Many of us were raised with authoritarian parents and even if we rebelled, we turned out okay. On some level, our fond memories of our parents urge us to honor them by raising our children the same way. Much anecdotal evidence tells us that children are becoming more spoiled, self-centered, or out of control, which leads some people to believe that we should return to traditional, stricter styles of discipline. Some people even advocate a return to physical punishment, though ample evidence indicates this is harmful. If nothing else, physical punishment makes children feel like victims and interferes with their learning a lesson. While they have been punished, they have not been truly disciplined or taught anything.

I could not say it better than Thomas Gordon, who wrote in his classic book, *Parent Effectiveness Training*, "Each and every time they [parents] force a child to do something by using their power or authority, they deny that child a chance to learn self-discipline and self-responsibility." Precisely because self-discipline and self-responsibility are such important ingredients of resilience, I will discuss discipline in detail here.

Giving Yourself Permission *Not* to Be Permissive

In any given moment, children seem most appreciative of permissive parents. They get more. They have fewer rules to follow. What's not to love from any child's perspective? Let's be honest—sometimes we do things simply because they differ from the way our parents did them. Many parents today who were raised in authoritarian homes vow to be very different—looser, more laid-back…permissive.

This style feels good in the short run but may raise more neurotic children because they are forced to self-monitor through guilt. When parents don't set boundaries, children have to set their own, without the wisdom or life experience that says where those boundaries should be drawn.

Even though it doesn't feel as comfortable, parents do children a great service by setting appropriate limits. We don't have to swing in the opposite direction, either; we can be different from our authoritarian parents. With an authoritative approach, we can shower children with affection and still explain and monitor the rules. This is vital because kids will only acquire a sense of control if they understand that their actions lead to consequences.

When you feel conflicted about not always giving in to your child's impulsive requests, remember 2 things. First, clear boundaries create a sense of safety; kids want to know where they stand. Second, sometimes saying "no" is the best way of showing your love for your child.

Making Boundaries Acceptable

Children crave boundaries so they can know if they're pleasing you and because they're eager to prove they are good. Adolescents need boundaries so they can better learn to define themselves. Boundaries allow teens to experience and test their limits, while knowing deep down that they will be protected. Still, don't count on your children thanking you for setting boundaries, at least until they have children of their own.

The challenge is to give clearly defined rules and boundaries in a way that is acceptable to children. Judith Smetana's book, *Adolescents, Families, and Social Development,* helps parents consider how to do just that. It suggests we move away from the belief that monitoring is as simple as asking your children where they are, who they're with, and when they will be home. Instead, it discusses what adolescents consider "legitimate authority" of parents and reveals that parents really only know what their teens choose to tell them. Armed with this knowledge, we then have to consider what it is that will make teens more likely to share.

In previous chapters when we discussed connection, we talked about the importance of listening as the best guarantee to keep teens talking—listening without judgment; listening while offering unconditional support; listening while honoring a young person's intelligence and serving as a sounding board while she develops her own solutions. Dr Smetana's work takes it a step further. She reveals what teens find to be acceptable areas for parental guidance and intervention and which areas they expect a hands-off approach. Teens believe that parents have an obligation to be involved with their safety and a responsibility to teach them how to interact with society, while respecting other people's rights and following the law. Teens also believe that parents do not have free reign to transcend on personal territory. If the issue is about their friends or about behavior that doesn't affect safety or their "getting along" with society, it may be out of bounds.

This information informs us how we need to present rules and boundaries. We must make it clear to our children that we have rules because we love them deeply and care for their safety. The rules are not frivolous and certainly don't exist to control them. In fact, we cherish their growing independence and recognize their growing skills and competencies. While some rules are *always* or *never* rules, most are in place only until children gain more experience or demonstrate the responsibility that shows they need less supervision. *"Always* wear a seat belt; *never* drive intoxicated." "You may not drive after dark until you gain more experience driving during the daytime."

Certainly the toughest area for setting rules and boundaries involves your child's friends. Adolescents especially may not think you have a right to comment on their friendships or even what they do with their own time. I want to underscore this important point—rules and boundaries should be framed to be about safety whenever possible. If you condemn your teen's friends, you might just make their company more enticing. If you limit them from seeing particular friends, your child might choose to stop talking to you about who they're with and might make up stories that prevent you from knowing where they're going. After all, they think, "This is my personal life and not your business."

Although some believe that peers control teens' behavior more than parents, I disagree. Our strategy has to be to influence peers' affects in a way teens find acceptable. First, be selective in your comments and rules about friends. Your children really do deserve privacy when issues do not involve safety or negative influence. On the more "controlling" side, you should set general rules that will keep your children safer and won't feel like they were made to counter any of their friends. Curfew, for example, keeps your child off the streets when things get wild. When you make sure that adults appropriately supervise parties your child attends, you protect him from untold risks and pressure. Next, be subtle about promoting positive relationships. You can make it easier for your child to be with friends you trust by creating opportunities for them to get together. Third, always bear in mind that your child probably wants to do the right thing; he just needs the skills to follow his own internal compass. That's why giving him the tools to navigate the peer world, as discussed in chapters 11 through 13, is so important. The check-in rule and code word allow your child to have face-saving techniques to follow his own values even in the midst of peer pressure.

Finally, remember there is less to rebel against when teens know their parents care about them. Sometimes it takes an extra effort to help your teen understand that the limits and structure you impose come from your concern for his welfare and safety. The truth is, there are situations in which peers' influence can lead to destructive decisions and others in which they innocently make a situation more dangerous because they create distractions or generate heightened emotions that make teens lose focus. Driving serves as an example again. We know that peer passengers in a car driven by a new driver substantially increase the risk of crashes. But how do you make a rule about something that, on the surface, seems as innocent as driving friends to the movies? If you say, "I don't want you to have any friends in the car while you are driving," your teen will think, "My friends are my business." *(In other words, "My parents have no legitimate authority.")* "Why do my parents hate my friends? I'll take them anyway and my parents will never know."

Instead, be clear about your motives. "I care about your safety, and because teen passengers distract new drivers, you may not drive with passengers until you have at least 6 months' experience behind the wheel."

Expect pushback. It's perfectly normal, even a good thing, for teens to test their boundaries. "My friends are really good; that's probably because other kids act wild."

You respond, "Actually, even great kids get excited talking when they're having a good time. It's too much to expect you to have your eyes on the road, control of the car, and control of your friends. This is nonnegotiable, but it's also temporary. When you have more experience driving and you've shown me you continue to be responsible, you'll be able to drive your friends. In the meantime, I'm happy to get you all where you want to go."

Making It Easier on Both of You

Remember, it's a teen's job to explore limits. Teens compare themselves with peers to see what they can handle. They want to at least keep up because they're always trying to answer one of those fundamental questions of adolescence—"Am I normal?"

When your rules are different than those of other parents, you'll be seen as strict and unreasonable, and your child is set up to rebel. If you work with your community or with the parents of your child's circle of friends to set up common rules and boundaries, everything will go more smoothly. Your child will just expect the rules because everybody else has similar boundaries. He can meet your expectations, stay safe, and be "normal" all at the same time.

Positive Discipline Strategies

The word *discipline* means teach or guide. It doesn't mean punish or control. Parents who discipline successfully see discipline as an ongoing responsibility to teach. The best disciplinarians (or teachers) hold high expectations for children and give appropriate consequences, or allow them to occur naturally, rather than dole out arbitrary punishments when children fall short of those expectations.

Several disciplinary strategies can help children develop control of behaviors and their outcomes. Some of these approaches can be used to spotlight and further encourage positive behaviors. Others can be used to steer children away from negative behaviors. While some discipline is a reaction, depending on the situation at hand or your child's particular need at the moment, the most important aspect of discipline is positive attention, and it should be ongoing.

Paying Positive Attention

When infants cry and a parent's face soon appears above the crib, babies learn their first lesson about how they control their environment. They can't yet articulate it, but they know, "If I cry, someone will come and pick me up, feed me, change me, and take care of me." As they get older, children become masters at controlling our attention.

You may have seen this joke (which has been e-mailed around cyberspace) that captures a child's attention-grabbing control. A small boy is sent to bed by his father. Five minutes later—"Da-ad." "What?" "I'm *thirsty.* Can you bring me a drink of water?" "No, you had your chance before lights out." Five minutes later—"Da-aaaad." "WHAT?" "I'm *thirsty.* Can I have a drink of water?" "I told you, no! If you ask again, I'll have to spank you!" Five minutes later— "Daaaa-aaaad." "WHAT?!?" "When you come in to spank me, can you bring a drink of water?"

Children crave parents' attention. When they don't get enough of it, they find ways to make us pay attention by doing something we cannot ignore, like interrupt, yell, whine, talk back, or pick a fight with a sibling. Then our attention is usually paid in negative ways, like scolding, criticizing, lecturing, threatening, or punishing. These negative ways of paying attention are ineffective and instill powerlessness rather than a sense of control. The cycle continues because kids begin to see that type of attention as what they expect and learn to need from parents.

As we list a litany of reasons why children shouldn't have done something, they don't think about how correct we are. In fact, our efforts tend to backfire because we make them feel inadequate and incompetent. They want to prove our dire predictions or assessment of their behavior wrong. This doesn't build resilience.

If we want to diminish negative behaviors, we can short-circuit them by giving kids more frequent doses of positive attention. Unfortunately, we tend to focus primarily on their undesirable behaviors and fall into a pattern of responding only to those. If this has been your experience, here's a simple way to break the pattern. Keep a diary for a week and note all your interactions with your child. When he wants your attention, how does he get it each time? Begin to recognize that many of his annoying or undesirable behaviors may be attention-seeking ploys. How do you respond? Once you become more aware of your pattern, you'll be better able to replace negative attention with positive attention.

I've already mentioned some ways to pay positive attention. Catch kids being good. Show appreciation for the little things they do or say, things we often overlook, such as sharing toys with other children, getting their school gear together on time, or helping with daily chores. Praise them with words that show you have really noticed and appreciated something they have done, rather than generalized phrases like, "You're so terrific." I'm certainly not against telling kids they're terrific, but let them know *why*. "I think you're terrific to help your little brother learn to ride a bike."

Other ways to pay positive attention can occur in simple, daily encounters—share a joke, play guessing games while waiting in line, tell or read bedtime stories, or ask kids to help you with something pleasant that is not a chore. Children appreciate being invited to participate in grown-up activities, which also helps them feel more competent. "I have to mail a lot of letters. Can you help me put the stamps on the envelopes, please?" "I could use some help hanging these pictures. Could you please help me line them up straight?" "I need to get a present for someone at work. Want to help me pick out something?"

These minor occasions are wonderful opportunities to pay loving attention to our children. The more positive attention we give them, the less they feel a need to capture our attention by behaving in less desirable ways. But let's face it, all the positive attention in the world won't guarantee a child will never misbehave. What do we do then?

Appropriate Consequences

From an early age, children should learn that certain misbehaviors bring unwanted consequences. Hitting younger siblings means a *time-out,* sitting quietly for a certain amount of time away from the center of the action, and losing that positive attention that they crave. Failing to finish homework means loss of television time. Leaving piles of dirty laundry around their rooms means their favorite clothes won't be clean the next time they want to wear them.

These consequences are appropriate because they fit the crime. When parents have to discipline by using a punishment, it should be reasonable and related to the offense so that children understand the direct consequence. When they spill or break something, for example, they have to clean it up or fix it. A consequence that is too stiff or unrelated to the offense (say, they cannot attend a friend's birthday party because they haven't picked up their socks) takes their focus off the misbehavior and prevents them from thinking about how to correct it. They become defensive or feel like victims. They become angry, focus on your unfairness, and sometimes even want to get even ("I'll show them! I'll never..."). More relevant to our discussion of control, overly harsh or arbitrary punishments send the messages, "You aren't in control. We, your parents, control what happens to you. There's no logical connection between your actions and consequences."

Certain patterns typically emerge between children and parents when parents try to guide kids toward a safe behavior (such as, "I need to know where you're going and who you'll be with."), get them to adhere to safety rules ("Bike riding requires a helmet."), or contribute to smooth operations of the home ("Fold your clothes; clean the dishes."). The diagram that follows illustrates the flow of communication between parents and children, when it works productively and when it breaks down. As I describe the interactions, try to see what portion of the diagram applies to you. It may be that you have different interactions with different children or that you and your spouse have different patterns.

Discipline Cycle

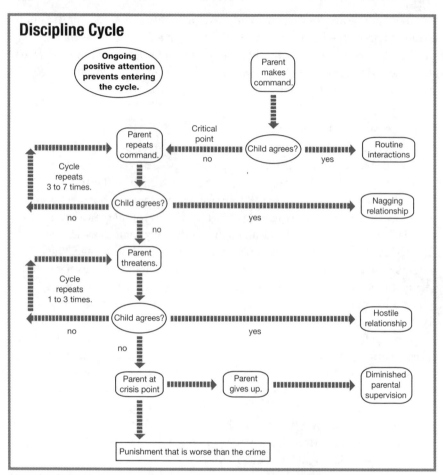

Adapted from Barkley RA. *Hyperactive Children: A Handbook for Diagnosis and Treatment.* New York, NY: Guilford Press; 1981. Copyright Guilford Press. Reprinted with permission of The Guilford Press

First we issue an order like, "Clean up your room!" The child may follow the command, and all is well. If the child ignores our command or argues with us, everyone's stress level increases. We may repeat the order several times. Most kids know their parents' threshold for repeating commands. Some parents repeat them 3 times; others repeat 5, 6, or even 7 times. Children know just how far to push us and how many refusals they can get away with before we give in or get tough.

Why do they do this? Because they are engaging us, holding our attention. The problem is that parents and children caught in this repetitive cycle of commands waste a lot of time nagging and refusing, nagging and refusing.

If they don't comply after our first, second, or seventh request, we move up a notch to the threat level. "If you don't clean up your room, you can't go to the birthday party!" Now the child must decide to accept the threat and obey or call our bluff ("I don't want to go to the dumb party anyway!") because if he buys into the threat and complies, our attention will disappear. Either way, the tone in the household moves from nagging to hostile.

If we let confrontations get to this point, we get angry because the child is disobedient and defiant. We are at a lose-lose crossroad. We have 2 options— we can follow through on the threat, or we can cave in. If we follow through with the threat, children don't learn useful lessons. They feel like victims of mean parents; they learn nothing about taking responsibility or solving a problem. They focus instead on how we made them pick up their rooms or kept them from going to a party. The punishment shifts away from the original request or command and now focuses on their rising defiance and disobedience. Missing a party because socks are left on the floor seems unfair to them.

When we get to this point with teenagers, we are sometimes talking about problems and consequences much more serious than cleaning up and going to birthday parties. They may be out after curfew, we may not know where they are, and we're so frantic that our threats become almost hysterical. Most parents are unlikely to say, "You are 25 minutes late. I have been worried sick. I was ready to call the police! I'm going to come up with a consequence so fair and so directly related to your lateness that you will really learn this lesson!" No, hysterical parents instead have adrenaline coursing through their veins and say, "That's it, young lady! You are grounded for 2 weeks!" Parents may consider grounding a gift to themselves because it means they will know where their child is. To adolescents, grounding feels like being sent to prison, and they don't see how 25 minutes even begins to compare to 2 weeks. They learn nothing and become increasingly hostile.

Parents often realize that their initial threats were too harsh, so in a more rational state they take the second option, caving in ("Okay, I give up. You can pick up your room after the party," or "All right, never mind. You're not grounded. Just be home on time tomorrow, okay?"). When we cave in, children learn that they can manipulate us, hold our attention even in a negative way, and still win by not obeying our original request. Children who learn to manipulate parents or simply endure our nagging and anger because they know they'll win in the end are headed for trouble.

To prevent these lose-lose situations, try to avoid getting to that critical point in the first place. The critical turning point is immediately after you make the initial command. Don't let children pull you into these spiraling negative cycles. Instead, make it clear from the beginning that certain behaviors are not negotiable and consequences are immediate. It may seem harsh to have immediate consequences, but it is far better than wasting so much of your valuable relationship time on nagging, hostility, or empty threats.

A word to the wise here—pick your battles. On those things that really matter to you, have clear and immediate consequences. But remember that part of growing up involves kids' negotiating boundaries and figuring out what they can handle. Parents who make rules about everything or hold a rigid sense of exactly how children should behave in every situation prevent them from benefiting fully from their own experiences of decision-making and boundary-setting.

Advance Planning

You can avoid negative punishment cycles by planning fair, consistent, and predetermined consequences that will occur if your child refuses to comply with your request or behaves irresponsibly. (More about this in a few more pages.) Make these consequences known in a concise, clear way. If you plan ahead, you can set consequences that are reasonable and linked to the problem, and your child will be disciplined instead of punished.

When you are in the middle of a problem or confrontation, give your child options in a calm, straightforward tone. "If you don't pick up your toys, we won't go to the playground." "You can continue to whine or, when you stop, I'll play a game with you." "If you want a ride to the mall, you'll have to finish your chores first." Then stick to your statement. Don't let your child pull you into the old pattern. By making consequences immediate and linked to his choices or actions, you help him understand that he has some control. You, the parent, set the limits, but he controls his choices and consequences within those limits.

With younger children, trying times may arise when they act out in public or in front of friends, and you'll need to issue a consequence in a way that won't embarrass your child or yourself. We want our children to keep their dignity even when they are misbehaving, so we can take them aside and have a brief, firm private discussion. ("How do you think your remark made her feel? Apologize or leave the room.") With very young children, we may need to remove them physically from the scene—take them out of the store when they toss a tantrum.

These challenges take patience and a cool head. We don't want to embarrass kids because that not only instills a sense of shame, but it also puts them in a defensive position ("Why are you picking on me?") so they don't reflect on what they've done wrong. They become hysterical, the adrenaline courses through their veins, and it becomes unlikely they'll behave rationally. Again, we want them to learn that they have control over outcomes, good and bad.

Family Meetings

Sitting down together to solve problems is a great way to allow children to experience more control of their behaviors. Family meetings don't have to be (and certainly *shouldn't* have to be) saved for problem occasions only. They can be used for pleasant purposes, such as discussing family vacations, whether to get a new pet, or what color to paint the house. They can be brainstorming sessions—what to get Grandpa for his next birthday or where to send letters to get the local government to plant more trees.

Family meetings can be reactive. "We have a problem, now what can we do to solve it?" They can also be viewed as a preventive strategy. As advance planning sessions, they go a long way in addressing how to respond to situations clearly and directly when they arise. Encourage everyone to brainstorm the potential problem and its possible solutions.

Family meetings give children a safe, relaxed environment in which to think in advance about their behaviors. This is an opportunity for them to develop more abstract, cause-and-effect thinking as they discuss benefits and disadvantages of possible actions and consequences. Everyone's contribution should be heard and respected in these family discussions. The more input children have, the more likely they will be to comply with decisions. You want your child to propose reasonable, fair solutions and consequences, but don't forget that parents are the final arbiters and ultimately set the limits. You can do this without issuing threats or commands.

The consequences you agree on should be spelled out clearly so that when the time comes to test them, they will be understood and effective. It may be helpful to allow your child to run through some what-if scenarios. "What if I come home too late and I haven't called?" "What if I get in trouble with...?" "What if I am going to be late, but call to tell you what the problem is and how I'm handling it?" This process will help your child clarify the purpose of the rules and more importantly, understand the limits of your flexibility.

Increasing Kids' Control

When discussing problems and solutions with your child, encourage her to negotiate. You are the ultimate limit-setter and certain misbehaviors are non-negotiable, such as hitting another person, verbal abuse, stealing, or whatever you deem unacceptable. But the majority of issues that you will consider with your child will probably not be of the nonnegotiable quality. When you're discussing individual family members' responsibilities, such as taking care of pets or sharing computer time, it's healthy for children to negotiate schedules, rules, and the consequences for not following them. By actively negotiating, kids reap several benefits. They exert some control of events. They will be more likely to follow through on compromises that they've had a role in reaching. As teenagers and young adults, they will have learned give-and-take skills that will come in handy when they must negotiate with peers, teachers, or bosses.

Whatever consequences you and your child agree on, expect that problems will inevitably arise, so be ready for them with the appropriate consequence. Don't make children feel that they have ever made a mistake in coming to you when they've messed up or fallen into trouble. Let the consequence teach the lesson, but don't let your disappointment in their behavior or your anger take over.

When children do mess up, let your essential message be, "Yes, you've done something wrong, but I still love you." Statements like this don't erase or diminish the disciplinary consequence, but they will help ensure that your child feels secure enough to come to you with problems. If we don't send a strong message of unconditional love, even in the face of disappointment over behavior, kids may turn away from us the next time they do something wrong or find themselves in trouble.

A Rein in Each Hand

As children grow, we parents often feel that we're holding 2 reins. We grip one tightly to keep them safe, while the other is looser as we gradually give them a little more slack to move away from us and explore increasing freedom. We're constantly jiggling these reins, pulling one a bit tighter, letting the other out an inch or two. We don't want to overprotect or control children too strictly, yet we don't dare let them have too much freedom or they may make serious mistakes. It requires a delicate balance, but the trick is to increase their freedom gradually, while at the same time minimize chances that they'll make unsafe or unwise choices.

We typically think of teenagers as pulling away from parents and asserting their independence and autonomy. That's true; it is their job to develop their own identities apart from us. But the process actually begins at a much earlier age. Even the toddler whose favorite word is "No!" is asserting her independence. By age 3 years or so, she may be saying, "No, I do it myself," when you try to get her dressed faster than she's dressing herself. Some children, of course, have innate temperament traits that make them more independent, persistent, or outgoing than other kids. Very few children want their parents to hover over their shoulders, overprotect them, make all their decisions, or otherwise curtail their burgeoning independence.

Earned Freedoms

We can take advantage of children's natural desire for independence by guiding them along safely if we put some safety nets in place. I call one of those nets *earned freedoms,* which are built on the foundation that parents don't hand out privileges and freedoms lightly, and neither do we use them as bribes. Earned freedoms are just that—earned. Here's how to institute this practice in your family.

Sit down with your child and explain the concept that you and she can come up with a plan that serves you both well by ensuring 2 things—her greater freedom and privileges and your need to be sure she's safe and responsible. Together, you draw up lists of what you each want and need. You'll discuss these, negotiate, put them in writing, and come up with a written contract.

Your child may want to stay up later at night, but you need to be sure she gets enough sleep to be healthy and alert for school and play. She may want a new bicycle, but you need to be sure she wears a helmet and rides safely. Your child may plead for a larger allowance, but you want to be sure she knows how to handle money responsibly. She may want to go somewhere with her friends, but you need to know where they'll be, if there will be adults present, and when and how she'll get home. She may be ready to drive, and you may be eager to let her drive, but you need to put into place the restrictions that have been proven to save lives—limiting the number of teenagers in the car, no driving after a certain hour, no cell phone use while driving, exposure to more complex driving situations (like 4-lane highways or bad weather conditions) only after the easier ones have been mastered, and driving on her own only after a significant amount of adult supervision.

From both your lists, you can draft a contract of sorts. Her wants should be linked to your expectations of her responsible behavior. If your child requests a later bedtime, for example, she can earn it by meeting your expectation of being wide-eyed and bushy-tailed enough to get up in the morning, meet the bus on time, and earn good grades in school. If she wants to go places with friends, she can earn this privilege by calling you at an appointed time to check in and let you know where they are, who they're with, and how she's getting home. If she is ready to drive, you will allow this if she follows your safety plan.

Your contract will work most effectively if you reevaluate it from time to time to see how it's working. You'll probably hit several snags, but try to stick with it and tailor it to be more effective when necessary. As you work through the earned freedoms process, your child will enjoy having more control and will undoubtedly act more responsibly to keep that control and gain greater freedom and privileges. It's a reinforcer of good behavior as well as a deterrent of negative behavior.

The earned freedoms technique works best when you make the privileges and freedoms measurable and verifiable. For example, a new privilege can be earned when it is monitored or verified by some measure, such as a certain length of time (say, the number of hours spent watching television or doing homework). If your side of the contract says, "I need to know you're keeping up with your schoolwork," that can be measured by the report card or amount of time your child spends on homework. If kids aren't keeping up their side of the bargain and their grades are slipping, the consequence is to decrease the amount of time they spend on the television, computer, phone, or other amusements.

In the case of teenagers and safety concerns ("I want to know where you're going, who you're with, whether parents will be present, and who's bringing you home and when."), adolescents should be very clear—before they earn freedoms to go out on their own—about how strongly you feel about following the rules. They should know which freedoms and privileges will be unearned (otherwise known as *lost*) if they don't act responsibly to prove they are capable of those freedoms. For example, a parent could say, "I want you to understand that if you are late, I will not allow you to stay out until 11:00 again. You have already proven to me that you're capable of following a 10:00 curfew. You will return to that earlier curfew if you are not able to follow the later one. I think you are ready to handle an 11:00 curfew, so go have a great time."

When your family has worked out an earned freedoms contract, go back and consider its effect on the interaction patterns shown in the Discipline Cycle diagram on page 288 in the previous chapter. Recall the importance of having immediate consequences at the critical point after your first command, so your family isn't dragged into a fruitless cycle of repeating and threatening, nagging and arguing. Pick your battles and don't overregulate your child's choices. For the big items that involve safety and responsibility, though, parents must have clear guidelines, stick to them, and make the consequences immediate. This stick-to-itiveness and immediate response will be far easier when the consequences are understood in advance—easier still because children (usually beginning at about 10 years, depending on the individual child) have helped formulate that understanding.

Essentially the contract says, "I know that I will earn this freedom or privilege by being willing to show responsibility and keep this freedom by proving my responsibility. I also know that I will lose this freedom when I do not show I can be responsible." Parents have the consequence in advance and at their disposal to use when necessary ("You have not shown responsibility here. You have lost this freedom."). The advantage of revising the contract every few months, perhaps at the start of each new season, is that you have a history of past successes—freedoms your child has proven she is capable of handling. When you need to come up with a fair consequence, you could revert to a freedom your child proved able to handle in the past. For example, "You said that if you stayed out until 8:00, you would have time to finish your homework. You didn't finish your homework. I'm afraid that you'll have to begin coming in at 7:30 again. You were able to have fun then and still complete your homework."

Improved Communication

The earned freedoms technique can improve communication in your home for several reasons. Most obviously, it will improve because you will be discussing how to help your family function better on a regular basis, but also because you will be hearing your child's self-assessment of what she believes she can handle and you will calmly be able to share concerns.

Perhaps the most important reason is this—when you write down your need to know she's safe and responsible, you are sending your child the message that you're willing to trust her, negotiate, hear her side, and consider her ideas. Most children expect parents to tell them what to do. They think we want to control them, rather than delegate some measure of control to them. When you first propose the earned freedoms concept, your child may look at you skeptically. As you work through it, she will realize that your motivation is to help her grow safely and that you are willing to listen to her. It is convenient to have a contract to refer to when children misbehave or disappoint you, but realistically, children will make requests for privileges or misbehave in ways you simply didn't anticipate.

Whether you are in a family meeting responding to a child's request or on the spot with a crisis at hand, don't feel that you must make an instant decision. It's fine to say, "Mom/Dad and I need to think about this. We'll let you know after we discuss it." That statement not only buys you some valuable time to reflect without an instant overreaction, but it also models for your child a thoughtful way to deal with challenges.

In 2-parent families, it's ideal, of course, when both parents present a unified front in decision-making. But it's not unheard of for parents to disagree! Partners often have differing philosophies about or styles for raising children. After all, we had different sets of parents and different childhoods ourselves. So when we disagree or are unclear about how our partner sees a problem, it's wise to take time out to discuss it. This also heads off the all-too-frequent strategy that children learn early in life—divide and conquer, otherwise know as, "If Mom says no, ask Dad."

Delaying Gratification and Trusting Their Decisions

Resilient adults can delay gratification. So many things that feel good for a moment can get in the way of success. Especially when we're stressed, we may look for easy answers, quick fixes, and feel-good solutions that end up creating more stress in the long run. Adults are more likely to succeed when they postpone immediate gratification and deal with a temporary stressor because the time delay helps them keep their eyes on the ball. Those who can maintain self-control while striving toward a larger goal are more likely to move beyond obstacles and adversity. Adults who can build a foundation slowly, painstakingly, brick by brick, are able to create a solid base from which success can be launched.

But children? Kids start out being all about instant gratification. "I want it when? *Now!*" They arrive in the world as self-centered pleasure machines, using their charm and sheer cuteness to get big lumbering adults to meet their every need. Children are quickly socialized to learn that not every desire can be granted immediately, of course. The rice pudding comes after the strained peas. (Nothing against peas here.) They must learn to wait in line for the carnival ride or their turn at T-ball. They have to do homework before going outside to jump rope or skate.

As every parent knows, it's an ongoing challenge to teach children that they often must wait to get what they want, and sometimes they never get what they want. Parents who are committed to raising resilient children know that it is a critical part of a child's developing self-control.

Control and delaying gratification are not usually considered aspects of discipline, but when we remember that discipline is teaching and not punishing, it becomes clearer that teaching control is a cornerstone of preparing children to have self-discipline for life.

I know you want to make your children smile, giggle, hug you, and say, "Thanks, this is exactly what I wanted," as much as I do. On some level, I just want to be loved endlessly by my daughters. I have to stop myself from showering them with things that make them smile ear to ear. When I learn what they want for their birthdays, I have to tie myself to a chair to keep from running out to get it. When they say they want to go out instead of doing homework, the little boy in me wants to say, "Neat, I want to play too." Fortunately, I am restrained from being so absurdly indulgent because of some adults I know. These adults who never learned to delay gratification are quite obnoxious. They push ahead in line, leave work for colleagues to finish while they go off and play, and are unconcerned about others. Not so cute.

So I overcome my impulses and teach my girls that sometimes pleasures are earned, sometimes we have to wait for them, and other times we may never get them. As children, that meant special toys usually had to wait for special occasions, and others were too expensive to buy at all. It meant that finishing homework came first, or that as much as they loved ice cream, it followed a meal. While they always have known they are the absolute priority in my life, they also know that after huge hugs, they sometimes had to wait until I returned some patients' phone calls before I could play with them. Now that they are teens, I am careful to make sure they have earned the special electronics or sports equipment they crave. But because I am busier, I try even harder to let them know they remain my top priority, and I will be wholeheartedly available to them as soon as I am able.

These small delays of gratification when children are young will prepare them to put in the necessary, sometimes boring effort and time that will reap success later. They learn, for example, that lots of research and homework can create a science project that they can show with pride. The knowledge that an investment of time and effort produces desirable results is also key to choosing positive coping strategies instead of easier, quick-acting, but dangerous ones that perpetuate stress.

Trusting Their Own Decision-Making Skills

Children and adolescents who are able to make wise decisions learn to trust their ability to control their own lives. They are less afraid of taking the appropriate risks that resilient people must take to meet and rise above obstacles and adversity. They don't fear failure. They don't assume they are powerless because they have seen the fruits of good decisions. They learn from mistakes and don't repeat the pattern of decisions that led to those mistakes.

Parents can be instrumental in helping kids learn that they control their destiny through their choices. You have already learned many ways to support positive, independent decisions and thwart less wise ones. Here is a brief review, but if you feel that your child needs an enhanced sense of control, you may want to revisit the particular sections of this book.

* For children to learn the consequences of their decisions and actions, they occasionally have to experience some emotional bruises. As difficult as it is, good parents get out of the way while still protecting kids from the big hurts (Chapter 5).

* Children who are lectured about what they should do never have the opportunity to figure out for themselves how to handle challenging situations. Lectures backfire by making them want to prove to parents that they can handle everything by themselves and in their own way. They need guidance delivered in a way that puts them in the driver's seat, in control of their own wise decisions (chapters 10 and 11).

* Parents who learn to listen effectively give children just enough security, safety, and support to allow them to trust their own judgment. When children's plans go astray, parents can engage more active listening skills and move into choreographed conversations or other methods to help kids make wiser choices (Chapter 18).

* Children need confidence to be able to make a decision and stick to it. They may need even more confidence to be able to be flexible, to shift to a new path when they have figured out that an initial strategy is unsuccessful or even harmful. We must help children understand that they are capable of sound decisions, and avoid at all costs the shameful messages that tell them they are incompetent (Chapter 16).

* So much of childhood is about negotiating with peers to fit in. Children usually know the right decisions to make but find it too difficult to follow through on them because they worry about losing friends. Children equipped with the ability to handle peers while still maintaining those friendships will feel more comfortable about making their own, perhaps unpopular decisions. They will be more in control of their own behavior (chapters 12 and 13).

* Children who learn that their actions are linked directly to consequences learn to evaluate their choices and behaviors. Parents who understand that discipline is about active, loving teaching and not punishment will nurture children who are prepared to adjust their decisions (chapters 29 and 30).

One Rung at a Time

Sometimes a decision to take a positive step seems so huge or a goal so difficult to reach that young people feel they can't even think about trying. They feel powerless and scared. They think they have no choices. They sense that they're controlled by outside forces that just push them along.

When young people have no deep-seated belief that they are capable of changing, I use a ladder technique. I've used it with kids who never thought they could succeed in school or never considered that they could become healthier by losing weight or exercising. I've even used it with youngsters burdened with drug addiction and trapped in gangs. They all have in common the sense of being so overwhelmed, so stuck, that they believe they can't take the first small step, that they have no control at all in their lives.

When your child is at an impasse, use choreographed conversations and active listening on a regular basis and decision trees occasionally. Save this ladder technique for when your child is really stuck and feeling hopeless. Here's how to begin.

Explain that you sometimes get overwhelmed yourself. The first step is to think about where you are in the present moment. Draw out the base of the ladder and write in the dilemma at hand.

Tell your child that you don't have all the answers, but you do know there are a couple of different possible futures. Write them at the top ends of the ladders as 2 distant but real destinations. One is the positive, hopeful future and the other is what might happen if he doesn't start to make wise choices. Repeat that you don't know all the answers, but you do know that each ladder has several rungs along the way, leading to the ultimate outcome. Ask your child to suggest what steps will lead to the less desirable end. Because he's feeling overwhelmed and helpless, don't be surprised if he knows exactly what steps lead to the negative outcome. He feels expert at those decisions and actions. Unfortunately, he may see no alternatives for the other, positive ladder.

As you write the steps he suggests, tell him that you find it easier when you divide difficult tasks into many small steps. You keep an eye on the future dream to keep you motivated, but you worry about only one step at a time so you don't become weighed down and have a better chance of success.

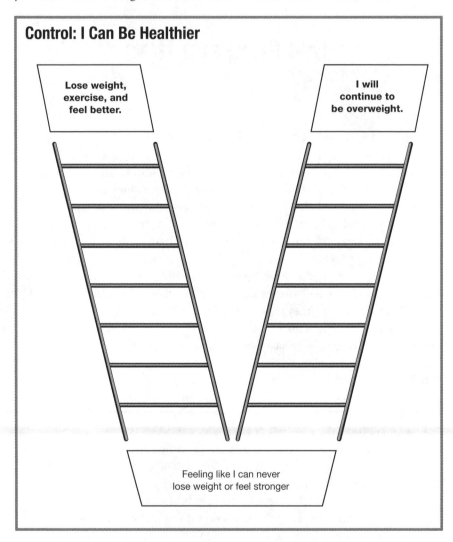

Control: I Can Be Healthier

Lose weight, exercise, and feel better.

I will continue to be overweight.

Feeling like I can never lose weight or feel stronger

I used this ladder technique with Jung, a 12-year-old boy who was very overweight and unable to participate in the sports he loved. His parents nagged him to lose weight, and some of his peers teased him. Jung desperately wanted to lose weight, but he could only admit that with his gaze on the floor. Until our conversation, he had never talked about how much he wanted to shed the extra pounds. Instead, he'd put on a bravado front—"I don't care. Why do you?" He confided to me that the thought of losing weight frightened him because every time he'd tried in the past, he failed and gained more. He didn't even want to try again; he felt doomed to failure.

I sketched out 2 ladders and asked him what he had to do to keep gaining weight. He knew exactly what to do. He named all the unhealthy habits he had and said he would simply continue them. I noted these habits on different rungs of the ladder. Then I asked him to name one step he could take to get on a healthier path. I assured him that once he was on that ladder, each successive rung would be easier. Jung struggled to come up with a single step, but he eventually decided that he could stop drinking candy water (soda pop). When he returned to my office a month later, Jung had lost 3 pounds—a huge success! The greater difference was in his attitude. He realized that he had control. He could make a decision and follow it. He had gained the confidence to take further control and began telling me what his next step would be (walking the dog for 20 minutes after dinner each night).

I used another ladder diagram with Leslie, a 14-year-old girl who was trapped in a gang run by her 16-year-old cousin. Leslie was a bright, engaging girl who felt too overwhelmed to escape her dangerous circumstances. She wanted to become an architect when she got older so should could build buildings in her community to keep children off the streets. I tried my best to offer her my "adult wisdom." She appreciated my well-intentioned ideas but told me that I just didn't get how hard it would be to break from her cousin's gang—"That's family!" she explained.

The ladder diagram allowed Leslie to visualize 2 different futures. She knew which steps would continue to propel her toward trouble, but the ladder technique took away the broad, vague nature of "turning your life around" by helping her see that ladders are climbed one rung at a time.

On her first visit, I could not even get Leslie to the first rung of the positive ladder. After a week, she returned and said she was ashamed that she could still not think of one right step. When I told her that just returning to see me was a positive step, she realized that she had some control over events in her life. Her sudden awareness that she had some control melted away her belief that she was powerless, blown by the winds of fate and trapped by her fellow gang members.

The same girl who spent a week wallowing in her inability to come up with any possibilities immediately began brainstorming ideas she could use to break with the gang. She engaged her mother in a "Just blame me" conspiracy (Chapter 13). When she was facing the most trouble, she would call her mother, who would demand that she come home. Her cousin respected her mother and would allow Leslie to have that special mother-daughter time. Leslie broke from the gang and later attended college.

The key point of these examples is that Jung and Leslie overcame their sense of powerlessness, utter lack of control, and beliefs that only fate determined their futures when they experienced success in one small first step. The success that gave them an inner sense of control was achieved by using the first part of the coping plan—they broke down a daunting task into manageable steps (see "Identify and Then Address the Problem" in Chapter 26). Once they felt successful, the expectation of failure that had paralyzed their ability to act disappeared. They could take control. They could succeed.

When children become responsible for their own decisions and actions, they learn to face joyful and disappointing results. They learn that mistakes happen; sometimes they could have prevented them, but the next time they will be more prepared for them. If they are given many chances to exercise control in their lives, they are far less likely to see themselves as passive victims and blame others. This is the core of resilience—when faced with adversity, failure, or stress, kids who have a true center of control will be able to bounce back. Ultimately they will be happier, more optimistic, and better equipped to face the next challenge.

Not Everything Is Within Our Control

When children know that they can control their environments and influence what happens to them, they hold a powerful key to resilience. It's also important for them (and for adults) to know when they don't have control. Otherwise, we would be banging our heads against walls and wasting vital resources and energy needed to handle those things we can control. People who are overly and unrealistically optimistic will take on unreachable challenges and perhaps miss opportunities to take on those they can conquer. The key is to assess realistically what can and can't be controlled.

My mother-in-law, Regina Schwarcova Pretter, is a case study in resilience. A Czech Jew, she was taken to Auschwitz in the first major transport when she was 16 years old. She survived 3-and-a-half years of hell and went on to raise wonderful, loving children and experience a great deal of joy in her life. When asked the secret of surviving, she says simply, "You fight for the things you can do something about, and you don't waste your energy on the things you can't control."

To overcome any adversity, large or small, children must know when they have the power to change something and when they should reserve their energy. Think about anxiety. At some level, it results from the confusion about what we can and can't control. Like all emotions, anxiety can be helpful, but when it's out of control, it can be paralyzing. Isn't it better to know what we can handle, know our confidence is well earned, and have the good sense to recognize what *not* to worry about?

We've discussed the power of discipline to help children gain inner control and understand their control of consequences. When we incorporate clear boundaries into our disciplinary practice, we also teach kids that they sometimes have no control. Any parent would be a fool to watch an 18-month-old who reaches toward the stove and say, "Now, dear, I want you to understand that if you place your precious little fingers on the stove, you will experience a very nasty consequence." Of course you'd shout, "No!" and grab her. Then you would act out big owies as you pretend to touch the stove. That's setting clear, distinct boundaries—no choices, no negotiation.

A 4-year-old has no choice about crossing the street to chase down a wayward ball. A 9-year-old has no choice about bicycling without a helmet. A 16-year-old has no choice to stay out all night. Clear, distinct boundaries. Long-winded explanations or negotiations would be a waste of energy. Children learn not to expend energy on choices over which they have no control.

We can also teach the lesson about conserving energy in no-control situations by modeling. If we do a little self-talk aloud when our children are present, we can model real but selected, well-choreographed conversations. For example,

Mother: "Ms Brown is so difficult to work with. She makes me feel awful every day. She keeps nagging me to turn in my reports faster. I'd really like to tell her off."

Father: "I don't blame you one bit. You are already working so hard. What would happen if you let her know what you think?"

Mother: "I'd feel a lot better!"

Father: "For how long?"

Mother: "About a minute, I guess."

Father: "Then what would happen?"

Mother: "I'd lose my job, or she'd keep me on but become nastier."

Father: "Whoa. You're really stuck between a rock and a hard place. Is there anything you could do that would make things better?"

Mother: "I can't fix her bad personality or management style. I'm just going to try to remember that it's her problem. You know, I could try a little harder to grind out a report a bit faster each day and plop it on her desk before she has a chance to nag me. But if she does, I'll just smile at her and let it go."

Father: "Sounds like a plan. You'll do what you can do and let go of the stuff you can't change anyway."

Previous chapters introduced strategies that can also be used to help children learn the limits of their control. The first is listening. (Are you surprised?) If we create a zone of safety by using empathetic listening skills, children will come to us during their most frustrating and vulnerable moments. We'll naturally want to fix them and their problems, but we cannot. Even if we could, we shouldn't. We can guide them to come up with their own solutions by using a choreographed conversation or decision tree to help them imagine the end points of various situations. We can go back to the beginning and walk through the situation to see what parts they can control or improve. Children usually will be able to arrive at solutions that fix or improve the problem.

They may instead reach an impasse—just like real life. That's the moment to put an arm around them, support them, give them a hug, and remind them that when life gets tough, at least they can always rely on your unwavering presence. Help them understand that some things are simply beyond our control, for grown-ups and kids alike, and the only thing we can really control is how we choose to react. Often the best thing we can do in these situations is conserve our energy and move ahead without tearing ourselves apart.

PART 6

When Resilience Is Challenged Beyond Reasonable Limits

Extreme Circumstances

Parents can do everything in their power to help children develop resilience, but major challenges can test even the most resilient young people. When we know in advance that a crisis is looming, such as a divorce or the terminal illness of a beloved grandparent, we try to prepare children. In times of unforeseen crisis, we'd like to be able to give them a quick booster shot of resilience.

All our good intentions may not be enough because these events put enormous pressure on us and leave us little energy or time to support our children. For that reason, resilience building should be an ongoing, preventive practice of parenting—a routine that builds a child's strength and stores it for unusually critical times. This chapter goes a step further than the 7 Cs model to address circumstances (divorce, death, terrorism, and natural disasters) that require a resilience boost. In each situation, parents make a major difference in how children weather the storm.

Divorce

As much as we want children to be our top priority, parents going through separation and divorce experience such enormous stress themselves that some find it difficult to focus on their children's needs. Some children suffer serious social and psychologic repercussions, but many children of divorced couples thrive after an initial adjustment period. Parents who are sensitive to children's needs, despite their own overwhelming stress, are more likely to have children who bounce back.

Research demonstrates certain keys about why children do well after their parents separate or divorce. For example, a child's optimistic versus catastrophic thinking style can be a determining factor in how he gets past the divorce. Parents can have a great deal of influence in helping children realistically assess situations and avoid catastrophic thinking patterns (see Chapter 9). Children also prove to be more resilient when there is less residual conflict between their parents and they continue to be able to spend time with both parents (assuming both parents are safe, capable caregivers). Consistent parental discipline has been shown to be important because it ensures clear boundaries that don't vary widely between homes. During times of change, even turmoil, it is important that children maintain as many routines as possible.

It's Not All Bad

Parents often experience guilt around divorce because their relationship has failed, and they worry about the effect on their children. Certainly it is best when families remain well functioning, but when there is hostility in the home, it is stressful for parents and kids. If parents will be much happier living separately, they will have more time for themselves and their children without wasting so much negative energy sparring with each other. Children may experience mixed feelings, including relief at the reduced tensions between their parents.

It is helpful to make the following points to children:

- Mommy and Daddy will both be happier.
- There will be 2 homes where you will be loved.
- Each of us will be able to spend special time with you.

Talking About Divorce

Children at varied developmental levels naturally have a different understanding of divorce, the reasons for it, and what the future will bring. For all kids, their parents' message should be clear and simple. It should leave out messy details that could lead children to believe that they need to fix the problem or that they are the cause of the divorce. Parents—ideally together—should explain in a calm tone something like, "We have decided that we can't live together anymore and do not want to stay married. This was not an easy decision, but it was an adult decision. It has absolutely nothing to do with you; we both totally love you."

It is important to listen and pay attention to children's reactions. For older children, this news may not come as a surprise. They may have friends with divorced parents. They may have worried with every argument that their parents would be next. For other children, the news may come as a shock. Prepared and unprepared children have many questions that they are afraid to ask. Some questions will be immediate, and others will evolve over time. For this reason, it is important to give children repeated opportunities to ask questions and express their worries.

Children usually focus on whether they will remain secure and safe. Other major concerns may remain unspoken. Most children worry about whether they were responsible for the dissolution of their parents' marriage, but few find the nerve to ask directly. Asked and unspoken questions should be addressed.

* Was this my fault?
* Could I have done anything to make you stick together?
* If I promise to behave, will that make you get back together?
* Will you still love me, even if you don't live with me?
* How often will I get to see you?
* Do I have to move?
* Do I have to change schools?
* Will we have enough money?

The keys to answering these questions are clarity, honesty, and reassurance that they will remain safe and loved. Children must know that there is absolutely nothing they have done that caused their parents to decide to split. It must be reinforced repeatedly that the decision to separate was an adult decision, based on adult problems. This may be a hard point to convey convincingly if child-rearing issues were often a point of contention. Nevertheless, it is a vital point to make. Children also must know that there is nothing that they can do to fix this adult problem. That is not their responsibility. Neither angelic behavior nor acting out will bring their parents together.

Traps to Avoid

If parents want to be sure that children rebound as well as possible after divorce, they can work to avoid some common traps. First, it is vitally important that children not feel caught in the middle between parents. Divorced couples often harbor a lot of resentment toward each other. Children should be spared from witnessing hostility between 2 people they so deeply love. Even fine people can get ugly during these fights, and this is very confusing to children. Words spoken in anger might be seared into children's memory and interfere with their ability to remain close to both parents.

Another trap to avoid—use every ounce of restraint not to tell your children how you've been hurt by your spouse. It is important that they can continue to relate well with both parents. They need to be able to see each parent without worrying about hurting the other or leaving the other feeling jealous or angry. Children have to be able to continue to build a relationship with each parent without feeling disloyal to the other. (This assumes that both parents have reasonable capabilities to care for the children.)

Even if communication is at a standstill between spouses, children should not be used as go-betweens or pumped for information as they move between homes.

It is also important not to force children to grow up too soon. Separated or divorced parents sometimes turn to their children for emotional support. This can be very confusing for children if they have to assume a caregiver role for a parent. Be careful not to make statements to older children like, "You are the man of the house now." That can put an unreasonable amount of pressure on children and leave them feeling guilty when they are unable to fill that role. You can let them know how important their contribution is to the family by saying, for example, "I need you to help me make sure that your little sister is handling this." That's fine as long as you also check in with that older child about his well-being too.

Because children are a combination of both parents, some kids worry that if their mother rejected their father or vice versa, they will be rejected if they act like the "offending" spouse. On many occasions, I have met parents who dislike attributes in a child who reminds them of their former spouse. This is very dangerous for the child's well-being. If you ever feel the urge to say in anger, "You are just like your [father/mother]!" stop yourself in your tracks. Children who hear that not only feel ashamed, but they also wonder when they will be rejected.

Creating Shared Experiences

No matter how amicable a divorce, parents struggle to honor each others' desire to spend as much time as possible with their children. When they are separated by distance, this is particularly difficult. Telephone calls, video chatting, and conversations by social networking sites or e-mail can keep parents and children close, but that kind of communication often feels unsatisfactory. Although it allows parents to stay informed, it may not fill their need to experience life more directly with their children.

I suggest a possible solution from a father who is separated from his children by nearly 2,000 miles. He can't be with his children nearly as often as he desires, but he creates shared experiences by arranging to do the same things at the same times. Father and children plan in advance to see a certain movie, read a book, or watch a televised game. After every shared experience, he phones them and they have long discussions.

The most important take-home lesson is that for children to be able to rebound from divorce, it is vital that they know their parents will go out of their way—no matter the distance—to include them in their lives as fully and as often as possible.

Sickness and Death

Paula K. Rauch, MD, author of *Raising an Emotionally Healthy Child When a Parent is Sick,* encourages parents to tell children not to worry alone but to share their worries with a parent or other designated caring adult. Parents can let children know that the most productive worrying happens as a team. If children share concerns with a parent, those concerns can be addressed together. When children do not share their worries, parents cannot worry with them and can only worry about them. Being worried about often does not feel good to a child and is not very useful. Worrying with a child, so that challenges are faced as a parent-child team, prevents children from feeling alone or overwhelmed, models good problem-solving skills, and improves resilience.

Many parents and children need help to start a conversation about emotionally challenging situations. Children are most likely to talk to caring adults who listen with curiosity and respect. Asking a child to tell a parent what he has heard or noticed is often a good place to start. After hearing from the child, the parent can connect the child's observations to the situation being faced. Other approaches to opening a conversation could be to ask the child to tell the parent how he would explain this challenging experience to a friend or classmate or to ask a child what others who haven't lived this experience would be surprised to learn or might not understand about it. An older child who is reluctant to show sadness about an upsetting experience may respond to the question, "What is the dumbest thing anyone has said to you?" The best parent-child conversations are those in which the child does 3 times as much talking as the parent.

Children will be exposed to death at some point in their young lives because death is part of the natural cycle of life. Even young children who may not understand death react to grieving parents. Older children grieve themselves. As with all grieving, time eventually heals. Parents need to support children through the grieving process to help them resume their lives.

At various developmental levels, children have a different understanding of the finality of death. Preschoolers see death as something temporary. Their misconception is reinforced by cartoons where characters pop back to life moments after anvils drop on them from the sky. Because young children are concrete thinkers, seeing things exactly as they appear and hearing things literally, it is important that they are told about death in simple, clear language. Do not use euphemisms like, "She has gone to sleep," "...traveled to the great beyond," or "...passed away." These phrases will not be understood and may even generate fears of sleeping or taking long trips. Instead, young children should be told that their loved one has died and "that means we will no longer be able to see her."

This firm but clear message can be softened with the knowledge that memories last forever. It is up to individual parents, of course, whether they will also use religious explanations. School-aged children begin to understand death as a final event. Adolescents may understand death on the same level as adults but may be resistant to expressing emotions about it.

Once again, it is more important to listen than to say the perfect words. Children grieve in stages much as adults do. We can't push them to come to terms with their feelings; it takes time. The most important factor is that they have you as a sounding board to meet them at their level. Sometimes a hug and a simple statement like, "I miss him too," gives children the opportunity to share their feelings or at least know that all of their confusing emotions are acceptable. Younger children's thoughts and fears often will come out during play. Remember that play can be the language of childhood, so remain alert to what kids may be trying to tell you through their play.

Children worry that they will be left alone, especially by the death of a significant adult. When an aunt dies, for example, a young child may ask her mother, "Mommy, when are you going to die?" Don't be surprised if your child becomes cuddlier, more watchful, and more possessive of your time. Reassure him of your health. Let him know how many people in his life care for him. Take care of yourself and make sure you have support. Your child is watching you closely. When he sees that you're okay, he becomes more comfortable. This is yet another circumstance in which parents take care of their children by caring for themselves. Keep as many routines as possible intact. Routine is a protective force for children amid major disruptions.

Children and teenagers fear permanent loss, just as adults do. They need to do something to memorialize the person they miss. They may satisfy this need through prayer, reminiscing over pictures, recounting stories, or planting trees in honor of the person who died. When I work with teens who have suffered a loss, I try to help them create a living memorial. I start by asking them, "What are you going to do to honor his/her life?" Sometimes their answer is obvious and immediate; other times, they flounder. If they lost a friend or peer, I ask, "What was his/her dream?" The young person may be able to fulfill part of that dream in honor of the friend. If they've lost a dear relative (a grandmother, for example), I ask, "What was her dream for you?" I then help my patients come up with a goal that is consistent with a grandmother's dreams—one that is reachable but will take genuine effort to fulfill that dream in her name.

I did that with a young patient whose favorite older cousin had been killed in an accident. Tyra was inconsolable and talked of wanting to kill herself to be with her cousin. I knew she wanted me to talk her out of her suicidal feelings. Many of us might have near-hysterical reactions like, "You can't do that!

What good would killing yourself do? That's ridiculous! You'd only add to your family's grief with another death! Now your grandmother would have 2 grandchildren to bury!"

I took another approach. As we talked, I sketched a decision tree that forked in 2 directions. One took the negative direction, the series of events that would likely unfold if she did harm herself. I led her through a series of hypothetical questions—"Who would you leave behind? How would your mother and father feel? What would your younger cousins think and feel? Your friends? What things would you leave unfinished or untried?"

Tyra filled in the answers. "No high school diploma, no job, no marriage or family of my own. I'd never get to see my little sister grow up." She saw these options sketched out, but concluded, "I don't feel any better."

Then I drew a tree branch in another direction and led her through questions that would lead her to a more positive outcome. "What was your cousin like, Tyra? What were his dreams? What were his dreams for you?"

As she answered, I scribbled down her answers. Her cousin had been a musician. He'd written poetry. He had recently become a father and left behind a wife and 6-month-old daughter. He had told Tyra that he hoped she'd be a mother some day, that he knew she'd be a good mother.

Then I asked her, "How can you honor him and his memory?" As she offered answers, I wrote them down. She would make sure his daughter knew who he was. She would put together a book of his poems and songs and give the book to his daughter when she was older.

This simple technique of sketching a decision tree helped Tyra realize that she had better options than killing herself. I knew she never wanted to, but her grief prevented her from seeing another alternative. As soon as she recognized other possible paths, she knew which direction to take. Our conversation didn't erase her grief or anger at her cousin's tragic early death, but she found a way to embrace her grief and honor her cousin. As sad and distressed as a child is whenever a loved one dies, you can help her focus on the person's qualities and give something back in the person's honor. This gives a young person a coping strategy and knowledge that she has some control. Ultimately, this contributes to her resilience.

Terrorism, War, and Natural Disasters

As much as we don't want to think about it, we must prepare for the possibility of helping children bounce back from catastrophes such as acts of terror, war, or natural disasters, whether they affect us directly or we witness them through the media. Here are some considerations to think of in advance of eventualities that we hope will never happen.

Take Care of Yourself

Children sense adults' fears and insecurity. Babies, toddlers, and young children don't understand disasters, but they do understand security. They seek that security in their parents. If we feel disjointed, confused, or traumatized, they feel insecure. We cannot be superhuman, but we need to take care of ourselves in these circumstances. Think of a flight attendant who instructs us to put on an oxygen mask before putting one on our precious child. We can't take care of our child if we cannot breathe ourselves.

In a major crisis, you'll be shaken, furious, and scared. The first thing you will do is hug your family and remind yourself that they are okay. You will know you're ready to talk to your child when your adrenaline has run its course. Maybe you'll need to exercise or scream it out of yourself. Then when you can think more clearly, you can talk with your child in a calmer, more reassuring way that will help all of you process the events and reestablish some sense of security.

Remember That Each Child Is Different

Every child will have unique needs in a crisis and will express how and when you can meet those needs. Much will depend on how closely a child is affected or whether he knows anyone who was personally involved, how much he's been exposed to the news, as well as his age, developmental level, and individual temperament. Let children give you clues about how to meet their separate needs, and don't assume that one size fits all.

When America was attacked on 9/11, my twin daughters had just celebrated their sixth birthdays. After rushing home to be with my family, I suggested that each girl could have some private daddy time because I assumed they would need extra comfort. I walked one daughter around the block, and we settled on a park bench. She asked many questions about the planes and the reasons why something like that could happen. I answered as best I could, although I was totally rattled and confused myself. Then she pulled out some paper and pencils she'd brought along, began drawing intense pictures, and explained them to me.

Drawing and talking really helped her work it out, and I felt that I had learned how to navigate this impossible task. When we arrived back home, I suggested to my other daughter that we also take a walk. "Great," she said, "let's get a pizza."

Incidentally, the pizza daughter is one of the most intense humans I know. She had exactly the same exposure to the event as her sister but didn't want to discuss anything. She just wanted normalcy, the security of feeling that life was going on.

Whether we're trying to help children deal with their emotions in the face of terrorism, war, or a natural disaster, keep in mind one notable difference—the direction of their anger or confusion. With terrorism, it's typical to ask, "How could people be so cruel?" and have justified anger. With natural disasters, we are often more confused about how to vent anger. Many adults as well as older children turn it inward—"We could have prepared better," or "I am being punished." Others may express anger outwardly or have a crisis of faith—"How could our government fail to protect us?" or "How could a loving God do this to us?" Wherever that anger and confusion is directed, our first response is to listen, not to deny it or try to talk kids out of it.

Listening

Throughout this book, I've stressed the importance of listening as a way to express love and acceptance and help children figure out dilemmas. In the context of crises, listening takes on another vital role. Because children react to crises differently, we must look for clues from them about what they know, how they interpret the events, and what they need from the adults around them. After the hugs, ask children what they understand about what has happened. When they finish talking, ask them how they are doing and how you can be helpful to them.

Helping Them Express Their Fears and Worries

Just asking children what they understand or how they feel may not be enough to get them to voice their feelings. Sometimes simply sitting with them while they draw a picture or play with their toys will help them find a way to communicate what they're feeling, even if they are not fully aware of it themselves.

Older children and adolescents might find it easier to talk about what others think. "My friend Monica said that she just keeps following her mom around to make sure they never get separated. Isn't she a freak?" When this occurs, don't destroy the mask by saying, "I'll bet you're feeling this too." Instead, talk about what Monica must be feeling and how it is understandable. Ask your child what Monica's mom could do to make her feel more secure.

Some children will act as if they aren't bothered at all. They don't seem particularly interested in or moved by the event. If so, there's no reason to push them to express anything at this time. Your child may be deeply moved or upset but actually needs a sense of normalcy. Model that your own way of gaining comfort is by talking about the situation. Let your child see you talking to other adults and observe your relief as you connect with others. Leave the door open for future conversations. They may happen at any time.

What to Say

Our ability to communicate that we feel safe through our body language and tone may be more important than our exact words. In the face of a crisis, gather the family in the part of your home where you spend good times together, or take a walk to a favorite spot that will remind children of comfort. You may want to begin the conversation with everyone present to feel more secure when you are all together. Depending on your children's age and developmental level, more in-depth conversations might occur with just one child and one or both parents.

More than anything else, adults must be honest about what has happened. Sadly this is not the kind of truth that we can protect our children from, but the truth doesn't need to include every horrid detail. How much detail to share will depend on their ability to understand. If they have a gross misunderstanding of events, correct them. But if they explain the story in a way that implies, "It's all over now, the bad guys are all dead, and this happened very far away," do not correct them or add more nuanced details. Their simple explanations may be exactly what they need to believe to feel safe. Don't take away that sense of security they're constructing for themselves.

Don't worry about saying the perfect words, either. Nothing we can say in these circumstances will make everything better. In fact, there's a reasonable chance that adult conversation may upset children further, but keep in mind that it is the situation that is upsetting them, not our talking about it.

As we try to explain tragic events, the main goal is to reinforce that you and your children are safe. If it isn't clear that you are safe, don't lie. Focus instead on the steps you are taking to become safer. If you can, point out things like the distance you are from the event or the fact that police, soldiers, and rescue workers are prepared to take care of everyone.

Attempting to Restore Balance

If your family has been directly involved in an act of terror, war, or a natural disaster, you will have spent weeks or months—hopefully with adequate support—in recovering your lives. If your family has been on the periphery of these crises as witnesses via the media, you will also need time to restore some emotional balance. During these periods, a few small things can help children.

As soon as reasonably possible, try to follow old routines because they provide comfort and a familiar structure to a child's daily life. For example, get him back in school and do not cancel celebrations like birthday parties or after-school activities that he enjoys. Follow as normal a schedule as possible.

Try to monitor and limit your child's exposure to the news. As compelling as it may be during a disaster, news coverage is often overwhelming because today's 24-hour news cycle replays dramatic footage hour after hour, day after day. This barrage can sear images into the mind and increase the trauma. Depending on your child's age, shield him entirely or limit the time he spends watching the news.

Children rely on us so heavily to figure out how to interpret dire events that we need to be aware of the many different ways they learn from us. They listen to our words, notice the level of stress that our bodies communicate, watch whether we follow routines, and see whether we change our tone or attitude when we talk to others. If we cannot maintain a consistent air of calm with friends or other adults, we should have those conversations in private, away from children, and preferably without children knowing that adults are speaking secretly, which will only raise their anxiety and undercut the sense of security we're trying to communicate.

Other Unforeseen Circumstances

Our greatest fear is that our children could be kidnapped, exploited, or abused. Because children who are exploited deserve a professional assessment, strategies for recovery are beyond the scope of this book. For parents to feel safe even letting children navigate this world, we have to know that we have done everything in our power to prevent these terrors. We watch our children as closely as possible, of course, but we also need to build their competencies so that they know what to do to avoid exploitative adults and dangerous situations. Free materials offered by the National Center for Missing & Exploited Children are thoughtful and comprehensive. See Resources for contact information.

Turning for Help

One of my intentions in writing this book has been to give parents strategies to ensure that children know how to rebound from difficult circumstances. The security that derives from a strong connection with parents is the key to resilience. It gives children a deep sense of safety and the constant reminder that things will be okay, no matter what, because your love will always be there. But even if you have the strongest connection and the most competent, confident children equipped with the best possible coping strategies, your children still have limits that can be exceeded when life gets too tough to manage.

We must never believe that resilience means invulnerability. All people, even the most stable and resilient, reach their limits sometimes. It is not a sign of weakness on our children's part, nor is it a sign of poor parenting on our part, when children show their human limitations. When children are no longer coping well, they may come to their parents silently with telltale signs like tears or a furrowed brow. At other times, they may verbalize their feelings clearly and express exactly why they are troubled and what they need. But usually, parents have to remain alert to subtle indications that children are troubled.

Signs of trouble can include regression. A classic example of regression is a 3-year-old reacting to the birth of a new baby by becoming infantile, sucking her thumb, and demanding much more attention from her parents. Other children regress by bedwetting. Older children and adolescents might have the kind of tantrums they haven't had since they were toddlers—anything to let their parents know they are out of control. Sometimes a child will show signs of regression by being overwhelmingly lovable. Be thrilled when your child needs to cuddle or just wants to snuggle up the way she did as a toddler, but if it is a change of behavior and her need feels intense, allow her the opportunity to open up about something that may be troubling her. A child who has heightened anxiety when a parent is out of sight may have an increased need to have you near, perhaps to guarantee her safety or security. Or she may be worried about you and only feels comfortable with you in close range.

Children experience stress through their bodies just as we do. They get bellyaches, headaches, muscle strains, fatigue, and even chest pain and dizziness when they're stressed. Don't assume they are faking to avoid school or get out of responsibilities. If you approach children as if they are faking, they will feel ashamed. It is likely that they do not yet understand the connection between their emotions and their bodies' responses. In these situations, it is important to have them examined by a pediatric caregiver to be sure there is not an illness that needs treatment. It is equally important to consider that children with frequent aches and pains that can't be explained by a virus or other illness may be stressed. Pay attention when your child has frequent complaints that prevent her from going to school. Pay particular attention if symptoms are less frequent on weekends or vacations. That will be helpful information for your pediatrician, who will consider the possibility of school being a stressor in your child's life.

Some children who are troubled also show signs of sleep disturbances—sleeping too much or having trouble falling asleep. They may have nightmares or a renewed need to sleep in your bed. Sometimes children don't even know that they're having trouble sleeping. Look for signs of fatigue or difficulty waking up in time for school.

School-aged children often reveal their levels of stress through school performance. Remember, school is the job of childhood. Just as adults' performance at work declines with increasing stress, children find it difficult to focus on schoolwork. Anytime a child's grades are slipping significantly, it should be a red flag that alerts caring adults to explore what is going on in the child's life.

In older children and adolescents, always look for changes in their behavior. A new circle of friends or radical change in dress style are certainly signs that merit a supportive conversation. Any suspicion that your child may be turning to substance use, including cigarettes, deserves your intensive involvement as well as professional guidance.

Many parents are very attentive to signs of depression, but they make the mistake of believing that childhood and adolescent depression appears the same as adult depression. Adults who are particularly sad or depressed tend to have sleep disturbances, become withdrawn, lack energy, seem to have a lower capacity to experience pleasure, and often express hopelessness. This is true of some children and adolescents, but nearly half of adolescents who are depressed are irritable instead of withdrawn. They may have boundless energy and are likely to act out with rage. I have taken care of many depressed teenagers whose parents are loving and attentive but missed their child's depression because it is sometimes difficult for parents to tell a normal teenager from a depressed one. Normal teenagers have phases where they're irritable at home and have occasional outrageous outbursts. Because parents may have adjusted to this moodiness, they can miss a teen whose rage and irritability are signals of emotional turmoil or depression. This is a critical reason that parents need to feel comfortable turning to a professional for an evaluation.

Finding Help

When a child does reach the limits of her resilience, she has to deal with a sense of inadequacy. It is important that she not also have to deal with the feeling that she is somehow letting her parents down. If you want to make sure that this never happens in your family, let go of the fantasy that your child will be able to handle everything as long as you do everything right. If you view your child's problems as a reflection of you, you won't be able to help her through the toughest of times because you'll have to work through your own feelings of failure.

Whenever your child does seem to be troubled, the first step is always to reinforce that you are there to be fully supportive. Listen, be a sounding board, perhaps even offer advice, but certainly give hugs or do whatever you can to ensure that her most important source of security remains constant. If your child seems to need more than you, it is time to turn to professional help.

At this point, most parents have to work through their own disappointment that their child needs something more than they can give. But think of it as an act of love, not of failure. You love your child so much that you will get whatever help she needs to be able to thrive.

Be assured that professionals who evaluate young children have the training to ensure it is a safe, even enjoyable, experience for your child. Ask your child's pediatrician, school counselor, or clergyperson for recommendations, and then speak to the professional to find the right match for your child.

It may be tougher to guide a teenager to agree to seek professional guidance. Adolescents may feel ashamed that they can't handle their own problems and worry that going for help confirms that they are weak or "crazy." If you have any ambivalent thoughts about seeking professional help, I strongly suggest you try to resolve them before talking to your teen. She will pick up on your mixed emotions easily and become even more resistant. If you genuinely believe that seeking professional help is a positive action, your adolescent is more likely to see it that way.

It is important for adolescents to understand a few key points about professional help. First, they need to understand that they deserve to feel good. Seeking help is an act of strength because strong people know they are capable of feeling better, deserve to feel better, and will take the steps to feel better. They also need to know that professionals do not give answers or solve problems but instead try to find the strengths of each person and build on them. Adolescents should understand they will only be guided to become stronger by using skills they already have and new ones that they will be taught to put into place for themselves.

Possible Signs of Trouble

Remember that no single sign should make you panic. Often, children and adolescents have some of these signs and are fine. But they are signals that you should check in with your child and consider seeking professional help.

* Slipping school performance
* Sleep problems
* Nightmares
* Returning to less mature behaviors (thumb sucking/tantrums)
* Renewed separation anxiety
* New bedwetting
* Irritability, outbursts, or tantrums
* Hopelessness
* Change in eating habits
* Anger
* Isolation/withdrawal
* Loss of friends
* New circle of friends
* Radically new style of dress
* Physical symptoms
  - Belly pain
  - Headaches
  - Fatigue
  - Chest pain
* Missing school because of frequent physical symptoms
* Drug, alcohol, or cigarette use

When Your Own Resilience Reaches Its Limits

When you became a parent, you felt indescribable love for your infant. You began living for someone else. Your drive to protect this precious gift sometimes overrode your desire to meet your own needs. But if your goal has been to build a happy, resilient child who is prepared to thrive through good times and bad, it's critical that you care for yourself with the same degree of commitment you give your child. This is always true, but it becomes essential when your own resilience reaches its limits.

We parents are role models. By viewing challenges as opportunities for growth, we display a resilient mindset. We're the models who demonstrate healthy coping strategies. We're the ones who, through our example, make it safe to admit vulnerability and personal limitations. When we acknowledge and address problems, we reject stigma associated with imperfection. When we reach our limits and reach out to others, we model that strong people seek support and guidance.

Parents who instinctually grasp the importance of modeling when the topic is substance use, inappropriate language, or even how to be neighborly are sometimes resistant to demonstrating self-care—why? Perhaps it is because our generation of overstretched parents devotes every last drop of energy to making sure children's material, educational, and emotional needs are met. It seems like a small sacrifice to forgo our "selfish" needs. This is especially true for those of us who harbor the unspoken but deep fear that because we work so hard, we aren't giving our children the time we think "good" parents should offer.

As a child and adolescent advocate, I *know* that the well-being of your child rests on your health and personal resilience as well as on the strength of the partnership between you and your spouse. If I thought I could sell you on caring for yourself by telling you that you deserve to be happy, I would. But after years of experience with parents, I know that an approach that centers on you will be appreciated for the moment but forgotten during stressful times. I therefore need to stress that caring for yourself is *not* selfish—it is a selfless and strategic act of good parenting.

Your child wants you to be okay. For you to care for your child properly, you need to be okay. For this reason, it is a selfless act to take care of yourself so you can maintain the strength needed to care effectively for others. Parenting is a long-haul proposition; burnout is simply not an option. Maintaining your interests, addressing your needs, and relieving your stress with healthy coping strategies are precisely what give you the energy to give to others.

Let's take this a step further. Do you want your child to grow up and focus all of her energies on caring for her children and lose herself in the process? You are the model. Show that good parents are child-centered but maintain an adult existence. Keep in mind that your ultimate parenting goal is to raise a healthy 35-year-old.

The greatest gifts you can give your child are to live a balanced life and to demonstrate that when life inevitably offers us challenges, we take active steps to get back on track.

Falling Back in Love

The best parents reach their limits at times. You might reach that point because parenting sometimes feels like a mystery; no matter what you do, you are not getting the results you want. Maybe you're at your rope's end for other reasons and your patience is wearing thin. Possibly external forces, like peers or media, are influencing your child, her behavior is unacceptable, and you grow frustrated trying to counter those forces. Perhaps something troubles your child so deeply that she takes out her anger on you because only you are safe enough to dump on. It could be that precisely because of how deeply she loves you, she needs to rebel to test her own wings. Remember, our teens rarely hate us; they only hate how deeply connected they feel to us.

No matter what pushes us there, most of us reach our limits and often don't like ourselves when we do. Those flashing moments when we don't like our kids can be even more unsettling. The fact is, one of parents' greatest challenges is being confronted with a situation that leaves them seriously disappointed in their children's behavior or desperately worried about their safety. These moments most directly challenge our resilience and our relationships.

What can we do at these moments? A first step is to reassure yourself that normal development is full of fits and starts, bumps and bruises. Just because you are in the midst of a crisis doesn't mean you have lost your child. On the other side of the crisis may be a deeper relationship and a son or daughter who has once more learned to turn to you. It may be that your steady presence is all your child needs to right herself, but don't forget that the best of families sometimes need professional guidance. The health of your relationship is worth investing in; assuming that "it will all work out in the end" might be a mistake.

The best resilience-based advice I can offer to weather these storms is to never lower your expectations. Children are fully aware when parents' disappointment and anger overwhelms them. I have cared for countless teens who have told me they have nothing to lose anymore because their parents have already lost trust in them. I have heard this used as an excuse to use drugs, cut school, even to have a baby. I have seen it lead to depression. Other teens ratchet up their behavior a notch to continue to get the only kind of reaction they can still get from their parents. They notice that their exhausted parents have given up and begun to display that dangerous "Kids will be kids, what can I do?" attitude. As a result, teens learn that the only way to get attention is to provoke a strong-enough reaction to shake their parents' complacency. A very different but ineffective approach is to lower your standards and decide to be your kid's friend. Especially in times of crisis, your child needs a parent with strong, predictable values more than he needs a friend.

These parenting traps can be avoided if we return to 2 of the core messages of resilience. First, children need unconditional love, absolute security, and a deep connection to at least one adult if they are going to be prepared to overcome life's challenges. Second, and most importantly here, children live up or down to adults' expectations of them.

Unconditional love gives children the knowledge that all will be okay in the long run. Even when we dislike or disapprove of their behaviors, our children must always know we stand beside them. Keep in mind that unconditional love doesn't mean unconditional approval. You can reject a behavior without rejecting your child. Love is never withdrawn or withheld based on a behavior. If you deal with even alarming concerns with this approach, your adolescent will not go down the dangerous path of believing she has nothing to lose. Even as she may send you strong signals of rejection, she will eventually want to return to the greatest security she knows, your unwavering presence.

Despite our anger and disappointment, we must never lower our expectations. When parents hold children to high expectations, kids tend to strive for those standards. I am not referring to achievements; rather, we expect consideration, respect, honesty, a sense of fairness, generosity, and responsibility.

This might sound logical intellectually, but it's not easy to turn off the anger when we're confronted with a major crisis or deep disappointment. It's hard to heed the advice to maintain constant love and high expectations when you're worried out of your mind or seething with anger. You need something that will allow you to draw that deep breath to reassess how best to approach the situation. It is time to give yourself the gift of falling back in love.

You fell in love the moment you looked into your child's eyes and were swept away when your baby grasped your finger. Well, your child might be a teen now, but inside is the baby you held, the toddler you chased, and the child you took to the first day of school. He may be ornery at times and need deodorant (badly!), but inside your 14-year-old is the 1-year-old who looked to you for cheers as he took his first steps, the 2-year-old who ran down the sidewalk to greet you as you came home, and the 4-year-old who could only be comforted by you when his bike toppled over. It is not just the memories of childhood that should remind you of how passionately you feel toward your child. Hasn't it been wonderful to watch your child learn to question rather than always accept? Hasn't it been wonderful to see her sense of humor evolve?

The knowledge of who your child *really* is can remind you of the highest expectations and greatest dreams you hold for your child. It may give you the fortitude to continue to blanket your child with unconditional love even as you are being pushed away. Not smothering "I can fix this" love, just the reassurance that you are not going anywhere. Re-owning this love may be just what you need to break the cycle of condemnation, excuses, threats, and anger that can easily overtake your home in challenging times.

Seeing the little boy inside of the young man causing you grief may be just the ticket that will allow you to change the negative pattern of interactions between you that pushes you to your limits of parenting resilience. You need a reset button, but perhaps your self-righteousness and your adolescent's pride and sense of indignation may be getting in the way of starting over. You can't count on him to make the first move. The love that blossomed the day of his birth is precisely what you can draw from to restore your relationship and begin to turn him around. It may allow you to set aside your disappointment and request a vacation from the stress you are experiencing in your relationship. You need some time together with no friction; the opportunity to enjoy each other again. Go out to dinner, a beach, or a theme park. Promise each other a vacation from arguments. Let him see that he is not rejected. Hopefully he will learn there is something to be gained by restoring your relationship and modifying his behavior. I can't guarantee this will work, but I can assure you it will not make things worse, whereas more fighting and displays of disappointment will.

I can genuinely state that I am blessed to have 2 wonderful, rather easy daughters. But even guys who write parenting books have their moments. My girls are creative, independent, confident, and occasionally strong-headed (which will serve them well). But let me tell you who they *really* are—they are the children who at the age of 3 made me stop at the side of the road to rescue a soiled, worn, pink teddy bear that was "lost." It was scared and lonely, and they wanted to protect it.

One of them became attached to Eeyore at 2½ because "Eeyore seems so sad, I want to make him happy." They are the girls who begged me to catch bugs and then free them outside so they could be with their friends. When they were 4, we were traveling and saw a roadside chef preparing dinner. They saw a whole chicken in a pot with its feet poking out. Awareness flashed across their innocent faces. "Daddy, did you know that when some people eat chicken, they eat real chickens?!? Why would they do that, don't they even like chickens?"

When I took my 10-year-old daughters shopping one day, I considered buying one of those memory foam pillows that promises to improve sleep. I wanted it, but the sticker price dissuaded me. The next day, one of my girls spent all her money and gave me the pillow because "I know that if you sleep well it will change your whooooole life."

That is who my girls are. Genuinely good people. Faithful friends. Stewards of the environment. People who have a deep capacity to love and an instinct to protect the vulnerable. Funny, funny girls. Sometimes they drive me crazy, but I can usually sift through their behaviors to uncover the girls I know and love. My knowledge of their essential makeup makes it easier to occasionally absorb their expressed frustrations because I can (rightly or wrongly) reframe it as the flip side of the sensitivity I cherish in them. It's not always easy, but my recollection of who they are restores my senses when my patience wears thin. Most importantly, my understanding of their makeup allows me to always hold them to the very highest expectations—in terms of sensitivity, warmth, and empathy. They usually prove me right.

There is no magic formula for good parenting, and no words of wisdom exist to guarantee children won't stray toward some worrisome behaviors. I would never tell you that you don't have the right to be angry and display that anger. Just always remember that the power of your influence lies in the unconditional love you maintain for your child. There is only one place in the world where a child can count on that depth of security. You must remain a stable force so your child can securely navigate a challenging world. Finally, precisely when worrying about your child consumes every drop of energy within you, remember to care for yourself. Your child needs your strength to last; he is learning from you how to recover from adversity.

The takeaway line of this chapter is, take care of yourself and model healthy coping strategies for your children. But when your resilience reaches its limits, it may be difficult to take a breath and think about which specific steps to take. At those moments, you may not realize that you have the answers. You know the steps to take because you have been absorbing them throughout these pages. You have been integrating healthy coping strategies as you've been learning how to use them with your children. I don't need to repeat those lessons about changing catastrophic thinking, stress-reduction methods, or the many ways to take care of your physical health. While you've been helping your children enhance their resilience, you have been indirectly strengthening your own. When you reach your limits, you have the strategies to fall back on.

PART 7

Especially for Communities and Individual Teens

Community-based Resilience-building Strategies

Our goal must be to create a world in which every child has the supports and encouragement to develop to his potential. We can visualize that support as concentric circles of guidance, protection, and opportunities. The first and most important protective layer must be parents' high expectations, enduring love, and unwavering support. Other protective layers include extended family, positive peers, school, and community. Whether the community encompasses civic groups, religious organizations, schools, sports leagues, or any and all groups that serve youth, it can promote healthy development by creating conditions in which families can thrive and by offering community-based resources including youth development and enrichment programs.

The first edition of this book was written exclusively for parents, but many community-based programs, schools, and parenting groups used it as a framework to discuss resilience and youth development. This new chapter was added so this broader audience can more effectively use the principles and strategies on these pages.

If you're reading this primarily as a parent, you may find this chapter useful in better understanding how community-based programs can develop extra layers of support for your child. You can also join other parents to create a community of concerned families, one that shifts your locale into being one where all youth are prepared to thrive. Be assured that as your community takes on the challenge of creating an environment where all children will reach their potential, each child, including your own, will be better prepared to succeed and lead us into the future.

This chapter focuses on 2 points. It discusses steps that a community as a whole, or a community-based program, can take to shift toward a strength-based, resilience-building philosophy and practice. It also suggests specific strategies that parenting programs can use to engage and empower families to build resilience in their children.

The 7 Cs Model: Usefulness and Limitations

This book is not designed to be a full-scale intervention; rather, it's meant to give parents tools to build strengths in their children and give communities a common language and philosophy to build on the inherent strengths of youth while lowering risks. If you represent a school, community, or program that's thinking about using a positive youth development or resilience-based strategy to transform the way young people are approached, I congratulate you. I suggest that you consider organizations that will work closely with you to evaluate needs, suggest infrastructure changes, and frame interventions. Although there may be many such programs, I would like to highlight 4 well-respected groups that can rise to meet your needs: the Search Institute (www.search-institute.org); Communities That Care (www.communitiesthatcare.net); Kids at Hope (www.kidsathope.org); and the Penn Resiliency Project (www.ppc.sas.upenn.edu/prpsum.htm).

This book is a translational work intended to take the best of the literature and research and make it easy for parents and communities to act on it. The 7 Cs allow people from many viewpoints and disciplines—from parents to teachers to youth workers to policy makers to professors—to ask, "What are we doing to promote (fill in any of the Cs), and how can we do more?" Nobody needs to change their framework or approach if it is already strength-based; the goal is to use a common language so we can better hold conversations. This common language can break down the silos that so often prevent people from different disciplines with a shared purpose from joining together to take effective action.

The 7 Cs are a minor adaptation from the positive youth development movement; they're changed subtly to allow us to address risk while promoting strengths. Rick Little and colleagues at the International Youth Foundation first described the 4 Cs of confidence, competence, connection, and character. This group holds my respect and gratitude because they determined that these were the key ingredients needed to ensure a healthy developmental path. Later they added contribution because it was clear that youth with these essential 4 characteristics were poised to contribute to society, and reflexively that youth who contributed further developed the essential 4 Cs.

The resilience movement is tightly linked to and largely overlaps the positive youth development philosophy, but it focuses on the importance of recovery from and overcoming adversity. Although coping is usually included as a part of competence-building in positive youth development programs, I felt it needed to be highlighted here as one of the best ways of reducing risks. Positive coping strategies allow youth to be able to manage stress without turning to those quick, easy, but dangerous fixes that we call risk behaviors. Finally, one of the keys to a person's willingness to enter the positive behavioral change process is to hold the belief in one's ability and skills to tackle a problem; this is called *self-efficacy*. The final C, control, includes self-efficacy in that people with control understand that actions they take can control, or at least alter, their destiny.

For more information on the 7 Cs resilience model and downloadable and printable materials that complement this book (including a teen stress-reduction plan and summary sheets that can be used in school and community forums), visit www.fosteringresilience.com.

Youth Will Live Up or Down to Community Expectations

The first step your community, school, or program can take is to decide how you choose to portray youth. Although we hope that schools and communities are uniformly protective of children and adolescents, the truth is that healthy development can be undermined. Youth can receive subtle and blatant messages that they aren't deserving of resources and high expectations. If we are to build the resilience of this generation, we must enhance the supports surrounding children while simultaneously making a concerted effort to address toxic undermining messages.

These messages are not intentional. That's why we need to bring awareness to how negative portrayals get inadvertently transmitted. As discussed earlier and in greater depth in Chapter 4, unflattering portrayals of youth create self-fulfilling prophecies for 2 key reasons. First, because adolescents focus so much unspoken energy on answering the question, "Am I normal?" teens do what they think is normal. When we focus on problems without paying greater attention to what is going well, teens mistakenly see the behaviors that generate crises as "normal." Second, teens will live up or down to the expectations they believe we hold for them.

A painful example is youth in underperforming schools who have incorporated the toxic message into their self-image that academics are not for them. These youth often have resources directed toward them in the form of prevention programs, but they may not have adequate enrichment activities. Despite noble intentions, they may receive a message that kids like them are expected to engage in worrisome behaviors. If prevention programs were better balanced with strength-building and academic enrichment programs, teens would have the positive alternatives clearly defined and a better understanding of what our dreams for them are.

Remember that all children, even teens, want recognition and attention. What does it mean if limited resources in schools go toward teen mother programs while the academically oriented girls get little additional support, recess is eliminated, and the sports and arts programs are cut to bare bones? Kids might sometimes do what they learn gets attention; when that happens, our prevention efforts may backfire. Do not misread this as a statement *against* risk-based intervention programs. To the contrary, they are essential. But I believe we err when we don't put as great an effort into promoting and recognizing the positive as we do in correcting the negative.

The reverberations associated with low expectations are not limited to adolescents. For example, schools should be places where every young person can find his area of strength. Some youth will be artistically inclined, others academically. Some will excel on the playing field, others in the computer laboratory. It's important to maintain a wide variety of opportunities in schools so that no young person receives the message that he is incapable or without a special gift. A child whose gifts are not noticed will quickly lose confidence. Think about how tracking may tell even a 7-year-old precisely where he stands. A child learns quickly about expectations when he's placed in either the "minnows" or "sharks" reading group. I'm not taking a position on tracking here, only on the care that needs to be taken to ensure each child feels valued and receives the opportunity each needs to excel in something.

Youth need to know that most kids are active, contributing, positive community members. But public health messages illuminate the problems of youth, creating a crisis mentality that may be disconnected with reality. Youth absorb the messages that normal teens engage in the kind of behaviors that alarm adults and earn attention on the news. So most of our attention has to focus on noticing and extolling the positive behaviors around us. What can you do as a parent within your community or as a community leader?

- Notice the acts of generosity and compassion shown by youth and spread these good news stories. Don't notice only the heroic acts, but also the everyday acts; recognize kindness and contribution as the norm.
- Advocate for the positive portrayal of youth in the community. Ask for a shift away from media coverage where only the highest achievers and delinquents get airtime.
- Advocate for public health messages that don't just tell kids what *not* to do but fervently tell kids *what* to do, and recognize that most youth are already doing the right thing.
- Advocate for enrichment programs in communities and schools, especially in those areas most at risk that currently only have prevention programs. This doesn't mean you should suggest that risk-based programs be cut.

- Give youth opportunities to contribute to their communities. When they're out serving others, their value will be noticed and they'll receive those vital reinforcing displays of gratitude.
- Work with the parents in your community so that young people have appropriate role models, rules, and boundaries that ensure safety. If these are seen as normal in your community, adolescents will have less reason to rebel.

Connection to School and Community-based Programs as a Key Protective Factor

Connection is a key protective factor for young people. Connection to adults within the home, school, and community make a young person feel valued and protected. Youth with multiple connections have somewhere to turn when times are rough. Adults will notice when connected youth are no longer thriving or when they're headed for trouble. Despite this, some young people slip through the cracks. Efforts at ensuring that each young person is noticed by several adults gives each a combined level of protection higher than could ever be offered by just one caring adult. Think of a block of Swiss cheese slices. It is easy to fall through one hole without notice, but if several slices are aligned, a child is unlikely to slip through the whole block.

Schools and programs can take steps to ensure that no young person slips through unnoticed. One program of interest was started under the leadership of principal Richard Simon in a New York school. The school determined that no child should be left without adequate connections. It prepared an index card with a picture of each student, posted it in a private faculty space, and asked teachers to initial if they had formed a positive connection with the student. The cards that had no initials, or only one, were referred to the guidance department and interventions were made, including referral to the Jared Project, a group of volunteer teachers and staff (including custodians and secretaries) who made one-to-one mentor-type connections. In that way, they ensured that all students formed a positive relationship with an adult in the school. This simple exercise is now being used in schools and programs around the nation to ensure a caring environment and prevent crises. Some schools are placing rosters on the walls, and teachers place dots next to those young people with whom they feel they have formed a connection. Students without ample connections are assigned adults to reach out to them.

Ideally, young people would also have the opportunity to assign a dot to adults with whom they feel connected. A youth unable to comfortably place a dot on an adult name needs a higher level of attention. Some kids find it harder to reach out because they may be shy or find passing under the radar beneficial; they may not be the superstar or delinquent and just pass through our walls with relative anonymity. But no child is anonymous. It is our job to find the special attributes and uncover the unspoken needs of each child in our midst.

Including Youth Wisdom

Youth retain the idealism we need. Within those idealistic thoughts lie tomorrow's solutions for today's problems. We foster that idealism when we listen to the wisdom of youth.

Young people who contribute to the well-being of their community and are noticed for their efforts will be more likely to stay engaged. We must never forget that youth are the experts on themselves. We increase the quality of the program and the benefits to the participants when we ask youth for advice in designing a program. Young people who help programs design services may become leaders in those same or future programs.

If you want to guide the youth of a community toward positive behaviors, consider creating peer educators and positive role models. Messages hold a certain resonance when transmitted from someone to whom peers can relate. At the same time, peer educators have more credibility when they're linked with respected adult experts. Understand also who the peer opinion leaders are (not necessarily the best students or class officers) and influence them to model appropriate behaviors.

Every Kid Is Within Reach

The motto of Kids at Hope is "All Children are Capable of Success, No Exceptions!" It is essential that community-based agencies strive to live by that bold imperative. But to really believe that and create programming that suggests we believe it, we have to check in with ourselves and view kids a bit differently, especially those who are heavily invested in alienating adults.

Some young people do an excellent job of pushing adults away. This is particularly true of kids who have been hurt or traumatized. They have earned the right not to trust easily. Another group of kids who push adults away are perfectionists who aren't meeting their own standards and therefore invest heavily in the mask of indifference. Sometimes young people join a subculture to show clearly how they fully reject adult culture. Remember that all of these kids grew from the same small children who craved attention. Maybe they didn't get it, or maybe they were bullied or hurt. Maybe their sensitivity hurts so badly that having their consciousness clouded in drugs feels like the perfect answer; even better if their behavior perpetuates the myth that they really don't care.

Sometimes all it takes is the right adult being there at the right time to help them acknowledge that they actually care so much it hurts.

Not every individual can reach every young person—perhaps because of what you look like, your age, what you say, what you don't say, or who you remind the kid of. That's okay. It is the reason why our programs often use a team approach. It is really a positive thing when you engage a colleague who you think might better connect with a young person. Don't make those connections solely based on gender, age, ethnicity, or race. Rather, link child professionals with kids based on interests, life experience, and temperament. The only thing that really matters is that we don't give up.

Community-based Programs

Every child possesses unique gifts. That is why "one size fits all" programming never works. If each young person is to have the opportunity to thrive, a variety of programs are needed so each child can find his niche. Safe play spaces are necessary so children can exercise while developing their own innate curiosity and creativity. Communities need academic enrichment programs to help some excel and to prevent others from falling behind. Healthy child-centered communities also have spiritual and recreational centers with a wide variety of programs. And finally, any community-based activities that promote family connection (like recreation centers) or effective parenting magnify the benefit.

How Can Programs Build on the Strengths of Youth?

Some youth programs still exist on the deficit model—they are designed solely to decrease risk and focus on education. Others instinctively understand that young people respond better when their strengths are recognized, but even these programs struggle to shift toward a strength-building approach.

I care deeply about risk and about keeping kids safe, but I've learned from so many youth that the transformative moment in their lives came when a caring adult first really believed in them, when a youth worker or counselor "made me first understand that I wasn't trash, and that changed everything." Our challenge is to pay attention to the positive, the traits that really make us care for a young person, with the same level of intensity that we focus on the behaviors we want to address.

The following pages have questions, grouped by the 7 Cs, that youth professionals and programs can ask themselves as they shift toward a resilience-building, strength-based approach to youth. Feel free to copy these for your center or download them from www.fosteringresilience.com or from the American Academy of Pediatrics (AAP) Web site for parents, www.HealthyChildren.org.

The Resilience-based Philosophy: Reflections on Our Program

The Essential 2 Questions

Within our walls, do we believe in every young person unconditionally and hold them to high expectations? Do we sincerely believe that every child can succeed?

Competence

❂ Do we see what a young person has done right? Or do we focus on their mistakes?

❂ Do we help our youth recognize what they have going for themselves?

❂ Do we help them focus on those strengths and build on them?

❂ Are we helping to build the authentic skills that make them competent in the real world?

Educational skills	Work skills
Social skills	Interview skills
Anger management skills	Stress-reduction skills

❂ Do we communicate in a way that empowers them to make their own decisions, or do we undermine their sense of competence by lecturing them, thereby giving them information in a style they cannot grasp? Rather than talking down to them, do we instead deliver information in a manner they understand?

❂ Do we let them make safe mistakes so they have the opportunity to right themselves, or do we protect them from every bump and bruise?

❂ Do we praise in a way that notices effort more than it rewards the product?

From Ginsburg KR, Jablow MM. *Building Resilience in Children and Teens: Giving Kids Roots and Wings*. 2nd ed. Elk Grove Village, IL: American Academy of Pediatrics; 2011

Please feel free to copy this handout or download from www.fosteringresilience.com or the American Academy of Pediatrics Web site for parents, www.HealthyChildren.org.

Confidence

* Do we see the best in our youth so that they can see the best in themselves?
* Do we clearly express that we expect the best in them?
* Do we help them recognize what they have done right? (Confidence comes from knowing that one has competence.)
* Do we help them understand that they have authentic survival skills?
* Do we treat them as incapable children or young adults learning to navigate a difficult world?
* Do we catch them when they are doing the right thing?
* Do we encourage them to strive just a little bit further because we believe they can succeed?
* Do we avoid instilling shame?

From Ginsburg KR, Jablow MM. *Building Resilience in Children and Teens: Giving Kids Roots and Wings*. 2nd ed. Elk Grove Village, IL: American Academy of Pediatrics; 2011

Please feel free to copy this handout or download from www.fosteringresilience.com or the American Academy of Pediatrics Web site for parents, www.HealthyChildren.org.

Connection

- ◈ Do we recognize that adults' unconditional belief in young people—and holding them to high expectations—is the single most important factor determining whether those young people will be able to overcome challenging circumstances?
- ◈ Do we enter young people's lives without permission, or do we give them time to understand we are worthy of their trust?
- ◈ Do we build a sense of safe community within our walls?
- ◈ Do we encourage young people to take pride in the various ethnic, religious, or cultural groups they belong to?
- ◈ Do we recognize that for many of our most troubled youth, the firm attachment to a stable family might be missing? Further, do we know that our role as stable, caring adults takes on an even greater importance?
- ◈ Do we have a television and self-contained entertainment system in every room, or do we create a common space so people share time together? Does everyone exist in their own world, hiding behind earphones and texting distant friends, or is communication happening here?

From Ginsburg KR, Jablow MM. *Building Resilience in Children and Teens: Giving Kids Roots and Wings.* 2nd ed. Elk Grove Village, IL: American Academy of Pediatrics; 2011

Please feel free to copy this handout or download from www.fosteringresilience.com or the American Academy of Pediatrics Web site for parents, www.HealthyChildren.org.

Character

- Are we helping our youth to recognize themselves as caring people?
- Do we allow them to clarify their own values?
- Do we allow them to consider right versus wrong and look beyond immediate needs?
- Do we help them understand how their behavior affects others?
- Do we help them develop a sense of spirituality that fits into their (not our) belief system?
- Do we value them so clearly that we model for them how important it is to care for others?
- Do we value each other so clearly that we demonstrate the importance of community?
- Do we value each young person and promote the understanding that when all reach their potential, every child benefits?

From Ginsburg KR, Jablow MM. *Building Resilience in Children and Teens: Giving Kids Roots and Wings.* 2nd ed. Elk Grove Village, IL: American Academy of Pediatrics; 2011

Please feel free to copy this handout or download from www.fosteringresilience.com or the American Academy of Pediatrics Web site for parents, www.HealthyChildren.org.

Contribution

* Do we make clear that we believe our youth can make the world a better place?
* As we create programs that serve youth, do we include them in the planning process, appreciating that they are the experts on themselves and their own needs?
* Do we create opportunities for each youth to contribute to the community?
* Do we share how important a value it is to serve others?
* Do we help our young people recognize that precisely because they have come through difficult times, they are positioned to guide others in how to improve their lives?
* Do we search in each person's life for another individual for whom they might serve as a role model? Do we use this to encourage them to be the best person they can possibly be?
* Do we help them to understand that if they have messed up in their past, their recovery serves as a model?

From Ginsburg KR, Jablow MM. *Building Resilience in Children and Teens: Giving Kids Roots and Wings.* 2nd ed. Elk Grove Village, IL: American Academy of Pediatrics; 2011

Please feel free to copy this handout or download from www.fosteringresilience.com or the American Academy of Pediatrics Web site for parents, www.HealthyChildren.org.

Coping

- Do we recognize that so many of the risk behaviors youth engage in are attempts at reducing the stress or pain in their lives?
- Do we condemn young people for their behaviors? Do we increase their sense of shame and therefore drive them toward those behaviors?
- Do we believe that telling youth to "just stop" the negative behaviors will do any good?
- Do we guide youth to develop positive, effective coping strategies?
- Do we help young people understand when their thoughts are magnifying problems? Do we help them to make realistic assessments?
- Do we model positive coping strategies on a daily basis?
- Do we encourage caring for our bodies through exercise, good nutrition, and adequate sleep?
- Can children safely play and exercise outdoors or in recreational centers in our community?
- Do we encourage creative expression? Does our community offer resources and programs in which children and teens are able to learn and practice creative expression?
- Do we encourage written and verbal expression in a way that allows each youth to reveal thoughts in a comfortable manner, whether through talking, journaling, poetry, or rap?
- Do we create an environment in which talking, listening, and sharing are safe and productive?
- Do we model relaxation techniques?
- As we struggle to compose ourselves so we can make the fairest, wisest decisions, do we model how we take control rather than respond impulsively?

From Ginsburg KR, Jablow MM. *Building Resilience in Children and Teens: Giving Kids Roots and Wings*. 2nd ed. Elk Grove Village, IL: American Academy of Pediatrics; 2011

Control

- Do we help young people understand that life is not purely random?
- Do we help them to understand that they are not responsible for many of the bad circumstances that may have plagued them?
- Do we help them think about the future but take one step at a time?
- Do we help them recognize their mini-successes so they can experience the knowledge that they can succeed?
- Do we help youth understand that while no one can control all of his circumstances, each person can shift the odds by choosing positive or protective behaviors?
- Do we understand that youth who have been hurt emotionally or physically may think they have no control and therefore have no reason to take positive action?
- Do we understand that discipline is about teaching, *not* punishing or controlling? Do we use discipline as a means to help someone understand that their actions produce consequences (in other words, life is not random)?

From Ginsburg KR, Jablow MM. *Building Resilience in Children and Teens: Giving Kids Roots and Wings.* 2nd ed. Elk Grove Village, IL: American Academy of Pediatrics; 2011

Please feel free to copy this handout or download from www.fosteringresilience.com or the American Academy of Pediatrics Web site for parents, www.HealthyChildren.org.

Strategies for Teaching and Engaging Parents

If a community-based agency or school wants to maximize its yield in enhancing youth resilience, among the most important things it could do would be to engage and empower parents. It is beyond the scope of this chapter to discuss best practices in adult educational strategies, but I would like to offer a few that have been shared with me by parenting groups, schools, and agencies that have used this book to teach parents.

Suggestions about how to incorporate the 7 Cs model into your parenting programs do not substitute for well-evaluated parenting programs. One place to find proven parenting programs that enhance resilience is through Communities That Care (www.communitiesthatcare.net).

The 7 Cs of Resilience as Parent Empowerment/Skill-building Lessons

First, let's assume that your community has an ongoing parenting seminar series or would like to design one. Then let's assume that your seminar is a one-time event or a book club.

If Your Community Has a Seminar Series

You know your community best, so you can determine whether parents are more likely to invest in a preventive strength-building model like the 7 Cs or a topic-driven series that focuses on risks. Generally it takes a philosophic shift to have the ongoing focus be strength-based prevention. It will involve convincing opinion leaders that in fact, one of the best ways to address risk is through building strengths. Parents of adolescents never tire of topical subjects related to risk—sex, drugs, bullying, eating disorders, driving safety—because these are the areas that generate so much parental anxiety.

Communities That Wish to Focus on Resilience/Strength Building

It is unlikely that your parents will have the time to invest in 7 sessions, one for each of the Cs. A more realistic series has 4 sessions. I recommend the following groupings:

Session 1: Connection and Control

So much parental anxiety focuses on maintaining a strong connection with their child and losing that connection during adolescence. Much of the news here is reassuring and relieves them of pressure. For example, parents who are able to listen well are relieved of the need to find the perfect words and maintain a stronger connection with their child.

Parents care deeply about discipline because it creates so much tension in households. Parents who use discipline as punishment will likely drive their children away, whereas those who use it as guidance are more likely to maintain effective, loving connections.

Session 2: Confidence and Competence

Confidence and competence are fully intertwined. Children build confidence when adults continue to notice their competencies. This is the session where parents can discuss the importance of letting kids make some of their own mistakes and talking to kids in ways that encourage them to arrive at their own wise decisions. It is also a session where you can discuss how to praise and criticize children in ways that help them become authentically successful.

Session 3: Character and Contribution

Parents need to determine for themselves the character traits they wish to build in their children, but a parenting seminar can be a great place to promote discussion. A wonderful way for young people to build character is to contribute to their families and community. The praise they will receive for their contributions will reinforce ongoing positive behaviors and protect children from negative undermining messages that may interfere with their positive development.

Session 4: Coping

This session offers an effective way to tee off successive sessions that focus on topical areas of risk. Once parents understand that risk-taking behavior is often a child's attempt to put away the uncomfortable feelings associated with stress, they will feel better prepared to take on risk behaviors. This session is also a good opportunity to help parents understand their vital role as models of appropriate behaviors. Perhaps most importantly, this is the session where you can focus on the importance of parents taking care of themselves as one of the greatest gifts they can give their children. Parents need to hear this message; they don't always believe it, but it is critical that parents remain strong and whole to take care of their children. The coping strategies offer healthful alternatives to manage stress and can be used by adults as well.

Ongoing Sessions

Further sessions can focus on risk topic areas. At this point, parents will be well prepared to think about averting risk behaviors by parenting with an eye toward recognizing and reinforcing strengths and building resilience.

Communities That Wish to Focus on Risk Topics

Some communities may not want more than one general session introducing them to the language of resilience. The following strategies can maximize the effectiveness of that session:

Your goal can be to incorporate the language and philosophy of resilience into all of your ongoing parenting seminars, even if topics are risk specific. For example, discipline is a subject that parents want to learn about at every developmental stage. It is important that they shift their understanding of discipline away from punishment and toward guidance. Each discipline lesson can reinforce the importance of children learning control by understanding that they earn privileges through demonstrated responsibility. Similarly, if you want parents to become part of the solution preventing risk behaviors, always include coping as part of the discussion. Reinforce as often as you can that parents may do their greatest good when they model appropriate behaviors and when they tell kids what to do in reaction to stress rather than just deliver facts about what *not* to do. Further, use each risk prevention session to teach parents how to build competency skills in dealing with peer pressure.

At each session that addresses risk, be aware that some people in the room are attending because their children are actively engaged in worrisome behaviors. Reinforce for them that they should never lower their expectations of their children and that opportunities always exist to turn their child's life around. Help them understand that their love remains the pivotal force with the greatest potential to affect change. The opposite is not true; you do not want them believing their children engaged in the activity for lack of love. Finally, always include in each session the importance of turning to professional guidance. You may use Chapter 36 as a guide on how to determine when someone needs professional guidance and how seeking help can in itself be an act of great strength.

The 7 Cs of Resilience as One Session or a Book Club

One Session: Parents Need to Know How Much They Matter

No single parenting session can be expected to make a permanent change in parents' approach to parenting, especially if it differs from how they were raised. What it can do is empower them to understand that parents really matter and can make a large difference to the well-being of children. Although this statement—*parents matter*—seems so intuitive to child experts and professionals that it borders on the condescending, please understand that society often reinforces that parents become powerless when puberty hits. They believe that once the tween years begin, peer influence takes over. Some books fan this incorrect assumption and sell thousands of copies to parents who wish to eliminate any potential guilt by accepting their powerlessness. Media messages often suggest parents have no control; in many shows with teen stars, the parents are nearly absent. It is no coincidence that so much public health effort is invested in counteracting these messages and letting parents know how much they do matter.

The most dangerous and influential force suggesting parents are powerless comes from parents who have lost control of their children and who are emotionally invested in the belief that there's nothing they could have done. They stir anxiety and hopelessness in other parents. For these reasons, it is imperative that parents receive reinforcement of the fact that they remain the most influential forces in their children's lives continuing through adolescence.

The real goal of a single session, therefore, is to inspire, empower, and motivate attendees to continue learning. That means that you should draw on their emotions of how deeply they love their children. Be prepared for parents who enter saying, "I am ready to find out that everything I have been doing has been wrong." It's imperative that they learn that the 7 Cs model usually only reminds them of what they already know. It may give them a language to better discuss this with their partners and friends, but it is likely they already possess the wisdom. You also want parents to walk away knowing that self-care is the greatest gift they can give their children.

Taking Home a Reminder

Because there is no way that the message of resilience can be "owned" in one session, it's nice for parents to be able to walk away with a reminder. Please feel free to distribute the take-home handout at the end of this chapter or download it from www.fosteringresilience.com or the AAP Web site for parents, www.HealthyChildren.org. In addition, here are 3 strategies recommended by the Military Child Education Coalition that it has found helpful in its sessions.

The Grid

This new language and perhaps philosophy need reinforcement. Parents need opportunities to catch themselves being good when they break from old habits and instead use resilience-building strategies. They can leave the sessions with a resilience grid to track their progress. The 7 Cs can be listed across the top. Depending on the goal, there are different possibilities of what to list on the side. One grid could focus on children's resilience and list each of their names along the side. Parents can fill in the resilience-building traits each child already possesses and which need further support and development. Another grid could focus on the parents themselves and allow a self-assessment of what they already are doing well and clarify which areas might benefit from improvement. Remember, resilience is uneven, and so is resilience-based parenting! Another grid might be used to reinforce the parenting behaviors they use to build resilience in their children. They will catch themselves using resilience-based strategies. Chances are they will notice that they are already doing many things well and this will reinforce their desire to build new skills.

Books and Movies

There is a strong case for approaching human beings from a direction of recognizing their strengths; it matches our deep-seated instincts about what should be used to motivate people. It also feels good to see people overcome challenges. There are few things more stirring than seeing people rise above adversity and meet their highest potential. Movies and books often portray such stories. One of the most powerful ways you can boost the resilience lesson, therefore, is to send attendees home with a list of books they can read to their children or movies they can watch as a family or by themselves. Parents may be more willing to experience their feelings fully in private or with their child, and those emotions will reinforce their commitment to putting into place the strategies that will help their child thrive despite adversity.

The Resilience Hand

Parents are taught about the 7 Cs and then asked to trace a spread hand on a piece of paper. They are asked to write *confidence* and *competence* on their thumb and *connection, character, contribution,* and *coping* on each of the fingers. On their palm, they write *control.* Putting control in the palm reinforces that they have control over how they choose to parent and how their children will be raised. They do this near the beginning of the session so that they can write critical notes by each topic. Placed somewhere in their home, the hand serves as a reminder. This memory tool holds personal resonance for me because in Judaism, the hand is often used as a symbol of the protective nature of G-d. Muslims also use this hand as a similar symbol. We put the gift of resilience into children's lives to protect them and ultimately to build in them the strength to protect themselves and overcome adversity.

◈·◈·◈·◈

Take-home Handout

The 7 Cs: The Essential Building Blocks of Resilience

Bottom Line #1: Young people live up or down to expectations we set for them. They need adults who believe in them unconditionally and hold them to the high expectations of being compassionate, generous, and creative.

Competence: When we notice what young people are doing right and give them opportunities to develop important skills, they feel competent. We undermine competence when we don't allow young people to recover themselves after a fall.

Confidence: Young people need confidence to be able to navigate the world, think outside the box, and recover from challenges.

Connection: Connections with other people, schools, and communities offer young people the security that allows them to stand on their own and develop creative solutions.

Character: Young people need a clear sense of right and wrong and a commitment to integrity.

Contribution: Young people who contribute to the well-being of others will receive gratitude rather than condemnation. They will learn that contributing feels good and may therefore more easily turn to others, and do so without shame.

Coping: Young people who possess a variety of healthy coping strategies will be less likely to turn to dangerous quick fixes when stressed.

Control: Young people who understand privileges and respect are earned through demonstrated responsibility will learn to make wise choices and feel a sense of control.

Bottom Line #2: What we do to model healthy resilience strategies for our children is more important than anything we say about them.

From Ginsburg KR, Jablow MM. *Building Resilience in Children and Teens: Giving Kids Roots and Wings.* 2nd ed. Elk Grove Village, IL: American Academy of Pediatrics; 2011

Please feel free to copy this handout or download from www.fosteringresilience.com or the American Academy of Pediatrics Web site for parents, www.HealthyChildren.org.

Just for Kids: A Personalized Guide for Managing Stress

The following chapter is written specifically for young people from 12 to 18 years of age. It explains how stress affects bodies and emotions and suggests ways to manage and reduce stress. I hope you will also give teens an opportunity to read Part 4, Coping, because it will fill in many of the details that can't be included in this brief overview.

This chapter also includes a personal stress plan. The plan is available at www.fosteringresilience.com and on the American Academy of Pediatrics Web site for parents, www.HealthyChildren.org. There you and your adolescent can learn about and complete his or her personal stress-reduction plan.

A Teen's Personal Guide for Managing Stress

What Is Stress?

Stress is the uncomfortable feeling you get when you're worried, scared, angry, frustrated, or overwhelmed. It is caused by emotions, but it also affects your mood and body. Many adults think that teens don't have stress because they don't have to work and support a family. They are missing the point and are wrong!

What Causes Stress?

Stress comes from many different places.

- *From your parents.* "Don't disappoint me, clean up, hurry up, finish this, do your homework, go out for the team, practice your music, try out for the school play, do your best, stay out of trouble, make more friends, don't ever try drugs."
- *From your friends.* "How'd you do on the test, try this, prove you're not a loser, don't hang out with them, don't wear that."
- *Even from yourself.* "I need to lose weight, build my muscles, wear the right clothes, get better grades, score more goals, show my parents I'm not a kid anymore."
  And from
- Watching parents argue
- Figuring out how to be independent
- Feeling pressure to get good grades
- Thinking about the future
- Being pressured to do something you know is bad for you, like smoking
- Not being good enough at sports
- Worrying about how your body's changing
- Dealing with sexual feelings
- Worrying about neighborhood or world problems
- Feeling guilty

How Does the Body Handle Stress?

First, here are 2 short definitions.

- *Hormone:* a chemical made by one part of the body that travels through your blood to send messages to the rest of the body.
- *Nervous system:* the brain, spinal cord, and all of the nerves. The nerves send messages between your brain and the rest of your body.

The body is a finely tuned machine that can change quickly to do what we need it to do, like react to stress. The body has 2 nervous systems. The *voluntary* system does what you choose to have it do—walk, talk, move. The *involuntary* system keeps the body running without your even thinking about it—breathe, sweat, digest. The body actually has 2 different nerve pathways in the involuntary system. One works while we're relaxed, and the other works when there's an emergency. These 2 systems can't work together at the same time. It's important to know this because we can shut off the emergency system by flipping a switch and turning on the relaxed system.

Is Stress Always Bad?

Even though stress is uncomfortable, it's not always a bad thing. Sometimes stress helps us deal with tough situations. A lot of stress changes our bodies quickly and helps us react to an emergency. A little stress keeps us alert and helps us work harder.

Ages ago, when people lived in the jungle—where a tiger might leap out at any moment—the emergency nervous system was key to survival. Imagine your great, great, great ancestors, Sam and Zelda, munching on some berries. Suddenly they saw a tiger and had to *run!* Hormones gave them the burst of energy they needed to escape.

How did their bodies react? First, Sam and Zelda got that sinking feeling in their stomachs as the blood in their bellies quickly went to their legs so they could take off. Then when they jumped to their feet, their hearts beat faster to pump more blood. As they ran from the tiger, they breathed faster to take in more air. Their sweat cooled them as they ran. Their pupils became bigger so they could see in the dark, in case they needed to jump over a log while running away. They didn't think about anything but running because they weren't supposed to stop and figure out a friendly way to work it all out with the tiger.

Our ancestors never would have survived without the stress reaction, but stress helps us do more than run. It keeps us alert and prepared for the next lurking tiger.

Few of us need to outrun tigers today, but we all have problems and worries that turn on some of those exact same stress responses, like that panicky feeling you sometimes get when you're studying for a big test. Your heart beats fast. Your breathing becomes heavier. You sweat and get flashes of heat because your hormones are confused about why you aren't listening to them. Why are you standing still when they are telling you to run?

If Stress Is a Survival Tool, Why Does It Make Us Feel Awful?

Sam and Zelda had few choices when the tiger chased them. Either the tiger ate them or they escaped. As sick as it sounds, if they'd been eaten, they wouldn't have had much to worry about anymore, right? If they lived, you can be sure their burst of energy allowed them to outrun the tiger or at least outrun Zok (their slower friend who was eaten by the tiger). In their run for survival, Sam and Zelda used up every drop of their hormone burst and then took a well-deserved nap.

In the modern world, our biggest worries aren't usually about life or death. We don't really have to run away from our problems. But those same stress hormones stay in our bodies because unlike Sam and Zelda, we don't use them up by running. Instead, those hormones continue to hang around, unused and confused. They seem to be asking, "Why did my body stand still when that 'tiger' attacked?"

It would be better if we had different hormones for different stresses. Hormones to deal with parental pressure would make you love chores. Hormones related to school stress would make you focus longer and shut down your kidneys so you wouldn't need bathroom breaks. But we only have those hormones that prepare us to flee or fight. So it's really important to use your brain to decide what's a real emergency and to use exercise to use up those hormone bursts.

Even when there are no real emergencies, our emotions make our bodies act like there is a huge crisis because the brain controls emotions and stress hormones. If your brain thinks something terrible is happening, your body will react as if it really is! Even a little bit of stress that never seems to go away can confuse the body. It makes the body work harder to prepare for an emergency that may not really be there.

A tiger running at you is a real crisis. If you believe a mild stress (like a math test) is an emergency, you will not be able to study. Your body will be preparing to deal with a real tiger, and you won't be able to concentrate on anything but escaping. The trick is to figure out when something really is an emergency and when your emotions are only treating it like one.

A Review

- Stress is an important survival tool and can keep you alert and focused. But when you're not dealing with a real survival issue, it can make you uncomfortable and interfere with your ability to think through the problem.
- Stress hormones are telling us to run, so exercise uses them up.
- The body reacts to stress when the brain tells the body to prepare for an emergency.
- Emotions play an important role in how our bodies experience stress. How we think about a stressful situation and what we choose to do about it affect how it makes us feel.

How Do People Deal With Stress?

Nobody can avoid all stress, but you can learn ways to deal with it. When you are stressed, it is normal to want to feel better. Anything that makes you feel better is called a *coping strategy*. Negative strategies can be quick fixes, but they're harmful because they can be dangerous and make stress worse in the long run. Think about some of the ways people cope with stress that can really hurt them.

- Drugs
- Cigarettes
- Alcohol
- Bullying
- Fighting
- Sex
- Cutting/self-mutilation
- Skipping school
- Eating disorders
- Running away
- Isolating themselves or withdrawal
- Gangs

Dealing With Stress

These harmful choices may help you feel good for a little while, but some can be really dangerous. They also end up making people worried about you or angry with you. This messes up your life, and you become a lot more stressed. They're especially worrisome if they are a major way you deal with stress because you may turn to these behaviors more often during hard times. This is one of the ways addiction starts. If you are doing some of these things, ask yourself, "Why?" If it is to deal with problems, consider other ways of dealing with the same problems.

There are many healthy ways of coping. Healthy coping strategies are safe and can help you feel better without messing up your life.

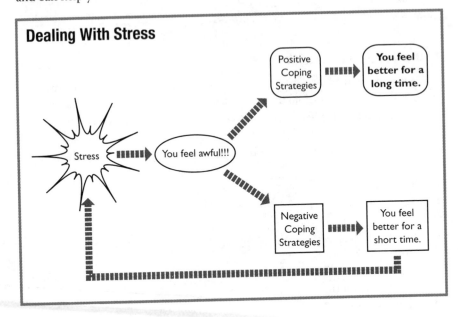

Dealing With Stress

Creating Your Personal Stress-Management Plan

Following is a 10-point plan to help you manage stress. All of these ideas can lower stress without doing any harm. None are quick fixes, but they will lead you toward a healthy and successful life. The plan is divided into 4 parts.

1. Tackling the problem
2. Taking care of my body
3. Dealing with emotions
4. Making the world better

When you read over the plan, you'll notice that you can come up with a bunch of ideas for each point. PLEASE don't think you should try them all. This plan is supposed to help you reduce stress, not give you more. Try out some ideas, then stick to one or two for each point.

You might notice that this plan is almost like building a college or work résumé. This is the sane way to build a résumé; you are doing it to manage your life and remain happy and prepared for success, not to cram in activities to impress someone else. It will ensure you're healthy and balanced, and that's very attractive to colleges and employers.

Part 1: Tackling the Problem

Point 1: Identify and Then Address the Problem.

First decide if a problem is a real tiger or just feels like one. If it can't hurt you, chances are that it can be better handled with clear thinking. This means turning off those thoughts that make you interpret the situation as a disaster.

1. A lot of people cope by ignoring problems. This doesn't make them go away; usually they just get worse.
2. People who cope by trying to fix problems tend to be emotionally healthier.
3. When it comes to studying or chores, it is best to get the work done first. Because work or studying produces stress, many people put it off and choose to do fun things first. The problem with that is they're not really having fun because they're worrying about the work they're ignoring. And of course, the longer they put it off, the more they worry. The cycle is endless.
4. Fights with parents and friends don't go away unless you deal with what upset you in the first place, or unless everyone apologizes and decides to forgive each other.

Three ideas can help you manage a lot of work.
1. Break the work into small pieces. Then do one small piece at a time, rather than look at the whole huge mess. As you finish each piece, the work becomes less overwhelming.
2. Make lists of what you need to do. This will help you sleep because your head won't spin with worry about whether you can do everything. At the end of the day, you'll have less to worry about as you check off the things you have finished. You will look at the same huge amount of work and realize you can handle it.
3. Timelines can help with big projects.

Point 2: Avoid Stress When Possible.

Sometimes we know exactly when we are headed for trouble. Avoiding trouble from a distance is easier than dealing with it up close. You know the people who might be a bad influence on you, the places where you're likely to get in trouble, and the things that upset you. Choose not to be around those people, places, and things that mess you up.

Point 3: Let Some Things Go.

It's important to try to fix problems, but sometimes there is nothing you can do to change a problem. For example, you can't change the weather, so don't waste your energy worrying about it. You can't change the fact that teachers give tests, so just study instead of complaining about how unfair they are. You can't change the fact that your parents need to know where you go, so prove that you're responsible and deserve more freedoms. People who waste their energy worrying about things they can't change don't have enough energy left over to fix the things they can. Also learn when not to take things personally. You feel badly for no reason when you take something personally that really has little to do with you.

Part 2: Taking Care of My Body

Point 4: The Power of Exercise.

Exercise is the most important part of a plan to manage stress. When you are stressed, your body is saying, "Run!" So do it. Exercise every day to control stress and build a strong, healthy body. You may think you don't have time to exercise when you are most stressed, but that is exactly when you need it the most. If you are stressed about an assignment but too nervous to sit down and study—exercise! You will be able to think better after you have used up those stress hormones. Some people exercise before school so they can focus and learn better.

Point 5: Active Relaxation.

You can flip the switch from being stressed to relaxed if you know how to fool your body. Because your body can only use the relaxed or emergency nervous system at any one time, you can turn on the relaxed system. You do this by doing the opposite of what your body does when it is stressed. Here are 2 ideas.

1. Breathe deeply and slowly. Try the 4–8 breathing technique. Lie on your back and place your hands on your belly with your fingers loose. Deep breaths first fill the belly, then the chest, then the mouth; the breath expands the belly and your hands pull gently apart. Take a full breath while counting to 4. Then hold that breath for about twice as long, or an 8 count. Slowly let it out to the count of 8, or even longer if you can. This will relax your body after a few breaths, but just as importantly, it requires your full concentration. Your mind is too focused on breathing to focus on worries. Do this 10 times and you will feel much more relaxed. Yoga, martial arts, and meditation also teach great breathing skills. When you get good at this, you can even do this in a chair during a test and nobody will know.

2. Put your body in a relaxed position.
    - Your body knows when you're nervous. If you sit down to take a test and your legs are shaking, you are saying, "I want to run!" Remember, you can't concentrate and run at the same time, so you are making it harder to take the test. Instead, take those deep breaths, lean back, and tell your body there is no emergency.
    - When you're angry, the natural thing to do is stand up and face some-one shoulder-to-shoulder and chest-to-chest. You do this without even thinking, but this subconsciously tells the other person that you're angry and ready to fight. It also may prevent you from thinking clearly. Do the *opposite* of what you would do if you were really going to fight—sit down, take deep slow breaths, and tell your body there is no danger. Then use your brain to get out of the situation.

Point 6: Eat Well.

Everyone knows good nutrition makes you healthier. Only some people realize that it also keeps you alert through the day and your mood steady. People who eat mostly junk food have highs and lows in their energy level, which harms their ability to reduce stress. Instead of eating greasy or sugary foods, eat more fruits, vegetables, and whole grains—they keep you focused for a longer time. Go to MyPyramid.gov to learn more.

Point 7: Sleep Well.

Most kids don't get the sleep they need to grow and think clearly. Tired people can't learn as well and can be impatient and irritable. Here are some ideas to improve your sleep.

- Go to sleep about the same time every night.
- Exercise 4 to 6 hours before bedtime. Your body falls asleep most easily when it has cooled down. If you exercise right before bed, you will be over-heated and won't sleep well. A hot shower 1 hour before bedtime also helps your body relax to fall asleep.
- Use your bed only to sleep. Don't solve your problems in bed. When you think about all the things that bother you, you have trouble falling asleep and wake up in the middle of the night to worry more. Instead, have another spot to think, like a *worry chair.* Give yourself plenty of time to think things through, make a list if you need to, and then *set it aside!* Go to bed to sleep.
- Don't do homework, watch television, read, or use the phone while in bed.

Part 3: Dealing With Emotions

Point 8: Take Instant Vacations.

Sometimes the best way to de-stress is to take your mind away to a more relaxing place.

1. *Visualize.* Have a favorite place where you can imagine yourself relaxing. The place should be beautiful and calm. When you're stressed, sit down, lean back, take deep breaths, close your eyes, and imagine yourself in your calm place.
2. *Take time out for yourself.* Everyone deserves time for themselves—a bath or something that allows time to think and de-stress. Try a warm bath with your ears just underwater. Listen to yourself take deep, slow breaths. Take your pulse and count as your heart rate goes down.
3. Enjoy *hobbies* or creative art as an instant vacation.
4. Look at the beauty around you and get *pleasure from the small things* you may have stopped noticing.
5. Take *mini-vacations.* Sometimes we forget that the park around the corner is a great place to hang out. A walk outside can be a mini-vacation if you choose to forget your worries.
6. *Reading* a good book is an escape from reality. You have to imagine the sights, sounds, and smells—you are somewhere else for a while.

Point 9: Release Emotional Tension.

Sometimes feelings become so overwhelming that we cram them all away in an imaginary box and think we'll deal with them later. But later, there's so much stuff in the box that there is too much to deal with. This can make your head feel as if it is spinning. Sometimes you get angry or frustrated without even knowing why. You just know there is too much stuff going on in your head. It's good to pick just one problem to work on and forget the rest for the moment. When we decide to deal with only one problem at a time, it's much less scary to open the box.

Here are some ideas to release your thoughts or worries one at a time.

- **Creativity.** People who have a way to express themselves don't need to hold it inside. Creative outlets like art, music, poetry, singing, dance, and rap are powerful ways to let your feelings out.
- **Talking.** Every young person deserves a responsible adult to talk to and some friends to trust. Hopefully, you can talk to your parents. If you do not want to tell your parents everything, make sure to find an adult who'll listen and whom you can ask for advice.
- **Journaling.** Write it out!
- **Prayer.** Many young people find prayer or meditation helpful.
- **Laughing or crying.** Give yourself permission to feel your emotions fully.

Part 4: Making the World Better

Point 10: Contribute to the World.

Young people who work to make the world better have a sense of purpose, feel good about themselves, and handle their own problems better. It's important to understand that you really can make a difference in other people's lives. The role of teenagers is to recognize the mistakes adults have made and build a better world.

❖❖❖❖

Now that you have read about the kind of things a person can do to reduce stress, you may be ready to create a plan for yourself. Just check off the ideas you think would work best for you. There are spaces for you to write down your own ideas.

My Personal Stress Plan

Part 1: Tackling the Problem

Point 1: Identify and Then Address the Problem.

When I have too many problems, I will work on just one at a time. For example, I am going to pick one huge problem and break it into smaller pieces.

* I will seek advice from family members and learn from their experience how to better handle problems.
* I will take big assignments and learn to make lists or timelines.
* I will work in teams so that I will learn that when people work well together they can do much more than if they each work alone.

Point 2: Avoid Stress When Possible.

I know that everyone has stress, but there are things that I could stay away from that really stress me out. I will

* Avoid certain people, like _____
* Avoid certain places, like _____
* Avoid certain things, like _____
* Avoid certain memories that create pain for me, like _____

Point 3: Let Some Things Go.

I realize that I waste some of my energy worrying about things I can't fix. Here are some things that I will try to let go so I can focus on the problems I can change.

* _____
* _____
* _____

    I know I waste some of my energy when I take things personally that really have nothing to do with me. I am going to learn this lesson by remembering a time I did this and by choosing not to repeat that mistake.

_____

_____

_____

_____

Part 2: Taking Care of My Body

Point 4: The Power of Exercise.

I will do something that makes my body work hard for at least 20 minutes every other day—more is better. I know that strong bodies help people better deal with stress, and this will keep me in shape. The kinds of things I like to do include

* _____
* _____
* _____

    I can commit to _____ minutes of exercise a day. If I have trouble focusing in school, I will try exercising before school for _____ minutes (recommended minimum: 20) to see if it helps me concentrate better.

    I know that a really hard physical workout will help me calm down when I am feeling most worried, stressed, or fearful. This is especially true when I can't concentrate on my homework because it feels like too much. The kinds of things I might do include

* _____
* _____
* _____

Point 5: Active Relaxation.

I will try to teach my body to relax by using
* Exercise that controls the body and releases tension like tai chi or boxing.
* Deep breathing.
* Yoga.
* Meditation.
* Warm, long baths or showers.
* My imagination. I will imagine I am someplace peaceful and relaxing. The place I could imagine myself being is _____

Point 6: Eat Well.

I know that having a healthy body helps people deal with stress better. I have already agreed to exercise more. I understand that good nutrition also makes a difference in my health and how well I deal with stress. The changes I am ready to make include
* Eating a good breakfast
* Skipping fewer meals
* Drinking fewer sodas and sugary drinks
* Drinking more water

- Eating smaller portions
- Eating less greasy meals or snacks
- Eating more fruits, vegetables, and whole grain foods
- Going to MyPyramid.gov to learn more
- _____
- _____

Point 7: Sleep Well.

I know that people who get a good night's sleep do a better job of dealing with stress and do better in school. For me to get the sleep I need, I will try to go to bed at ____:____.

I will consider the following plan to help me get the best night's rest:

- Avoid caffeine at least 6 hours before bed.
- Exercise 4 to 6 hours before bed.
- Finish homework after exercise because I will be my calmest, clearest, and most focused.
- Take some time to relax or hang out after homework.
- Shower or bathe 1 hour before bed.
- Begin to dim the lights 30 minutes before bed.
- Let go of my emotional tension before bed in a place other than bed (see point 9). If I am really troubled, I will do this earlier in the evening.
- Use my bed only for sleeping. I will use another place to do some of the things I do in bed now. I will
  - Stop reading in bed.
  - Stop doing homework in bed.
  - Stop watching television in bed.
  - Stop talking to my friends or instant messaging in bed.
  - Stop worrying in bed.
- Dock my cell phone in a charger that is not in my bedroom.
- Deal with the things that stress me out by having a time to let go of my thoughts and feelings in a place other than my bed.

Part 3: Taking Care of Emotions

Point 8: Take Instant Vacations.

Everyone needs to be able to escape problems for a while by taking an *instant vacation.* I will

- Read a book.
- Take a mini-vacation to a local park or recreation center.

* Imagine I am someplace peaceful and relaxing. The place I could imagine myself being is _____
* Watch television.
* Listen to music.
* Play video games that are not violent or stressful.
* Take a warm bath.
* _____

Point 9: Release Emotional Tension.

I will try to let my worries go, rather than letting them build up inside.

* I will talk to a friend I have chosen wisely because I know he or she will give good advice.
* I will talk to my
  - Mother.
  - Father.
  - Teacher.
  - _____
  - I will ask my parents or a teacher to help me find a counselor to help me work out my problems.
* I will pray to gain strength.
* I will meditate.
* I will write out my thoughts in a diary, journal, or blog.
* I will let myself laugh more.
* I will let myself cry more.
* I will make lists to get organized.
* When it seems that I have too many problems and they seem like more than I can handle, I will work on one at a time.
* I will express myself through
  - Art
  - Music
  - Creative writing
  - Poetry
  - Rap
* _____
* _____

Part 4: Helping Can Make Your World—And the Way You Feel—Better

Point 10: Contribute.

I know that people who realize they are needed feel better about themselves because they can make a difference in other people's lives. I plan to

☀ Help a member of my family by _____

☀ Volunteer in my community by _____

☀ Help the environment (or animals) by _____

When to Turn for Help

Even if you are great at dealing with problems, there may be times when stress feels like it is getting to you. You are not alone. This does not mean you are crazy or a failure. Strong people turn to others for support when they have too much to handle. It's okay to turn to wise friends for advice, but it is also important to turn to your parents or another adult to help you. Nobody will solve your problems; they might just help you figure out how to better deal with them. *You deserve to feel good.*

The following signs suggest that you should seek some extra guidance:

- Your grades are dropping.
- You worry a lot.
- You easily get moody or angry.
- You feel tired all the time.
- You get a lot of headaches, dizziness, chest pain, or stomach pain.
- You feel sad or hopeless.
- You feel bored all the time and are less interested in being with friends.
- You are thinking about using alcohol or drugs to try to feel better.
- You ever think about hurting yourself.
- You are using unhealthy coping strategies and are having trouble replacing them with healthier ones.

Remember that one of the best ways to be happy and successful is to manage stress well. You can do it!

Parting Thoughts

Several years ago, as I was completing the first edition of this book, I was strolling along a quaint street with my wife and 2 of our closest friends, both pediatricians, as our combined 5 children happily tagged along behind us. We were enjoying our children and noting how much they sprouted over that summer.

I was sharing my attempt to capture the essence of resilience in a book. Vicky looked at her children and said, "Quick, tell me the answer. How do you make sure your kids are resilient? Give me a sneak peek at the last page!" I laughed nervously and stumbled because I knew the answer wasn't that easy. So here we were, 3 pediatricians and the best mother I know—4 child experts, one of whom was writing a book on resilience—and we didn't know the simple answer.

I've had several more years to contemplate resilience, and I still haven't found a simple solution that guarantees children will be consistently resilient. In truth, I have never met a human being who has the capability to bounce back from every difficult circumstance. Yet I remain humbled on an almost daily basis by children, teenagers, and adults who demonstrate an ability to rise above challenges and maintain their spirit and optimism in the face of adversity. While I can't promise you that if you follow every piece of advice on these pages, your children will easily negotiate every challenge, I do feel confident that they will be more resilient, more capable, and happier.

I hope that this book has challenged you to come up with the kind of strategies that will fit your individual child. When you revisit this book as your child grows, I hope it will reinforce what you already know about parenting and spur you to come up with approaches that I may have left out but would more perfectly meet your child's needs. Have the confidence in yourself and the courage to trust your own instincts, to know that your knowledge of your child outweighs any opinion that I or any "expert" may offer.

If I had to summarize the essence of resilience-building while standing on one foot, I think I would add a new C—*caring.*

- Care so deeply that your children know that you are absolutely crazy in love with them.
- Care so fervently that you hold them to high expectations to be good people—because they will rise to your expectations.
- Care so intensely that you are willing to let them learn that they control their own world and that the solutions to most problems lie within their developing wisdom. Trust in their natural strengths and resilience to nurture their problem-solving capabilities rather than solve their problems for them.
- Care by teaching children to care for themselves. Teach them what to do to relieve stress and move beyond just telling them what *not* to do.
- Care enough about your children so that you really know who they are. Rather than hoping they fit into a plan or idealized image you have for them, know their individual temperaments, limitations, and potential. If you know this, you will be able to exhibit the flexibility and wisdom necessary to allow them to thrive.
- Care for yourself. When you model how important self-care is, you give children the gift of learning that it's okay to have feelings, human to reach a limit, and necessary to rejuvenate.
- Care so much about our future that you work to make this world better not only for your own child, but for all of our children.

No book can teach caring. You began caring the day you found out that a baby was coming into your life. You were overcome with caring when that baby grasped your finger, squeezed tightly, and seemed to say, "I'm yours; please protect me." As children grow, our greatest challenge is to learn how to say, "You are strong; you can stand on your own." I have tried to give you some ideas to build your children's resilience so that you can comfortably prepare them to stand on their own, even to run. But never forget that they draw the security and confidence to be able to thrive from the safety and guidance you offer them.

Let them try out their wings and soar toward independence. When they trust that they can navigate the world on their own, they will return to you for the interdependence that has no age boundaries and offers security for a lifetime.

Resources

The following resources are offered so you can further explore areas of particular interest or concern. These resources are by no means exhaustive; many fine resources are not included. While I cannot endorse each point in every listed book or Web page, they all are high-quality resources.

Adolescent Development

Ginsburg KR, Fitzgerald S. *Letting Go With Love and Confidence: Raising Responsible, Resilient, Self-sufficient Teens*. New York, NY: Avery Press, Penguin Group; 2011
This book guides parents to develop concrete step-by-step strategies to help adolescents navigate life's challenges. It also addresses the emotional journey parents take as their children become increasingly independent.

Adolescent Health Information

Children's Hospital Boston offers www.youngwomenshealth.org, a site to provide health information for teen girls and young women, and www.youngmenshealthsite.org for teen boys and young men.

Nemours, a pediatric health system, has an online teen and parent health Web site at www.teenshealth.org/teen.

Goryeb Children's Hospital offers a teen information site with peer advice and oversight from clinical social workers, health educators, adolescent medicine physicians, and other health professionals at www.teenhealthfx.com, and the Adolescent/Young Adult Center for Health at www.atlantichealth.org/Goryeb/Patient+Care+Services/Adolescent+-+Young+Adult+Center +for+Health.

Students Against Destructive Decisions (SADD) (www.sadd.org) is a peer-to-peer education, prevention, and activism organization dedicated to preventing destructive decisions, particularly underage drinking, other drug use, risky and impaired driving, teen violence, and teen suicide.

The Covenant House Nineline, a national, 24-hour, toll-free hotline for kids and parents across the United States, handles crisis and runaway issues. Counselors are available to offer guidance and support as well to link to community services. Visit www.nineline.org or call 800/999-9999.

The National Youth Anti-Drug Media Campaign offers a site, www.theantidrug.com, that offers far more than ideas to counter drug use.

The National Campaign to Prevent Teen and Unplanned Pregnancy site is www.thenationalcampaign.org

The American Medical Association (AMA) has published 2 paperback books especially for teens: *AMA Girl's Guide to Becoming a Teen* (Kate Gruenwald Pfeifer, LCSW, author; Amy B. Middleman, MD, MSEd, MPH, editor; 2006); and *AMA Boy's Guide to Becoming a Teen* (Kate Gruenwald Pfeifer, LCSW, author; Amy B. Middleman, MD, MSEd, MPH, editor; 2006).

The Web site www.fosteringresilience.com offers an overview of the 7 Cs model of resilience. It includes downloadable and printable materials that complement this book, including a teen stress-reduction plan and summary sheets that can be used in school and community forums.

Character Development/Raising Children Without Prejudice

Raising Children Without Prejudice

Mathias B, French MA. *40 Ways to Raise a Nonracist Child.* New York, NY: HarperPerennial; 1996

Stern-Larosa C, Bettman EH. *The Anti-Defamation League's Hate Hurts: How Children Learn and Unlearn Prejudice.* New York, NY: Scholastic, Inc; 2000

The Southern Poverty Law Center has a program entitled "Teaching Tolerance" that offers a variety of resources. Visit www.splcenter.org/what-we-do/teaching-tolerance.

The following Web page contains links to children's books on diversity, multiculturalism, prejudice reduction, and related topics: www.understandingprejudice.org/readroom/kidsbib.htm.

A World of Difference Institute of the Anti-Defamation League recommends multicultural and antibias literature for children at www.adl.org/bibliography.

Child Development

The American Academy of Pediatrics publishes authoritative books to help parents understand and support healthy development through a child's life span. These books can be previewed at www.healthychildren.org/bookstore.

Child Play (and Adult Play)

Hallowell EM. *The Childhood Roots of Adult Happiness: Five Steps to Help Kids Create and Sustain Lifelong Joy.* New York, NY: Ballantine Books; 2002

Hirsh-Pasek K, Golinkoff RM, Eyer DE. *Einstein Never Used Flash Cards: How Our Children Really Learn—and Why They Need to Play More and Memorize Less.* Emmaus, PA: Rodale Books; 2003

Elkind D. *The Power of Play: Learning What Comes Naturally.* Cambridge, MA: Da Capo Lifelong; 2007

Brown, SL, Vaughan CC. *Play: How It Shapes the Brain, Opens the Imagination, and Invigorates the Soul.* New York, NY: Avery; 2009

The Alliance for Childhood promotes policies and practices that support children's healthy development, love of learning, and joy in living. Visit www.allianceforchildhood.org.

Child Safety

De Becker G. *Protecting the Gift: Keeping Children and Teenagers Safe (and Parents Sane).* Dell Pub; 2000

Prevention of Child Abuse and Exploitation

The National Center for Missing & Exploited Children offers a wide range of outstanding materials for children, teenagers, and parents to prepare them to navigate a world that can be exploitative to children. Visit www.ncmec.org.

Emotional Intelligence

Goleman D. *Emotional Intelligence: Why It Can Matter More Than IQ.* London, England: Bloomsbury; 1996

Gottman JM, DeClaire J. *Raising an Emotionally Intelligent Child.* New York, NY: Simon and Schuster; 1997

Extreme Circumstances

Illness, Death, and Grief

The Journey of Hearts Web site offers information and links to a wide variety of resources and organizations that help children through loss, change, and grief. Visit http://journeyofhearts.org.

Rauch PK, Muriel AC. *Raising an Emotionally Healthy Child When a Parent is Sick.* New York, NY: McGraw-Hill; 2006

Divorce

The Nemours Foundation offers online information for children and teenagers. Visit www.kidshealth.org/kid/feeling/home_family/divorce.html.

The American Association for Marriage and Family Therapy offers advice on managing divorce in a manner that protects children. Visit www.aamft.org/families/consumer_updates/childrenanddivorce.asp.

Terrorism and Disaster

Several authoritative organizations have published online materials for dealing with disasters. They often update materials for specific disasters. Go to the Web sites of the following organizations and follow prompts for terrorism or disasters:

- American Academy of Pediatrics (www.HealthyChildren.org)
- Substance Abuse and Mental Health Services Administration, National Mental Health Information Center (www.samhsa.gov)
- National Center for Missing & Exploited Children (www.missingkids.com)

- American Academy of Child and Adolescent Psychiatry (www.aacap.org)
- American Psychological Association (www.apa.org)

Internet Safety

O'Keeffe GS. *CyberSafe: Protecting and Empowering Kids in the Digital World of Texting, Gaming, and Social Media*. Elk Grove Village, IL: American Academy of Pediatrics; 2011

Wired Kids, Inc. is a US charity dedicated to protecting all Internet users, especially children, from cyber-crime and abuse. Visit www.wiredkids.com.

The National Center for Missing & Exploited Children has materials written for teenagers (Don't Believe the Type) at http://tcs.cybertipline.com and for parents (HDOP: Help Delete Online Predators) at www.missingkids.com/adcouncil.

Listening

Faber A, Mazlish E. *How to Talk So Kids Will Listen & Listen So Kids Will Talk*. New York, NY: Perennial Currents; 2004

Gordon T. *Parent Effectiveness Training: The Proven Program for Raising Responsible Children*. New York, NY: Three Rivers Press; 2000

Media Literacy and Safety

Kilbourne J. *Can't Buy My Love: How Advertising Changes the Way We Think and Feel*. New York, NY: Simon & Schuster; 2000

Steyer JP. *The Other Parent: The Inside Story of the Media's Effect on Our Children*. New York, NY: Atria Books; 2003

Strasburger VC, Wilson BJ. *Children, Adolescents, and the Media*. Thousand Oaks, CA: Sage Publications; 2002

The Center on Media and Child Health at Children's Hospital Boston, Harvard Medical School, and Harvard School of Public Health is dedicated to understanding and responding to the effects of media on the physical, mental, and social health of children through research, production, and education. Visit www.cmch.tv.

The Center for Media Literacy offers information, resources, and links at www.medialit.org.

Mental Health

The American Academy of Child & Adolescent Psychiatry offers information for psychiatrists and families about developmental, behavioral, emotional, and mental disorders affecting children and adolescents. Visit www.aacap.org.

The American Psychological Association Web site offers information for psychologists and families on a wide variety of mental health concerns and special circumstances such as dealing with death, terrorism, or natural disasters. Visit www.apa.org.

The National Institute of Mental Health offers free, easy-to-read brochures and fact sheets on mental health issues at http://nimh.nih.gov/health/publications/index.shtml.

The National Institute on Alcohol Abuse and Alcoholism offers easy-to-read material for the public covering a wide range of alcohol-related topics. Visit www.niaaa.nih.gov/publications.

The National Institute on Drug Abuse has materials developed specifically for students and young adults at http://nida.nih.gov/students.html. More information about specific drugs is available at http://nida.nih.gov/drugpages.

Finding a Mental Health Professional

Your child's pediatrician or other health care professional, school counselor, or clergyperson can help you find a mental health professional who would be the right match for your child and family. If this is difficult, however, most mental health professional organizations have online referral networks.

United States

American Academy of Child & Adolescent Psychiatry: www.aacap.org/cs/forFamilies

American Association for Marriage and Family Therapy: www.aamft.org/TherapistLocator/index.asp

American Mental Health Counselors Association: www.amhca.org

American Psychiatric Nurses Association: www.apna.org

American Psychological Association: http://locator.apa.org

National Association of Social Workers: www.socialworkers.org

Canada

Canadian Academy of Child and Adolescent Psychiatry: www.cacap-acpea.org

Canadian Association of Social Workers: www.casw-acts.ca

Canadian Psychiatric Association: www.cpa-apc.org

Canadian Psychological Association: www.cpa.ca

Parenting Books and Information

The American Academy of Pediatrics Web site, HealthyChildren.org, has information for parents of babies, children, teens, and young adults. Visit www.healthychildren.org.

Perfectionism

Elliott M, Goldberg J, Price C. *Perfectionism: What's Bad About Being Too Good?* Minneapolis, MN: Free Spirit Pub; 1999

Greenspon TS. *Freeing Our Families from Perfectionism.* Minneapolis, MN: Free Spirit Pub; 2001

Greenspon TS. *What to Do When Good Enough Isn't Good Enough: The Real Deal on Perfectionism: A Guide for Kids.* Minneapolis, MN: Free Spirit Pub; 2007

Physical Health

Ratey JJ, Hagerman E. *Spark: The Revolutionary New Science of Exercise and the Brain.* Little, Brown; 2008

Stricker PR. *Sports Success R$_X$! Your Child's Prescription for the Best Experience: How to Maximize Potential and Minimize Pressure.* Elk Grove Village, IL: American Academy of Pediatrics; 2006

Nutrition

Jana LA, Shu J. *Food Fights: Winning the Nutritional Challenges of Parenthood Armed With Insight, Humor, and a Bottle of Ketchup.* Elk Grove Village, IL: American Academy of Pediatrics; 2008

The US Department of Agriculture interactive MyPyramid.gov site allows users to individualize a nutrition plan.

The National Institute of Diabetes and Digestive and Kidney Diseases offers information on nutrition for parents (WIN: Weight-control Information Network) at www.win.niddk.nih.gov/publications/child.htm.

The Canadian Public Health Agency offers a guide for nutrition and activity for children and adolescents at www.phac-aspc.gc.ca/hp-ps/hl-mvs/pag-gap/index-eng.php.

Resilience

Building Resilient Communities

At the heart of the Search Institute's work is the framework of 40 developmental assets that are positive experiences and personal qualities young people need to grow up healthy, caring, and responsible. To see the listed assets, go to www.search-institute.org/assets. The assets are modified for each developmental level.

Communities That Care is a system developed by J. David Hawkins and Richard F. Catalano that empowers communities to use advances from prevention science to guide their prevention efforts. The *CTC Prevention Strategies Guide* lists 56 tested and effective prevention programs and policies shown to increase protective factors, reduce risk factors, and reduce adolescent problem behaviors in well-controlled studies. These are the preventive interventions recommended in the Communities That Care system. The Communities That Care Web site is www.communitiesthatcare.net.

Kids at Hope is interested in helping families, youth-serving organizations, and communities create the kind of environment where all kids will thrive. Visit www.kidsathope.org.

Healthy, Optimistic, and Hopeful Thinking

Reivich K, Shatté A. *The Resilience Factor: 7 Essential Skills for Overcoming Life's Inevitable Obstacles.* New York, NY: Broadway Books; 2002

Seligman MEP, Reivich K, Jaycox L, Gillham J. *The Optimistic Child: A Proven Program to Safeguard Children from Depression and Build Lifelong Resilience.* Boston, MA: Houghton Mifflin Co; 2007

Parenting Books

Brooks RB, Goldstein S. *Raising Resilient Children: Fostering Strength, Hope, and Optimism in Your Child.* Lincolnwood, IL: Contemporary Books; 2001

Cohen-Sandler R. *Stressed-Out Girls: Helping Them Thrive in the Age of Pressure.* New York, NY: Viking; 2005

Mogel W. *The Blessing of a Skinned Knee: Using Jewish Teachings to Raise Self-Reliant Children.* New York, NY: Penguin Compass; 2001

Mogel W. *The Blessing of a B Minus: Using Jewish Teachings to Raise Resilient Teenagers.* New York, NY: Scribner; 2010

Benson PL. *Sparks: How Parents Can Help Ignite the Hidden Strengths of Teenagers.* San Francisco, CA: Jossey-Bass; 2008

Lerner RM, Israeloff R. *The Good Teen: Rescuing Adolescence from the Myths of the Storm and Stress Years.* New York, NY: Three Rivers Press; 2007

Sexual Minority Youth

Parents, Families and Friends of Lesbians and Gays (PFLAG) offers guidance and support if you believe that a young person you care for may be struggling with his or her sexual identity, or if he or she shares a homosexual or bisexual orientation with you and you wish to learn how best to be supportive. Visit www.pflag.org or call 202/467-8180.

The GLBT National Health Center offers the GLBT National Youth Talkline at 800/246-7743 and online support and information at www.glnh.org for the gay, lesbian, bisexual, and transgender community.

The Trevor Lifeline, a 24-hour crisis hotline for sexual minority youth, is available at 866/488-7386.

Stress and the Mind-Body Connection

Sapolsky RM. *Why Zebras Don't Get Ulcers.* 3rd ed. New York, NY: Henry Holt and Co; 2004
This classic book translates scientific evidence to help the reader understand the intricate connections between the mind and body.

Benson H, Klipper MZ. *The Relaxation Response.* New York, NY: HarperTorch; 2000
Herbert Benson coined the phrase *relaxation response* that is used in the stress-reduction plan offered here.

Sterling P. Principles of allostasis: optimal design, predictive regulation, pathophysiology and rational therapeutics. In Schulkin J. *Allostasis, Homeostasis, and the Costs of Physiological Adaptation.* Cambridge, UK: Cambridge University Press; 2004
This chapter is written for a scientific audience. If you can survive some of the jargon, it brilliantly and clearly makes the connection between the mind, emotions, and the body's response.

Stress Reduction for Teens

Hipp E. *Fighting Invisible Tigers: Stress Management for Teens.* 3rd ed rev. Minneapolis, MN: Free Spirit Pub; 2008
This book offers teenagers easily digestible information and concrete skills for stress reduction. It uses the same metaphor of tigers chasing us that is used in Chapter 39 of this book, and therefore may be a natural next step for your adolescents.

Seaward BL, Bartlett LK. *Hot Stones & Funny Bones: Teens Helping Teens Cope with Stress & Anger.* Deerfield Beach, FL: Health Communications; 2002
This book may be particularly helpful for teenagers who feel isolated and may not know how common stress is among their peers.

Success, Pressures That Interfere With Authentic Success, and Opportunities to Achieve It

Elkind D. *The Hurried Child: Growing Up Too Fast Too Soon.* 3rd ed. Cambridge, MA: Perseus Publishers; 2001

Hallowell EM. *The Childhood Roots of Adult Happiness: Five Steps to Help Kids Create and Sustain Lifelong Joy.* New York, NY: Ballantine Books; 2002

Hirsh-Pasek K, Golinkoff RM, Eyer DE. *Einstein Never Used Flash Cards: How Our Children Really Learn—and Why They Need to Play More and Memorize Less.* Emmaus, PA: Rodale Books; 2003

Rosenfeld AA, Wise N. *The Over-Scheduled Child: Avoiding the Hyper-Parenting Trap.* New York, NY: St. Martin's Griffin; 2001

Warner J. *Perfect Madness: Motherhood in the Age of Anxiety.* New York, NY: Riverhead Books; 2005

Levine M. *The Price of Privilege: How Parental Pressure and Material Advantage are Creating a Generation of Disconnected and Unhappy Kids.* New York, NY: Harper Paperbacks; 2008

Pope DC. *Doing School: How We are Creating a Generation of Stressed-Out, Materialistic, and Miseducated Students.* New Haven, CT: Yale University Press; 2003

The Challenge Success organization is committed to championing a broader vision of success for youth. Its mission statement follows: "We believe that real success results from attention to the basic developmental needs of children and a valuing of different types of skills and abilities. In particular, we endorse a vision of success that emphasizes character, health, independence, connection, creativity, enthusiasm, and achievement.

"Accordingly, we have created Challenge Success with a mission to inform, inspire, and equip youth, parents, and schools to adopt practices that expand options for youth success." Visit www.challengesuccess.org.

Dweck C. *Mindset: The New Psychology of Success.* New York, NY: Ballantine Books; 2008

Csikszentmihalyi M. *Flow: The Psychology of Optimal Experience.* New York, NY: HarperPerennial; 1991

Teen Driving

The Web site www.teendriverssource.org is produced by the Center for Injury Research and Prevention at The Children's Hospital of Philadelphia. It has a portal for teens, parents, and educators. It includes a site (http://parentingmyteendriver.org) that teaches parents how to apply authoritative parenting strategies to teen driving.

Temperament

Carey WB, Jablow MM. *Understanding Your Child's Temperament.* Bloomington, IN: Xlibris; 2004

Index